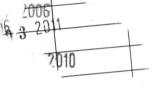

HUMAN
AGGRESSION

HUMAN
AGGRESSION

THEORIES, RESEARCH,

AND IMPLICATIONS FOR SOCIAL POLICY

EDITED BY

RUSSELL G. GEEN
Department of Psychology
University of Missouri
Columbia, Missouri

EDWARD DONNERSTEIN
Department of Communication
University of California, Santa Barbara
Santa Barbara, California

ACADEMIC PRESS
San Diego   London   Boston   New York   Sydney   Tokyo   Toronto

Copyright © 1998 by ACADEMIC PRESS

Academic Press
a division of Harcourt Brace & Company
525 B Street, Suite 1900, San Diego, California 92101-4495, USA
http://www.apnet.com

Academic Press Limited
24-28 Oval Road, London NW1 7DX, UK
http://www.hbuk.co.uk/ap/

Library of Congress Card Catalog Number: 98-84364

International Standard Book Number: 0-12-278805-2

PRINTED IN THE UNITED STATES OF AMERICA
98 99 00 01 02 03 EB 9 8 7 6 5 4 3 2 1

CONTENTS

2

METHODOLOGY IN THE STUDY OF AGGRESSION:
INTEGRATING EXPERIMENTAL
AND NONEXPERIMENTAL FINDINGS

BRAD J. BUSHMAN AND CRAIG A. ANDERSON

3

AFFECTIVE AGGRESSION:
THE ROLE OF STRESS, PAIN, AND NEGATIVE AFFECT

LEONARD BERKOWITZ

4

THE ROLE OF SOCIAL INFORMATION PROCESSING AND COGNITIVE SCHEMA IN THE ACQUISITION AND MAINTENANCE OF HABITUAL AGGRESSIVE BEHAVIOR

L. ROWELL HUESMANN

5

AGGRESSION AND THE SELF: HIGH SELF-ESTEEM, LOW SELF-CONTROL, AND EGO THREAT

ROY F. BAUMEISTER AND JOSEPH M. BODEN

6

PSYCHOACTIVE DRUGS AND HUMAN AGGRESSION

STUART P. TAYLOR AND MICHAEL R. HULSIZER

7

HARMFUL EFFECTS OF EXPOSURE TO MEDIA VIOLENCE: LEARNING OF AGGRESSION, EMOTIONAL DESENSITIZATION, AND FEAR

STACY L. SMITH AND EDWARD DONNERSTEIN

8

MALE VIOLENCE TOWARD WOMEN: AN INTEGRATED PERSPECTIVE

JACQUELYN W. WHITE AND ROBIN M. KOWALSKI

9

THE CONFLUENCE MODEL AS AN ORGANIZING FRAMEWORK FOR RESEARCH ON SEXUALLY AGGRESSIVE MEN: RISK MODERATORS, IMAGINED AGGRESSION, AND PORNOGRAPHY CONSUMPTION

NEIL M. MALAMUTH

10

TEMPERATURE AND AGGRESSION: PARADOX, CONTROVERSY, AND A (FAIRLY) CLEAR PICTURE

CRAIG A. ANDERSON AND KATHRYN B. ANDERSON

CONTRIBUTORS

Craig A. Anderson (23, 247), Department of Psychology, University of Missouri, Columbia, Missouri 65211

Kathryn B. Anderson (247), Department of Psychology, Our Lady of the Lake University, San Antonio, Texas 78285

Roy F. Baumeister (111), Department of Psychology, Case Western Reserve University, Cleveland, Ohio 44106

Leonard Berkowitz (49), Department of Psychology, University of Wisconsin—Madison, Madison, Wisconsin 53706

Joseph M. Boden (111), Department of Psychology, Case Western Reserve University, Cleveland, Ohio 44106

Brad J. Bushman (23), Department of Psychology, Iowa State University, Ames, Iowa 50011

Edward Donnerstein (167), Department of Communication, University of California, Santa Barbara, Santa Barbara, California 93110

Russell G. Geen (1), Department of Psychology, University of Missouri, Columbia, Missouri 65211

L. Rowell Huesmann (73), Research Center for Group Dynamics, University of Michigan, Ann Arbor, Michigan 48106

Michael R. Hulsizer (139), Department of Psychology, Kent State University, Kent, Ohio 44242

Robin M. Kowalski (203), Department of Psychology, Western Carolina University, Cullowhee, North Carolina 28723

Neil M. Malamuth (229), Department of Communication Studies, University of California, Los Angeles, Los Angeles, California 90023

Stacy L. Smith (167), Department of Communication, University of California, Santa Barbara, Santa Barbara, California 93110

Stuart P. Taylor (139), Department of Psychology, Kent State University, Kent, Ohio 44242

Jacquelyn W. White (203), Department of Psychology, University of North Carolina, Greensboro, North Carolina 27412

PREFACE

We live in a violent society. As a nation, we rank first among all developed countries in the world in homicides. The statistics on violence are staggering, particularly with regard to children and adolescents. Consider, for example, the following:

- Among individuals 15 to 24 years old, homicide is the second leading cause of death.
- Adolescents account for 24% of all violent crimes leading to arrest.
- Every 5 minutes a child is arrested for a violent crime.
- Gun-related violence takes the life of an American child every 3 hours.
- Every day over 100,000 children carry guns to schools.
- In a recent survey of fifth graders in New Orleans, more than 50% of the children reported being a victim of violence, and 70% of these kids have seen weapons being used.

What accounts for these alarming figures? There is universal agreement that many factors, including gangs, drugs, guns, poverty, and racism, contribute to violent behavior in society. Many of these variables may independently or interactively affect antisocial responding. We realize that there is no single cause of violent behavior. Fifteen years ago we published a two-volume series with Academic Press aimed at addressing the causes and prevention of violence. Since that time two things have changed. First, violence in our society has not subsided and, in fact, in some areas has increased. Second, and perhaps more importantly, we know much more today about the causes of violence. Because of a continuing increase in research over the years, we now have more information on ways to control and mitigate aggressive behavior. This current volume, 15 years after the first, will address this research and its implications.

This book has a number of defining characteristics. First and foremost, it is built on contemporary theories and research evidence. Its major emphasis is on summarizing what is currently known about the causes of aggressive behavior from current ongoing research programs. Second, its chapters are written by psychologists and present psychological viewpoints and theories on aggression. Finally, it seeks to point out from its theoretical–empirical base the possible implications for and applications of this research to public policy. We believe that these implications can be best addressed by those who are at the forefront of the research and theorizing in this area, that is, the contributors to this book. We believe we have succeeded on all accounts, and this current volume will add significantly to our understanding of human aggression. Most importantly, for the researcher and practitioner alike, the applications of this research to public policy on aggression will have significant benefits for years to come.

Russell G. Geen
Edward Donnerstein

1

PROCESSES AND PERSONAL VARIABLES IN AFFECTIVE AGGRESSION

RUSSELL G. GEEN

University of Missouri

The literature in human aggression has become so large that truly comprehensive overviews are no longer feasible. Some of it is theory-driven, but much is addressed more to solving social problems than to building general models and research paradigms. It is too diverse to permit easy generalizations. However, a review of this literature reveals some convergences among research programs and theoretical emphases, and these provide a base on which we may eventually build a unified theory of human aggression. This chapter consists of a few observations on some of the directions being taken in the contemporary study of aggression, along with a brief introduction to the chapters that follow. A few preliminary points must be made regarding the definition of aggression.

1. "Aggression" is not a scientific term. It is taken from everyday English and used to describe a number of functionally different behaviors that have in common the infliction of harm upon another person.[1] In the animal kingdom, several kinds of aggression have been observed, e.g., predatory, maternal, and territorial. Although such distinctions do not characterize most social psychological or clinical research on human subjects,[2] certain varieties of aggression have been identified, such as angry retaliation, self-defense, and violence carried out for purposes

---

[1]A useful working definition of aggression is: "Aggression is any form of behavior directed toward the goal of harming another living being who is motivated to avoid such treatment" (Baron & Richardson, 1994, p. 5).

[2]The emerging psychoevolutionary approach to behavior (e.g., Cairns, 1986) may stimulate a more diversified search for determinants of human aggression than the one usually taken by social psychologists.

of coercion, punishment, and profit. It is customary among those who study aggression in humans to observe two broad distinctions: (a) angry, or *affective,* aggression in which harming the victim is the main motive of the aggressor, and (b) *instrumental* aggression, which may involve strong emotions but is motivated primarily by concerns other than the harmdoing itself. Because affective aggression has received more attention from researchers than instrumental, it will be the subject of this chapter.

2. Affective aggression is a response to some event or change in the environment, or to the mental representation of such an event (e.g., a memory of having been insulted). Most social psychologists consider aggression to be not spontaneous, but reactive. Some studies have reported apparently spontaneous "seizure-like" rage related to underlying brain pathology (e.g., Pontius, 1984). These are certainly intriguing investigations, but they involve intensive case studies of relatively small numbers of people and must be considered preliminary. Furthermore, even some of the research reported in this literature suggests that brain pathology may serve more as a predisposing variable than as a determinant of aggression and that situational events are the proximal cause of actual aggressive behavior (Lewis, Moy, Jackson, Aaronson, Restifo, Serra, & Simos, 1985). The same may be true of research on hormonal antecedents of aggression, such as testosterone levels (e.g., Van Goozen, Frijda, & Van de Poll, 1994, 1995). This treats biological factors in aggression as contributors to a disposition to aggress, given suitable provocation, or, as called elsewhere (Geen, 1990), part of a group of "background variables."

For purposes of explication, this chapter is organized along the lines of a diagram (Figure 1.1) in which some of the variables currently generating interesting and important research on human aggression are spelled out. This diagram is not a formal theoretical model but only a device that may be useful in organizing information. Two assumptions underlie this diagram. The first is that human aggression is a joint product of both instigating conditions and variables related to a disposition to behave aggressively. The second is that the aggressive act occurs within a sequence of events beginning with the provocation and terminating in some condition that follows the act and can be understood only with reference to this sequence. In other words, explanations for aggression must be built on considerations of intervening *processes* that connect the instigating condition to the aggressive response.

PROCESSES IN AGGRESSION

Let us begin by considering the instigators, or eliciting conditions, of aggression. Several instigators have been identified in research begun in the 1960s. Frustration, insult, and interpersonal attack were among the first to be studied. Later, a number of investigations identified environmental stressors such as noise, heat, and

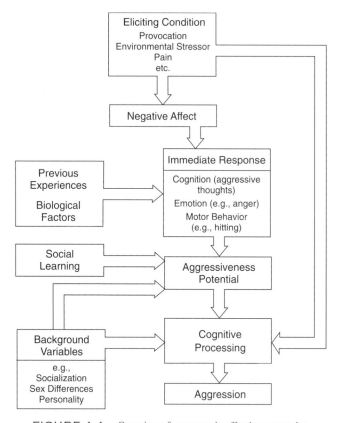

FIGURE 1.1   Overview of processes in affective aggression.

air pollution as effective antecedents of aggression, even when the target person was not responsible for the subject's stress in any way. Zillmann (1988) later defined aggression as a response to any condition that poses a threat to the well-being of the person. More recently, aggression has been linked to depressed mood states (Capaldi, 1991) and to physical pain (Berkowitz & Heimer, 1989). This is certainly an odd assortment of variables, leading one to wonder whether they share any characteristics that may account for their common potential for evoking aggression. To answer that question we must go beyond the mere identification of antecedents and attempt to discover those intervening processes referred to earlier.

COGNITIVE NEOASSOCIATIONISM

In what ways are threat, pain, insult, stress, and negative mood states similar? One possibility is that all produce highly unpleasant experiences or, in correct psychological terminology, lead to increased levels of a negative affect. The theory of cognitive neoassociationism developed by Berkowitz (1993) explains a person's initial reaction to any of the conditions noted earlier, including interpersonal conflict and provocation, as a function of such negative affect. At this level cognition is required only to recognize the stimulus. Even at this initial stage, however, negative affect does not automatically evoke aggression. It may engender instead an impulse to flee from the unpleasant situation. The immediate first reaction to a condition of negative affect is therefore either "fight or flight." Berkowitz (1993) argues that both tendencies are elicited simultaneously but that one usually tends to prevail, depending on (a) the person's genetic endowment, (b) prior conditioning and learning, and (c) recognition of aspects of the situation that either facilitate or inhibit aggression.

Biological factors in aggression therefore make an important contribution at this point by contributing to the probability of a person's reacting to increased negative affect with impulsive aggression. Several studies have established a link between hormone levels and aggression (e.g., Berman, Gladue, & Taylor, 1993; Gladue, 1991; Van Goozen et al., 1995). Moreover, behavior genetic studies that have revealed a heritability component in aggressive behavior (Ghodsian-Carpey & Baker, 1987; Miles & Carey, 1997) are probably best understood as reflecting an immediate, preconscious response tendency to aversive stimulation.

The heart of the cognitive-neoassociationist theory deals with the larger syndromes of cognition, affect, and motor behaviors that are activated by negative affect. Following associationist models of memory, Berkowitz asserts that negative affect elicits associated cognitive and emotional states and expressive motor patterns linked to it along directional pathways. The theory has a number of implications for the study of aggression. As Berkowitz observes in his chapter, it explains certain phenomena that have previously been explained in terms of other constructs, such as frustration. Work by Anderson and colleagues has also built upon, and extended, the theory in isolating the effects of temperature on aggression (Anderson, Anderson, & Deuser, 1996). The theory also provides an explanation for individual differences in aggressiveness as a function of the depth and extent of associative networks that underlie aggressive behavior (Bushman & Geen, 1989; Bushman, 1996). Finally, it can explain the often-reported connection between aggressive behavior and prior exposure to violence in the mass media (Berkowitz, 1984).

COGNITIVE PROCESSES IN AGGRESSION

It must be emphasized that the theory of cognitive neoassociationism describes reactions that antedate cognitive processing. Berkowitz has stated clearly that the initial impulsive reaction to negative affect is only a potential first stage in aggression. The anger, hostile thoughts, and aggressive motor patterns evoked at this stage are only "rudimentary." Beyond this point, cognitive processes play an important role in what happens. We must now turn our attention to the processes involved in cognitively controlled aggression, and when we do we begin by noting a truism: aggressive acts, like any others, have consequences. These conse-

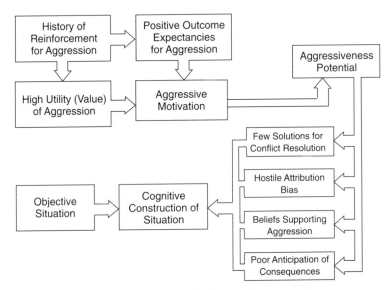

FIGURE 1.2   General summary of social-cognitive processes in aggression.

quences—the rewarding or punishing outcomes of aggression—constitute the basis for the social learning process (Figure 1.2).

The processes involved in social learning are familiar from motivation theory, involving the variables of expectancy and value. Aggression that is rewarded produces an increased expectancy that such behavior will be useful in the future under similar conditions. The expectancy-value analysis of aggression has received some empirical support. Perry, Perry, and Rasmussen (1986) asked children to express their level of confidence that various types of outcome would follow aggressive behavior. Children who had been classified on the basis of peer ratings as highly aggressive were more confident than their less aggressive counterparts that aggression would produce tangible rewards and would also cause other people to stop behaving in aversive ways. High expectancies of desired outcomes following aggression were therefore shown to be correlated with levels of general aggressiveness. In a subsequent study, Boldizar, Perry, and Perry (1989) found that peer-rated aggressiveness also predicted the values that children associated with the outcomes of aggression. Children rated as high in aggressiveness attached greater positive value than did less aggressive children to "control of the victim" resulting from aggression against the latter. In addition, highly aggressive children placed less negative value on such outcomes as the victim's suffering, threat of retaliation, rejection by peers, and negative feelings about themselves. In short, children who were highly aggressive saw more good outcomes arising from aggression, and fewer bad ones, than less aggressive children.

Expectancy and value are the determinants of an immediate incentive or motivational state. Eventually, children use information regarding the consequences of aggression in developing internal standards of right and wrong and in regulating their behavior according to such standards (Perry, Perry, & Boldizar, 1990). Over time, the standards, the situational stimuli that activate them, and the behaviors that result become encoded in *cognitive scripts* that prescribe behavior under appropriate conditions (Huesmann, 1988). Frequent enaction of aggressive behaviors under conditions of conflict or provocation increase the probability of similar enactments under those conditions in the future, and each enactment results in a more elaborated script. The end result is a child described by teachers, peers, and other observers as "aggressive," meaning that the child manifests a high potential for behaving aggressively under provocative conditions.

SOCIAL INFORMATION PROCESSING

Among the consequences of this acquired potential for aggression are several that have to do with how people understand and interpret social interactions. Because behavior in situations of interpersonal conflict is guided by one's cognitive representations of events, whether aggression occurs depends on how social information is processed. A person who is deficient in the ability to receive and respond to social cues may manifest reactions to social information that are inappropriate and possibly maladaptive. Such behavior may cause other people to reject the person, and this outcome may in turn have several undesirable consequences, including further rejection by peers, depression, and chronic and characteristic aggressiveness. Dodge and colleagues have developed a model that identifies several stages, at any one of which faulty processing may be predicted by the person's level of maladjustment. In the most recent version of the model (Crick & Dodge, 1994), six stages are described: (1) *encoding* of cues arising from the actions of oneself and others; (2) *interpretation* of those cues; (3) clarification of the *goals* of the interaction after the relevant information has been assimilated; (4) the search for, and gaining of *access* to, responses to the situation as defined; (5) the *decision* to select one of the available responses for the present situation; and (6) behavior *enactment* of the chosen response. Finally, feedback from the person's behavior at stage 6 contributes to the encoding of stimulus input at the beginning of a new round of processing. The model therefore describes the basis for an ongoing interactive process.

When social information is generated by a provocative interpersonal exchange, any bias that the person brings to the situation can influence the cognitive construction of the exchange and the response that one makes to it (i.e., stages 1 and 2). Studies have shown that boys classified as highly aggressive (e.g., through peer nominations and teacher ratings) react more aggressively to the frustrating actions of other boys than their less aggressive peers when the intentions of the frustrator were ambiguous (Dodge, 1980) or even benign (Nasby, Hayden, & DePaulo, 1979). This tendency of aggressive children to misread the intentions of others has been called the *hostile attribution bias*. It may be the product of some of the processing deficiencies described by Dodge and associates, such as inefficient encoding and interpretation of social cues. For example, aggressive boys pay less attention to available social cues than their less aggressive counterparts, react to situations more quickly, and, when responding quickly, are more likely to commit the hostile attribution bias (Dodge & Newman, 1981). In addition, aggressive boys, although not less attentive overall than less aggressive peers, are more likely to be selectively attentive to aggressive cues in the social situation (Gouze, 1987). They are also more likely than nonaggressive boys to reach a conclusion regarding the intent of others on the basis of personal beliefs and schemata rather than information about the situation (Dodge & Tomlin, 1987). Consistent with this finding, Slaby and Guerra (1988) found that highly aggressive boys and girls sought less information, generated fewer solutions, and foresaw fewer consequences of aggression in processing interpersonal encounters than did less aggressive children. High aggressiveness was also associated with agreement with statements of belief supporting aggression. Thus high aggressiveness is linked to poor social information processing, a hostile attribution bias, and endorsement of beliefs sanctioning aggression.

The relationship between aggressiveness and social competence is a reciprocal and cyclical one. Aggressive children and adolescents interpret cues in potentially provocative situations in such a way that they attribute hostile motives to others and, in general, react in aggressive ways that may not be the most effective under the circumstances. Such behavior invites social rejection that may make the child even more aggressive (Dodge, Coie, & Brakke, 1982; Huesmann, 1988). Among these reasons is a continued deficiency in the processing of relevant information associated with social rejection; some studies have shown that rejection by peers leads to processing problems similar to those observed in highly aggressive children (Crick & Ladd, 1990).

INDIVIDUAL VARIABLES IN AGGRESSION

The discussion so far has been of how potentially provoking situations are constructed by the person and of the processes whereby personal constructions are likely to lead to aggressive outcomes. Of course, situations account for only part of the variance in aggressive behavior. Variables associated with the person also produce variance, in part through their interaction with situational effects. Any discussion of aggression must therefore seek to identify individual variables and to explore possible interactions. Three such individual variables are reviewed: sex, personality, and socialization within norm-setting systems.

SEX DIFFERENCES

Although it is commonly believed in our society that men are more aggressive than women, research has shown effects that are more complex. Most investigators would probably agree that men are typically more *physically* aggressive than women (e.g., Reinisch & Sanders, 1986), but the basis for this effect, the conditions under which it is found, and the nature of the cognitive and affective processes that mediate it are subjects of some disagreement. One of the longest standing theories of sex differences in aggression attributes these differences to inherent physical differences between men and women (Maccoby and Jacklin, 1974). This viewpoint has been challenged by critics (e.g., White, 1983) who emphasize instead the importance of differential socialization practices as the basis for male–female differences in aggression. It should be noted that Maccoby and Jacklin (1974) do not attribute all sex differences to biological differences, but insist only that the latter provide the background within which situational variables operate.

Sex differences in aggression have been linked to several processes. One important source of such differences is in the ways in which men and women construe potentially provoking situations. In an early review of the literature, Frodi, Macaulay, and Thome (1977) concluded that women are more likely than men to consider aggression inappropriate, to repress aggression, and to experience guilt or anxiety in connection with aggressive actions. These findings indicate that the two sexes respond to normative prescriptions in judging aggression and in the affective states that accompany it. There is also some evidence that conditions which evoke anger in women tend to be different from those that elicit anger in men. Harris (1993) found that women are more angered than men by insensitive or condescending behavior from a man and by verbal abuse and condescending behavior from another woman, whereas men are more angered than women by physical attack from another man. Sexual infidelity by a partner has also been shown to excite greater anger and desire for punitive action in women than in men. Paul, Foss, and Galloway (1993) found that women reported being more angry than men toward both their unfaithful partners and their rivals for the partner's affections. Women also were more likely than men to react to infidelity by such actions as "badmouthing" and harassing their rivals (Paul & Galloway, 1994).

Eagly and Steffen (1986) conducted a meta-analysis which revealed that a large amount of the sex difference in aggression can be traced to beliefs about the negative consequences of aggression. Women are less aggressive than men when they believe that acting aggressively will harm the victim, pose a danger to themselves, or evoke intense feelings of guilt or anxiety. This set of affective and cognitive processes may all conspire to inhibit expression of aggressive behavior. Eagly and Steffen (1986) also found that the beliefs of men and women regarding the consequences of aggression become especially divergent under conditions that involve physical aggression. This may explain why most studies show that men are especially likely to be more aggressive than women when the aggression is physical and assaultive and why male–female differences are attenuated when aggression is less physical (e.g., verbal abuse). Such findings indicate that men and women differ in terms of the mode of aggression that they typically use. Even though most reviewers conclude that the evidence for such preferences does not constitute the most important variable underlying sex differences (e.g., White, 1983), none deny that the response mode is involved. Research with children reported by Crick and associates indicates that girls engage in what has been termed *relational* aggression to a greater extent than boys (Crick & Grotepeter, 1995). This aggression consists of activity that "harms others through damage to their peer relationships or to the threat of such damage . . ." (Crick, 1995, p. 313), such as excluding the victim from one's playgroup or threatening withdrawal of friendship and acceptance. In many respects, relational aggression resembles physical aggression. Children who typically use relational aggression to control or hurt others are more prone to form hostile attribution biases in situations involving relational conflicts than children who are not usually aggressive in this way and are also more emotionally distressed by such conflicts (Crick, 1995). Children also label relationally manipulative behaviors as "aggressive," i.e., as an appropriate accompaniment to feelings of anger and intent to harm (Crick, 1996).

Bettencourt and Miller (1996) reported that sex and provocation interact in predicting aggression: men are more aggressive than women under neutral conditions, whereas provocation attenuates sex differences. In addition, Bettencourt and Miller (1996) found that although provocation reduces sex differences in general, specific types of provocation differentially affect the degree to which this attenuation occurs. For example, threats to self-esteem have little effect on women's aggression whereas insults or physical attacks lead to relatively high aggressiveness. Threats to self-esteem provoke men as much as physical attack and are more provocative than insult. Bettencourt and Miller (1996) also found that men are more aggressive than women when physical aggression is the method made available to subjects, but are no more aggressive than women when verbal or written aggression is involved.

The results of a recent series of studies conducted in Finland add further support to the idea that differences in the method of aggressing contribute to sex differences in aggressive behavior. These studies involved young children, adolescents, and adults. Some clear developmental trends were found, as well as sex differences. From a cohort of 8 year olds, Björkqvist, Lagerspetz, and Kaukiainen (1992) obtained peer- and self-reports of what children in a class do when they are angry. A factor analysis of the behaviors listed by the children yielded factors of direct and indirect aggression and a third factor of nonaggressive withdrawal behaviors. Direct aggression included such behaviors as physical assault and verbal abuse carried out by the aggressor against the target. Indirect aggression involved either using other people to carry out aggressive intentions against the target or other manipulations of the social network designed to exclude and isolate the target. Boys reported engaging in significantly more direct aggression than girls, whereas girls were slightly, but not significantly, more prone than boys to use indirect aggression and to withdraw peacefully from anger-inducing settings. In the 11-year-old cohort, boys were higher on the direct aggression factor than girls and girls were higher on both indirect aggression and nonaggression factors. In addition, girls were found to be organized into smaller, tighter friendship groupings than boys, a condition that might facilitate the manipulation of the social environment for purposes of indirect aggression (Lagerspetz, Björkqvist, & Peltonen, 1988); a similar difference in the organization of friendship groupings was not found in the study of 8 year olds. Thus, whereas sex differences in the use of direct aggression were found in young children, the emergence of parallel sex differences in indirect aggression came later. Indirect (e.g., relational) aggression obviously involves the learning of tactics and strategies that can come only after a certain level of gender-role socialization has been attained. In a study of adult subjects, Björkqvist, Österman, & Lagerspetz (1994) found that men and women also tend to report being the *victims* of different kinds of indirect aggression. Men report a high level of aggression against them that is indirect, but is also personal in that it is disguised to seem rational and non-malicious (such as having their work evaluated unjustly), whereas women report high levels of socially manipulated aggression, like having false rumors spread about them.

The factor analysis of reported behaviors in the 15-year-old cohort yielded four factors: direct physical aggression, direct verbal aggression, indirect aggression, and nonaggressive withdrawal. Boys showed more direct physical aggression than girls whereas girls manifested more indirect aggression and withdrawal than boys while no sex differences in direct verbal aggression were found. Again, friendship units tended to be smaller among girls than among boys, with a larger number of pair friendships. The study of 18-year-old subjects revealed significant sex differences for both indirect and direct verbal aggression and for nonagrressive acts, with girls showing higher levels than boys in each case (Lagerspetz & Björkqvist, 1994). No sex differences in direct physical aggression were found, mainly because the levels of such aggression among both boys and girls were very low. In fact, one of the most striking findings to emerge from the studies involving adolescents was the dramatic decline in physical aggression among boys from the ages of 15 to 18. The decreased use of physical aggression among boys was accompanied by increased verbal and indirect aggression, which raises the possibility that aggression does not change as a function of age so much as it merely changes in the way in which it is expressed. If men become less directly and more indirectly aggressive with age while women remain more prone to use indirect than direct aggression, this could account for the finding that sex differences decrease with age (Eagly & Steffen, 1986).

The findings of the Finnish studies show sex differences in preferred modes of aggressing for boys and girls, with these differences tending to become attenuated with age. Among adults, sex differences appear to be manifested more in the cognitive constructions that people place on provoking events, on the affect elicited by these events, and in the anticipated consequences of aggression. As has been noted earlier, the cognitive constructions that are placed on provocation and aggression mediate to a large extent the degree of aggression that such events evoke. A similar conclusion has been drawn from research in Great Britain by Campbell and associates (Campbell, 1993; Campbell & Muncer, 1987) which shows that men and women interpret their own aggressiveness in different ways. Whereas men tend to define their aggression as instrumental behavior that allows them to control other people, women tend to regard theirs more as emotionally uncontrolled behavior. Thus, while men characteristically see aggression as useful and satisfying, women tend to react to it with guilt and repression. Campbell, Muncer, and Coyle (1992) have developed a self-report scale by means of which subjects can describe their aggressive behavior in either instrumental or expressive (i.e., emotional) terms. Instrumentality versus expressivity is reflected in several dimensions, such as the form that aggression takes, the social value of aggression, and the specific cognitions and emotions that accompany conflict and aggression. Campbell and Muncer (1994) administered the scale to samples of respondents that varied in terms of sex as well as occupation (soldiers or nurses) and found that both variables were related to beliefs in expressivity versus instrumentality of aggression. Women were more expressive in their self-descriptions and men less expressive. In addition, nurses, whether male or female, were more expressive than male and female soldiers. Thus, the sex role identity influences the social construction that is placed on aggression in much the same way as sex identity. The findings of Campbell and associates all involve adults. Archer and Parker (1994) have extended the findings of differential social construction of aggression by showing that the same sex difference is found in children of grammar-school age, indicating thereby that the socialization process that underlies the typical male–female difference begins early in life. Archer and Parker (1994) have also shown the same boy–girl difference in the case of indirect, verbal aggression. The tendencies of males to regard aggression as instrumental behavior and of females to regard it as undesirable emotionality therefore appear to emerge fairly early.

PERSONALITY AND AGGRESSION

Social psychologists do not usually study the role played by personality variables in aggression. This indifference to personality has been the result of certain characteristics of the study of human aggression. First, a relative scarcity of reliable and valid personality scales to measure aggressive tendencies—for many years the Buss–Durkee Hostility Inventory (BDHI) was a lone exception to this generalization—has discouraged researchers who might otherwise have included personality variables in their research designs (Edmunds & Kendrick, 1980). Second, much of the research that has shown an effect of personality on aggression has been designed mainly to identify personality markers in applied settings, not to test theories of person–situation interactions (e.g., Bersani, Chen, Pendleton, & Denton, 1992; Julian & McKenry, 1993). For that reason, they have not addressed the status of personality traits as moderator variables. Third, social psychologists have tended to explain behavior in terms of situational demands and to relegate individual differences to a secondary explanatory status, if indeed they use such explanations at all.

Arguments against the role for personality in aggression are usually based on the contention that aggressive behavior is unstable across time and conditions. However, evidence for the consistency of aggression has been reported by investigators in several countries (e.g., Deluty, 1985; Eron & Huesmann, 1990; Farrington, 1994; Rushton & Erdle, 1987; Stattin & Magnusson, 1989). In a major investigation, Olweus (1979) reviewed a large number of longitudinal studies of aggressive behavior and patterns of responding in children, noting in each study the coefficient of stability in aggressive behavior from one assessment period to another. The lengths of time intervening between measurements varied from study to study, as did the ages of the children at the outset of each study. Measures of aggressiveness included direct observation, teacher ratings, clinical ratings, and judgments made by other children.

Olweus (1979) found considerable evidence for the stability of aggressive behavior. Clear individual differences in the level of aggressiveness emerged as early as the age of three, and this stability lasted for as long as 12–18 months. Children aged 8–9 showed aggressive behavior patterns that were correlated with aggressiveness as long as 10–14 years later. In some instances, the magnitude of correlation was sufficient to account for 25% of the variance at the later age. Aggressive behavior at ages 12–13 also showed a high degree of stability for periods of 1 to 5 years, with between 50 and 90% of the variance accounted for. Such findings indicate that aggressive behavior is to some degree a function of generalized aggressiveness.

Showing stability in aggressive behavior does not necessarily prove that certain people behave aggressively most of the time. Olweus (1979) suggests instead that individual differences contribute to aggression in concert with cognitive appraisals of the situation, emotional reactions, and tendencies to inhibit aggression. Personal aggressiveness interacts with situational variables to predict aggressive behavior. An interactional approach is also the basis for a two-factor theory of antisocial behavior proposed by Moffitt (1993), who notes that whereas most antisocial behavior begins and ends during adolescence, some people manifest antisocial activity over the entire life span, beginning in early childhood. This latter group is the one that is most relevant to the present discussion. The origins of life course persistent antisocial behavior lie in neuropsychological deficits that may be prenatal or perinatal in nature. These deficits may involve verbal deficits as well as deficits in "executive" function such as inattention and impulsivity; they may be the result of a host of factors, among them genetic inheritance, maternal drug abuse, poor prenatal nutrition, and postnatal understimulation. The product of these conditions is an infant that is cognitively, affectively, and behaviorally "difficult."

If the difficult child is placed in an environment that is nurturant and supportive, the problems are often overcome. However, if the child is reared in a less friendly environment, his or her behavior may become progressively antisocial. At the same time, prosocial skills do not develop. Thus, through an interaction between neuropsychological deficits and early experiences with the environment, the beginnings of an antisocial personality are formed. This personality is maintained past childhood through two subsequent interactions with the environment. One is the tendency of antisocial people to construct a functional environment that is consistent with their personality by means of the hostile attribution bias. The other is the tendency to select or create environments that conform to antisocial behavior patterns (e.g., Patterson, Reid, & Dishion, 1992). As a result of these on-going reciprocal person–situation interactions, antisocial behavior becomes stable and consistent (cf. Caspi, Elder, & Bem, 1987).

Attempts to assess stable individual differences in aggressiveness with tests and inventories have yielded mixed results. Several inventories for the assessment of hostility and manifest aggressiveness have been published, but solid evidence of reliable and valid personal moderators of situational causes of aggression is not commonplace (for a review, see Edmunds & Kendrick, 1980). Of the personality measures that have been used in research on aggression, the most popular has been the Buss–Durkee Hostility Inventory (Buss & Durkee, 1957). Factor analytic studies of the seven subscales that comprise the BDHI have typically yielded two factors: one described usually as "aggressiveness" (i.e., revealing tendencies toward aggressive physical and/or verbal behavior) and the other as "hostility" (i.e., revealing tendencies toward attitudes of suspiciousness and resentment and toward wishing to see others come to harm). In a meta-analysis of several large factor analyses of the BDHI, Bushman, Cooper, and Lemke (1991) identified these same factors and labeled them, respectively, *overt* and *covert* hostility.

Citing several psychometric weaknesses in the BDHI as the reasons, Buss and Perry (1992) developed a new inventory built on a factorial structure similar to that of the original. Instead of the seven subscales of the original inventory, the new Aggression Questionnaire consists of four: physical aggression, verbal aggression, hostility, and anger. The four scales are positively correlated with each other to a moderate degree, with the highest r values reflecting the relation of anger to both physical and verbal aggression and hostility. Thus, as was the case with the BDHI, aggressiveness and hostility emerge as factors in the new scale, with anger serving as a "psychological bridge" between the two components. Scale scores were also positively correlated with peer ratings of physical and verbal aggression, anger, and hostility in a sample of male college students, with correlations ranging from $r = .20$ for verbal aggression to $r = .45$ for physical aggression. The Aggression Questionnaire therefore holds some promise as a predictor of aggressiveness and hostility.

A major program of research into individual difference variables in human aggression has been reported by Caprara and associates, who have conceptualized a number of personality variables as antecedents of aggressive behavior and have developed scales to assess these variables. Intercorrelations among the several variables have yielded a preliminary factorial structure of the aggressive personality, and the factors of the system have been shown to articulate with measures from other systems and theories, such as the five-factor model (Caprara, Barbaranelli, Pastorelli, & Perugini, 1994). The three scales most consistently related to aggressive dispositions have been irritability, emotional susceptibility, and dissipation–rumination. The first of these scales is defined as a "readiness to explode at the slightest provocation, including quick temper, grouchiness, exasperation, and rudeness" and the second as "the tendency to experience feelings of discomfort, helplessness, inadequacy, and vulnerability" (Caprara, Cinanni, D'Imperio, Passerini, Renzi, & Travaglia, 1985, p. 667). Dissipation–rumination refers to a tendency to retain or augment feelings of anger over time following provocation, as opposed to a tendency to dissipate such feelings and become less angry (Caprara, 1986). In several studies in laboratory settings, Caprara and colleagues have shown main effects on aggression for each of these variables, often paralleling main effects of frustrating or provoking treatments, such as task failure or insults (e.g., Caprara, 1982; Caprara, Renzi, Alcini, D'Imperio, & Travaglia, 1983).

The study of how the various personality scales relate to aggressive behavior raises the question of their status as moderator variables. As noted, several experimental studies have shown main effects for the personality variables. However, for personality to moderate situational effects, it is necessary to show an interaction between these variables and experimental treatments. Research done by Caprara has shown that such interactions are specific to certain combinations of treatment and personality variables. The variable shown most often to moderate the effects of provocation on aggression is irritability, provided that the provocation is operationalized in terms of failure at a task. In studies in which subjects have been given false feedback about task performance, those who are high in irritability have reacted to negative feedback with more intense aggression against a target than those who score low on that variable (Caprara et al., 1983). Emotional susceptibility has been shown not to interact with the feedback treatment variable, and when interpersonal insult is used as a means of provoking the subject, neither irritability nor emotional susceptibilily serves as a moderator variable, but dissipation–rumination does, with persons classified as high ruminators–low dissipators showing greater retaliatory aggression than low ruminators–high dissipators (Caprara, 1986).

In three studies, Bushman has reported a moderator effect of the trait of physical aggressiveness on both aggressive behavior and cognitive processing. Bushman and Geen (1990) found that male subjects who had scored high on the irritability scale of the BDHI listed a greater number of hostile and aggressive thoughts after seeing a moderately violent videotape than did those who had scored low on irritability. The authors invoked Berkowitz's theory of cognitive neoassociationism in concluding that a high level of personal irritability may reflect a large and highly articulated network of aggressive associations that is likely to be primed by stimuli related to violence. Bushman (1996) confirmed this supposition by showing that highly aggressive subjects made more aggressive verbal associations to ambiguous words than did less aggressive subjects. Bushman (1995) also demonstrated a link between personal aggressiveness and aggressive behavior in response to provocation following the observation of televised violence. Provoked subjects who were shown a violent videotape were more aggressive in their level of retaliation than those shown a less violent tape only if they were also high in physical aggressiveness as assessed by the Buss–Perry Aggression Questionnaire. Bushman's findings are especially significant because they show clear situation–person interactions and do so within the context of a well-developed theory.

The research described here stipulates some fairly straightforward effects of personality variables in aggression. Personality may also enter into aggression in more subtle ways through processes related to maintenance and enhancement of self-esteem. To the extent that being provoked threatens or weakens self-esteem and retaliation helps to restore it, such behavior might be expected to vary as a function of existing levels of the variable. Protection or restoration of self-esteem has been cited as a cause of aggression by numerous reviewers (e.g., Averill, 1982), but whether high or low self-esteem is most seriously affected by threats has not been clear. In a review on the subject, Baumeister, Smart, and Boden (1996) have concluded that aggression is usually an outcome of threats to highly favorable views of the self, i.e., high self-esteem. They suggest that the person with high self-esteem may direct anger toward others as a means of avoiding a downward revision of self-concept (see chapter by Baumeister and Boden). This is especially true of people whose high self-esteem is fragile, unstable, and susceptible to challenge (Kernis, Granneman, & Barclay, 1989). A related finding has been reported by Tangney, Wagner, Fletcher, and Gramzow (1992) that people who are relatively prone to experience shame are also more likely to express anger and hostility and to blame others for bad things that happen to them. Shame is an aversive emotion that brings about a negative evaluation of the self and a temporary breakdown in self-esteem. The corresponding tendency to blame others shown by shame-prone people may cause them to become angry and hostile toward those whom they see as the cause of their poor self-esteem. Thus shame may be an intervening variable that moderates the effects of provocation on self-esteem.

SOCIALIZATION DIFFERENCES

Aggression is moderated to a large degree by social and cultural factors. A provocation that evokes a violent and destructive response in one culture or society may elicit a more controlled reaction in another that follows different norms for aggressive behavior. The nature of a person's socialization therefore provides another basis for individual differences in aggression within given situations. In this final section of the chapter, two examples of socialization differences are described.

The analysis of social and cultural influences on aggression and violence has been facilitated by cross-cultural studies. These have taken two forms: those that compare *national cultures* and those that compare *subcultures within nations*. An example of the first type is the research program reported by Archer and Gartner (1984). This work involved the creation of a Comparative Crime Data File (CCDF) from statistics on 110 nations and 44 major cities over the period from 1900 to 1970. From this file, comparative rates of several crimes (e.g., homicide, rape, and criminal assault) were calculated and cross-national comparisons were made. One comparison revealed that the United States has the highest rate of homicides among the industrial nations of the world. Further analysis of cross-national data suggests that one cause of this high rate is the relatively easy availability of firearms in the United States (Archer, 1994), a conclusion supported by other findings showing that countries that enacted major controls over access to firearms showed overall decreases in rates of violent crime following implementation of those controls (Podell & Archer, 1994). Another possible explanation for the relatively high incidence of violence in the United States is a tendency for Americans to generate aggressive solutions to interpersonal conflicts to a greater degree than people from some other nations. Archer and McDaniel (1995) reported findings from a cross-national study that support this conclusion. Subjects in 12 countries— 10 western countries, Japan, and Korea—were asked to write stories describing the resolution of a number of hypothetical interpersonal conflicts; these stories were later analyzed for violent and nonviolent themes. Slightly more than 30% of the themes written by American subjects contained some type of violence, which was the fourth highest among the 12 nations, after New Zealand, Australia, and Northern Ireland. This finding indicates that Americans may be more likely to think of violent solutions to problems than persons from most other industrial nations.

Another finding reported by Archer and Gartner (1984) suggests that nations may come to be characterized by different levels of aggressiveness to the extent that they participate in collective violence through war. Participation in wars, especially as major combatants, can cause countries to bestow some legitimation on violence, with an increase in postwar violence, relative to prewar levels, as a consequence. From data in the CCDF, Archer and Gartner (1984) found that countries that participated in World War I and II were more likely than neutral control nations to experience a postwar increase in homicide rates. Participation in smaller wars, such as the Vietnam War, produced a similar, although less pronounced, outcome. The effect of war on subsequent social violence was also greater in countries that had suffered large combat losses than in those that had been less heavily involved and greater in the victorious countries than in the losers. A nation that engages in intensely violent activity and is rewarded for such behavior with victory may be providing a strong message regarding the instrumental value of violence to its people. It would not be surprising, therefore, if attitudes toward conflict resolution were affected to some degree by this lesson.

Violence may therefore become embedded in social norms that prescribe the conditions under which aggression is an acceptable, and even socially desirable, behavior. Such a prescriptive process is manifested not only in national cultures, but also in what Wolfgang and Ferracuti (1982) have called *subcultures of violence* within larger societies. The origins of various subcultures of violence depend on the history and circumstances of the society, but regardless of origins, the subculture dictates the values, beliefs, and attitudes of its members. Some studies indicate the existence of regional subcultural differences in aggression within the United States associated with differential norms for aggressive behavior (Cohen & Nisbett, 1994; Nisbett, 1993). Nisbett and colleagues have found that homicide rates among white non-Hispanic males living in rural or small town environments in the southern part of the country are higher than corresponding rates in similar settings in other regions. Southern white males do not endorse violence in general to a greater degree than non-Southerners, but they are more likely to favor aggressive behavior in defense of human life and property and in response to insults. Attitudes favoring punitive discipline of children also tend to be more strongly held in the South than elsewhere. Furthermore, white male homicide rates are higher in those parts of the rural South in which the herding and tending of animals is the main basis for agriculture than in those regions characterized by farming.

The concept of subcultures of violence has been criticized on grounds that certain of its central assumptions are open to question. Tedeschi and Felson (1994) have argued that the concept rests on two sequential relationships: demographic factors must be closely linked to certain values and these values must in turn mediate aggressive and violent behavior. After surveying a number of relevant studies, Tedeschi and Felson (1994) concluded that the evidence for these assumed relationships is weak at best. In a variant of the original hypothesis, Baumeister and Heatherton (1996) have proposed that subcultures do not promote or encourage aggressive behavior as much as they define the conditions under which such behavior is acceptable, i.e., they disinhibit aggressive reactions to situations that in other subcultures would be restrained. The regional effects documented by Nisbett may therefore reflect the influence of culture on the rules by which anger is expressed and displayed behaviorally.

CONCLUSION

This introductory chapter has discussed only a few of the variables in human aggression, but it is hoped that it has given some indication of the basic processes that are involved. The sequence of actions that begins with impulsive reactions to provocations and culminates in controlled and deliberate aggression describes the way in which aggression becomes part of the person's behavioral repertoire. What follows is a characteristic way in which the person construes social situations, making the person more or less likely to react to future provocations with aggression. Personal variables, of which sex, personality, and socialization are representative, moderate this latter process. In the chapters that follow, many of these underlying variables and processes are reflected.

REFERENCES

Anderson, C. A., Anderson, K. B., & Deuser, W. E. (1996). Examining an affective aggression framework: Weapon and temperature effects on aggressive thoughts, affect, and attitudes. *Personality and Social Psychology Bulletin, 22,* 366–376.

Archer, D. (1994). American violence: How high and why? *Law Studies, 19,* 12–20.

Archer, D., & Gartner, R. (1984). *Violence and crime in cross-national perspective.* New Haven, CT: Yale University Press.

Archer, D., & McDaniel, P. (1995). Violence and gender: Differences and similarities across societies. In R. B. Ruback & N. A. Weiner (Eds.), *Interpersonal violent behaviors: Social and cultural aspects* (pp. 63–87). New York: Springer.

Archer, J., & Parker, S. (1994). Social representations of aggression in children. *Aggressive Behavior, 20,* 101–114.

Averill, J. R. (1982). *Anger and aggression: An essay on emotion.* New York: Springer-Verlag.

Baron, R. B., & Richardson, D. (1994). *Human aggression.* New York: Plenum.

Baumeister, R. F., & Heatherton, T. F. (1996). Self-regulation failure: An overview. *Psychological Inquiry, 7,* 1–15.

Baumeister, R. F., Smart, L., & Boden, J. M. (1996). Relation of threatened egotism to violence and aggression: The dark side of high self-esteem. *Psychological Review, 103,* 5–33.

Berkowitz, L. (1984). Some effects of thoughts on anti- and prosocial influences of media events: A cognitive-neoassociationist analysis. *Psychological Bulletin, 95,* 410–427.

Berkowitz, L. B. (1993). *Aggression: Its causes, consequences, and control.* New York: McGraw-Hill.

Berkowitz, L., & Heimer, K. (1989). On the construction of the anger experience: Aversive events and negative priming in the formation of feelings. In L. Berkowitz (Ed.), *Advances in experimental social psychology* (Vol. 22, pp. 1–37). New York: Academic Press.

Berman, M., Gladue, B., & Taylor, S. (1993). The effects of hormones, Type A behavior pattern, and provocation on aggression in men. *Motivation and Emotion, 17,* 125–138.

Bersani, A., Chen, H. T., Pendleton, B. F., & Denton, R. (1992). Personality traits of convicted male batterers. *Journal of Family Violence, 7,* 123–134.

Bettencourt, B. A., & Miller, N. (1996). Sex differences in aggression as a function of provocation: A meta-analysis. *Psychological Bulletin, 119,* 422–447.

Björkqvist, K., Lagerspetz, K. M. J., & Kaukiainen, A. (1992). Do girls manipulate and boys fight? Developmental trends in regard to direct and indirect aggression. *Aggressive Behavior, 18,* 117–127.

Björkqvist, K., Österman, K., & Lagerspetz, K. M. J. (1994). Sex differences in covert aggression among adults. *Aggressive Behavior, 20,* 27–33.

Boldizar, J. P., Perry, D. G., & Perry, L. (1989). Outcome values and aggression. *Child Development, 60,* 571–579.

Bushman, B. J. (1995). Moderating role of trait aggressiveness in the effects of violent media on aggression. *Journal of Personality and Social Psychology, 69,* 950–960.

Bushman, B. J. (1996). Individual differences in the extent and development of aggressive cognitive-associative networks. *Personality and Social Psychology Bulletin, 22,* 811–819.

Bushman, B. J., Cooper, H. M., & Lemke, K. M. (1991). Meta-analysis of factor analyses: An illustration using the Buss-Durkee Hostility Inventory. *Personality and Individual Differences, 17,* 344–349.

Bushman, B. J., & Geen, R. G. (1990). Role of cognitive-emotional mediators and individual differences in the effects of media violence on aggression. *Journal of Personality and Social Psychology, 58,* 156–163.

Buss, A. H., & Durkee, A. (1957). An inventory for assessing different kinds of hostility. *Journal of Consulting Psychology, 21,* 343–349.

Buss, A. H., & Perry, M. (1992). The Aggression Questionnaire. *Journal of Personality and Social Psychology, 63,* 452–459.

Cairns, R. B. (1986). An evolutionary and developmental perspective on aggressive patterns. In C. Zahn-Waxler, E. M. Cummings, & R. Iannotti (Eds.), *Altruism and aggression: Biological and social origins* (pp. 58–87). Cambridge, UK: Cambridge University Press.

Campbell, A. (1993). *Men, women, and aggression.* New York: Basic Books.

Campbell, A., & Muncer, S. (1987). Models of anger and aggression in the social talk of women and men. *Journal for the Theory of Social Behavior, 17,* 489–512.

Campbell, A., & Muncer, S. (1994). Sex differences in aggression: Social representation and social roles. *British Journal of Social Psychology, 33,* 233–240.

Campbell, A., Muncer, S., & Coyle, E. (1992). Social representation of aggression as an explanation of gender differences: A preliminary study. *Aggressive Behavior, 18,* 95–108.

Capaldi, D. M. (1991). Co-occurrence of conduct problems and depressive symptoms in early adolescent boys. I. Familial factors and general adjustment. *Development and Psychopathology, 3,* 277–300.

Caprara, G. V. (1982). A comparison of the frustration–aggression and emotional susceptibility hypotheses. *Aggressive Behavior, 8,* 234–236.

Caprara, G. V. (1986). Indicators of aggression: The Dissipation-Rumination Scale. *Personality and Individual Differences, 7,* 763–769.

Caprara, G. V., Barbaranelli, C., Pastorelli, C., & Perugini, M. (1994). Individual differences in the study of aggression. *Aggressive Behavior, 20,* 291–303.

Caprara, G. V., Cinanni, V., D'Imperio, G., Passerini, S., Renzi, P., & Travaglia, G. (1985). Indicators of impulsive aggression: Present status of research on Irritability and Emotional Susceptibility Scales. *Personality and Individual Differences, 6,* 665–674.

Caprara, G. V., Renzi, P., Alcini, P., D'Imperio, G., & Travaglia, G. (1983). Instigation to aggress and escalation of aggression examined from a personological perspective: The role of irritability and emotional susceptibility. *Aggressive Behavior, 9,* 345–351.

Caspi, A., Elder, G. H., Jr., & Bem, D. J. (1987). Moving against the world: Life-course patterns of explosive children. *Developmental Psychology, 23,* 308–313.

Cohen, D., & Nisbett, R. E. (1994). Self-protection and culture of honor: Explaining Southern violence. *Personality and Social Psychology Bulletin, 20,* 551–567.

Crick, N. R. (1995). Relational aggression: The role of intent attributions, feelings of distress, and provocation type. *Development and Psychopathology, 7,* 313–322.

Crick, N. R. (1996). Gender differences in children's normative beliefs about aggression: How do I hurt thee? Let me count the ways. *Child Development, 67,* 1003–1014.

Crick, N. R., & Dodge, K. A. (1994). A review and reformulation of social information-processing mechanisms in children's social adjustment. *Psychological Bulletin, 115,* 74–101.

Crick, N. R., & Grotepeter, J. K. (1995). Relational aggression, gender, and social-psychological adjustment. *Child Development, 66,* 710–722.

Crick, N. R., & Ladd, G. W. (1990). Children's perceptions of the outcomes of aggressive strategies: Do the ends justify being mean? *Developmental Psychology, 26,* 612–620.

Deluty, R. H. (1985). Consistency of aggressive, assertive, and submissive behavior for children. *Journal of Personality and Social Psychology, 49,* 1054–1065.

Dodge, K. A. (1980). Social cognition and children's aggressive behavior. *Child Development, 51,* 162–170.

Dodge, K. A., Coie, J. D., & Brakke, N. P. (1982). Behavior patterns of socially rejected and neglected preadolescents: The roles of social approach and aggression. *Journal of Abnormal Child Psychology, 10,* 389–410.

Dodge, K. A., & Newman, J. P. (1981). Biased decision making processes in aggressive boys. *Journal of Abnormal Psychology, 90,* 375–379.

Dodge, K. A., & Tomlin, A. M. (1987). Utilization of self-schemas as a mechanism of interpretational bias in aggressive children. *Social Cognition, 5,* 280–300.

Eagly, A. H., & Steffen, V. J. (1986). Gender and aggressive behavior: A meta-analytic review of the social psychological literature. *Psychological Bulletin, 100,* 309–330.

Edmunds, G., & Kendrick, D. C. (1980). *The measurement of human aggressiveness.* New York: Halsted Press.

Eron, L. D., & Huesmann, L. R. (1990). The stability of aggressive behavior: Even unto the third generation. In M. Lewis & S. M. Miller (Eds.), *Handbook of developmental psychopathology* (pp. 147–156). New York: Plenum.

Farrington, D. P. (1994). Childhood, adolescent, and adult features of violent males. In L. R. Huesmann (Ed.), *Aggressive behavior: Current perspectives* (pp. 215–240). New York: Plenum.

Frodi, A., Macaulay, J., & Thome, P. R. (1977). Are women always less aggressive than men? A review of the experimental literature. *Psychological Bulletin, 84,* 634–660.

Geen, R. G. (1990). *Human aggression.* Pacific Grove, CA: Brooks/Cole.

Ghodsian-Carpey, J., & Baker, L. A. (1987). Genetic and environmental influences on aggression in 4- to 7-year-old twins. *Aggressive Behavior, 13,* 173–186.

Gladue, B. A. (1991). Aggressive behavioral characteristics, hormones, and sexual orientation in men and women. *Aggressive Behavior, 17,* 313–326.

Gouze, K. R. (1987). Attention and social problem solving as correlates of aggression in preschool males. *Journal of Abnormal Child Psychology, 15,* 181–197.

Harris, M. B. (1993). How provoking! What makes men and women angry? *Aggressive Behavior, 19,* 199–211.

Huesmann, L. R. (1988). An information processing model for the development of aggression. *Aggressive Behavior, 14,* 13–24.

Julian, T. W., & McKenry, P. C. (1993). Mediators of male violence toward female intimates. *Journal of Family Violence, 8,* 39–58.

Kernis, M. H., Grannemann, B. D., & Barclay, L. C. (1989). Stability and level of self-esteem as predictors of anger arousal and hostility. *Journal of Personality and Social Psychology, 56,* 1013–1022.

Lagerspetz, K. M. J., & Björkqvist, K. (1994). Indirect aggression in boys and girls. In L. R. Huesmann (Ed.), *Aggressive behavior: Current perspectives* (pp. 131–150). New York: Plenum.

Lagerspetz, K. M. J., Björkqvist, K., & Peltonen, T. (1988). Is indirect aggression typical of females? Gender differences in aggressiveness in 11- to 12-year-old children. *Aggressive Behavior, 14,* 403–414.

Lewis, D. O., Moy, E., Jackson, L. D., Aaronson, R., Restifo, N., Serra, S., & Simos, A. (1985). Biopsychological characteristics of children who later murder: A prospective study. *American Journal of Psychiatry, 142,* 1161–1167.

Maccoby, E. E., & Jacklin, C. N. (1974). *The psychology of sex differences.* Stanford, CA: Stanford University Press.

Miles, D. R., & Carey, G. (1997). The genetic and environmental architecture of human aggression. *Journal of Personality and Social Psychology, 72,* 207–217.

Moffitt, T. E. (1993). Adolescence-limited and life-course-persistent antisocial behavior: A developmental taxonomy. *Psychological Review, 100,* 674–701.

Nasby, W., Hayden, B., & DePaulo, B. M. (1979). Attributional bias among aggressive boys to interpret unambiguous social stimuli as displays of hostility. *Journal of Abnormal Psychology, 89,* 459–468.

Nisbett, R. E. (1993). Violence and U.S. regional culture. *American Psychologist, 48,* 441–449.

Olweus, D. (1979). Stability of aggression patterns in males: A review. *Psychological Bulletin, 86,* 852–875.

Patterson, G. R., Reid, J. B., & Dishion, T. J. (1992). *Antisocial boys.* Eugene, OR: Castalia Press.

Paul, L., Foss, M. A., & Galloway, J. (1993). Sexual jealousy in young women and men: Aggressive responsiveness to partner and rival. *Aggressive Behavior, 19,* 401–420.

Paul, L., & Galloway, J. (1994). Sexual jealousy: Gender differences in response to partner and rival. *Aggressive Behavior, 20,* 79–100.

Perry, D. G., Perry, L. C., & Boldizar, J. P. (1990). Learning of aggression. In M. Lewis & S. Miller (Eds.), *Handbook of developmental psychopathology* (pp. 135–146). New York: Plenum.

Perry, D. G., Perry, L. C., & Rasmussen, P. (1986). Cognitive social learning mediators of aggression. *Child Development, 57,* 700–711.

Podell, S., & Archer, D. (1994). Do legal changes matter? The case of gun control laws. In M. Costanzo & S. Oskamp (Eds.), *Violence and the law* (pp. 37–60). Thousand Oaks, CA: Sage.

Pontius, A. A. (1984). Specific stimulus-evoked violent action in psychotic trigger reaction: A seizure-like imbalance between frontal lobe and limbic system? *Perceptual and Motor Skills, 59,* 299–333.

Reinisch, J. M., & Sanders, S. A. (1986). A test of sex differences in aggressive response to hypothetical conflict situations. *Journal of Personality and Social Psychology, 50,* 1045–1049.

Rushton, J. P., & Erdle, S. (1987). Evidence for aggressive (and delinquent) personality. *British Journal of Social Psychology, 26,* 87–89.

Slaby, R. G., & Guerra, N. G. (1988). Cognitive mediators of aggression in adolescent offenders. 1. Assessment. *Developmental Psychology, 24,* 580–588.

Stattin, H., & Magnusson, D. (1989). The role of early aggressive behavior in the frequency, seriousness, and types of later crime. *Journal of Consulting and Clinical Psychology, 57,* 710–718.

Tangney, J. P., Wagner, P., Fletcher, C., & Gramzow, R. (1992). Shame into anger? The relation of shame and guilt to anger and self-reported aggression. *Journal of Personality and Social Psychology, 62,* 669–675.

Tedeschi, J. T., & Felson, R. B. (1994). *Violence, aggression, and coercive actions.* Washington, DC: American Psychological Association.

Tedeschi, J. T., & Nesler, M. S. (1993). Grievances: Development and reactions. In R. B. Felson & J. T. Tedeschi (Eds.), *Aggression and violence: Social interactionist perspectives* (pp. 13–45). Washington, DC: American Psychological Association.

Van Goozen, S. H. M., Frijda, N. H., & Van de Poll, N. E. (1994). Anger and aggression in women: Influence of sports choice and testosterone administration. *Aggressive Behavior, 20,* 213–222.

Van Goozen, S. H. M., Frijda, N. H., & Van de Poll, N. E. (1995). Anger and aggression during role playing: Gender differences between hormonally treated male and female transsexuals and controls. *Aggressive Behavior, 21,* 257–273.

White, J. W. (1983). Sex and gender issues in aggression research. In R. G. Geen & E. I. Donnerstein (Eds.), *Aggression: Theoretical and empirical reviews* (Vol. 2, pp. 1–26). New York: Academic Press.

Wolfgang, M. E., & Ferracuti, F. (1982). *The subculture of violence: Towards an integrated theory in criminology.* Beverly Hills, CA: Sage.

Zillmann, D. (1988). Cognition-excitation interdependencies in aggressive behavior. *Aggressive Behavior, 14,* 51–64.

2

METHODOLOGY IN THE STUDY

OF AGGRESSION: INTEGRATING

EXPERIMENTAL AND

NONEXPERIMENTAL FINDINGS

BRAD J. BUSHMAN

Iowa State University

CRAIG A. ANDERSON

University of Missouri

Consider the following news story (McKinley, 1990).

> A gang of young men wielding knives and bats went on a Halloween rampage Wednesday night, assaulting several homeless people on the footbridge to Wards Island and leaving one of them dead among the garbage-strewn weeds, his throat slashed. The group of about 10 young men, some wearing Halloween masks, apparently attacked the homeless men for thrills.

Now consider the following description of a laboratory aggression experiment. In this experiment (Zimbardo, 1969), college women were told that the researchers were studying "empathic responses to strangers." Individuals participated in groups of four. By the flip of a coin, participants were assigned to anonymous or identifiable conditions. In the anonymous condition, participants wore large laboratory coats, wore hoods over their heads, and were not referred to by name. In the identifiable condition, participants did not wear laboratory coats, wore large name tags, and were referred to by name. The room lights were turned off in the anonymous condition or only dimmed in the identifiable condition. Participants then listened to one of two tape-recorded interviews between the experimenter and another "participant" (who was actually an accomplice to the experimenter). In one of the tapes, the accomplice behaved in a nice, altruistic, and accepting manner. In the other tape, she behaved in an obnoxious, self-centered, and critical manner.

Participants then shocked the accomplice by holding down a button as long as they wanted her to be shocked. The results showed that participants in the anonymous condition gave the accomplice longer shocks than did participants in the identifiable condition, especially when the accomplice was obnoxious.

What is the relation between the news report and the laboratory aggression experiment? Is there any reason to believe that "artificial" laboratory studies of aggression can inform us about gang violence or any other kind of "real world" aggression? That is, do the measures of aggression that are typically used in laboratory studies truly measure "aggression"? There are two related issues embedded in this question. First, do different laboratory measures of aggression measure the same underlying conceptual variable? Second, do laboratory measures of aggression measure "real" aggression, as found in the natural environment? The major purpose of this chapter is to answer these important questions. First, however, we must discuss what is meant by "aggression" and how aggression is measured in the laboratory.

MEASUREMENT OF AGGRESSION

Buss (1961, p. 1) defined aggression as "a response that delivers noxious stimuli to another organism." Geen (1990) clarified this definition by adding two elements: (a) the aggressor delivers the noxious stimuli with the intent to harm the victim, and (b) the aggressor expects that the noxious stimuli will have their intended effect. Buss further proposed that acts of human aggression can be classified using combinations of three dichotomous variables: physical versus verbal, direct versus indirect, and active versus passive. Although there are eight possible combinations of the three dichotomous variables proposed by Buss, none of the four "passive" types of aggression are common in experimental studies of aggression. This review therefore focuses on the four "active" types of human aggression. In *physical* aggression, noxious stimuli delivered to the victim are pain and injury, whereas in *verbal* aggression, noxious stimuli delivered to the victim are rejection and threat. In *direct* aggression the aggressor is easily identified by the victim, whereas in *indirect* aggression the aggressor is not easily identified by the victim. There are two ways in which an aggressive act can be indirect. First, the victim is not present and noxious stimuli are delivered via the negative reactions of others. Second, the victim is not injured or threatened, but his or her belongings are stolen or damaged. The next section describes prototypical procedures for measuring each type of active aggression.

DIRECT PHYSICAL AGGRESSION

The aggression machine paradigm (Buss, 1961) has been the primary laboratory procedure used to measure direct physical aggression. In this procedure, a participant and a confederate are told that the study is concerned with the effects of punishment on learning. Using a rigged lottery, the real participant is selected to be the "teacher" whereas the confederate is selected to be the "learner." The participant presents stimulus materials to the confederate who (supposedly) attempts to learn them. In some experiments, the participant is angered by the confederate prior to the beginning of the learning task.

When the confederate makes an incorrect response on a trial, the participant is supposed to punish him or her by means of electric shock. By using different buttons, the participant can control the intensity and duration of shock given to the confederate. The shocks, for example, may range in intensity from just perceptible (e.g., button 1) to excruciatingly painful (e.g., button 10). In some experiments, shock duration is controlled by holding down the shock button for the desired amount of time. The two measures of aggression then are intensity and duration of shock "given" to the confederate by the participant. Some researchers have used noxious stimuli other than electric shocks, such as noise blasts and heat pulses.

Another commonly employed method to study direct physical aggression is to place the participant and the confederate in a situation that requires the confederate to evaluate the participant and *later* requires the participant to evaluate the confederate. In Berkowitz's (1962) paradigm, for example, participants are led to believe that they will be evaluating another student's performance on an assigned task. Solutions are evaluated using anywhere from 1 to 10 electric shocks, where 1 shock indicates a very favorable evaluation and 10 shocks indicates a very unfavorable evaluation. First, the confederate evaluates the participant's solution. Generally, half of the participants receive a positive evaluation from the confederate (e.g., 1 shock), whereas the other half receive a negative evaluation (e.g., 7 shocks). After exposure to some treatment (e.g., a violent or nonviolent film), the participant then evaluates the confederate's solution. The measure of aggression is the number of shocks the participant gives the confederate.

The competitive reaction time paradigm (Taylor, 1967) is a third common method employed in the laboratory to study direct physical aggression. In this procedure, the participant competes with an ostensible opponent on a reaction time task in which the slower responding person receives electric shock. At the beginning of each trial the participant sets the intensity of shock he or she wants the opponent (confederate) to receive if the opponent's response is slower. At the end of each trial, the participant is informed of the level of shock the opponent set for him or her to receive on the trial. The slower responding person then supposedly receives the shock. In actuality, the experimenter determines both who wins and loses and the feedback/shocks delivered. Sometimes provocation is manipulated by increasing the intensity of shock set by the "opponent" across trials on the reaction time task. The measure of aggression is the intensity of shock the participant sets for the opponent. Some researchers have included duration as a second measure of aggression. Other researchers have used noise rather than shock as the noxious stimuli.

INDIRECT PHYSICAL AGGRESSION

The laboratory paradigms used to measure direct physical aggression also have been modified to measure indirect physical aggression. In one study (Barnett, 1979), for example, male college students were given $2.00 and course credit for their participation. Participants were told to subtract between 0 cents (button 0) and 9 cents (button 9) from a confederate whenever he made a mistake on a trial. This paradigm measures indirect physical aggression because the participant takes the confederate's belongings (i.e., his money).

The free-operant paradigm (e.g., Cherek, 1981) is another method commonly employed to measure indirect physical aggression. In this procedure, the participant can press one of two buttons on an apparatus. Pressing button A results in the accumulation of points exchangeable for money. Pressing button B results in the subtraction of points from a fictitious second participant. Sometimes provocation is manipulated by subtracting points from the participant; the point loss is attributed to the fictitious second participant. The fixed ratios associated with each button also can be manipulated (e.g., a fixed ratio of 100 responses might be required for button A, whereas a fixed ratio of 10 responses might be required for button B).

DIRECT VERBAL AGGRESSION

In the laboratory, verbal aggression is often assessed by recording a participant's vocal comments to a confederate and counting the frequency of attacks or other negative verbal statements. For example, in a study by Wheeler and Caggiula (1966), male naval recruits evaluated opinions expressed by a confederate on various topics (e.g., religion, war, sex, liquor). On most of the topics, the confederate expressed socially undesirable opinions. On the topic of religion, for example, the confederate said: "I think my religion is best, and I don't think the others are worth a damn. . . . If I had my way, all other religions would be illegal." The participant then was given an opportunity to comment on the confederate's opinions. Because the confederate could presumably overhear the participant's evaluations of him, it was possible for the participant to make direct verbal attacks against the confederate. The dependent variable was whether or not the participant made extremely aggressive evaluations of the confederate (that he was an "ass," "idiot," "crazy," "nuts," "insane," etc.; that he should be "locked up," "shot," "deported," "beaten up," "tortured," etc.).

INDIRECT VERBAL AGGRESSION

Indirect measures of verbal aggression are more common in laboratory experiments than are direct measures of verbal aggression. Generally, a confederate or experimenter first provokes the participant. Rather than confronting the confederate or experimenter face to face, the participant uses a pencil-and-paper measure to evaluate him or her. The participant is led to believe that negative ratings will harm the confederate or experimenter in some way. In one study (Rohsenow & Bachorowski, 1984), for example, a male participant was told to trace a circle as slowly as possible. After this task was completed, a male experimenter burst into the room, introduced himself as the supervisor who had been observing through a one-way mirror, and contemptuously stated, "Obviously, you don't follow instructions. You were *supposed* to trace the circle as slowly as possible without stopping but you clearly didn't do this. Now I don't know if we can use your data." The experimenter paused, then continued (interrupting the participant if he or she tried to respond), "Do it over again." After the experiment, the participant completed an evaluation form for each member of the laboratory staff, including the obnoxious experimenter. The form asked the participant to rate each staff member on seven-point scales as to whether he or she was effective in performing duties, was a capable employee, was likeable, made the participant feel comfortable, showed respect for the participant, and should be rehired. The evaluations were placed in a sealed envelope and were allegedly sent to the principal investigator to be used in future hiring decisions. Therefore, the participant could harm the experimenter's chance of being rehired by evaluating him in a negative manner.

CONVERGENCE OF LABORATORY AGGRESSION MEASURES

The first question—Do different laboratory measures of aggression measure the same underlying conceptual variable?—has been addressed in a meta-analytic review of laboratory aggression measures by Carlson, Marcus-Newhall, and Miller (1989). These researchers used three different approaches to examining this question. The first focused on the correlations among measures of direct physical aggression assessed within the same study. They reasoned that, "If the different dependent measures that are used to assess aggression have a common conceptual component, then positive correlations between them should be present within studies that include multiple measures" (p. 378). They found that the average within study correlations of intensity, duration, and number of physical punishments were all positive and statistically significant ($ps < .05$).

As impressive as these results are, we believe them to underestimate the true comparability of these different laboratory measures of physical aggression. The within-subjects nature of these correlations may well reduce their magnitude in two different artificial ways. First, when people have multiple ways of aggressing against another person, they may well choose to use only one of them to "get back" at their target. That is, most will see one "payback" method as being "best" and will therefore use only that one. Different participants will likely choose

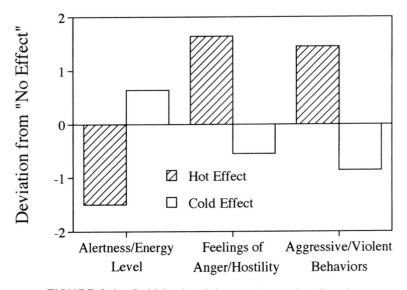

FIGURE 2.1 Social theories relating temperature to three dimensions.

different payback methods as the "best," thus reducing intermeasure correlations. Second, in our experience, many participants forget that there is more than one way to aggress against their target. There are so many things going on in these studies (i.e., the participants are very involved and cognitively busy) that they remember only one payback method.

A second approach used by Carlson et al. (1989) to examine the comparability of laboratory measures of aggression involved examining the between-subjects effects of theoretically relevant negative affect-related independent variables on physical versus verbal measures of aggression in laboratory studies. They reasoned that if artificial laboratory measures of physical and verbal aggression were not measuring the same underlying construct, then ANOVAs examining the effects of negative affect manipulations (anger, frustration, aggression directness, personal attack) should differ as a function of the type of aggression measure used. More specifically, meta-analyses on these effects should yield significant aggression type × negative affect interactions if laboratory measures of physical and verbal aggression are not measuring the same underlying type of aggression. Across the four different types of negative affect manipulations (listed earlier), results strongly contradicted this "different types" proposition; none of the interactions was significant.

A third approach used by Carlson et al. (1989) examined the correlations between the effect of various independent variables on different types of laboratory measures of aggression in laboratory studies that had more than one aggression-dependent variable. The types of aggression measures included were intensity, number, or duration of punishments, "other" measures of physical aggression (e.g., latency), and written. Figure 2.1 clearly reveals that different measures of aggression are significantly positively related to each other across a wide range of laboratory studies. For instance, correlations of number, duration, and intensity of punishments ranged from .70 to .88. Written and physical response measures of aggression were also positively correlated (overall $r = .71$).

Overall, the Carlson et al. (1989) results clearly demonstrate that the most commonly used (and "artificial") laboratory measures of aggression tap the same underlying conceptual variable, which leads us to the second question posed at the outset: Do laboratory measures of aggression measure "real" aggression, as found in the natural environment?

SIMILARITY OF REAL-WORLD AND LABORATORY AGGRESSION

Table 2.1 gives "real world" and laboratory examples of each of the four types of active aggression proposed by Buss (1961). In the real world, most extreme acts of aggression are violent crimes, which the FBI classifies as murder, aggravated assault, forcible rape, and robbery. According to Buss's framework, murder, forcible rape, and aggravated assault are examples of direct physical aggression, whereas robbery is an example of indirect physical aggression. As can be seen in Table 2.1, laboratory measures of aggression have few surface features in common with real world measures of aggression. It is this lack of surface similarity that leads to the overly pessimistic critiques of the value of laboratory aggression paradigms.

TABLE 2.1   "Real World" and Laboratory Examples of the Types of Aggression Proposed by Buss (1961)

Type of aggression	"Real world" examples	Laboratory examples
Direct physical	Assaulting someone with body parts (e.g., limbs, teeth) or weapons (e.g., clubs, knives, guns)	Shocking a confederate on a task
Indirect physical	Stealing or damaging someone's property Setting a booby trap for someone Hiring an assassin to kill someone	Subtracting money from a confederate on a task
Direct verbal	Criticizing, derogating, or cursing someone Threatening someone	Making negative verbal statements to a confederate
Indirect verbal	Spreading vicious rumors about someone	Evaluating a confederate negatively on a questionnaire

CAN ONE GENERALIZE THE RESULTS FROM THE ARTIFICIAL CONFINES OF THE LABORATORY TO THE REAL WORLD?

Now back to the question at hand: Is there any reason to believe that the results from laboratory aggression studies can inform us about "real world" aggression? We believe that the answer to this question depends on whether aggression in the laboratory paradigm has the same meaning as it does in the real world (also see Berkowitz & Donnerstein, 1982). If laboratory aggression "means" the same thing to people as real world aggression, then there should be considerable correspondence between the effects of the same conceptual independent variables on laboratory and real world aggression measures. Likewise, individual differences in aggressiveness observed in the real world should also be observed in the laboratory.

We began this study by creating a list of situational and individual difference variables that we believed a priori to relate to real world aggression (see Anderson & Bushman, 1997). We then examined the published literature to compare the effects of these variables on real world and laboratory aggression. Table 2.2 lists the situational and individual difference variables we examined. Also indicated for each variable in Table 2.2 is whether there was sufficient empirical support to warrant a comparison.

Meta-analytic procedures were used to integrate the results from studies conducted inside and outside the laboratory.[1] Although meta-analytic procedures can be used to combine the results from two studies, in this chapter meta-analytic procedures were used only if there were at least three independent studies. When possible, we also tested whether the mean effect-size estimates differed for studies conducted inside and outside the laboratory. A .05 significance level was used for all tests.

Because laboratory researchers study more homogeneous populations (e.g., college students), individual differences should vary more outside the laboratory. In other words, individual difference variables have a restricted range in laboratory studies. Thus, stronger effects for individual difference variables are expected outside the laboratory than within it. The opposite pattern of results is expected

---

[1]To obtain a weighted average of the sample correlations, r_+, we first obtained a weighted average of Fisher's r-to-z transformation values in which each z value was weighted by the inverse of its variance (i.e., $N - 3$). Thus, correlations based on larger sample sizes received more weight than did correlations based on smaller sample sizes. Once a 95% confidence interval was obtained for the population z value, it was transformed to a 95% confidence interval for the population correlation, ρ (see Hedges & Olkin, 1985, pp. 235 and 236). The standardized mean difference was defined as $d = (M_E - M_C)/SD$, where M_E and M_C are the sample means for the experimental and control groups, respectively, and SD is the pooled estimate of the population standard deviation. To obtain a weighted average of the sample standardized mean differences, d_+, each d value was weighted by the inverse of its variance, $[2(n_E + n_C)n_En_C]/[2(n_E + n_C)^2 + n_En_Cd^2]$. A 95% confidence interval was also calculated for the population standardized mean difference, δ (see Hedges & Olkin, 1985, pp. 110–113). Cohen (1988) has offered conventional values for "small," "medium," and "large" effect-size estimates. For the standardized mean difference, the conventional values for small, medium, and large effects are $d = 0.20$, $d = 0.50$, and $d = 0.80$, respectively. For the correlation coefficient, the conventional values for small, medium, and large effects are $r = .10$, $r = .30$, and $r = .50$, respectively. According to Cohen, most of the effects in the social sciences are small to medium.

TABLE 2.2 Review Status of the Individual Difference and Situational Variables Originally Selected for Review

Individual difference variables			Situational variables		
Variable	Keywords	Review status	Variable	Keywords	Review status
Sex	NA	Kept	Provocation	NA	Kept
Trait aggressiveness	Buss, BDHI, Aggression Questionnaire, AQ, trait aggress[a]	Kept	Alcohol	NA	Kept
			Media violence	NA	Kept
Type A personality	Type A, Type B	Kept	Anonymity	anonym,[a] deindividuat[a]	Kept
Sex role orientation	sex, gender, sex role[a]	Dropped[b]	Temperature	NA	Kept
Attitudes toward violence	attitud[a]	Dropped[c]	Frustration	frustrat[a]	Dropped[e]
Rape myth beliefs	rape myth,[a] attitud,[a] belief[a]	Dropped[d]	Self-awareness	self awarene,[a] mirror	Dropped[b]
Biological differences	XYY, hormon,[a] insulin, serum cholesterol, glucose genetic,[a] biolog[a]	Dropped[d]	Weapons effect	weapon,[a] gun[a]	Kept

[a]Not applicable because an extant meta-analysis was used.

[b]These variables were dropped because there were too few correlational studies with similar measures to laboratory experiments.

[c]This variable was dropped because only two laboratory experiments were located and meta-analytic procedures were deemed inappropriate for such a small number of studies.

[d]These variables were dropped because only one laboratory experiment was located.

[e]This variable was dropped because it is frequently defined in different ways and because a more precise variable, provocation, was kept.

TABLE 2.3   Mean Effect Size Estimates and Confidence Intervals for Individual Difference and Situational Variables Studied Inside and Outside the Laboratory

Variable	N	Effect-size estimate	95% CI
Individual difference variables			
Sex[a]			
Studies conducted outside the laboratory			
Physical aggression	6	$d_+ = 0.40^b$	[0.25, 0.55]
Verbal aggression	3	$d_+ = 0.03^a$	[–0.15, 0.22]
Studies conducted inside the laboratory			
Physical aggression	37	$d_+ = 0.31^b$	[0.23, 0.38]
Verbal aggression	18	$d_+ = 0.13^a$	[0.03, 0.24]
Trait aggressiveness			
Studies conducted outside the laboratory	16	$r_+ = .42^b$	[.38, .47]
Studies conducted inside the laboratory	13	$r_+ = .24^a$	[.18, .29]
Type A personality			
Studies conducted outside the laboratory	3	$d_+ = 0.97^b$	[0.71, 1.23]
Studies conducted inside the laboratory	9	$d_+ = 0.34^a$	[0.18, 0.49]
Situational variables			
Provocation[a]			
Studies conducted inside the laboratory	66	$d_+ = 0.76$	[0.66, 0.85]
Alcohol[b]			
Studies conducted outside the laboratory	130	$r_+ = 0.16^a$	[0.14, 0.17]
Studies conducted inside the laboratory	42	$r_+ = 0.26^a$	[0.21, 0.30]
Weapons effect[c]			
Studies conducted outside the laboratory	5	$d_+ = 0.17^a$	[–0.05, 0.39]
Studies conducted inside the laboratory	16	$d_+ = 0.21^a$	[0.01, 0.41]
Media violence[d]			
Studies conducted outside the laboratory	556	$d_+ = 0.42^b$	
Studies conducted inside the laboratory	586	$d_+ = 0.87^a$	
Anonymity			
Studies conducted outside the laboratory	4	$d_+ = 0.44^a$	[0.25, 0.63]
Studies conducted inside the laboratory	18	$d_+ = 0.57^a$	[0.45, 0.69]
Temperature[e]			
Studies conducted inside the laboratory			
Overall	28	$d_+ = 0.06$	[–0.11, 0.23]
Neutral context	12	$d_+ = 0.25$	[–0.03, 0.53]
Extra-negative context	14	$d_+ = -0.09$	[–0.33, 0.15]

Note: N = number of effect size estimates. Statistical test was the unit of analysis for the media violence variable; study was the unit of analysis for all variables. CI, confidence interval. r_+, weighted average of the sample correlations. d_+, weighted average of the sample standardized mean differences. Mean effect-size estimates (inside the lab vs outside the lab comparisons) having the same subscript are not significantly different for that variable at the .05 level.
[a]Data from Bettencourt & Miller (1996).
[b]Data from Lipsey et al. (1997).
[c]Data from Carlson, Marcus-Newhall, & Miller (1990).
[d]Data from Paik and Comstock (1994).
[e]Data from K. Anderson & Anderson (1997).

for situational variables because the greater variability in individual differences outside the laboratory makes situational variables less predictive.

LITERATURE SEARCH PROCEDURE

Whenever possible, extant meta-analytic literature reviews were used. In those cases where such reviews did not already exist, we attempted to conduct an exhaustive search of the literature. Table 2.2 also indicates whether a new literature search was conducted for each variable. The PsycINFO computer data base was searched (1974–1996) using the key words *aggress** and *violen**. The asterisk at the end of the key word gives all forms of the key words (e.g., *aggress, aggressive, aggressiveness, aggression, aggressed, aggressor*). The *aggress** and *violen** key words were paired with the key words for the individual difference and situational variables requiring a new search, as shown in Table 2.2. The search was restricted to studies published in English and to studies that used human participants.

RESULTS

INDIVIDUAL DIFFERENCES IN AGGRESSION

This section assesses the correspondence between findings from studies using real world and laboratory measures of aggression, focusing on the following individual difference variables: sex, trait aggressiveness, and Type A coronary-prone behavior pattern.

Sex Differences

Studies Conducted Outside the Laboratory

Archival data on violent crime rates clearly show that males commit more murders and assaults than do females. This sex effect occurs in virtually every murder and assault rate data set that can be found. For example, Dexter (1899) showed that the male rate of assault in New York city in the years from 1891 to 1897 was more than 11 times larger than the female rate. More recently, the 1993 FBI *Uniform Crime Report* showed that the male murder rate was almost 10 times larger than the female rate (U.S. Department of Justice, 1994).

To investigate sex effects in field studies, we recombined studies from Bettencourt and Miller's (1996) meta-analysis.[2] The results showed that males aggressed

---

[2]The main focus of the Bettencourt and Miller (1996) meta-analysis is sex differences in aggression as a function of provocation. For instance, they showed that males are more aggressive than females in both neutral and provoked conditions, but that the difference is smaller in provoked conditions. They also showed that the sex difference is larger when the aggressive behavior involves delivery of an aversive physical stimulus to the victim than when it involves some type of verbal aggression. As their analyses did not focus on laboratory versus field studies, we used their tabled results to conduct our own meta-analyses.

more than females when the aggression was a physical act such as horn honking, but not when the aggression was a verbal act such as making negative remarks (see Table 2.3).

Studies Conducted Inside the Laboratory

To investigate sex effects in laboratory studies, we also recombined studies from Bettencourt and Miller's (1996) meta-analysis (see Table 2.3). The results showed that males were more physically and verbally aggressive than females. Sex differences in verbal aggression, however, were quite small.

In summary, our analysis suggests that males are more physically aggressive than females both inside and outside the laboratory. Sex differences in verbal aggression are small to trivial in both settings. The setting did not significantly influence the magnitude of sex differences found for either type of aggression.

Trait Aggressiveness

Informal observation suggests that some people are especially likely to become involved in aggressive interactions. The personality trait of aggression is referred to as trait aggressiveness. Trait aggressiveness can be defined operationally using (a) self-report personality scales, (b) aggression nominations by others (e.g., peers, teachers, counselors), or (c) violent histories. The most widely used self-report measure of trait aggressiveness is the Buss–Durkee Hostility Inventory (BDHI; Buss & Durkee, 1957). Sample items from this scale include, "Once in a while I cannot control my urge to harm others" and "I often find myself disagreeing with people."

In most field studies, participants are individuals with histories of violence. In most laboratory studies, participants are college students. Because of greater variability in trait aggressiveness in field studies, stronger relations were expected for field studies than for laboratory studies.

Studies Conducted Outside the Laboratory

The BDHI has been used to successfully discriminate between violent and nonviolent criminals (Gunn & Gristwood, 1975; Selby, 1984; Syverson & Romney, 1985), between domestically violent and nonviolent men (Maiuro, Cahn, Vitaliano, Wagner, & Zegree, 1988), between violent and nonviolent patients (Lange, Dehghani, & De Beurs, 1995; Maiuro et al., 1988), between violent and nonviolent alcoholics (Renson, Adams, & Tinklenberg, 1978), and between violent and nonviolent adolescent offenders (Boone & Flint, 1988; Lothstein & Jones, 1978). Scores on the revised BDHI also are positively correlated with peer-nominated aggression in college students (Buss & Perry, 1992) and with self-reported involvement in physical fights (Archer, Holloway, & McLoughlin, 1995; Stanford, Greve, & Dickens, 1995). Meta-analysis revealed a substantial positive correlation between trait aggressiveness, as measured by the BDHI, and real world aggression (see Table 2.3).

Studies Conducted Inside the Laboratory

Scores on self-report trait aggression questionnaires have been found to correlate positively with laboratory measures of physical aggression (Bushman, 1995;

Giancola & Zeichner, 1995; Hammock & Richardson, 1992; Knott, 1970; Larsen, Coleman, Forbes, & Johnson, 1972; Leibowitz, 1968; Pihl, Lau, & Assaad, 1997; Scheier, Buss, & Buss, 1978; Shemberg, Leventhal, & Allman, 1968), although null results have been reported (Muntaner, Walter, Nagoshi, Fishbein, Haertzen, & Jaffe, 1990). Physical aggression in the laboratory was higher for male adolescent delinquents with a history of violence than for male adolescent delinquents with no history of violence (Hartman, 1969) and for young male offenders in maximum security than for male college students (Wolfe & Baron, 1971). Physical aggression in the laboratory was higher for high school students nominated by their counselors to be aggressive than for high school students nominated by their counselors to be nonaggressive (Shemberg et al., 1968) and for third-graders nominated by their peers to be aggressive than for third-graders nominated by their peers to be nonaggressive (Williams, Meyerson, Eron, & Semler, 1967). Meta-analytic procedures found a medium-sized correlation between trait aggressiveness and laboratory aggression (see Table 2.3).

In summary, trait aggressiveness was positively correlated with aggression inside and outside the laboratory. As expected, stronger correlations were found for field studies than for laboratory studies.

Type A Coronary-Prone Behavior Pattern

The Type A pattern is characterized by three major behavioral components: excessive competitive achievement striving, exaggerated time urgency, and aggression or hostility (Glass, 1977). The latter component has the most relevance to the present discussion (and to heart disease as well). A Type A personality can be assessed using either a self-report personality test or a structured interview. The most popular self-report personality test is the Jenkins Activity Survey (JAS; Jenkins, Zyzanski, & Rosenman, 1979). A sample item from the college student form of the JAS is "When you are studying and somebody interrupts you, how do you usually feel inside?" Response options include (a) "I feel OK because I work better after an occasional break," (b) "I feel only mildly annoyed," or (c) "I really feel irritated because most such interruptions are unnecessary." Type B's tend to choose response (a), whereas Type A's tend to choose response (c). For reasons similar to those given for trait aggressiveness, we expected larger aggression differences between Type A's and Type B's in field studies than in laboratory studies.

Studies Conducted Outside the Laboratory

Strube and colleagues (Strube, Turner, Cerro, Stevens, & Hinchey, 1984) compared JAS scores for violent and nonviolent women. The sample of violent women was selected from a population of women under treatment for child abuse; the sample of nonviolent women was selected from a preschool population in the same city. The nonviolent and violent women were matched according to the age of their child. The violent women were classified as Type A more often than were nonviolent women. In another study (Schell, Cachon, Ganjavi, & Porporino, 1986), inmates with a violent criminal background were classified as either assaulters or nonassaulters depending on whether they had been charged with some act of physical aggression (murder, attempted murder, or a physical assault of a guard or fellow inmate) over the past year. Inmates completed the Behavior Activity Profile (Matteson & Ivancevich, 1979), a self-report measure of the Type A pattern, as part of a battery of questionnaires. The results showed that most assaulters were classified as Type A's, whereas most nonassaulters were classified as Type B's. In another study (Hurlbert, Whittaker, & Munoz, 1991), abusive husbands were classified as Type A's, as measured by the JAS, significantly more often than were nonabusive husbands. Meta-analysis of the results from studies conducted outside the laboratory found a strong relation between Type A personality and aggression (see Table 2.3).

Studies Conducted Inside the Laboratory

Most laboratory studies have found that Type A's, in comparison to Type B's, are more physically aggressive (Baron, Russell, & Arms, 1985; Carver & Glass, 1978; Check & Dyck, 1986; Holmes & Will, 1985; Llorente, Bernardo, de Flores, & Valdes, 1985; Strube et al., 1984), although a few studies have found null results (Berman, Gladue, & Taylor, 1993; Muntaner, Llorente, & Nagoshi, 1989). Meta-analytic procedures found that, on average, Type A's behaved significantly more aggressively in the laboratory than did Type B's (see Table 2.3).

In summary, Type A's behaved more aggressively than did Type B's both inside and outside the laboratory. As expected, stronger effects were obtained for field studies than for laboratory studies.

SITUATION VARIABLES AND AGGRESSION

This section assesses the correspondence between findings from field studies and laboratory studies, focusing on situational variables. The effects of the following situational variables on human aggression were examined: provocation, alcohol, the presence of weapons, media violence, anonymity, and temperature.

Provocation

By provocation, we mean acts of harm committed by the target against the person whose aggressive behavior is eventually assessed. In the real world, provocations are quite common. They may involve cutting off another driver on the freeway, stealing someone's property, verbally insulting someone, or physically attacking someone. In most laboratory studies, provocations consist of physical attacks (e.g., painful shocks or noise blasts) or verbal insults.

Studies Conducted Outside the Laboratory

Crime statistics clearly demonstrate that provocation is the major source of real world aggression. In the breakdown of murders, for instance, the vast majority are the result of some intense, personal provocation. In the United States in 1993, only 27% of all murders were the result of some other felony activity, such as robbery. Of the remaining 1993 murders for which the circumstances are known, 73% were classified by the FBI as being due to arguments. Another 5% were due to romantic triangle disputes, and another 7% resulted from alcohol- and drug-related brawls (U.S. Department of Justice, 1994). Thus, the common circumstances surrounding murder involve attacks on one's self-esteem, public image, or family structure, all of which are types of provocation.

Several more formal studies have examined effects of provocation on violence in natural settings. For example, Curtis (1974) examined a U.S. national sample of police reports and found that provocation was common in homicide and aggravated assault, less common in robbery, and least common in forcible rape. Similarly, Davis (1991) examined psychiatric inpatient violence and found provocation to be an important situational predictor.

Searching for tests of provocation in field experiments is a difficult task because field experiments do not typically include a "no provocation" control condition. Indeed, Bettencourt and Miller (1996) could find no field experiment with a control condition to include in their meta-analysis of sex differences in the effects of provocation on aggression.

Studies Conducted Inside the Laboratory

The meta-analysis by Bettencourt and Miller (1996) also examined provocation effects in the context of sex effects. They found that high provocation increased aggression for all possible combinations of sex of confederate and sex of participant. Overall, the provocation effect was quite large (see Table 2.3). In summary, provocation has a large effect on aggression both inside and outside the laboratory.

Alcohol

Studies Conducted Outside the Laboratory

Co-occurrence statistics are often used to establish a relation between alcohol use and violent crime. For example, numerous studies have reported that at least 50% of the perpetrators of violent crimes were intoxicated at the time of the offense (e.g., Beck, 1991; Beck, Kline, & Greenfield, 1988; Greenberg, 1981; Innes, 1988; MacDonald, 1961; Murdoch, Pihl, & Ross, 1990; Pernanen, 1991). The problem with co-occurrence statistics is that they provide no base rate information about the level of alcohol use among comparable people who were not violent. Lipsey, Wilson, Cohen, and Derzon (1997) correctly point out that without the "other half" of the data, one cannot determine the strength of the relation between alcohol use and violent crime. Thus, Lipsey and his colleagues combined the results from studies that examined whether individuals with higher alcohol use also exhibit higher levels of violent behavior. The results of their meta-analysis found a small to medium-sized correlation between alcohol and violent behavior (see Table 2.3).[3]

---

[3]Lipsey et al. (1997) provided separate correlations for criminals with chronic alcohol consumption, criminals with acute alcohol consumption, and domestic offenders with chronic alcohol consumption. We combined these correlations.

Studies Conducted Inside the Laboratory

Numerous laboratory studies have investigated the relation between alcohol and aggression. Meta-analytic reviews of these studies have found that intoxicated participants are significantly more aggressive than are sober participants (Bushman, 1993, 1997; Bushman & Cooper, 1990; Ito, Miller, & Pollock, 1996; Lipsey, Wilson, Cohen, & Derzon, 1997; see Table 2.3). The type of aggression measure used does not appear to influence the magnitude of effects (Bushman, 1997; Bushman & Cooper, 1990). The correlation between alcohol and aggression is medium-sized in laboratory studies. Larger effects might be obtained if ethical considerations did not prevent researchers from using higher doses of alcohol in their laboratory studies (i.e., the target blood alcohol level is at most .10). In summary, alcohol appears to increase aggression inside and outside the laboratory.

Weapons Effect

According to Berkowitz (1968), "Guns not only permit violence, they can stimulate it as well. The finger pulls the trigger, but the trigger may also be pulling the finger" (p. 22). Carlson, Marcus-Newhall, and Miller (1990) conducted a meta-analytic review of the effects of aggression-related cues, including weapons, on aggression. We reanalyzed data from studies testing the effects of weapons on aggression inside and outside the laboratory. Carlson et al. (1990) found that the weapons effect was reversed when participants were suspicious or experiencing evaluation apprehension, so studies with such artifactual features were not included in our analysis.

Studies Conducted Outside the Laboratory

A few studies have investigated the presence of weapons in naturalistic settings (Boyanowski & Griffiths, 1982; Turner, Layton, & Simons, 1975, Studies 2 and 3). For example, in one study (Turner et al., 1975, Study 2), a confederate in a pickup truck stalled at a traffic signal light for 12 seconds. For some of the motorists, a .303-calibre military rifle was placed in a gun rack mounted on the back window of the confederate's truck. Among those motorists who saw the gun, half saw a bumper sticker attached to the tailgate that said "VENGEANCE" and half saw a bumper sticker that said "FRIEND." Motorists in the control group saw no gun or bumper sticker. The results showed the highest level of horn honking among motorists who saw a gun and the VENGEANCE sticker, followed respectively by motorists who saw a gun and the FRIEND sticker and by motorists who saw no gun or sticker. Four of the five comparisons yielded positive effects.[4] Meta-analysis of the five results from these studies showed a small effect, but it was not significantly different from zero (due to the small number of studies). These results are depicted in Table 2.3.

---

[4]For the Turner, Layton, and Simons (1975) study, Carlson, Marcus-Newhall, and Miller (1990) compared the rifle, vengeance bumper sticker group to the no rifle, no bumper sticker group. In this meta-analysis, to test the presence of a weapon, the rifle, vengeance bumper sticker group was compared to the no rifle, vengeance bumper sticker group.

Studies Conducted Inside the Laboratory

In the first laboratory test of the weapons effect (Berkowitz & LePage, 1967), a participant and a confederate took turns working on a problem and then evaluating each other's work using anywhere from 1 to 10 electric shocks. The confederate evaluated the participant's work first by giving him either 1 shock (nonangry condition) or 7 shocks (angry condition). The participant was then taken to a room that contained the shock apparatus and was given the confederate's solution to the problem to evaluate. In one condition (*weapons*), there was a .38-caliber revolver and a 12-gauge shotgun on the table next to the shock apparatus. In another condition (*neutral objects*), there were two badminton racquets and some shuttlecocks on the table next to the shock apparatus. In both of these conditions, the experimenter pushed the objects aside and said that they had been left there by another experimenter who was engaged in a different study. The results showed that provoked men who saw the guns on the table gave the confederate significantly more shocks than did provoked men who saw neutral objects or no objects on the table. The objects on the table did not significantly influence the number of shocks unprovoked men gave the confederate. Meta-analysis of the laboratory studies testing the weapons effect (Berkowitz & LePage, 1967; Buss, Booker, & Buss, 1972; Caprara, Renzi, Amolini, D'Imperio, & Travaglia, 1984; Ellis, Weiner, & Miller, 1971; Fischer, Kelm, & Rose, 1969; Fraczek & Macaulay, 1971; Page & Scheidt, 1971; Simons & Turner, 1976; Turner & Simons, 1974) found a small effect-size estimate (see Table 2.3). In summary, the mere presence of weapons can cause a small increase in aggression inside and outside the laboratory.

Media Violence

There are more televisions sets in the United States than there are toilets. Over 98% of American homes have at least one television set (APA, 1993). In the United States, adults spend more time watching television than they spend on any other activity except sleeping and working, and children spend more time watching television than they spend at school (Huston et al., 1992). About 60% of television programs contain violence (National Television Violence Study, 1996, 1997). By the time the average child graduates from elementary school, he or she will have seen at least 8,000 murders and more than 100,000 other assorted acts of violence on television (Huston et al., 1992).

The effect of violent media on aggression was expected to be larger for laboratory studies than for field studies. There are at least three reasons for making this prediction. First, laboratory studies are more effective at controlling extraneous variables than are field studies. Second, the violence shown is generally more concentrated in laboratory studies than in field studies. Third, the time between exposure to violent media and measurement of aggression is generally shorter in laboratory studies than in field studies.

Studies Conducted Outside the Laboratory

It is not hard to find anecdotal examples that suggest a relation between exposure to violent media and real world aggression. Consider the following news story.

On April 22, 1974, three people were murdered in a store in Ogden, Utah, by two armed men who forced them to drink liquid Drano, a caustic drain cleaner. In the court proceedings, the Assistant State Attorney General said that the accused murderers "had seen the movie *Magnum Force,* in which liquid Drano was used to kill a woman, the same month of the killings and took Drano to the (store) as a premeditated lethal weapon" ("Selby Makes One Last Plea," 1987). Another witness testified that the two men saw *Magnum Force* "three times in one day" the same month of the killings ("Still at a Loss for 'Why'," 1987).

In a recent meta-analysis, Paik and Comstock (1994) reported that violent media have a small to medium effect on aggression in field studies (see Table 2.3).

Studies Conducted Inside the Laboratory

Paik and Comstock (1994) reported that violent media have a large effect on aggression in laboratory studies (see Table 2.3). In one study (Bushman, 1995), for example, undergraduate psychology students were randomly assigned to view a 15-minute videotaped film segment that was either violent or nonviolent. The two videotapes were selected from a large pool of tapes because they were judged to be equally exciting but differentially violent. In addition, there were no significant differences between the two tapes on cardiovascular measures of arousal (i.e., systolic blood pressure, diastolic blood pressure, heart rate). After viewing the videotape, participants competed with an ostensible opponent on a reaction time task in which the slower responding person received a blast of noise. The results showed that participants who had seen the violent videotape set significantly higher noise levels for their "opponent" than did participants who had seen the nonviolent videotape.

In summary, violent media increased aggression both inside and outside the laboratory. As expected, the effect of violent media on aggression was larger for laboratory studies than for field studies.

Anonymity

What factors influence people to engage in such uninhibited antisocial behaviors as those described in the news story at the beginning of this chapter? Festinger, Pepitone, and Newcomb (1952) proposed that when group members are not seen as individuals, a state of deindividuation may result, with a consequent lowering of social restraints. The terms *deindividuation* and *anonymity* often are used interchangeably (Lightdale & Prentice, 1994). An individual can achieve anonymity by being part of a group, by wearing a mask, or by performing behaviors in the dark. This may partially account for why bank robbers and members of the Ku Klux Klan wear masks when committing violent crimes, why crowds attending sporting events sometimes become violent (e.g., Dunand, 1986), and why violent crimes are more frequently committed during nighttime hours than during daytime hours (e.g., Tamura, 1983; Meyer, 1982). Deindividuation leads to a reduced sense of accountability.

Studies Conducted Outside the Laboratory

We found four studies that examined the role of deindividuation on real world aggression. Mullen (1986) conducted an archival analysis to determine whether the atrocities committed by lynch mobs could be accounted for in terms of self-attention processes. Sixty newspaper reports of lynching events were coded for information regarding group composition (i.e., number of victims, number of lynchers) and atrocity (i.e., occurrence or nonoccurrence of hanging, shooting, burning, lacerating, or dismembering the victim, as well as the duration of the lynching). The results showed that as lynchers became more numerous relative to the victims, atrocities increased. Mann (1981) analyzed 21 cases in which crowds were present when a disturbed person threatened to jump off a building, bridge, or tower. Analysis of newspaper accounts of the episodes showed that large crowds were more likely to taunt and urge the victim to jump than were small crowds. In addition, more baiting episodes occurred in nighttime hours than in daytime hours. Wilson and Brewer (1993) reported that the amount of conflict police encountered while on patrol was higher when a large number of bystanders (six or more) were present than when a small number of bystanders (five or less) were present. Ellison, Govern, Petri, and Figler (1995) found that drivers in convertibles or 4 × 4s with their tops up honked more at a stalled motorist than did drivers with their tops down. Meta-analysis of these results yielded a medium-sized effect (see Table 2.3).

Studies Conducted Inside the Laboratory

Several laboratory studies have shown that aggression is increased when participants are placed in a deindividuated state (Diener, 1976; Diener, Dineen, Endresen, Beaman, & Fraser, 1975; Lightdale & Prentice, 1994; Mann, Newton, & Innes, 1982; Paloutzian, 1975; Prentice-Dunn & Rogers, 1980, 1982; Prentice-Dunn & Spivey, 1986; Rogers, 1980; Rogers & Ketchen, 1979; Rogers & Prentice-Dunn, 1981; Spivey & Prentice-Dunn, 1990; Worchel, Arnold, & Harrison, 1978; Zimbardo, 1969), although a few null results have been reported (Propst, 1979; Worchel & Andreoli, 1978). Meta-analysis of these laboratory results showed that anonymous participants behaved more aggressively than did nonanonymous participants. The average effect-size estimate for laboratory experiments was medium in size (see Table 2.3).

Thus, anonymity increased aggression both inside and outside the laboratory. The type of setting (i.e., inside versus outside the laboratory) did not significantly influence the magnitude of the effect of anonymity on aggression.

Temperature

Heat has historically been associated with anger and aggression. Common phrases such as "hot under the collar," "my blood is boiling," and the use of the word "hot" as a synonym for "angry" convey both the increase in physiological arousal that results from feeling angry and the conceptual linking of hot temperature with anger.

Real World Aggression

The most comprehensive review of temperature effects on real world aggression found strikingly consistent results for different types of field studies (Anderson, 1989). Although formal meta-analytic statistical procedures were not used in that review, meta-analytic strategies of exhaustively sampling the literature, partitioning studies by important features, and combining results within these partitions were used. Time period studies, in which aggression rates are compared across time periods that differ in temperature, showed that aggressive behaviors such as murders, rapes, assaults, and wife battering were relatively more frequent during hotter periods of time than during cooler periods of time. More recent time period studies have shown that violent crime rates in the United States (from 1950 to 1992) are higher during hotter years than during cooler years and that the usual summer increase in violent crime is magnified in hotter years (Anderson, Bushman, & Groom, 1997). Similarly, geographic region studies from several different countries found that hotter regions tend to have higher aggression rates than do cooler regions. More recent analyses of U.S. violent crime rates (Anderson & Anderson, 1995) show that this region effect occurs even when numerous steps are taken to control for possible regional differences in "culture of honor" (Nisbett, 1993). Finally, the two concomitant studies of real world aggression reviewed by Anderson (1989), in which temperature and aggression were simultaneously assessed, also yielded significant temperature effects on aggression. In sum, real world aggression studies show that hot temperatures produce increases in aggression.

Laboratory Aggression

Laboratory studies of aggression have yielded quite inconsistent effects. Hot temperatures sometimes increase and sometimes decrease aggression (Anderson, 1989). To interpret these discrepancies, Anderson and Anderson (1997) conducted a meta-analysis on the laboratory studies of aggression. When all of the laboratory effects of hot versus comfortable temperatures are combined, the average effect size is about zero (see Table 2.3). One possible factor that might account for this null effect concerns whether there were other manipulated variables that raised or lowered the participant's feelings of anger, annoyance, or friendliness. Specifically, Baron's (1979) negative affect escape (NAE) model predict that hot temperatures will increase aggression when there are no other negative factors present, but will decrease aggression when there are other factors present which, taken together, would tend to heighten negative feelings. In laboratory studies, the most common factor used to heighten the negative affect has been an anger manipulation.

To test the NAE model, Anderson and Anderson (1997) categorized the 26 separate effects of hot temperatures (i.e., in the 90s°F versus low to mid-70s°F) on the basis of whether other experimental factors could be expected to produce a net increase in the negative affect. The results were in the direction predicted by the NAE model, but they were not statistically significant (due to the small number of studies). These results are depicted in Table 2.3.

DEALING WITH REAL-WORLD/LABORATORY DISCREPANCIES

Discrepancies between real world and laboratory studies should arise when key conceptual variables or processes (a) are prevalent and operate freely in the "real world" but are controlled in the laboratory or (b) are prevalent and operate freely in the laboratory but are infrequent or less prevalent in the real world. When the conceptual variables or processes are the same, parallel results should be obtained in the laboratory and real world. Two imprudent approaches to dealing with discrepancies between real world and laboratory findings involve simple rejection. One can reject real world findings as being the result of the confounds or the lack of control that typifies such studies. Alternatively, one can reject laboratory findings as being the result of suspicion problems, trivial manipulations, or trivial measures of aggression. The former approach appears to characterize the theoretical, experimental perspective, whereas the latter appears to characterize the applied, nonexperimental perspective.

Our view is that such discrepancies should serve as signals that additional conceptual work is needed, to be followed by additional empirical work on the new understandings that result from the additional conceptual work. In other words, rather than take the perspective that one "side" or the other is wrong, it may be more prudent to try to locate the source of the discrepancies in psychological processes that may differ in the two settings. One then could try to discover the conditions that lead to one versus the other type of finding (cf. Greenwald, Pratkanis, Leippe, & Baumgardner, 1986). The analysis of the temperature/aggression discrepancies was the result of such a conceptual reanalysis.

GENERAL DISCUSSION

At the outset, we presented two aggression scenarios—one real world example of gang violence and one laboratory example of "trivial" aggression—and asked if there was any reason to believe that the findings from the latter could inform us about the former. In our view, the answer must be a resounding "yes." When careful conceptual analyses of both types of situations are conducted and when solid empirical research methods are employed, findings about the relations between conceptual variables will generalize from the laboratory to the real world, and vice versa.

The various aggression literatures sampled for this chapter provide strong empirical support for the laboratory researchers' faith in their "trivial" laboratory aggression paradigms. All of the individual difference variables (sex, trait aggressiveness, Type A pattern) and most of the situational variables (provocation, alcohol, the presence of weapons, media violence, anonymity) consistently influenced aggressive behavior in real world and laboratory paradigms in the same way. Such a convergence of findings in such disparate settings confirms the validity of both types of studies. Even in the one case where real world and trivial aggression differed, the temperature domain, the differences appear to be a function of different psychological processes at work. Once such processes were identified and at least partially equated, comparable findings emerged.

It is important to note that real world aggression measures (e.g., violent crime) share few surface features with laboratory aggression measures (e.g., delivery of electric shock). However, these aggression measures do share the conceptual features of delivering a noxious stimulus to a victim with the intent and expectation of causing harm. As noted by Mook (1983), Berkowitz and Donnerstein (1982), and others, what we should expect to generalize are theories. In other words, the conceptual relations among variables are expected to be similar in quite dissimilar situations. The aggression literature, often the most volatile domain in this external validity debate, clearly shows considerable consistency between real world and trivial aggression measures. In summary, we believe the studies that we have reviewed conclusively demonstrate that the trivial laboratory paradigms of aggression are not at all trivial; they are quite high in external validity at this conceptual level of generalizability.

REFERENCES

References marked with an asterisk indicate studies included in the meta-analyses.

American Psychological Association (1993). *Violence and youth: Psychology's response.* Washington, DC: Author.

Anderson, C. A. (1989). Temperature and aggression: Ubiquitous effects of heat on occurrence of human violence. *Psychological Bulletin, 106,* 74–96.

Anderson, C. A., & Bushman, B. J. (1997). External validity of "trivial" experiments: The case of laboratory aggression. *General Psychology Review, 1,* 19–41.

Anderson, C. A., Bushman, B. J., & Groom, R. (1997). Hot years and serious and deadly assault: Empirical tests of the heat hypothesis. *Journal of Personality and Social Psychology, 73,* 1213–1223.

Anderson, K. B., & Anderson, C. A. (1997). Laboratory effects of hot temperatures on aggressive behavior: A meta-analysis. Manuscript under review.

*Archer, J., Holloway, R., & McLoughlin, K. (1995). Self-reported physical aggression among young men. *Aggressive Behavior, 21,* 325–342.

Barnett, R. K. (1979). The effects of alcohol, expectancy, provocation, and permission to aggress upon aggressive behavior. *Dissertation Abstracts International, 40,* 4993B. (University Microfilms No. ADG80-09229, 0000).

Baron, R. A. (1979). Aggression and heat: The "long hot summer" revisited. In A. Baum, J. E. Singer, & S. Valins (Eds.), *Advances in environmental psychology* (pp. 57–84). Hillsdale, NJ: Erlbaum.

*Baron, R. A., Russell, G. W., & Arms, R. L. (1985). Negative ions and behavior: Impact on mood, memory, and aggression among Type A and Type B persons. *Journal of Personality and Social Psychology, 48,* 746–754.

Beck, A. J. (1991). *Profile of jail inmates, 1989.* Washington, DC: Bureau of Justice Statistics.

Beck, A. J., Kline, S. A., & Greenfield, L. A. (1988). *Survey of youth in custody, 1987.* Washington, DC: Bureau of Justice Statistics.

Berkowitz, L. (1962). *Aggression: A social psychological analysis.* New York: McGraw-Hill.

Berkowitz, L. (1968). Impulse, aggression, and the gun. *Psychology Today, 2,* 18–22.

Berkowitz, L., & Donnerstein, E. (1982). External validity is more than skin deep: Some answers to criticism of laboratory experiments. *American Psychologist, 37,* 245–257.

*Berkowitz, L., & Le Page, A. (1967). Weapons as aggression-eliciting stimuli. *Journal of Personality and Social Psychology, 7,* 202–207.

*Berman, M., Gladue, B., & Taylor, S. (1993). The effects of hormones, Type A behavior pattern, and provocation on aggression in men. *Motivation and Emotion, 17,* 125–138.

Bettencourt, B. A., & Miller, N. (1996). Sex differences in aggression as a function of provocation: A meta-analysis. *Psychological Bulletin, 119,* 422–447.

*Boone, S. L., & Flint, C. (1988). A psychometric analysis of aggression and conflict-resolution behavior in black adolescent males. *Social Behavior and Personality, 16,* 215–226.

*Boyanowski, E. O., & Griffiths, C. T. (1982). Weapons and eye contact as instigators or inhibitors of aggressive arousal in police–citizen interaction. *Journal of Applied Social Psychology, 12*, 398–407.

Bushman, B. J. (1993). Human aggression while under the influence of alcohol and other drugs: An integrative research review. *Current Directions in Psychological Science, 2*, 148–152.

*Bushman, B. J. (1995). Moderating role of trait aggressiveness in the effects of violent media on aggression. *Journal of Personality and Social Psychology, 69*, 950–960.

Bushman, B. J. (1997). Effects of alcohol on human aggression: Validity of proposed explanations. In D. Fuller, R. Dietrich, & E. Gottheil (Eds.), *Recent developments in alcoholism: Alcohol and violence* (Vol. 13, pp. 227–243). New York: Plenum.

Bushman, B. J., & Cooper, H. M. (1990). Effects of alcohol on human aggression: An integrative research review. *Psychological Bulletin, 107*, 341–354.

Buss, A. H. (1961). *The psychology of aggression.* New York: Wiley.

*Buss, A. H., Booker, A., & Buss, E. (1972). Firing a weapon and aggression. *Journal of Personality and Social Psychology, 22*, 296–302.

Buss, A. H., & Durkee, A. (1957). An inventory for assessing different kinds of hostility. *Journal of Consulting Psychology, 21*, 343–349.

*Buss, A. H., & Perry, M. (1992). The Aggression Questionnaire. *Journal of Personality and Social Psychology, 63*, 452–459.

*Caprara, G. V., Renzi, P., Amolini, P., D'Imperio, G., & Travaglia, G. (1984). The eliciting value of aggressive slides reconsidered in a personological perspective: The weapons effect and irritability. *European Journal of Social Psychology, 14*, 313–322.

Carlson, M., Marcus-Newhall, A., & Miller, N. (1989). Evidence for a general construct of aggression. *Personality and Social Psychology Bulletin, 15*, 377–389.

Carlson, M., Marcus-Newhall, A., & Miller, N. (1990). Effects of situational aggression cues: A quantitative review. *Journal of Personality and Social Psychology, 58*, 622–633.

*Carver, C. S., & Glass, D. C. (1978). Coronary-prone behavior pattern and interpersonal aggression. *Journal of Personality and Social Psychology, 36*, 361–366.

*Check, J. V., & Dyck, D. G. (1986). Hostile aggression and Type A behavior. *Personality and Individual Differences, 7*, 819–827.

Cherek, D. R. (1981). Effects of smoking different doses of nicotine on human aggressive behavior. *Psychopharmacology, 75*, 339–345.

Cohen, J. (1988). *Statistical power analysis for the behavioral sciences* (2nd ed.). Hillsdale, NJ: Lawrence Erlbaum.

Cook, P. J., & Moore, M. J. (1993). Violence reduction through restrictions on alcohol availability. *Alcohol, Health, and Research World, 17*, 151–156.

Curtis, L. A. (1974). Victim precipitation and violent crime. *Social Problems, 21*, 594–605.

Davis, S. (1991). Violence by psychiatric inpatients: A review. *Hospital and Community Psychiatry, 42*, 585–590.

Dexter, E. G. (1899). Conduct and the weather. *Psychological Monographs, 11(10)*, 1–103.

*Diener, E. (1976). Effects of prior destructive behavior, anonymity, and group presence on deindividuation and aggression. *Journal of Personality and Social Psychology, 33*, 497–507.

*Diener, E., Dineen, J., Endresen, K., Beaman, A. L., & Fraser, S. C. (1975). Effects of altered responsibility, cognitive set, and modeling on physical aggression and deindividuation. *Journal of Personality and Social Psychology, 31*, 328–337.

Dunand, M. A. (1986). Violence and panic at the Brussels football stadium in 1985: Social psychological approach to the event. *Cahiers de Psychologie Cognitive, 6*, 235–266.

*Ellis, D. P., Weiner, P., & Miller, L. (1971). Does the trigger pull the finger? An experimental test of weapons as aggression-enhancing stimuli. *Sociometry, 34*, 453–465.

*Ellison, P. A., Govern, J. M., Petri, H. L., & Figler, M. H. (1995). Anonymity and aggressive driving behavior: A field study. *Journal of Social Behavior and Personality, 10*, 265–272.

Festinger, L., Pepitone, A., & Newcomb, T. (1952). Some consequences of deindividuation in a group. *Journal of Abnormal and Social Psychology, 47*, 382–389.

*Fischer, D. G., Kelm, H., & Rose, A. (1969). Knives as aggression eliciting stimuli. *Psychological Reports, 24*, 755–760.

*Fraczek, A., & Macaulay, J. R. (1971). Some personality factors in reaction to aggressive stimuli. *Journal of Personality and Social Psychology, 39,* 163–177.

Geen, R. G. (1990). *Human aggression.* Pacific Grove, CA: Brooks/Cole.

*Giancola, P. R., & Zeichner, A. (1995). Construct validity of a competitive reaction-time aggression paradigm. *Aggressive Behavior, 21,* 199–204.

Glass, D. C. (1977). *Behavior patterns, stress, and coronary disease.* Beverly Hills, CA: Sage.

Greenberg, S. W. (1981). Alcohol and crime: A methodological critique of the literature. In J. J. Collins (Ed.), *Drinking and crime: Perspectives on the relationships between alcohol consumption and criminal behavior.* New York: Guilford.

Greenwald, A. G., Pratkanis, A. R., Leippe, M. R., & Baumgardner, M. H. (1986). Under what conditions does theory obstruct research progress? *Psychological Review, 93,* 216–229.

*Gunn, J., & Gristwood, J. (1975). Use of the Buss–Durkee Hostility Inventory among British prisoners. *Journal of Consulting and Clinical Psychology, 43,* 590.

*Hammock, G. S., & Richardson, D. R. (1992). Predictors of aggressive behavior. *Aggressive Behavior, 18,* 219–229.

*Hartman, D. P. (1969). Influence of symbolically modeled instrumental aggression and pain cues on aggressive behavior. *Journal of Personality and Social Psychology, 11,* 280–288.

Hedges, L. V., & Olkin, I. (1985). *Statistical methods for meta-analysis.* New York: Academic Press.

*Holmes, D. S., & Will, M. J. (1985). Expression of interpersonal aggression by angered and nonangered persons with Type A and Type B behavior patterns. *Journal of Personality and Social Psychology, 48,* 723–727.

*Hurlbert, D. F., Whittaker, K. E., & Munoz, C. J. (1991). Etiological characteristics of abusive husbands. *Military Medicine, 156,* 670–675.

Huston, A. C., Donnerstein, E., Fairchild, H., Feshbach, N. D., Katz, P. A., Murray, J. P., Rubinstein, E. A., Wilcox, B. L., & Zuckerman, D. (1992). *Big world, small screen: The role of television in American society.* Lincoln, NE: University of Nebraska Press.

Innes, C. A. (1988). *Drug use and crime.* Washington, DC: U.S. Department of Justice.

Jenkins, C. D., Zyzanski, S. J., & Rosenman, R. H. (1979). *The Jenkins Activity Survey, Form C.* New York: The Psychological Corporation.

*Knott, P. (1970). A further methodological study of the measurement of interpersonal aggression. *Psychological Reports, 26,* 807–809.

*Lange, A., Dehghani, B., & De Beurs, E. (1995). Validation of the Dutch adaptation of the Buss–Durkee Hostility Inventory. *Behavioral Research Therapy, 33,* 229–233.

*Larsen, K. S., Coleman, D., Forbes, J., & Johnson, R. (1972). Is the subject's personality or the experimental situation a better predictor of a subject's willingness to administer shock to a victim? *Journal of Personality and Social Psychology, 22,* 287–295.

*Leibowitz, G. (1968). Comparison of self-report and behavioral techniques of assessing aggression. *Journal of Consulting and Clinical Psychology, 32,* 21–25.

*Lightdale, J. R., & Prentice, D. A. (1994). Rethinking sex differences in aggression: Aggressive behavior in the absence of social roles. *Personality and Social Psychology Bulletin, 20,* 34–44.

Lipsey, M. W., Wilson, D. B., Cohen, M. A., & Derzon, J. H. (1997). Is there a causal relationship between alcohol use and violence? In D. Fuller, R. Dietrich, & E. Gottheil (Eds.), *Recent developments in alcoholism: Alcohol and violence* (Vol. 13, pp. 245–282). New York: Plenum.

*Llorente, M., Bernardo, M., de Flores, T., & Valdes, M. (1985). Type A behavior and Buss's instrumental aggression paradigm (BIAP). *Activitas Nervosa Superior, 27,* 106–109.

*Lothstein, L. M., & Jones, P. (1978). Discriminating violent individuals by means of various psychological tests. *Journal of Personality Assessment, 42,* 237–243.

MacDonald, J. M. (1961). *The murderer and his victim.* Springfield, IL: Charles C. Thomas.

*Maiuro, R. D., Cahn, T. S., Vitaliano, P. P., Wagner, B. C., & Zegree, J. B. (1988). Anger, hostility, and depression in domestically violent versus generally assaultive men and nonviolent control subjects. *Journal of Consulting and Clinical Psychology, 56,* 17–23.

*Mann, L. (1981). The baiting crowd in episodes of threatened suicide. *Journal of Personality and Social Psychology, 41,* 703–709.

*Mann, L., Newton, J. W., & Innes, J. M. (1982). A test between deindividuation and emergent norm theories of crowd aggression. *Journal of Personality and Social Psychology, 42,* 260–272.

*Matteson, M. T., & Ivancevich, J. M. (1982). Behavior activity profile. In J. L. Gibson, J. M. Ivancevich, & J. H. Donnelly, Jr. (Eds.), *Organizations: Behavior, structure, processes* (pp. 169–173). Plano, TX: Business Publ.

McKinley, J. C. Jr. (1990, November 2). Gang kills homeless man in Halloween rampage. *New York Times,* pp. A1, B3.

Meyer, C. K. (1982). An analysis of factors related to robbery-associated assaults on police officers: I. *Journal of Police Science and Administration, 10,* 1–27.

Mook, D. G. (1983). In defense of external invalidity. *American Psychologist, 38,* 379–387.

*Mullen, B. (1986). Atrocity as a function of lynch mob composition: A self-attention perspective. *Personality and Social Psychology Bulletin, 12,* 187–197.

*Muntaner, C., Llorente, M., & Nagoshi, C. (1989). Evaluation instructions and interpersonal aggression in the Type A behavior pattern. *Aggressive Behavior, 15,* 161–170.

*Muntaner, C., Walter, D., Nagoshi, C., Fishbein, D., Haertzen, C. A., & Jaffe, J. H. (1990). Self-report vs. laboratory measures of aggression as predictors of substance abuse. *Drug and Alcohol Dependence, 25,* 1–11.

Murdoch, D., Pihl, R. O., & Ross, D. (1990). Alcohol and crimes of violence: Present issues. *International Journal of the Addictions, 25,* 1065–1081.

National Television Violence Study (1996). *National television violence study: Scientific papers 1994–1995* (Vol. 1). Thousand Oaks, CA: Sage.

National Television Violence Study (1997). *National television violence study: Scientific papers 1995–1996* (Vol. 2). Thousand Oaks, CA: Sage.

Nisbett, R. E. (1993). Violence and U.S. regional culture. *American Psychologist, 48,* 441–449.

*Page, M. M., & Scheidt, R. J. (1971). The elusive weapons effect: Demand awareness, evaluation apprehension, and slightly sophisticated subjects. *Journal of Personality and Social Psychology, 20,* 304–318.

Paik, H., & Comstock, G. (1994). The effects of television violence on antisocial behavior: A meta-analysis. *Communication Research, 21,* 516–546.

*Paloutzian, R. F. (1975). Effects of deindividuation, removal of responsibility, and coaction on impulsive and cyclical aggression. *Journal of Psychology, 90,* 163–169.

Pernanen, K. (1991). *Alcohol in human violence.* New York: Guilford Press.

*Pihl, R. O., Lau, M. L., & Assaad, J. M. (1997). Aggressive disposition, alcohol, and aggression. *Aggressive Behavior, 23,* 11–18.

*Prentice-Dunn, S., & Rogers, R. W. (1980). Effects of deindividuating situational cues and aggressive models on subjective deindividuation and aggression. *Journal of Personality and Social Psychology, 39,* 104–113.

*Prentice-Dunn, S., & Rogers, R. W. (1982). Effects of public and private self-awareness deindividuating situational cues and aggressive models on subjective deindividuation and aggression. *Journal of Personality and Social Psychology, 39,* 104–113.

*Prentice-Dunn, S., & Spivey, C. B. (1986). Extreme deindividuation in the laboratory: Its magnitude and subjective components. *Personality and Social Psychology Bulletin, 12,* 206–215.

*Propst, L. R. (1979). Effects of personality and loss of anonymity on aggression: A reevaluation of deindividuation. *Journal of Personality, 47,* 531–545.

*Renson, G. J., Adams, J. E., & Tinklenberg, J. R. (1978). Buss-Durkee assessment and validation with violent versus nonviolent chronic alcohol abusers. *Journal of Consulting and Clinical Psychology, 46,* 360–361.

*Rogers, R. W. (1980). Expressions of aggression: Aggression-inhibiting effects of anonymity to authority and threatened retaliation. *Personality and Social Psychology Bulletin, 6,* 315–320.

*Rogers, R. W., & Ketchen, C. M. (1979). Effects of anonymity and arousal on aggression. *Journal of Psychology, 102,* 13–19.

*Rogers, R. W., & Prentice-Dunn, S. (1981). Deindividuation and anger-mediated interracial aggression: Unmasking regressive racism. *Journal of Personality and Social Psychology, 41,* 63–73.

Rohsenow, D. J., & Bachorowski, J. (1984). Effect of alcohol and expectancies on verbal aggression in men and women. *Journal of Abnormal Psychology, 93,* 418–432.

*Scheier, M. F., Buss, A. H., & Buss, D. M. (1978). Self-consciousness, self-report of aggressiveness, and aggression. *Journal of Research in Personality, 12,* 133–140.

*Schell, B. H., Cachon, J., Ganjavi, O., & Porporino, F. (1986). A pilot study assessing Type A behavior in violence-prone inmates. *Psychological Reports, 59,* 371–382.

*Selby, M. J. (1984). Assessment of violence potential using measures of anger, hostility, and social desirability. *Journal of Personality Assessment, 48,* 531–544.

Selby makes one last plea. (1987, August 15). Ogden Standard Examiner, p. IA.

*Shemberg, K. M., Leventhal, D. B., & Allman, L. (1968). Aggression machine performance and rated aggression. *Journal of Experimental Research in Personality, 3,* 117–119.

*Simons, L. S., & Turner, C. W. (1976). Evaluation apprehension, hypothesis awareness, and weapons effect. *Aggressive Behavior, 2,* 77–87.

*Spivey, C. B., & Prentice-Dunn, S. (1990). Assessing the directionality of deindividuated behavior: Effects of deindividuation, modeling, and private self-consciousness on aggressive and prosocial responses. *Basic and Applied Social Psychology, 11,* 387–403.

*Stanford, M. S., Greve, K. W., & Dickens, T. J., Jr. (1995). Irritability and impulsiveness: Relationship to self-reported impulsive aggression. *Personality and Individual Differences, 19,* 757–760.

Still at a loss for "why." (1987, August 26). Ogden Standard Examiner, p. IA.

*Strube, M. J., Turner, C. W., Cerro, D., Stevens, J., & Hinchey, F. (1984). Interpersonal aggression and the Type A coronary-prone behavior pattern: Theoretical distinction and practical implications. *Journal of Personality and Social Psychology, 47,* 839–847.

*Syverson, K. L., & Romney, D. M. (1985). A further attempt to differentiate violent from nonviolent offenders by means of a battery of psychological tests. *Canadian Journal of Behavioural Science 17,* 87–92.

Tamura, M. (1983). Changes in the patterns of criminal homicide for recent three decades. *Reports of National Research Institute of Police Science, 24,* 149–161.

Taylor, S. P. (1967). Aggressive behavior and physiological arousal as a function of provocation and the tendency to inhibit aggression. *Journal of Personality, 35,* 297–310.

*Turner, C. W., Layton, J. F., & Simons, L. S. (1975). Naturalistic studies of aggressive behavior: Aggressive stimuli, victim visibility, and horn honking. *Journal of Personality and Social Psychology, 31,* 1098–1107.

*Turner, C. W., & Simons, L. S. (1974). Effects of subject sophistication and evaluation apprehension on aggressive responses to weapons. *Journal of Personality and Social Psychology, 30,* 341–348.

U.S. Department of Justice. (1994). *Uniform crime reports for the United States: 1993.* Washington, DC.

Wheeler, L., & Caggiula, A. R. (1966). The contagion of aggression. *Journal of Experimental Social Psychology, 2,* 1–10.

*Williams, J. F., Meyerson, L. J., Eron, L., & Semler, I. J. (1967). Peer-rated aggression and aggressive responses elicited in an experimental situation. *Child Development, 38,* 181–190.

*Wilson, C., & Brewer, N. (1993). Individuals and groups dealing with conflict: Findings from police on patrol. *Basic and Applied Social Psychology, 14,* 55–67.

*Wolfe, B. M., & Baron, R. A. (1971). Laboratory aggression related to aggression in naturalistic social situations: Effects of an aggressive model on the behavior of college student and prisoner observers. *Psychonomic Science, 24,* 193–194.

*Worchel, S., & Anderoli, V. (1978). Facilitation of social interaction through deindividuation of the target. *Journal of Personality and Social Psychology, 36,* 549–556.

*Worchel, S., Arnold, S. E., & Harrison, W. (1978). Aggression and power restoration: The effects of identifiability and timing on aggressive behavior. *Journal of Experimental Social Psychology, 14,* 43–52.

Zimbardo, P. G. (1969). The human choice: Individuation, reason, and order, versus deindividuation, impulse, and chaos. In W. Arnold & D. Levine (Eds.), *Nebraska Symposium on Motivation, 1969.* Lincoln, NE: University of Nebraska Press.

3

AFFECTIVE AGGRESSION:
THE ROLE OF STRESS, PAIN,
AND NEGATIVE AFFECT

LEONARD BERKOWITZ

University of Wisconsin—Madison

Over the ages, sensitive observers seeing the pain and torment often experienced by humankind have found some consolation in the belief that suffering can be beneficial. Long before our present western religions started assuring their followers that they will find ample compensation for their current misery in heavenly rewards, one of Aesop's fables proposed that people frequently find instruction in their suffering. In one way or another, our anguish somehow makes us into better persons.

However consoling is this belief in the ennobling consequences of pain and suffering, mounting evidence indicates that much of the violence and antisocial behavior in society can be traced to greatly unpleasant occurrences. This chapter will attempt to summarize the many research findings and theoretical accounts that focus on these adverse effects of aversive conditions and, in doing so, will expand upon previously published analyses of affective aggression.

AN OUTLINE OF THE
THEORETICAL FRAMEWORK

Before we embark in this review, however, a brief outline of the cognitive-neoassociationistic framework that will guide this literature summary may be helpful (see Berkowitz, 1990, 1993a). Basically, as can be seen in Figure 3.1, decidedly unpleasant conditions tend to activate, automatically and with relatively little thought, at least two sets of "primitive" inclinations: One to escape from or

A Cognitive-Neoassociationistic Conception of Anger

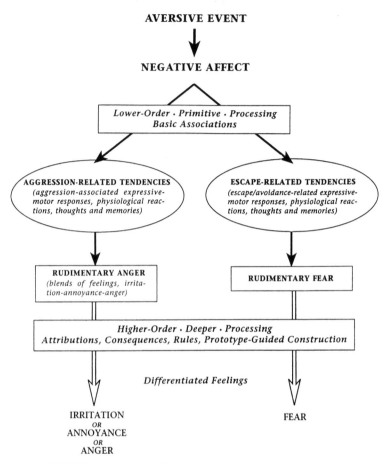

FIGURE 3.1   A cognitive-neoassociationistic conception of anger.

avoid the aversive stimulation and another to attack and even destroy the source of this stimulation. In other words, the aversive state of affairs presumably gives rise to *both* flight *and* fight tendencies. Genetic factors, prior learning, and situational influences all enter to determine the relative strengths of these opposing inclinations.

More important, both flight and fight tendencies should be regarded as syndromes, networks of associatively linked physiological, motoric, and cognitive components. The activated flight-associated syndrome (or network) is consciously experienced (perceived) as "fear," whereas the activated fight-linked syndrome is felt as "annoyance" or "irritation" at relatively weak levels or "anger" at more intense levels. These initial, fairly primitive reactions can also be modified and even substantially altered by cognitive processes that come into play after the first affective responses occur. It is in this second phase that appraisals, attributions, and the like can control reactions to the aversive incident. The present perspective emphasizes, nevertheless, that active information processing is required to bring these modifiers into operation so that particular appraisals and attributions are not necessary to produce the primitive experiences of fear and affective aggression. People can become angry and assault someone impulsively without the intervention of the complicated thought processes postulated by appraisal/attribution theorizing (see Berkowitz, 1993a,b).

In this last regard, this model suggests that persons exposed to decidedly unpleasant stressful conditions sometimes blame a salient available target for their troubles because of the hostile thoughts and angry feelings that had been generated within them; their attributions might then be the result rather than the cause of their affective reactions. Two recent investigations have provided supporting evidence. In the earliest of these, Keltner, Ellsworth, and Edwards (1993) induced angry or sad feelings in their participants and showed that the participants in the former condition were more apt to blame others for mishaps that occurred. In much the same vein, when Quigley and Tedeschi (1996) analyzed their respondents' self-reported angry incidents, they concluded that anger can lead to blame rather than being a consequence of blame.

Employing this general perspective, then, this chapter focuses largely on the stressful conditions that can activate the affectively generated, fight-related syndrome, an associatively connected network of angry feelings, hostile thoughts, and aggressive motor impulses. As most of the discussion will concentrate on the aggressive inclinations elicited by the unpleasant state of affairs, it may also be useful to think of the behavior of interrest as affective aggression.[1]

SOCIAL STRESS AND ANTISOCIAL CONDUCT

This section begins with the observation that those persons who are prone to extreme violence are often also disposed to engage in a wide variety of antisocial actions (Eron, Huesmann, Dubow, Romanoff, & Yarmel, 1987; Farrington, 1989). Among the several studies documenting this, Farrington's (1989, 1993) longitudinal investigations of a sample of London working class boys showed that (a) the

---

[1]Anderson (e.g., Anderson, Deuser, & DeNeve, 1995) has a very similar conception and also speaks of "affective aggression." However, unlike the present formulation, the Anderson model does not explicitly think of the various reactions produced by the aversive state as being associatively linked together and also does not hold that aversive stimulation tends to activate aggressive impulses fairly automatically.

social factors contributing to high levels of aggressiveness were also predictors of other patterns of antisocial conduct, and also (b) an index of "antisocial tendency" (composed of such measures as gambling, smoking, drunk driving, and drug use) was an excellent predictor of adult violence at 32 years of age. Analyses of the genesis of antisocial conduct can thus throw considerable light on the determinants of aggressive behavior, and vice versa.

"FRUSTRATIONS" AND "STRAINS" IN ANTISOCIAL BEHAVIOR STRAIN THEORY

A prominent line of thought in sociological criminology emphasizes the role of social stresses in generating antisocial inclinations. The strain theory of crime causation, initially advanced by Robert Merton (1957) and later adapted by other sociologists such as Albert Cohen (1955) and Richard Cloward and Lloyd Ohlin (1960), essentially traces antisocial deviancy to extremely unpleasant social experiences, mainly frustrations. First noting that United States society teaches its members to seek economic success, this formulation also points out that, largely because of its stratification system, society also effectively prevents segments of the population from achieving this goal. One result, according to this argument, is that poorly socialized people in those groups experiencing the strain of this disjunction between means and goals may turn to crime in trying to adapt to their frustrations. As Merton (1957, p. 146) observed, "a cardinal American virtue, 'ambition,' promotes a cardinal American vice, 'deviant behavior'" (quoted by Wilson & Herrnstein, 1985, p. 215). Although this analysis has been severely criticized, and obviously is seriously incomplete as a general account of all crime (see, e.g., Lilly, Cullen, & Ball, 1989), it apparently is useful in understanding some kinds of antisocial actions. Thus, for Bernard (1984, p. 366), "The data on serious gang delinquency virtually demand a strain type of explanation."

As the quotation from Merton readily illustrates, many of the discussions of the criminogenic effects of social strains basically envision these stresses as frustrations. The first question here is whether the strains postulated by these theorists should indeed be regarded as frustrations. It is argued that it is better, theoretically and practically, to think of strains more broadly as aversive experiences.

What Is Frustration?

Behavioral scientists are by no means agreed as to just what is a frustration. The term sometimes is applied to an external event, such as a situational obstruction to goal attainment, but at other times has to do with an internal, emotional reaction to some occurrence, as when people say they feel "frustrated." And then too, even when the reference is to an external condition, in many discussions this is a very general and even diffuse state of affairs, such as—as in the case of poverty—not having the pleasures that many persons typically experience in a given situation, whereas in other discussions the concept is much narrower, has a more specific scope, and has to do with some barrier preventing the person from obtaining an expected reward. A truly clear understanding of how social stresses and strains can promote antisocial conduct obviously requires a more precise definition of "frustration."

The 1939 Frustration–Aggression Hypothesis

The best known analysis of the effects of frustrations was spelled out in 1939 by a team of social scientists at Yale University led by John Dollard, Leonard Doob, and Neal Miller (Dollard, Doob, Miller, Mowrer & Sears, 1939). Rephrasing their behavioristic conception in more common sense terms, they basically defined "frustration" as an obstacle to the attainment of an expected gratification rather than as an emotional reaction. They also advanced two general propositions regarding the relationship between thwartings and the instigation to aggression: (1) Every frustration, they maintained, produces an instigation to aggression, an urge to harm someone, principally but not only the perceived source of the goal blocking, and (2) every aggressive action supposedly can be traced back to prior frustrations.

It should be recognized, however, that soon after the theory was first published, Miller (1941) amended the first proposition, acknowledging that the inability to reach an expected goal can have nonaggressive as well as aggressive consequences. There need not always be an open display of aggression. Still, he argued, if the affected persons continue to be thwarted, the nonaggressive reactions will diminish in strength and overt aggression will become more likely.

As for the second proposition, Berkowitz (1989, 1993a) has pointed out that much aggression is instrumental behavior in which the primary aim of the attack is to achieve some end other than the target's injury or destruction; the aggressor attempts to hurt or kill the victim, but seeks to do this in order to gain some objective such as money, social status, or a restoration of a favorable identity. This instrumental use of aggression can be learned, much as a person can learn to perform other useful actions, and does not necessarily stem from earlier thwartings. In my reformulation of the frustration–aggression hypothesis, I have therefore confined myself to the first proposition and contend that the frustration-produced urge to aggression should be regarded as an inclination to "hostile aggression" (Feshbach, 1964), a desire to hurt or destroy regardless of whatever other purposes might also be served. (Because the thwarted person is emotionally aroused, whatever aggression is displayed could also be called "affective aggression.")

In their 1939 monograph spelling out their analysis, Dollard and associates discussed a variety of factors affecting the strength of the frustration-engendered spur to aggression. They realized, for example, that thwarted persons are apt to refrain from striking at someone to the degree that they believe this aggression will be punished. However, the theorists also maintained that this self-restraint is frustrating to the extent that the would-be attackers' aggressive inclinations persist. As a consequence, the existing blocked instigation to aggression might actually be intensified (as long as the initial aggressive urge continues).

The Yale group's analysis of the role of the available target is especially interesting. Following the associationistic program then dominant in psychology, Dollard and colleagues held that the strongest urge is to strike at the perceived source of the frustration. But they also proposed that the threat of punishment could lead to displaced aggression in which substitute targets are attacked. Although the 1939 formulation did not say much about this displacement, Miller's (1948) later learning theory-based conflict model suggests that the intensity of the displaced aggression is a function of how strong are (a) the frustration-produced instigation to aggression and (b) the tendency to avoid performing that response, as well as (c) the degree of association between the perceived source of the frustration and the available target.

Some Research Findings

Social scientists apparently are no longer interested in this idea of displaced aggression, but there is evidence consistent with the Yale group's conception. Some of this support comes from a preliminary investigation reported by Hovland and Sears (1940, cited in Berkowitz, 1993, p. 77). The researchers reasoned that in the pre-World War II years, in which the economy of the U.S. South was greatly tied to the value of cotton, economic frustrations would have generated aggressive inclinations that could have then been displaced onto blacks. Consistent with their expectation, they found that sudden drops in the market price of cotton in this period were frequently followed by an increase in the number of blacks who were lynched in Southern states.[2]

There is even better evidence, especially for Miller's (1948) analysis, in a now all-but-forgotten experiment by Fitz (1976). Each of the undergraduate men serving in the study was led to think that he and his three partners in the session were to evaluate each other's creativity on assigned tasks. One of these three others (actually the experimenter's confederate) was very important in the study, called "P", whereas another one of the partners was said to be very similar to P in personality. P then "identified" this individual as a friend, who will be referred to as "P's friend." The third person supposedly was unknown to each of them (the "stranger"). After the naive participant worked on his task, in two-thirds of the cases he was provoked by P who derogated his work in "an obnoxious and know-it-all manner," whereas the remaining participants were treated in a neutral fashion by P. The naive subject was then required to evaluate each of his supposed partners' responses on an assigned task by administering a noise blast after each person's response, with higher intensity blasts signifying a less favorable judgment. Before this evaluation phase got underway, however, half of the angered men were frightened by letting them know that P would later judge their work by giving them electric shocks as his assessments of them (high fear condition). The remaining provoked subjects were not told about any later phase and thus had no reason to anticipate any punishment from P (low fear condition). The naive participant then embarked upon his judgments, with the order of presentation of the three "targets" being systematically varied.

---

[2]Hepworth and West (1988) reanalyzed the Hovland–Sears data employing a more sophisticated statistical procedure and essentially corroborated the original authors' conclusions.

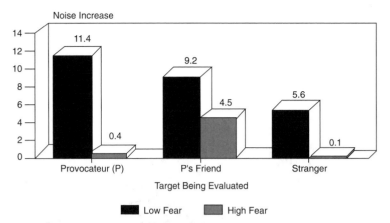

FIGURE 3.2   Punitive evaluations of targets by angered subjects. The scores given are differences from evaluations by nonangered subjects. Data from Fitz (1976).

Figure 3.2 summarizes the findings by showing *how much greater* was the mean intensity of the noise blasts delivered by the angered subjects to each of their partners than the mean intensity of the noises administered to these targets by the nonangry subjects. As can readily be seen, the results are entirely in line with Miller's associationistic analysis. We see, first of all, that the nonfearful-provoked subjects showed the expected declining gradient in the severity of the punishment they delivered to each target; they attacked the provocateur (P) most severely and were less punitive to P's friend but still gave that target stronger punishment than they administered to the stranger. However, the angered men led to fear P's possible retaliation did not attack P any more severely than they punished the stranger, but their most intense punishment was administered to the target associated with P: P's friend.

This last-mentioned experiment obviously says nothing about the effects of frustrations, but other investigations indicate that people can become aggressively inclined when they are thwarted (see Berkowitz, 1989, 1993a). As an example, Greenberg (1990) reported that employee theft rates increased in the manufacturing plants he studied when the workers' pay was temporarily cut by 15%. The employees had presumably regarded the pay reduction as unfair and expressed their resentment by stealing from the company. According to the investigator, "when the basis for the pay cuts was thoroughly and sensitively explained" to the employees, the theft rate declined (Greenberg, 1990, p. 561).

Does the Thwarting Have to Be "Illegitimate"?

This matter of a presumably unfair frustration brings us to the often-repeated contention (expressed, e.g., by Averill, 1983) that frustrations give rise to aggressive impulses only when they are regarded as illegitimate or somehow wrong. Although there can be little doubt that people can become highly aggressive when they believe they are improperly and deliberately blocked from reaching a desired goal, several experiments have found that even supposedly "legitimate" frustrations can give rise to aggressive tendencies.

In one of these supporting studies, Walters and Brown (1963) showed that after children had learned to perform make-believe aggressive responses, those who were then inadvertently frustrated, supposedly because a broken movie projector kept them from seeing a promised film, were subsequently especially aggressive while playing a game with another youngster. Inclined to be aggressive because of their prior training, they readily exhibited the aggressive tendencies generated by the accidental nonfulfillment of their expectations, even though they presumably did not blame anyone (other than the movie projector) for their frustration.

An experiment by Geen (1968) adds to this finding by indicating that socially "proper" frustrations can spur young adults to increased aggressiveness. In his study, male university students were individually first either reinforced or not reinforced for the punishment they gave a peer in a training session, and then were required to complete a jigsaw puzzle in the presence of another student (the experimenter's accomplice). Most of the participants were frustrated by being unable to complete the puzzle in the specified time, either because the confederate deliberately interfered with their work (Geen termed this the "personal frustration" condition) or because, unknown to them, the puzzle actually was insoluble so that they themselves apparently were responsible for their failure to get the job done (this is called the "task frustration" condition). In yet another condition (the "insult" group) the confederate insulted the subject as he struggled with the puzzle. Then, soon afterward, each participant had to shock the confederate whenever that person made a mistake on an assigned task and could vary the intensity of this punishment on a 10-step scale.

As we are not concerned with the influence of reinforcements for aggression, Figure 3.3 reports the mean intensity of the shocks administered by the *nonreinforced* subjects in the first and second halves of their shock opportunities (with each half composed of eight trials). As Figure 3.3 shows, and as would be expected, the men who were wrongly either frustrated or insulted by the "other student" were most punitive to that person, particularly in the second half of the trials (perhaps because their restraints against giving shocks had lowered in the later trials). More relevant to the discussion at hand, even those who had been thwarted by their own inability to do the task were significantly more aggressive to the confederate in the later half of the trials than were the nonfrustrated controls. Illegitimate interference with goal attainment clearly can instigate a relatively strong aggressive urge, but even a socially proper thwarting apparently can also evoke an aggressive inclination.

The Relationship May Be Inborn

Studies such as these obviously tell us little about the effects of prior learning on these frustration-produced aggressive reactions. Indeed, previous learning experiences undoubtedly can greatly modify the likelihood that an interference with

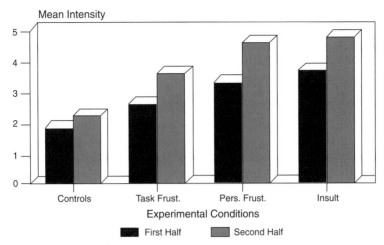

FIGURE 3.3   Shock intensity over trials when not reinforced for aggression. Data from Geen (1968).

goal attainment will promote an aggressive urge (see Bandura, 1973; Davitz, 1952). This does not mean that *only* those who have learned to react aggressively to frustrations will become assaultive when they are thwarted. Suggestive research with human infants indicates that frustrations can generate an instigation to aggression even in the absence of earlier training to be aggressive. Testifying to this, Stenberg, Campos, and Emde (1983) frustrated human infants by restraining their arms and legs and found that the babies then tended to display anger-like facial expressions. The researchers concluded that restraints of this type are inborn elicitors of anger.

Lewis (1993) has gone even further by proposing that anger is an unlearned reaction to the frustration of a goal-directed action. In his research he conditioned 2- to 8-month-old infants to pull one of their arms in order to see a picture of a baby's smiling face. An extinction phase was then established in which the arm pull no longer revealed the happy picture. Analysis of the infants' facial expressions demonstrated that the great majority of them displayed anger during this extinction period, whereas little anger was shown in the training phase. Furthermore, this pattern held for the 8-week-old babies as well as for the 8-month-old babies.

Long-Term Consequences

The investigations mentioned up to now had to do with the short-term consequences of the failure to attain an expected goal. Other studies investigating the long-run effects of repeated thwartings suggest that frequent frustrations can also increase the chances of antisocial behavior over a considerable period of time. Youngsters who were often frustrated during their formative years are especially apt to engage in criminal behavior in their adolescence and young adulthood. To cite only one example of many that could have been reported here, Farrington (1993) found that measures of the economic deprivation and poor parenting experienced by London boys were among "the most important predictors" of the likelihood that they would exhibit antisocial behavior as an adolescent and be "socially dysfunctional" as adults. Moreover, economic deprivation, indicated by low family income, poor housing, and large family size, was an especially good predictor of extreme aggressiveness in the youngsters' prepubertal years (Farrington, 1989). The frustrations these English youths had suffered as they were growing up because of their families' poverty and their parents' mistreatment of them (along with other adverse influences) evidently had contributed to the development of a fairly persistent pattern of antisocial conduct. For Berkowitz (1989, 1993a), but not necessarily for Dollard and colleagues (1939), these long-lasting effects of repeated frustrations are not due to the accumulation of an ever-active frustration-produced aggressive drive. Instead, the affected persons (a) have become quick to interpret other people's ambiguous actions in a hostile manner, (b) are disposed to respond to perceived threats and challenges with relatively strong aggression, and (c) tend to have weak self-restraints against aggression.

STRESS MORE THAN JUST FRUSTRATIONS

Despite all of this evidence (and the other studies that also could have been cited as well), there is reason to ask whether it is *frustration* that is the root of hostile (or affective) aggression, as Dollard and associates (1939) and other writers (e.g., Lewis, 1993) have proposed. Some concept other than "frustration" may be preferable if we are to develop an adequate account of this antisocial conduct. To spell this out in detail, let us go back to the often-reported connection between economic distress and crime (but see Wilson & Herrnstein, 1985, pp. 320 and 321 for a skeptical view of this often-claimed relationship).

Supporting the contention that economic hardships lead to relatively high levels of antisocial behavior, published studies have noted, among other things, that increases in unemployment in the United States between 1948 and 1985 were associated with jumps in homicide rates (Devine, Sheley, & Smith, 1988), poverty-stricken areas of the United States tend to have relatively high homicide rates (e.g., Williams, 1984; Williams & Flewelling, 1988), and unemployed young men are more likely to engage in wife battering (Howell & Pugliesi, 1988) or even to murder their women (Goetting, 1989) than are their better-off counterparts.

The question is, should the economic privations involved in these investigations properly be understood as frustrations? Consider the definition of frustration in the 1939 monograph mentioned earlier. Strictly speaking, the definition advanced by Dollard and associates, interference with the attainment of an expected goal, means that every privation is not necessarily frustrating. People are frustrated only if they are prevented from attaining the pleasures *they had been antic-*

ipating and not merely because they lack the good things in life that others enjoy. Thus, from this perspective, to employ the term "frustration" properly in connection with Merton's (1957) previously quoted observation regarding the societal thwarting of ambition, one would have to say: (1) that only those who had at least some hope or expectation of succeeding are frustrated when they cannot satisfy their ambitions and (2) that only these presumably become aggressively inclined. Many persons in the poverty-stricken areas of the United States with high homicide rates could well be frustrated in this strict sense, but others conceivably might resent their economic deprivations even though they actually had possessed little hope of improving their economic circumstances.

What is being suggested here, then, is that (a) sociological strain theory should be viewed as a theory about the effects of stress rather than about the consequences of frustration, and (b) it is social stress more than frustration that tends to give rise to inclinations to aggression and other forms of antisocial behavior. Indeed, as other writers (e.g., Agnew, 1989; Mawson, 1987) have also noted, a wide variety of highly stressful conditions are associated with relatively high levels of antisocial conduct.

Physical Pain

If frustrations are often stressful, physical pain is frequently even more disturbing. As Berkowitz (1983, 1990, 1993a,b) emphasizes, the experience of physical pain, like other stressful conditions, can generate aggressive inclinations. An impressive body of research with both animals and humans indicates that pain can be a fairly good stimulus to aggression (see Berkowitz, 1983, 1993b; Moyer, 1976).

Animal Research

Summarizing many of the investigations in this area, when two animals were cooped up together in a small chamber and exposed to decidedly unpleasant stimuli (such as physical blows, electric shocks, or loud noises), they frequently began to fight. Several experiments noted, however, that aggression is by no means an inevitable response to painful stimulation; many animals clearly would rather avoid or escape from the noxious event than attack an available target. Nevertheless, according to some studies, the afflicted animals are more likely to assault another animal when they do not know how to get away from the pain source.

A number of findings also contradict the contention that the pain-elicited aggression is only defensive aggression and/or only an attempt to lessen the noxious stimulation. Investigators have reported that the afflicted animals' assault can be offensive (i.e., appetitive) as well as defensive in nature (see Berkowitz, 1993b, p. 280; Hutchinson, 1983). Similarly, according to other results, pained animals sometimes expend effort to attack a suitable target (see Berkowitz, 1993b, p. 280). In general, then, as Moyer (1976) concluded on the basis of his review of the available literature, "there can be no doubt that under certain circumstances pain can lead to an intense attack. Such behavior has been demonstrated in the monkey . . . the cat . . . the rat . . . and the gerbil . . ." (p. 200).

Observations with Humans

As noted elsewhere (Berkowitz, 1993b, p. 281), there are quite a few reports in the medical literature indicating that people suffering from intense pain are often angry and even occasionally aggressive. As only one example, we find that patients tormented by severe episodic headaches are frequently described as angry and/or hostile persons. As supportive of the present thesis as these reports are, however, they obviously cannot demonstrate unequivocally that the pain produces anger and aggression instead of being only exacerbated by the patients' hostility. We therefore have to turn to controlled experiments for better evidence showing that painful experiences can indeed elicit affective aggression.

Much of this better evidence has to do with the nonbehavioral components of the affective aggression syndrome: the hostile cognitions, angry feelings, and bodily reactions that are usually, if only loosely, associated with the affectively generated impulse to strike at an available target. In one such case, research by Izard and associates (summarized in Izard, 1991, pp. 245 and 246) assessed the facial expressions activated by pain. Pointing out that infants' facial expressions during a number of emotional states are identical to those of adults, the investigators recorded how 25 babies reacted to painful immunization inoculations received over more than a year. According to these records, in early infancy (2 to 7 months) virtually all of the babies reacted to the injection with an expression of pain/distress accompanied by loud crying. However, in a few seconds "a clear-cut, full-faced anger expression" followed in fully 90% of these infants (p. 245). About a year later, when the babies were toddlers, "Every one of them showed clear, full-faced expressions of anger, and the anger expression was dominant on the face for a relatively long period of time" (p. 246), even though (we are told) they apparently did not remember the medical setting from their earlier experience. Izard concluded that "anger is a natural response to unanticipated pain" (p. 232).

Experiments with young adults indicate that the passage of years does not eliminate this kind of pain-induced effect. In a variety of investigations, college students exposed to physically very uncomfortable, and even somewhat painful, conditions were found to have more hostile thoughts and angry feelings than their counterparts placed in more comfortable circumstances (Anderson, Deuser, & DeNeve, 1995; Berkowitz, 1990).

The Aim of Pain-Elicited Aggression

Painful events apparently can evoke appetitive aggression in humans as well as in animals; suffering persons seem to be motivated to hurt someone as well as to lessen their own suffering.

Research by Baron (1977) on the aggression-stimulating influence of pain cues offers a suggestion along these lines. When angered persons were given an opportunity to attack their provocateur over a series of trials, information that they were hurting their target prompted them to increase the severity of the punishment they were delivering. It is as if the information about the target's suffering (i.e., the pain cues) essentially told them they were on their way to satisfying their aggressive "appetite," thereby intensifying their aggressive desires for the moment.

Two experiments by Berkowitz, Cochran, and Embree (1981) provide more direct evidence regarding the aim of pain-elicited aggression. Female undergraduates individually kept one hand in water that was either painfully cold or at a more comfortable room temperature while they evaluated the performance of a fellow student. After being told that any punishment they administered would either hurt the worker (in one condition) or help her by motivating her to do better (in the other condition), the participants delivered their evaluations of the supposed worker's performance on a series of trials in the form of either rewards (nickels) or punishments (noise blasts).

Figure 3.4 summarizes the results from the first of these studies, although both experiments yielded similar findings. As Figure 3.4 indicates, the women were generally unwilling to punish their fellow student, particularly when they were

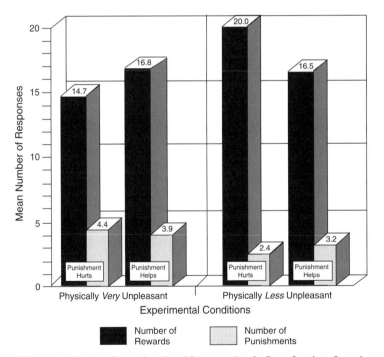

FIGURE 3.4   Number of rewards and punishments to "worker" as a function of aversiveness of situation and whether punishment will hurt or help the "worker." For each condition the maximum total number of responses possible was 50. Data from Berkowitz et al. (1981).

reminded that the punishment would be harmful. Those exposed to the relatively moderate water temperature delivered the most rewards and fewest punishments when they had been told that punishment would hurt their partner. However, as can also be seen in Figure 3.4, this pattern was reversed when the women's hands were in the painfully cold water. These suffering subjects administered fewer rewards and more punishments, especially when they believed the punishment would be hurtful. Apparently because they wanted to do injury, these latter people took some advantage of the opportunity to hurt the other individual.

The Effect of Stimuli Associated with Pain

A number of psychological theorists have recognized the aggression-eliciting effect of painful stimulation. Jeffrey Gray's (1987, 1991) formulation is especially interesting in this regard. He has postulated the existence of three "subsystems of emotion": an approach system, a behavioral inhibition system, and a fight/flight system. According to Gray (1991), this latter system, which is apparently somewhat similar to the conjectured aversively activated system summarized in Figure 3.1, "is specialized to respond to unconditioned punishing (typically painful) stimuli and to unconditioned termination of reward with either aggressive or flight behavior" (p. 283). Gray (1991) also suggested that "which of these outputs occur (i.e., attack or flight) seems to depend upon details of the environmental context (e.g., the availability of an escape route, the presence of an attackable target . . .)" (p. 283). What is especially pertinent to us now, for Gray only *unconditioned* aversive stimuli (i.e., only stimuli that are decidedly unpleasant in themselves) activate this fight/flight system. Stimuli that are only associated with an aversive state of affairs (i.e., conditioned aversive stimuli) presumably will only activate the behavioral inhibition system, and thus will suppress the responses that might bring punishment and not set the fight/flight system into operation (see, e.g., Gray, 1987, p. 244).

However, Gray's insistence that conditioned and unconditioned aversive stimuli have different effects is contradicted by a variety of studies with both animals (e.g., Vernon & Ulrich, 1966) and humans (Berkowitz, 1990, 1993a). Very much in accord with the present analysis, this research demonstrates that even stimuli that are only associated with decidedly unpleasant events can produce aggressive reactions even though they were not, in themselves, directly responsible for any aversive incidents.

One experiment with humans demonstrating this kind of effect was conducted by Fraczek (1974) in Poland. In the first, conditioning phase of the study, each of the male undergraduate participants pressed a button of a particular color whenever a light of that color flashed. For some subjects, in three-fourths of the trials a green light was quickly followed by a painful electric shock so that they learned to associate "green" with pain. In the next phase of the experiment, each participant had to "teach" a concept to a peer (in the standard Buss paradigm) and was required to punish the "pupil" for each of his mistakes by giving that person an electric shock. Importantly, for half of the subjects the shock-delivering apparatus was green in color, whereas it was a neutral color for the others.

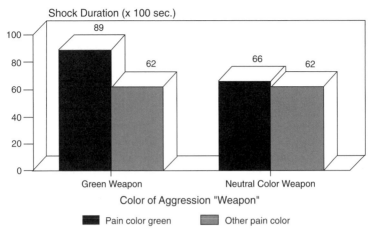

FIGURE 3.5   Duration of shocks as a function of "weapon's" association with pain. Data from Fraczek (1974).

Figure 3.5 summarizes the results for the measure based on how long the participants pressed the shock button when they administered the punishment. As Figure 3.5 shows, the subjects were most punitive when the "weapon" used in hurting the target was of the same color as the previous pain signal. Even though the "pupil" they were punishing had not been responsible for their earlier pain, they hurt this person most severely when they encountered a stimulus (the green shock apparatus) that was associated with the pain they had received just before.

Stress and Not Only Physical Pain

Other decidedly unpleasant conditions besides pain can also prompt aggressive reactions. In one of the macro-level investigations pointing to such an effect, Devine et al. (1988) reported that inflation-produced economic uncertainties and anxieties can lead to a jump in the U.S.'s homicide rate. Similarly, other studies (Blau & Blau, 1982; Williams, 1984) suggest that the income disparities within a metropolitan area can also be unpleasant enough to generate criminal violence. Other findings add to this list of social stressors. Research conducted in Israel found that increases in that country's national homicide level were related positively not only to the rapid modernization and sharply rising population that occurred from 1950 to 1981 (Landau & Raveh, 1987) but also to the number of highly salient threats to Israel's security (Landau & Pfefferman, 1988).

Even highly unpleasant atmospheric conditions apparently can give rise to aggressive inclinations. Following up on research by Baron (1977), Carlsmith and Anderson (1979) published a statistical analysis indicating that unusually hot weather had contributed to the urban riots in the United States during the 1960s. Craig Anderson and Dona Anderson (1984) then extended this finding by showing that hot weather in Houston, Texas, during the early 1980s was linked to a rise in violent crimes (murders and rapes) in that city, and especially to a high ratio of these violent crimes relative to property crimes. More recently, Craig Anderson and Kathryn Anderson (1996) pursued this line of investigation even further in two other analyses of the relationship between temperature and violent crime rates in U.S. metropolitan areas. These analyses demonstrated, among other things, that an index of arrests of whites for violent crimes was significantly related to the warmth of the cities even when "competitor" variables that also could affect the crime rate were taken into account. Similarly, an analysis of domestic disturbances reported to the Dayton, Ohio, police (Rotton & Frey, 1985) found that the greatest number of domestic assaults was received on or right after unusually hot days and when atmospheric pollution was high.

Individual-level investigations carried out in natural settings and in the laboratory also indicate how social stressors can promote violence. Making use of naturalistic observations, when Straus and colleagues (Straus, 1980a) asked the men and women in their nationally representative sample about the stressful events in their lives, the researchers found that the respondents experiencing the greatest number of stressors were most likely to report having abused their children in the past year. This stress–child abuse relationship held, for both men and women, even though the stressful occurrences were such things as having someone close die, moving to a different neighborhood, having trouble with other people at work, and having a family member with health or behavior problems. Furthermore (Straus, 1980b), over all of the couples in the sample, the greater the number of stressful events that was experienced by any one couple, the higher was the rate of both verbal and physical aggression in that couple.

Results from laboratory experiments provide further corroboration and also testify to the variety of unpleasant conditions that can give rise to an instigation to aggression. Some of these studies, dealing with the effects of physically aversive stimulation, also tend to rule out a possible alternative explanation for the previously mentioned connection between high temperatures and violent antisocial behavior: The hot weather conceivably might have driven large numbers of people onto the streets, thereby increasing the chances that they would be influenced by others and/or come into conflict with someone. In the experiments this possibility is excluded because the subjects came into contact with only one other individual (besides the experimenter). Even so, laboratory investigations dating back at least to the 1970s have demonstrated that people afflicted with unpleasantly high room temperatures are frequently more hostile to a stranger than they otherwise would have been under more comfortable conditions (Anderson, 1989; Anderson et al., 1995; Baron, 1977). A laboratory experiment by Rotton, Frey, and associates (1979) showed that foul odors can also promote a relatively high level of aggression.

Psychologically unpleasant states of affairs are also conducive to aggressive reactions. An experiment by Passman and Mulhern (1977) is illustrative. Each of the mothers serving in the experiment worked on an assigned task over a series of trials and, at the same time, was required to monitor her child as the youngster, in an adjoining room, tried to complete a puzzle. The child was to be punished whenever he or she made a mistake, but the woman could choose what level of punishment intensity she wanted to deliver. The researchers placed each mother under both high and low levels of stress as she worked by varying the clarity of the task requirements on any given trial. It was found that the women punished their children's mistakes more severely when they were under the stress of ambiguous requirements than when the situation was more comfortable for them.

Agitated Negative Affect as the Spur to Affective Aggression

Putting all of these findings together, it seems (e.g., Berkowitz, 1989, 1990, 1993a,b) that the stressful conditions involved in these investigations all had something in common: They probably all gave rise to an intense negative affect. I proposed that this common factor, this strong negative affect, was responsible for the affective aggression recorded in these studies. However, mostly because of some medical observations, I now believe that a particular type of negative affect is the spur that activates the affective aggression syndrome. According to some papers in the medical literature, those people who become openly angry are likely to be "affectively disturbed" by their condition (see Pilowsky & Spence, 1976; Wilson, Blazer, & Nashold, 1976), suggesting that anger and affective aggression result from the strong felt distress or experience of suffering produced by the physical sensations. More specifically, it may well be that the affective aggression syndrome is set into operation by an agitated negative effect.

RELATION BETWEEN THE EXPERIENCE AND BEHAVIOR

Where the present cognitive-neoassociationist formulation holds that the agitated negative affect activates an aggression-related motor program (as well as fear/escape-related motoric reactions), other theories do not postulate this direct connection between experience and motor responses. For some writers, such as Clore, Ortony et al. (1993) and Anderson et al. (1995), emotions influence actions only by affecting cognitive mechanisms, including attention, judgment, decision-making, and memory, rather than by directly activating a class of behaviors. Other theorists, most notably Frijda (1986), have taken a somewhat different position and maintain that an action priming occurs. According to Frijda (1986), an emotionally relevant appraisal elicits not only specific physiological and experiential reactions but also a particular action "readiness."

We might wonder, however, whether the term "readiness" adequately characterizes the anger-related effects. Although this word implies only a *latent disposition* to respond in a particular way, Frijda's own data indicate that the aversive experience can produce active motor responses such as impulses and involuntary skeletal muscular reactions (see Frijda, Kuipers, & ter Schure, 1989, p. 226). More than a mere readiness, then, there may be an active urge to attack, even to hurt, someone.

MORE THAN A DEFENSIVE REACTION

If we accept the existence of such an urge, the next question is what is the goal of this impulse? Some writers (e.g., Bandura, 1973) have suggested that the aggressive reactions arising under aversive stimulation are basically defensive responses aimed at reducing the unpleasant state of affairs. Contrary to such an interpretation, however, the aggressive behavior seen in many of the experiments just cited could not eliminate or even lessen the unpleasant conditions. The distressed participants apparently attacked their target fairly strongly because of their stress-generated aggressive urge and not in an attempt to better their condition. A number of theorists have recognized this, and so Frijda speaks of provoked people having a desire to "move against" someone, and Izard (1991) notes that anger is accompanied by "an impulse to strike out, to attack the [perceived] source of the anger" (p. 241). Spielberger's (1996, personal communication) factor analysis of responses to his latest questionnaire assessing individual differences in experienced anger testifies to such an aggressive urge. He found three intercorrelated clusters: one dealing with angry feelings (composed of items such as "I am furious"), one with a felt pressure to verbal expression (items such as "I feel like screaming"), and the third reflecting an urge to physical aggression (items such as "I feel like kicking somebody").

All of these observations suggest that aversive experiences promote aggressive-related motor impulses and that these motor reactions could have the aim of doing injury to an available target. Roseman, Wiest, and Swartz (1994) obtained evidence of this desire to hurt someone when they asked their respondents to indicate what they felt like doing when they were angry. Many of these people answered that in such a state they often thought "how unfair something was." More importantly, quite a few of them also said that they felt "like hitting someone" and that they "wanted to hurt someone."

INHIBITING THE ACTIVATED
AFFECTIVE AGGRESSION

The activation of the affective aggression syndrome obviously does not mean that there necessarily will be an open display of aggression. Various influences may operate to keep the aggressive reactions from becoming manifest. For one thing, as Figure 3.1 noted, because of the person's genetic background and/or prior learning history and/or the presence of situational influences, the aversive stimulation might evoke stronger flight-related than aggression-related reactions.

Because of space limitations, only the possible role of situationally induced restraints will be discussed.

THREAT OF PUNISHMENT

We have already touched on the threat of punishment as an aggression-inhibiting influence. As Fitz's (1976) previously mentioned experiment illustrates, unless people are exceedingly strongly instigated to attack their tormentor, the possibility that they will suffer severe consequences for assaulting this person may well keep them from aggressing openly (although they might displace their hostility onto a safer target). Years of research on the effectiveness of punishment as a disciplinary technique (summarized in Berkowitz, 1993a, Chap. 10) add detail to such a statement. By and large, this research indicates that punishment works best when it is (1) severe; (2) delivered quickly, before the individual whose behavior is to be disciplined can enjoy the benefits of his/her disapproved conduct; and (3) administered consistently and with certainty.

One might ask, however, whether these findings, mostly obtained from laboratory experiments, can be extended to our criminal justice system. Under what conditions is punishment most effective in controlling antisocial behavior?

The Importance of Punishment Certainty

A National Academy of Sciences-commissioned review of studies investigating the effectiveness of various types of judicial sentences for crimes (see Berkowitz, 1993a, p. 319) is suggestive. According to this review, the certainty of punishment (condition 3) is much more important than the severity of the sentence (condition 1) in deterring criminal behavior. The likelier it is that criminals will be apprehended and punished, the more likely it is that they will refrain from criminal conduct. This matter of punishment certainty can help explain why capital punishment does little to deter many murders. If we compare the homicide rates in regions (U.S. states or entire countries) that execute convicted killers with the rates in demographically matched regions (states or countries) not carrying out capital punishment, we generally find little evidence that many would-be murders are restrained by the threat of execution (see Berkowitz, 1993a, pp. 320 and 321).

One possible reason for the ineffectiveness of this ultimate penalty is that the punishment is by no means certain. Some murderers do get away with their crimes. Only about 70% of the homicides receiving police attention in recent years have resulted in arrests, and only about 7 in 10 of these cases led to convictions (see Berkowitz, 1993a, p. 323).

But capital punishment may also not deter many murders because a substantial fraction of these killings are emotionally charged and highly impulsive in nature. Most homicides grow out of conflicts between people who know each other (although there has been an increase in the proportion of cases in which a stranger is slain). The persons involved in these conflicts are apt to be highly enraged at the time they assault their antagonist (Berkowitz, 1993a, pp. 277–279). If so, furiously intent on inflicting pain, they might not think of the possible long-term consequences of their violence—the possibility of punishment is not apparent to them at that time—and they strike at their victim more or less impulsively with whatever weapon is available to them.

Minimizing Hostile Appraisals and Attributions

Although the present discussion has concentrated on the role of stressful circumstances in activating aggressive motor impulses, the present formulation recognizes that decidedly unpleasant conditions can also activate hostile thoughts and memories. Anderson's analysis of affective aggression (e.g., Anderson et al., 1995) has emphasized the part played by these cognitive reactions. This latter model notes, in accord with the previously cited findings by Keltner et al. (1993), that aversive conditions can generate hostile appraisals of other people's ambiguous behaviors. As a consequence, it is proposed that the afflicted persons are not only more strongly aroused but also are likely to think mostly of aggressive modes of reaction and then decide to assault the perceived offender.

However hostile appraisals and attributions operate, there is no doubt that they can increase the chances that stressful circumstances will lead to overt aggression. For this reason, cognitively oriented treatments of people who are prone to extremely violent reactions to disturbing conditions often attempt to teach these persons, among other things, to interpret their stresses in a nonhostile manner.

Attention Direction

The direction of an individual's attention can also influence the reaction to a stressful occurrence, sometimes heightening the likelihood of affective aggression but sometimes suppressing the violent inclinations. It is important to consider both of these possibilities.

We now know that strong emotional excitation tends to reduce the range of cues to which one pays attention (see, e.g., Christianson, 1992). Highly aroused people are apt to focus on the main features of the situation confronting them to the neglect of matters that are relatively peripheral for them at that time. Thus, persons who are emotionally aroused because of an aversive event might well focus their attention narrowly on those they blame for the unpleasant occurrence. They might then think only of the mistreatment they believe they have suffered, how the perceived culprit has wronged them, and how they want to lash out at this miscreant. Concentrating their attention on the wrongdoer, they might then totally disregard other considerations, such as the possibility of being punished for aggression, and therefore fail to restrain their activated aggressive urges.

However, the attentional focus might also lead to greater self-control and a reduced likelihood of open aggression, under some conditions. A series of experiments (Berkowitz, 1993a; Berkowitz & Troccoli, 1990) suggest this could happen when people become highly aware of their aroused feelings and think this arousal might influence them to act in socially improper or inappropriate ways.

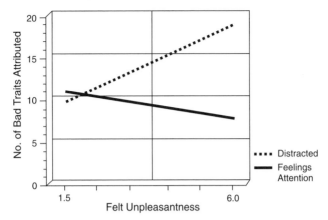

FIGURE 3.6   Relationship between felt discomfort and impression of target as influenced by attention direction. Calculated from multiple regression analysis.

Two experiments by Berkowitz and Troccoli (1990) point to some such process at work. Comparable results were obtained in both studies, but only the second experiment will be summarized here. Male undergraduates were given a physical activity to carry out that was decidedly uncomfortable in half of the cases and affectively neutral for the other men. Half of the subjects in each of these conditions were then distracted by giving them an irrelevant assignment, whereas the remaining participants were led to be highly attentive to their mood by asking them to rate their feelings on a series of items. Immediately after this, all of the subjects listened to a brief autobiographical statement supposedly made by a fellow student and gave their impressions of this individual's personality.

A multiple regression analysis was then carried out testing whether the experimental variations interacted with the participants' self-rated discomfort in predicting how many bad qualities the men assigned to the target person. Figure 3.6 shows that such a significant interaction was obtained. As Figure 3.6 indicates, when the subjects' attention was turned away from themselves, the worse they felt and the more unfavorable was their impression of the target. In contrast, those who were highly aware of their discomfort seemed to "lean over backwards" in their judgments: the greater their felt displeasure, the *fewer* was the number of bad qualities they attributed to the target. Presumably wanting to be "fair" and "objective" in their assessment, they apparently sought to minimize the possible distorting influence of their mood and then overcorrected for this possible source of bias.

All in all, the feelings attention in these studies apparently gave rise to a relatively careful consideration of what was socially appropriate under the given circumstances and, consequently, produced a heightened self-restraint. However, as was implied earlier, attention to one's feelings probably will not always have such an effect. The target person in these experiments clearly was not the source of the participants' displeasure, and wanting to be fair and proper, they realized they should not blame their distress on this other individual. However, under different circumstances, those who are highly aware of themselves and their bad feelings conceivably might become even more hostile toward an available target when (a) it is not clear to them that this person is not responsible for their distress and (b) they are not motivated to be fair and socially proper in their judgments and actions.

This brief overview of some of the ways in which cognitive processes can influence affective aggression obviously does not mean that cognitions have only a minimal role in the determination and regulation of emotional reactions. Indeed, the theoretical framework guiding the present discussion has been termed a "cognitive-neoassociationistic" perspective because an adequate account of affective aggression must employ both cognitive and associationistic ideas. Whether the concepts employed in such an analysis derive from a cognitive or associationistic tradition, it is also necessary to recognize the great degree to which the various components of the affective aggression syndrome operate in a largely automatic manner. Affectively aroused persons do not always decide what they should feel, think, and do.

REFERENCES

Agnew, R. (1989). A longitudinal test of the revised strain theory. *Journal of Quantitative Criminology, 5,* 373–387.

Anderson, C. A. (1989). Temperature and aggression: Ubiquitous effects of heat on occurrence of human violence. *Psychological Bulletin, 106,* 74–96.

Anderson, C. A., & Anderson, D. C. (1984). Ambient temperature and violent crime: Tests of the linear and curvilinear hypotheses. *Journal of Personality and Social Psychology, 46,* 91–97.

Anderson, C. A., & Anderson, K. B. (1996). Violent crime rate studies in philosophical context: A destructive testing approach to heat and southern culture of violence effects. *Journal of Personality and Social Psychology, 70,* 740–756.

Anderson, C. A., Deuser, W. E., & DeNeve, K. M. (1995). Hot temperatures, hostile affect, and arousal: Tests of a general model of affective aggression. *Personality and Social Psychology Bulletin, 21,* 434–448.

Averill, J. (1983). Studies on anger and aggression: Implications for theories of emotion. *American Psychologist, 38,* 1145–1160.

Bandura, A. (1973). *Aggression: A Social learning analysis.* New York: Prentice-Hall.

Baron, R. A. (1977). *Human aggression.* New York: Plenum.

Berkowitz, L. (1989). Frustration–aggression hypothesis: Examination and reformulation. *Psychological Bulletin, 106,* 59–73.

Berkowitz, L. (1990). On the formation and regulation of anger and aggression: A cognitive-neoassociationistic analysis. *American Psychologist, 45,* 494–503.

Berkowitz, L. (1993a). *Aggression: Its causes, consequences, and control.* New York: McGraw-Hill.

Berkowitz, L. (1993b). Pain and aggression: Some findings and implications. *Motivation and Emotion, 17,* 277–293.

Berkowitz, L., Cochran, S., & Embree, M. (1981). Physical pain and the goal of aversively stimulated aggression. *Journal of Personality and Social Psychology, 40,* 687–700.

Berkowitz, L., & Troccoli, B. T. (1990). Feelings, direction of attention, and expressed evaluations of others. *Cognition and Emotion, 4,* 305–325.

Bernard, T. J. (1984). Control criticisms of strain theories: An assessment of theoretical and empirical adequacy. *Journal of Research in Crime and Delinquency, 21,* 353–372.

Blau, J. R., & Blau, P. M. (1982). The cost of inequality: Metropolitan structure and violent crime. *American Sociological Review, 47,* 114–129.

Carlsmith, J. M., & Anderson, C. A. (1979). Ambient temperature and the occurrence of collective violence: A new analysis. *Journal of Personality and Social Psychology, 37,* 337–344.

Christianson, S-A. (1992). *Handbook of emotion and memory: Research and theory.* Hillsdale, NJ: Erlbaum.

Clore, G. L., Ortony, A., Dienes, B., & Fujita, F. (1993). Where does anger dwell? In R. S. Wyer, Jr., & T. K. Srull (Eds.), *Advances in social cognition: Perspectives on anger and emotion* (pp. 57–87). Hillsdale, NJ: Erlbaum.

Cloward, R. A., & Ohlin, L. E. (1960). *Delinquency and opportunity: A theory of delinquent gangs.* Glencoe, IL: Free Press.

Cohen, A. K. (1955). *Delinquent boys: The culture of the gang.* New York: Free Press.

Davitz, J. R. (1952). The effects of previous training on postfrustration behavior. *Journal of Abnormal and Social Psychology, 47,* 309–315.

Devine, J. A., Sheley, J. F., & Smith, M. D. (1988). Macroeconomic and social-control policy influences on crime rate changes, 1948–1985. *American Sociological Review, 53,* 407–420.

Dollard, D., Doob, L., Miller, N., Mowrer, O., & Sears, R. (1939). *Frustration and aggression.* New Haven, CT: Yale Univ. Press.

Eron, L. D., Huesmann, L. R., Dubow, E., Romanoff, R., & Yarmel, P. (1987). Aggression and its correlates over 22 years. In D. Crowell, I. Evans, & C. O'Donnell (Eds.), *Childhood aggression and violence* (pp. 249–262). New York: Plenum.

Farrington, D. P. (1989). Early predictors of adolescent aggression and adult violence. *Violence and Victims, 4,* 79–100.

Farrington, D. P. (1993). Childhood origins of teenage antisocial behaviour and adult social dysfunction. *Journal of the Royal Society of Medicine, 86,* 13–17.

Feshback, S. (1964). The function of aggression and the regulation of aggressive drive. *Psychological Review, 71,* 257–272.

Fitz, D. (1976). A renewed look at Miller's conflict theory of aggression displacement. *Journal of Personality and Social Psychology, 33,* 725–732.

Fraczek, A. (1974). Informational role of situation as a determinant of aggressive behavior. In J. De Wit & W. Hartup (Eds.), *Determinants and origins of aggressive behavior* (pp. 225–230). The Hague: Mouton.

Frijda, N. H. (1986). *The emotions.* Cambridge/New York: Cambridge Univ. Press.

Frijda, N. H., Kuipers, P., & ter Schure, E. (1989). Relations among emotion, appraisal, and emotional action readiness. *Journal of Personality and Social Psychology, 57,* 212–228.

Geen, R. G. (1968). Effects of frustration, attack, and prior training in aggressiveness upon aggressive behavior. *Journal of Personality and Social Psychology, 9,* 316–321.

Goetting, A. (1989). Men who kill their mates: A profile. *Journal of Family Violence, 4,* 285–296.

Gray, J. A. (1987). *The psychology of fear and stress* (2nd ed.). Cambridge, UK: Cambridge Univ. Press.

Gray, J. A. (1991). Neural systems, emotion and personality. In J. Madden (Ed.), *Neurobiology of learning, emotion, and affect* (pp. 273–306). New York: Raven Press.

Greenberg, J. (1990). Employee theft as a reaction to underpayment inequity: The hidden cost of pay cuts. *Journal of Applied Psychology, 75,* 561–568.

Hepworth, J. T., & West, S. G. (1988). Lynchings and the economy: A time-series reanalysis of Hovland and Sears (1940). *Journal of Personality and Social Psychology, 55,* 239–247.

Hovland, C., & Sears, R. (1940). Minor studies in aggression. VI. Correlation of lynchings with economic indices. *Journal of Psychology, 9,* 301–310.

Howell, M. J., & Pugliesi, K. L. (1988). Husbands who harm: Predicting spousal violence by men. *Journal of Family Violence, 3,* 15–27.

Hutchinson, R. R. (1983). The pain-aggression relationship and its expression in naturalistic settings. *Aggressive Behavior, 9,* 229–242.

Izard, C. E. (1991). *The psychology of emotions.* New York: Plenum.

Keltner, D., Ellsworth, P. C., & Edwards, K. (1993). Beyond simple pessimism: Effects of sadness and anger on social perception. *Journal of Personality and Social Psychology, 64,* 740–752.

Landau, S. F., & Pfeffermann, D. (1988). A time series analysis of violent crime and its relation to prolonged states of warfare: The Israeli case. *Criminology, 26,* 489–504.

Landau, S. F., & Raveh, A. (1987). Stress factors, social support, and violence in Israeli society: A quantitative analysis. *Aggressive Behavior, 13,* 67–85.

Lewis, M. (1993). The development of anger and rage. In R. A. Glick & S. P. Roose (Eds.), *Rage, power, and aggression* (pp. 148–168). New Haven, CT: Yale Univ. Press.

Lilly, J. R., Cullen, F. T., & Ball, R. A. (1989). *Criminological theory: Context and consequences.* Newbury Park, CA: Sage.

Mawson, A. R. (1987). *Transient criminality: A model of stress-induced crime.* New York: Praeger.

Merton, R. K. (1957). *Social theory and social structure.* Glencoe, IL: Free Press.

Miller, N. (1941). The frustration–aggression hypothesis. *Psychological Review, 48,* 337–342.

Miller, N. (1948). Theory and experiment relating psychoanalytic displacement to stimulus-response generalization. *Journal of Abnormal and Social Psychology, 43,* 155–178.

Moyer, K. E. (1976). *The psychobiology of aggression.* New York: Harper & Row.

Passman, R. H., & Mulhern, R. K., Jr. (1977). Maternal punitiveness as affected by situational stress: An experimental analogue of child abuse. *Journal of Abnormal Psychology, 86,* 565–569.

Pilowsky, I., & Spence, N. D. (1976). Pain, anger, and illness behaviour. *Journal of Psychosomatic Research, 20,* 411–416.

Quigley, B. M., & Tedeschi, J. T. (1996). Mediating effects of blame attributions on feelings of anger. *Personality and Social Psychology Bulletin, 22,* 1280–1288.

Roseman, I. J., Wiest, C., & Swartz, T. S. (1994). Phenomenology, behaviors, and goals differentiate discrete emotions. *Journal of Personality and Social Psychology, 67,* 186–205.

Rotton, J., & Frey, J. (1985). Air pollution, weather, and violent crime: Concomitant time-series analysis of archival data. *Journal of Personality and Social Psychology, 49,* 1207–1220.

Rotton, J., Frey, J., Barry, T., Milligan, M., & Fitzpatrick, M. (1979). The air pollution experience and physical aggression. *Journal of Applied Social Psychology, 9,* 397–412.

Stenberg, C. R., Campos, J. J., & Emde, R. N. (1983). The facial expression of anger in seven-month-old infants. *Child Development, 54,* 178–184.

Straus, M. A. (1980a). Stress and child abuse. In H. Kempe & R. E. Helfer (Eds.), *The battered child* (3rd ed.). Chicago, IL: Univ. of Chicago Press.

Straus, M. A. (1980b). Social stress and marital violence in a national sample of American families. *Annals of the New York Academy of Sciences, 347,* 229–250.

Vernon, W., & Ulrich, R. (1966). Classical conditioning of pain-elicited aggression. *Science, 152,* 668.

Walters, R., & Brown, M. (1963). Studies of reinforcement of aggression. III. Transfer of responses to an interpersonal situation. *Child Development, 34,* 563–571.

Williams, K. R. (1984). Economic sources of homicide: Reestimating the effects of poverty and inequality. *American Sociological Review, 49,* 283–289.

Williams, K. R., & Flewelling, R. L. (1988). The social production of criminal homicide: A comparative study of disaggregated rates in American cities. *American Sociological Review, 53,* 421–431.

Wilson, J. Q., & Herrnstein, R. J. (1985). *Crime and human nature.* New York: Simon & Schuster.

Wilson, W. P., Blazer, D. G., II, & Nashold, B. S., Jr. (1976). Observations on pain and suffering. *Psychosomatics, 17,* 73–76.

4

THE ROLE OF SOCIAL INFORMATION PROCESSING AND COGNITIVE SCHEMA IN THE ACQUISITION AND MAINTENANCE OF HABITUAL AGGRESSIVE BEHAVIOR

L. ROWELL HUESMANN

University of Michigan

INTRODUCTION

One of the essential ways in which humans are different from all other species is in their well-developed ability to represent, process, and communicate information. The psychological processes that humans invoke to perform these tasks are called cognitive processes, and the internal representations of information utilized in these processes are denoted as cognitions. Some reflexive behaviors may usually involve only peripheral processing, but more central cognitive processes often override these reflexes, e.g., one can will oneself to keep one's hand on a hot coal. From this perspective all human social behavior, including aggressive behavior, is mediated by the cognitions and cognitive processing of the participants. This does not mean that cognitive processes "cause" social behavior. Rather, as mediating processes, they connect biological, environmental, and situational inputs to behavioral outputs. However, as described in this chapter, different patterns of cognitive processing are more conducive to one kind of social behavior than to another.

Human Aggression: Theories, Research, and
Implications for Social Policy

73

In recent years theorists writing about aggression have generally accepted the importance of cognitions. All the chapters in the theoretical perspectives section of this book, in fact, deal with the role of cognitions in one way or another: hormones and conceptions of domination, cuing of aggressive thoughts, conceptions of self-esteem, and interpretations of arousal as anger. However, there have only been a few attempts to move the next step forward; that is, to integrate the large amount of empirical data accumulated about aggressive behavior and related cognitions into comprehensive *information processing models* for explaining aggressive behavior and how it develops. What do we mean by "information processing models?" An information processing model is a description of the cognitive data structures a person utilizes and the sequence of cognitive operations the person executes in order to generate the cognitions and behaviors that are output from given input. It is most analogous to a computer program that describes the output a computer produces from given input.

The major aim of this chapter is to show how the development and occurrence of human aggressive behavior are explained by social-cognitive information processing theory and to review the empirical evidence supporting the theory. However, the history and fundamentals of information processing models in general and of models for social cognition in particular must be reviewed briefly.

EMERGENCE OF INFORMATION PROCESSING MODELS OF SOCIAL BEHAVIOR

Early in 1996 a computer program named "Deep Blue" shocked the chess world by defeating the reigning champion, Gary Kasparov, in one game. Less than a year later, "Deep Blue" went on to defeat Kasparov in a match—an event that stimulated anew the discussion of the differences, if any, between artificial intelligence and human intelligence. This is not the place to pursue that argument in detail, but "Deep Blue's" victory is a mark of the advances that have been made in our understanding of how humans process information. Artificially intelligent programs like "Deep Blue" do not succeed in solving complex problems simply because they can compute very rapidly. They succeed because they also incorporate models of how human experts process information to solve problems.

It is not surprising that the use of information processing models to describe human behavior first flourished in studies of human problem solving (Newell, Shaw, & Simon, 1958; Newell & Simon, 1972; Simon, 1978). For one thing, the expertise in computer programming that such modeling requires tended to be concentrated in that area. However, as Herbert Simon, the father of information processing modeling, has cogently argued: the formalization and detailed specification of processes required in information processing models make them more valuable than either natural language or mathematical statistics for modeling any kind of human behavior (Gregg & Simon, 1967). In the early 1960s, two books—

Feigenbaum's (1963) *Computers and Thought,* and Miller, Galanter, and Pribram's (1960), *Plans and the Structure of Behavior* (1960)—stimulated thinking about information processing in many areas of psychology. By the mid-1960s, Abelson (1968), Gullahorn and Gullahorn (1963), Loehlin (1969), Simon (1957, 1967, 1969), and others had begun to describe psychological models of a variety of social behaviors in terms of underlying information processes. By the early 1970s more specific information processing theories of different kinds of social and abnormal behavior were appearing (Abelson, 1976; Carroll & Payne, 1976; Colby, Hilf, Weber, & Kraemer, 1972; Hastie & Carlston, 1980; Huesmann, 1978; Huesmann & Levinger, 1976; Wyer, 1974; Wyer & Srull, 1980). During this same period, the knowledge that cognitive psychologists were accumulating about basic human cognitive processes was also increasing exponentially and was being organized in an information processing framework. Textbooks by Neisser (1967), Lindsay and Norman (1977), and Anderson (1980) marked both this explosion in empirical knowledge and the progressive domination of cognitive psychology by the information processing approach. It should not be surprising then that the attention that social psychologists were giving to cognitions and information processing was also increasing dramatically during this period. The term social cognition became popular sometime in the late 1970s (Wyer & Carlston, 1979; Wyer & Srull, 1980), but it was really the publication of Fiske and Taylor's (1984) book on social cognition that marked the convergence of the cognitive and information processing trends into the mainstream of social theorizing.

For students of aggressive behavior the early 1980s also brought the first information processing analyses of aggression. Huesmann (1980, 1982b, 1986, 1988; Huesmann and Eron, 1984) offered a general information processing model for aggression, focusing particularly on observational learning, and Dodge (1980, 1986; Crick & Dodge, 1994; Dodge & Frame, 1982) offered a general information processing model for aggression, focusing particularly on perceptions and attributions. Since then, a variety of elaborations of the models have emerged and a reasonable consensus has developed about the ways in which human cognitions and cognitive processes mediate aggressive behavior. But before turning to a more detailed discussion of those models, we must review a number of general principles of information processing.

FUNDAMENTALS OF INFORMATION PROCESSING MODELS

What are the principles underlying information processing models of cognition and behavior? Information processing models formally lay out the sequence of cognitive processes involved in the occurrence of a behavior much as a computer program lays out the sequences of operations in a computer that produces a particular output. A basic assumption is that the human mind can be viewed as analogous to a computer. Behavior is the output of software programs operating within the biological hardware constraints of the brain. The difference between hardware and software is viewed as much less distinct than in most mechanical computers and the biological hardware is certainly less hard. It is the conceptual distinction of having more malleable programs and data stored and operating within less malleable processing systems that makes the analogy. A closely related assumption is that behavior is best modeled with hierarchical levels of explanation. For example, an aggressive interaction might most easily first be modeled in terms of relevant interacting behavior sequences (e.g., she shouted at him; he told her to shut up; she shouted again; he hit her). The behavior sequence might then be modeled in terms of a relatively high level program for behavior (e.g., follow rule to retaliate when insulted by a woman). The operation of these programs might then be modeled in terms of more fundamental cognitive processes, e.g., retrieval of rules by spreading activation; these more fundamental processes might be modeled in terms of neurophysiological reactions, which in turn might be modeled in terms of biochemical processes. Different theories of social behavior may use different levels of explanation within this hierarchy, but generally most theories adopt a level analogous to programming in a high level computer language. The formal properties and limitations these programming languages and symbol systems place on the modeled processes are well understood, and the natural language interpretations of the programs are also usually easily followed by other researchers.

Information processing models of social cognition assume that a person's social behavior is completely determined by the configuration of hardware, software, knowledge structures, and environmental inputs that the organism has experienced. Yet such models should not be called mechanistic. Process models sometimes include stochastic elements to model individual variations, but, even without them, complex variations in behaviors and cognitions are obtained because of the wide diversity of experiences encountered by different individuals. Information processing models are models of individuals' social cognitions and social behaviors, not of group means. Different individuals have different hardware, software, and data structures. Different situations generate different inputs. Most often models are developed that assume similar programs and structures for different individuals with well-defined loci for individual differences, e.g., perhaps the procedure for deciding whether to attribute hostility to another is the same for most individuals, but the database of past experiences on which they base their decision varies.

Every information processing model of social behavior must have a defined behavior space within which it operates. This space is characterized by a set of potential social behaviors (e.g., how one greets a stranger on the street) that the model is designed to explain and a set of potential inputs that define the variations in the current environment that the model is supposed to handle (e.g., location of meeting, characteristics of stranger, mood of person, etc.). In addition, every information processing model has an *executive program* (i.e., operating system) that specifies the overall flow of cognitive processes that are hypothesized, *subroutines* that represent the detailed operation of specific cognitive processes that are available, and multiple data structures in *memory* that represent the modeled individual's cognitions.

Some information processing models may include mechanisms for self-modification of the cognitions through a variety of learning processes. Others assume static cognitive structures. Generally, information processing models assume that humans employ the same basic kinds of processing operations and techniques that have been proven by IP mathematicians and theorists to be sufficient (or in some cases necessary) to do the kinds of cognitive processing that humans do, e.g., stored programs with branching instruction sequences, test–operate–test–execute sequences (TOTE), or node-link memory structures. In addition, the processes that have emerged as viable alternatives in computer science are usually the ones that are proposed as viable alternatives for human information processing models, e.g., top-down versus bottom-up tree searches, reproductive versus reconstructive retrieval from memory, or on-line calculation versus retrieval from stored schemas.

CONNECTIONIST ALTERNATIVES

One obvious limitation of information processing models is that the relations between the basic information processes and the underlying neurophysiological processes remain obscure. A second related problem is that information processing models of cognition most often hypothesize multiple programs that operate sequentially instead of in parallel (probably because until recently the machine languages available to simulate cognitive processes operated sequentially). However, there is significant evidence that many human cognitive processes occur in parallel.

One consequence of these problems has been the emergence of what have come to be called "connectionist" models of cognitive processing (Feldman & Ballard, 1982; Rumelhart & McClelland, 1986). Such models attempt to describe cognitive processes and related behaviors using simulated neural networks in which parallel processing is a natural property. Somewhat lost in the excitement over this "new" approach is the fact that it is actually a reemergence of a very old approach to pattern recognition called "perceptrons" (see McCulloch & Pitts, 1943; Minsky & Papert, 1969; Nilsson, 1965; Rosenblatt, 1960). Thus, arguments about the value of the two approaches have a long history (Newell & Simon, 1972).

Although neural network models undoubtedly bear a closer resemblance to the human central nervous system than information processing models, they do not have a one-to-one correspondence. More important, as Smolensky has argued (1988), it is still unclear that connectionist models offer a sound basis for modeling human cognition. The processes occurring in neural networks are usually as far removed from our empirical data on human cognitive processes as the processes in information processing models are removed from observed neurophysiological processes.

The parallel processing argument for connectionist modeling is also not as strong as it might seem at first. In fact, numerous information processing models of "parallel" processes have been proposed and even simulated over the past 25 years with information processing models that included parallel processing subroutines (e.g., Chase & Simon, 1973; Huesmann & Woocher, 1976; Townsend, 1976). Although simulations on nonparallel processing computers must, of course, simulate parallelism with sequential operations, that does not change the essential parallelism of the model. The related point is that serial processes inside the human head can appear to be parallel from outside the head (Simon, 1979, p. 4).

A third argument against information processing models is that they are "linear" (see, e.g., Crick & Dodge, 1994). This argument often reflects a confusion between linear and sequential. The fundamental structure of information processing models as described earlier allows outputs to be related to inputs in any nonlinear matter unless the model is specifically designed to produce linear outputs. Information processing models are "essentially" less linear and more readily falsifiable than path models and stochastic models of social behavior (Huesmann, 1982a) and less linear than many connectionist models that use only linear connections.

INFORMATION PROCESSING PRINCIPLES APPLIED TO SOCIAL COGNITION

Information processing models of social cognition have drawn on empirical knowledge about human cognition and human social behavior to define a set of basic processes and data structures that seem to characterize human cognitions about social behavior. As mentioned earlier, one can think of any information processing system as consisting of a *memory* in which *data and programs* can be stored and an *executive program* that distributes resources and has overall control over the system. The system processes *input* stimuli and cognitions and generates *outputs* that may be behaviors or cognitions. For social behavior, we conceive of this information processing system as accepting inputs of social stimuli that define a particular social situation. The executive program calls upon appropriate subroutines to process the inputs, search memory for relevant information, and generate output behaviors for that situation. Let us now examine several of the components involved in these processes in more detail.

MEMORY STRUCTURES
FOR SOCIAL-INFORMATION PROCESSING

Human memory can be thought of as a network of nodes and links that represents encoded propositions (Rumelhart, Lindsay, & Norman, 1972). The meaning of each node is defined by its associated links that represent labeled attributes whose values are other nodes. Thus, a male friend Sam may be denoted by a node with links such as gender = male, relation = friend, height = tall, works at = university. The meaning of male, friend, tall, and university, in turn, is defined by their links. Nodes can represent semantic constructs or episodic constructs (events, people, objects). Thus, one may refer to episodic or semantic memory.

Information is *encoded* by being integrated into the memory network. Encoding means the "formation of a representation of an external stimulus in the memory system" (Kintsch, 1977, p. 485). *Elaborative rehearsal* of information generates more links to the rest of the network and more firmly encodes information in the network. Elaborative rehearsal goes beyond simple repetition of information and involves consideration of how the new information fits with other knowledge already encoded.

Information is *retrieved* by being *activated*. One can imagine a *spread* of activation emanating out from one node to connected nodes. A cue, either an external stimulus or an internally activated schema or mood, activates the first node. As each successive node becomes activated it is said to be retrieved, but the strength of activation diminishes as greater distance separates linked nodes. Clearly multiple links enhance the likelihood of recall, although multiple nodes with similar links may produce inaccurate recall due to *interference*. However, retrieval of information generally is not viewed as a blind spreading activation process but rather as a more directed *heuristic search*. Particular branches of the network are followed that appear particularly promising, and the activated nodes are tested to see if they meet a criterion for what is being sought. Thus, memory search can be conceptualized as an example of the standard information processing technique of *generate and test*.

It is also clear that there are conceptually distinct *short-term* and *long-term* memory processes. Short-term memory has a very limited capacity and is sometimes called working memory because it contains the information currently being processed or being "activated." If information is activated long enough in short-term memory, it is likely to be integrated into the unlimited capacity long-term memory. Thus, attention to social information (i.e., maintaining it in short-term memory) can have a direct effect on the likelihood that it will be encoded in long-term memory (see, e.g., Hastie, 1988).

It is convenient to distinguish between two types of information about social behavior that one might store in memory: *declarative* and *procedural* (Anderson, 1983). Procedural knowledge can be thought of as knowledge about "how things are done" and is represented by stored programs. These programs are most commonly represented as sequences of if-then statements called *productions*. One can easily imagine many basic social skills being represented by short sequences of imperative productions, e.g., "if someone says hello to me, then I should say hello back." A production can be viewed as a particular type of link between an "input node" (the condition that must be satisfied) and an "output node" (the action).

Within this framework, *schema* is a term used to refer to any macro knowledge structure encoded in memory that represents substantial knowledge about a concept, its attributes, and its relations to other concepts. We can discuss our "self-schemas," which are organized knowledge about ourselves, "event schemas," which are organized knowledge about events, "belief schemas," which are organized sets of beliefs, and so on. Of course, we use such organized knowledge to make inferences and to draw conclusions in what is called *top-down* processing because our existing knowledge influences the conclusions we reach. One particularly important kind of inference in social cognition is *causal attribution*, which is an inference about why someone does something, believes something, or acts in a particular way. Attributions are often schema driven, i.e., they are influenced strongly by existing schemas (Fiske & Taylor, 1991), but often the outcome of an attribution process also leads to changes in schemas.

When a schema is formed that links together in a sequence many simpler event schemas representing expected events and actions, that schema is called a *script*. A script makes use of both *declarative* and *procedural* knowledge and may contain productions. This use of the term was first coined by Abelson (1976). A script serves as a guide for behavior by laying out the sequence of events that one believes are likely to happen and the behaviors that one believes are possible or appropriate for a particular situation. For example, almost everyone has a restaurant script that tells them that when they enter a restaurant someone will take them to a table and give them menus, that a waitress/waiter will appear to whom they should give an order, and so on.

Scripts have a strong influence on all sorts of social behavior, including aggressive behavior. For example, suppose you are sitting in a car alone on the New York subway when two tough-looking young men get on the train. The situation cues the retrieval of a script that might start out this way:

> The young toughs approach you with their hands in their pockets and ask "Can you give us 20 bucks?" Your script then branches. If you give them the $20, they leave, and you have lost $20. If you do not give them the money, they pull a revolver out of their pocket demand the money again, and your life is in danger.

The script could continue, but let us examine how it may influence your behavior to this point. Of course, the young toughs may never approach you, but the activation of the script has sensitized you to watch for signs of approach. The retrieval of the particular script has biased you toward making hostile intent attributions. If the toughs do start to approach, you may well watch their hands carefully. You may search for the consequences of alternative behaviors on your part. For example, if you have a gun in your pocket, you may retrieve the script sequence, "I shoot them before they can shoot me, and I don't lose my money or my life." If they approach you with their hands in their pockets and demand money, you may follow this script and shoot them, a la Bernard Goetz.

AUTOMATIC OR CONTROLLED
COGNITIVE PROCESSING

Studies of cognitive processing have revealed that at least two different modes of processing exist with quite different speeds and demands on conscious resources (Schneider & Shiffrin, 1977; Shiffrin & Schneider, 1977). *Automatic processes* occur very rapidly, without using many cognitive resources and without any conscious executive decisions being made about the process. Reading is one example. Many social-perception processes are automatic, including "schema-triggered affect" (Fiske, 1982), memory priming effects, and spontaneous trait inferences (Bargh, 1982). *Controlled processes* occur more slowly, require more cognitive resources, and demand conscious executive control. Conscious planning of how to deal with a social situation would be one example. The boundaries are sometimes fuzzy, and many controlled processes may become automatic either as part of a child's development or with repeated practice or rehearsal. For example, in a novel social situation, a person may engage in a controlled search for scripts that could be used in that situation. However, highly familiar situations quite probably automatically trigger scripts that fit the situation.

RETRIEVING SOCIAL INFORMATION

As described earlier, the ease with which any kind of information or response can be accessed in the human central nervous system depends on how elaborately it has been encoded. Even simple S–R pairings are more likely to be elicited if there are multiple paths from stimulus to response. Both controlled and automatic activation of information in memory can be viewed as spreading activation processes. The spread of activation is often guided by already encoded schemas (heuristic search). For example, if you see someone you know as a librarian walking down the street, your mental search for explanations for what he or she is doing will be influenced by your schema for librarians.

Such memory search is activated by immediate *social cues* that provide the input to begin the search, e.g., the librarian in the previous example. However, the speed and success of retrieving social information are also influenced by recent stimuli that may have activated relevant schemas in memory, making them more accessible. This process is known as *priming*. For example, you may be more likely to recognize the librarian on the street if you have just previously walked by the library and had the library schema activated. *Emotions and moods,* such as anger or depression, also serve as cues that activate related schemas or scripts.

The activation of a particular schema, script, or node in memory has automatic effects on social inference and behavior, but another process called *filtering* may limit the effect of any activated information. Filtering is the testing process through which the executive routine decides if the activated information is the information sought or whether the search should continue. Filters may be simple tests of accuracy for the information or they may be tests of appropriateness of the scripts or behaviors activated. For social behavior, filters represent what Bandura (1986) has called self-regulating internal standards or what Huesmann and Guerra (1997) have termed normative beliefs.

SOCIAL PERCEPTION

Whether a particular social cue will stimulate the retrieval of much social information depends to a great extent on its *salience* and the extent to which one *attends* to the cue. Cues need not be attended to consciously, but the human perceptual system distributes processing resources differentially, and inputs that do not have many resources directed at them (i.e., receive little attention) are unlikely to have much of an effect on the information processing system. For each information processing system there are certain properties of stimuli that attract attention (salient properties) and make the stimulus salient to the processor. However, what makes a stimulus salient to a person often varies from situation to situation. People who look strange or behave in different ways, for example, have high social salience for most people. What is most salient and attracts attention also depends on what moods and schemas are currently activated. A young female walking on the street who is worrying about being attacked will focus her attention on different cues in the males she sees than would a young female at a party who is thinking about potential mates.

In addition to being affected by the differential direction of attention, social perception is also affected by differential *interpretations* that may be given to the same cues. Most social cues are open to alternative plausible interpretations, e.g., "is the person smiling at you because she likes you," or "is the person smiling at you because he wants something." Of particular importance to social perception are the kinds of *causal attributions* one makes about others' social behaviors (Jones & Davis, 1965; Kelley, 1967; Weiner, 1986). As with stimulus salience, interpretations of social stimuli and causal attributions depend on the kinds of schemas that are activated in the processor as well as characteristics of the stimuli. The person who is "looking for trouble" may well "see trouble" where others would not.

Although social perception often involves "controlled" processes requiring the distribution of resources, many processes have been shown to operate "automatically" with little conscious control. For example, people make spontaneous inferences about the dispositions of those around them, e.g., are they angry or afraid, without consciously devoting cognitive resources to the processes (Bargh & Pietromonaco, 1982; Quattrone, 1982; Winter & Uleman, 1984). Again, the exact kind of interpretation that is made may depend on the schemas that are currently activated.

ENCODING MECHANISMS

Once social information is attended to and interpreted, it can be *encoded* into the node link memory structure. As described earlier, *elaborative rehearsal* of information builds many connections in memory and makes the information more accessible and more easily retrieved. However, the exact way in which information is integrated in memory depends on the information already there and the schemas that are activated. For example, if one's schema for Russia is that it is an aggressive, imperialistic country, it would be more difficult to encode any of its new peaceful actions into memory. A script may be closely associated with specific cues in the encoding context or may be an abstraction less connected to specific cues. To encode an observed sequence of behaviors as a script, a person must first attend to the sequence. Thus, scripts with particularly salient cues for the person are more likely to be encoded. However, many observed sequences might never be encoded because the person perceives them as inappropriate.

Social learning, i.e., the encoding of new connections between social stimuli and social schemas, scripts, or behaviors, occurs through either *enactive learning* or *observational learning* (Bandura, 1986). Enactive learning encompasses both instrumental and classical conditioning—a person engages in actual behaviors and experiences positive or negative consequences. Depending on the consequences, the social script employed to generate the behaviors becomes more or less accessible in the future. Observational learning occurs when a person encodes schemas, scripts, or behaviors that they have simply observed others utilizing. An important encoding principle is what is known as *encoding specificity* (Tulving & Thompson, 1973). This refers to the empirical fact that the specific context in which information appears when it is encoded becomes associated with the encoded information and can trigger its activation in memory better than other semantically related information. Thus, for example, the color of a room in which a violent act is observed may later trigger memories of that act. A variety of factors are known to affect the likelihood of observed social information being encoded, including, as described earlier, the saliency of the stimuli, the schemas already active, and the interpretation given to the information. In addition, however, the more the actor possesses characteristics valued by the observer, the greater is the likelihood of encoding (Huesmann, 1982b). The observer may also experience *vicariously* the reinforcements and consequences that the observed model experiences (Bandura, Ross, & Ross, 1963) and encode these outcomes as part of the social script derived from the observation. Of course, observed scripts that are not very salient and have observed consequences that are not very desirable are not very likely to be encoded as possible scripts for future use.

STRESS, MOOD, AROUSAL, AND INFORMATION PROCESSING

The level of arousal that the human information processor is experiencing seems to change information processing in a number of ways. As arousal levels become higher than normal, attention seems to be directed more narrowly at a few cues that seem to be the most salient (Broadbent, 1971; Easterbrook, 1959). Very high levels of arousal seem to decrease working memory capacity, narrow memory search, make activation of weakly associated schemas less likely, and make the activation of the best connected schemas and scripts most likely (Luria, 1973; Anderson, 1990). For simple tasks, this restriction can produce enhanced performance that may provide an evolutionary explanation for the phenomenon. For complex tasks requiring an extensive heuristic search for solutions, performance will worsen. Of course, stress is one of the most common causes of high arousal. As a result, in stressful social situations, one can expect that a person will focus on what seems to be the most salient social cues, activate only the schemas and scripts that are most closely connected to those cues, and generate a narrow range of behaviors. Thus, when stress is coupled with emotions such as fear or anger and coupled with situational cues linked to aggressive scripts, only violent schemas are likely to be activated. For example, a young male whose life is being threatened by another young male with a gun may find it very difficult to attend to any cues in the environment other than the gun or to retrieve any other scripts than simple scripts for fighting or fleeing.

AGGRESSIVE BEHAVIOR, ANGER, AND SOCIAL COGNITION

Let us now turn to more specific applications of these social information processing principles to understanding aggressive behavior. Our knowledge of human information processing and social cognition as outlined earlier provides important insights into the processes involved in many social behaviors, including aggression. But it is important to realize from the start that social cognition is *not* a cause of aggressive behavior. Social cognition is a *mediating* process that connects external situations, internal schemas, and social behavior in predictable ways.

AGGRESSIVE BEHAVIOR

Aggressive behavior means any behavior that is intended to injure or irritate another person (Berkowitz, 1993; Eron et al., 1971). Specifically excluded from this definition is the "assertive" behavior of dynamic sales people and executives that is often called "aggressive" by the public. Psychologists have long distinguished between the kind of aggressive behavior that is directed at the goal of obtaining a tangible reward for the aggressor (*instrumental or proactive*) and the kind of aggressive behavior that is simply intended to hurt someone else (at different times denoted *hostile, angry, emotional, or reactive aggression*) (Feshbach, 1964). However, an examination of the underlying cognitive processes involved (e.g., Dodge & Coie, 1987) has led to a realization that many of the same mechanisms are involved in both types of aggression. Clearly, anger plays a more important role in hostile aggression, but that does not mean that anger is not present in both types. One solution is to view the role of emotional anger in aggressive behavior as one that varies along a continuum. Instrumental aggression and hostile aggression are at opposite ends of this particular continuum but they are mediated by many common cognitive processes.

ANGER

What is anger then? From a social/cognitive perspective, anger occurs when one is emotionally aroused and the memory node labeled "anger" is activated. How does a node come to be labeled anger? Some argue from an evolutionary perspective that human infants (at least after a few months growth) become predisposed to respond to frustration (e.g., restraint) with a specific combination of general arousal, physiological responses, and muscle tensions that most observers would label anger (Stenberg & Campos, 1990). The node associated with this pattern of activation subsequently becomes labeled as anger by the growing organism. Others argue that the process involves more learning—that each person acquires a cognitive schema for anger defined in terms of a template of situational cues that must be matched (e.g., Fiske, 1982). Still others suggest that a node such as anger is defined in terms of the outcome of an "appraisal" process in which the person evaluates the current situation in terms of such characteristics as pleasantness (e.g., unpleasant), agency (e.g., another), uncertainty (e.g., certain), and attention (e.g., ruminating) (Smith & Ellsworth, 1985; Smith, 1989). In either case the activation of the "anger" node is the result of a cognitive evaluation of external and internal cues. For example, one may sense a variety of changes in muscles (e.g., facial expressions such as tensing, frowning, flaring nostrils) and internal physiology (release of epinephrine) in response to external social cues. Feelings of wanting to attack a target may also be present. The information processing executive perceives all or some of these components and labels the state as one of anger, which in turn may increase the component reactions present. Some theorists (e.g., Berkowitz, 1993) distinguish between anger and hostility. Hostile individuals are said to be those who are "typically quick to voice or otherwise indicate negative evaluations of others (p. 21)." Although such a distinction has pedagogic value, it is not a necessary distinction within a social cognitive framework. Different particular occurrences of anger may be connected to different specific targets. However, individuals can still vary in their disposition to experience anger because of the cognitions they hold and processes they employ.

BIOSOCIAL INTERACTIONS
AND THE DEVELOPMENT OF AGGRESSION

Three important facts about anger and aggressive behavior in humans need to be summarized before proceeding with our elaboration of the role of social cognition. First, habitual aggressive behavior usually emerges early in life, and early aggressive behavior is very predictive of later aggressive behavior and even of aggressive behavior of offspring (Farrington, 1982; 1985; Huesmann, Eron, Lefkowitz & Walder, 1984; Loeber & Dishion, 1983; Magnusson, Duner, & Zetterblom, 1975; Olweus, 1979). Process models for aggressive behavior need to explain this continuity over time and across generations. Second, severe aggression is most often a product of multiple interacting factors (Coie & Dodge, in press), including genetic predispositions (Cloninger & Gottesman, 1987; Mednick, Gabrielli, & Hutchins, 1984; Rushton et al., 1986), environment/genetic interactions (Lagerspetz & Lagerspetz, 1971; Lagerspetz & Sandnabba, 1982), central nervous system trauma and neurophysiological abnormalities (Moyer, 1976; Nachson & Denno, 1987; Pontius, 1984), early temperament or attention difficulties (Kagan, 1988; Moffitt, 1990), arousal levels (Raine & Jones, 1987), hormonal levels (Olweus, Mattsson, Schalling, & Low, 1988), family violence (Widom, 1989), cultural perspectives (Staub, 1996), poor parenting (Patterson, 1995), inappropriate punishment (Eron, Walder, & Lefkowitz, 1971), environmental poverty and stress (Guerra, Huesmann, Tolan, Eron, & VanAcker, 1995), peer-group identification (Patterson, Capaldi, & Bank, 1991), and other factors. No one causal factor by itself explains more than a small portion of individual differences in aggressiveness. Third, early learning and socialization processes play a key role in the development of habitual aggression (Bandura, 1973; Berkowitz, 1974; Eron, Walder, & Lefkowitz, 1971). Aggression is most likely to develop in children who grow up in environments that reinforce aggression, provide aggressive models, frustrate and victimize them, and teach them that aggression is acceptable.

More generally the existing research suggests that habitual aggressive behavior in young humans develops out of a combination of innate predisposing factors, the child's early interactions with the environment, and situationally specific precipitating factors. From a social cognitive perspective the variety of predisposing factors discussed earlier may make the emergence of certain specific cognitive routines, scripts, and schemas more likely, but these cognitions develop through interactions of the child with the environment and are designed to respond to different environmental situations.

ENVIRONMENTAL INSTIGATORS AND SOCIALIZERS

When examining how the human information processing system responds to environmental inputs relevant to aggressive behavior, one must distinguish between *situational instigators* that may precipitate, motivate, or cue aggressive cognitions and responses and those more lasting components of the child's *environment* that mold the child's cognitions (schemas, scripts, normative beliefs) over time and therefore socialize the child to respond in characteristic ways to the environment. An environment rife with deprivations, frustrations, and provocations is one in which habitual aggression readily develops, as is seen in the high level of aggression in our urban ghettos.

In summary, compelling empirical evidence suggests that the interaction of predisposing personal factors with environmental forces shape a child's cognitions to make aggressive behavior more or less likely when certain situational cues occur. Let us now review the processes through which these cognitions influence aggressive behavior and through which the cognitions are shaped by the interaction of the environment with predisposing personal factors.

COGNITIVE PROCESSES MEDIATING AGGRESSIVE BEHAVIOR

Since the early 1980s, two general cognitive/information processing models have emerged to explain how humans acquire and maintain aggressive habits.

One, developed by Huesmann and colleagues (Huesmann, 1977, 1982a, b, 1986, 1988; Huesmann and Eron, 1984; Huesmann & Guerra, 1997), initially focused particularly on scripts, beliefs, and observational learning, whereas the other, developed by Dodge and colleagues (1980, 1986, 1993; Crick & Dodge, 1994; Dodge & Frame, 1982), focused particularly on perceptions and attributions. However, both hypothesize a similar core of information processing, both rely heavily on the work of cognitive psychologists and information processing theory, and both draw from Bandura's (1977, 1986) earlier formulations of cognitive processing in social learning as well as Berkowitz's (1990) neoassociationist thinking.

According to Bandura's (1986) social/cognitive formulations, social behavior is under the control of internal self-regulating processes. What is important is the cognitive evaluation of events taking place in the child's environment, how the child interprets these events, and how competent the child feels in responding in different ways. These cognitions provide a basis for stability of behavior tendencies across a variety of situations. Internalized standards for behavior are developed from information conveyed by a variety of sources of social influence. Children have many opportunities to observe the standards of others, including through the mass media.

Berkowitz (1990), while not disputing the importance of internalized standards, has emphasized the importance of enduring associations among affect, cognition, and situational cues. He argues that such learned associations produce stable behavioral tendencies whenever specific situational cues occur.

The central core of processes hypothesized by both Huesmann (1986, 1988) and Dodge (Crick and Dodge, 1994; Dodge, 1986) are diagrammed in Figure 4.1. Both models draw on Berkowitz and Bandura's thinking. Both models suggest that any individual faced with a social problem evaluates and interprets situational cues, searches memory for guides to behavior, evaluates and decides on the best behavior, and enacts that response. The essential operations of encoding and interpreting cues, selecting a goal and behaviors for attaining it, and evaluating the behaviors on multiple dimensions are common to both models. Thus, in accord with Bandura's position, the cognitive interpretation of environmental events and the comparison of potential responses to self-regulating standards is important, whereas in accord with Berkowitz the associations between cues and encoded schemas are also important.

Huesmann's model focuses first on scripts, their acquisition and retrieval. His model assumes that people use a heuristic search process to retrieve a script that is relevant for the situation. More aggressive people are presumed to have encoded a larger number of aggressive scripts. The learning of scripts is assumed to be influenced both by observational learning and by conditioning, and more aggressive youth are expected to have more opportunities to observe aggression in others. Huesmann's model also hypothesizes a key role for what are called normative beliefs—internalized proscriptions about what is inappropriate behavior for the individual.

One of the most important elements in Dodge's model is cue interpretation. Aggressive individuals are presumed to have a bias toward interpreting ambiguous

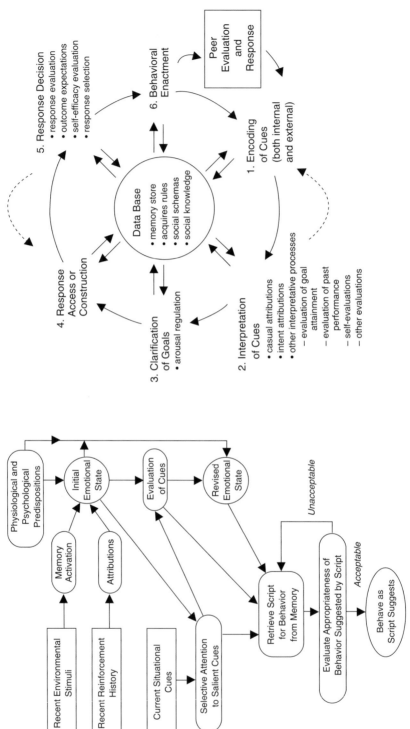

FIGURE 4.1 Huesmann's (1988) initial model (left) and Crick and Dodge's (1994) reformulated model (right).

cues as hostile. Another important focus of Dodge's model is the effect that society's (e.g., peers') responses to one's behaviors have on one's schemas. It is argued that an individual encodes and interprets peer's responses to one's behaviors and that those interpretations may change one's self-schema and thus one's future behaviors. For example, children who are rejected by their peers may develop schemas that deemphasize the importance of peers. In turn this may lead to the development of decision heuristics for social behavior (or the development of scripts, to use Huesmann's terminology) that emphasize tangible rewards over relationship rewards. Dodge's model also stresses the role of developmental changes in information processing *skills* in addition to the kinds of developmental changes in social knowledge (schemas, scripts, etc.) hypothesized by both models. It is presumed that attention span, speed of processing, encoding efficiency, heuristic search skills, and other basic information processes improve with age. Developmental delays may lead to less efficient information processing. Because nonaggressive, prosocial problem solving generally requires more complex information processing skills, this delayed development might well promote aggressive social behavior.

From their early formulations, these models of Dodge and Huesmann have evolved in parallel toward a common core model for the role of information processing and cognitive processes in aggressive behavior. Dodge's elaborations of the role of information processing in social behavior have attracted wide attention in the social development sphere where his model has had a major impact on the direction of the field; however, it has probably not received the attention it deserves among human and animal aggression researchers. Huesmann's elaborations have had an impact on core thinking about the observational learning of aggression and the role of media violence and to a lesser extent in the traditional aggression research domain, but have been missed by many developmental researchers on social adjustment. Yet taken together these elaborations define a powerful theory for how cognitive processes regulate aggressive behavior and for how aggressive behavior develops through early interactions between a child and the child's environment.

A UNIFIED INFORMATION PROCESSING MODEL FOR AGGRESSION

Figure 4.2 integrates the key elements of the two models in order to create a unified information processing theory of aggression that explains the role of cognition in aggressive behavior. This model incorporates the premise that social behavior is controlled to a great extent by cognitive *scripts* (Abelson, 1981) that are stored in a person's memory and are used as guides for behavior and social problem solving. As described earlier, a script incorporates both procedural and declarative knowledge and suggests what events are to happen in the environment, how the person should behave in response to these events, and what the likely outcome of those behaviors would be. It is presumed that while scripts are first being established they

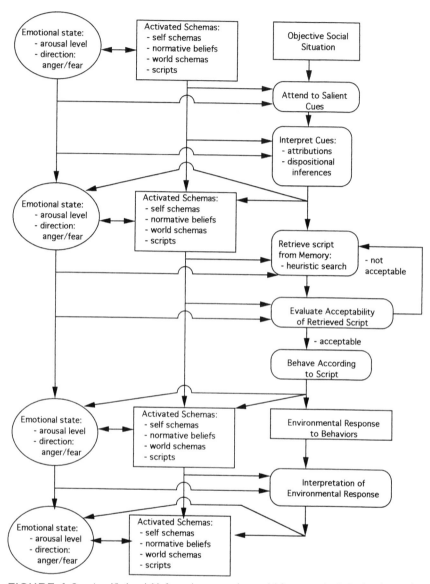

FIGURE 4.2   A unified social information processing model for aggressive behavior. Arrows indicate the direction of influence and flow of control. The diagram represents one cycle of social information processing. The terminal emotional state and activated schemas are the input for the next cycle.

influence the child's behavior through "controlled" mental processes (Schneider & Shriffrin, 1977; see earlier), but these processes become "automatic" as the child matures. Scripts that persist in a child's repertoire become increasingly more resistant to modification and change as they are rehearsed, enacted, and generate consequences. *Normative beliefs* are the second kind of cognitive schema hypothesized to play a central role in regulating aggressive behavior. Normative beliefs are cognitions about the appropriateness of aggressive behavior. They are related to perceived social norms but are different in that they concern what is "right for you." According to Huesmann and Guerra (1997), normative beliefs prime schemas used to evaluate other's behaviors, guide the search for social scripts, and filter out inappropriate scripts and behaviors.

Although this unified model does not adopt the circular form of the 1994 Crick and Dodge model, it is assumed that the internal states and external situations at the bottom of the diagram lead back into the top of the diagram. In other words, the process is continuous.

One can see within this model that there are four possible loci at which individual differences and situational variations can influence aggressive behavior.

Cue Attention and Evaluation

First, the objective situation is defined by the social problem and the environmental cues. However, which cues are given most attention and the interpretation of those cues may vary from person to person and may depend on a person's neurophysiological predispositions, current mood state, and previous learning history as reflected in activated schemas, including normative beliefs. Because emotional states may persist for some time, a person may enter a social interaction in an emotional state that is unrelated to the current situational cues. For example, a person exposed repeatedly to frustrating situations, who attributes the goal blocking to the actions of others, may enter a social interaction in an aroused state with hostile feelings toward everyone. Environmental stimuli may also directly trigger conditioned emotional reactions and may cue the retrieval from memory of cognitions that define the current emotional state. For example, the "sight of an enemy" or the "smell of a battlefield" may provoke both instantaneous physiological arousal and the recall of thoughts about the "enemy" that give meaning to the aroused state as anger. That emotional state may influence both which cues the person attends to and how the person interprets the cues to which he or she does attend. A highly aroused, angry person may focus on just a few highly salient cues and ignore others that convey equally important information about the social situation. Then the angry person's evaluation of these cues may be biased toward perceiving hostility when none is present. A person who finds hostile cues the most salient or who interprets ambiguous cues as hostile will be more likely to experience anger and activate schemas and scripts related to aggression

Script and Schema Activation and Retrieval

Second, the search for a script to guide behavior also accounts for substantial differences in aggressive responding. It is presumed that more aggressive individuals have encoded in memory more extensive, well-connected networks of social scripts emphasizing aggressive problem solving. Therefore, such a script is more likely to be retrieved during any search. However, the search for a script is also strongly affected by one's interpretation of the social cues, one's activated schemas including normative beliefs, and one's mood state and arousal. For example, anger, even in the absence of supporting cues, will make the retrieval of scripts previously associated with anger more likely; the presence of a weapon, even in the absence of anger, will make the retrieval of scripts associated with weapons more likely; and the perception that another person has hostile intentions will activate scripts related to hostility. Additionally, the schemas that have been activated, particularly the self-schema and normative beliefs, will influence the direction of the search for a script. The man who believes in "an eye for an eye" and perceives himself as "an avenger" is more likely to retrieve a script emphasizing aggressive retaliation.

Evaluation of Scripts

The third locus for the expression of individual differences and situational variation occurs after a script is activated. Before acting out the script, it is proposed that one evaluates the script in light of internalized activated schemas and normative beliefs to determine if the suggested behaviors are socially appropriate and possible to do and if the expected outcome is likely to be desirable. Different people may evaluate the same script quite differently, and the same person may evaluate the same script differently at different times. Persons under high stress and time pressures may devote much less time and resources to evaluation than they would otherwise.

On the average, however, habitually aggressive persons are expected to hold normative beliefs condoning more aggression and thus will employ more aggressive scripts. For example, if a man suddenly discovers that his wife has been unfaithful, he may experience rage and access a script for physical retribution. However, whether the man executes that script will depend on his normative beliefs about the appropriateness of "hitting a female." Even within the same person, different normative beliefs may be activated in different situations and different mood states. The person who has just been to church may have activated quite different normative beliefs than the person who has just watched a fight in a hockey game on TV. While evaluation of the script on the basis of one's normative beliefs is the most important filtering process, two other evaluations also play a role. First, one needs to be able to predict the desirability of the consequences of utilizing a script. Scripts include predictions about likely outcomes, but people differ in their capacities to think about the future, in their concern with the future, and in their evaluation of the desirability of an outcome. Information processing theory shows that the more a person focuses on immediate consequences and the less the person is concerned with the future, the more palatable a self-centered solution to a social problem may seem (Huesmann & Levinger, 1976). For example, if the man described earlier who hit his spouse was concerned about what his in-laws will think of him if they hear about it in a few days, he might not have hit her. Of course, people may also misperceive the likely consequences of aggressive acts simply because their scripts are inaccurate in predicting consequences for the current situation. Additionally, people differ in their evaluations of the desirability of an outcome. For some people the respect of their peers may be the most important evaluative dimension for an outcome from a social conflict while for others simply ending the conflict may be most important. The other dimension on which people evaluate generated scripts is the extent to which the behaviors in the script seem doable. A person with low perceived self-efficacy for prosocial behaviors may turn to aggressive scripts by default. A person with low perceived self-efficacy for aggressive behavior may avoid aggressive scripts at all costs.

Interpretation of Environmental Responses

Finally, as the bottom right box in Figure 4.2 shows, it is not simply society's response to a person's aggressive behavior per se that affects the person's future behavior, but the person's interpretation of society's response and how that interpretation affects the person's schemas and mood. This opens several important channels for explaining how aggressive scripts may be maintained even in the face of strong negative responses from society. For example, a boy who is severely beaten for behaving aggressively may attribute the beating to being disliked by the punisher rather than to anything he did. An aggressive teenage male, rather than changing his aggressive behaviors, which perhaps provide immediate gratification on some dimensions, may alter his normative beliefs to make the feedback he is receiving seem less negative. He might integrate some of the readily available aphorisms about aggression into his regulatory schemata. The boy who is told he is bad because he pushed others out of the way may shrug his shoulders and think, "Nice guys finish last." The boy who shoves a child who bumped into him may think, "An eye for an eye." Alternatively, he may mitigate society's punishments for his aggressive behavior by choosing environments in which aggression is more accepted. Thus, the more aggressive adolescent male may spend more time interacting with other aggressive peers who accept his behaviors as a way of life. Not only do such social networks provide adolescents with environments in which aggression is not discouraged, such social networks promote the internalization of normative beliefs favoring aggression. The important point sometimes lost on social engineers is that it is not just society's response to aggression that is important, but how the aggressor interprets that response.

EMOTIONAL AROUSAL, SCHEMA ACTIVATION, SCRIPT GENERATION, AND EVALUATION

Information processing models of social behavior are sometimes thought of as "cold" models with little room for affect. However, the evolving information processing model for the development of aggression described here hypothesizes a key role for emotion at each stage of information processing. An individual's absolute arousal level and the valence of the arousal affect aggressiveness at each stage. Existing negative affect interpreted as anger will bias cue interpretation toward hostility, will prime the retrieval of aggressive scripts, and will cue normative beliefs more supporting of aggression. As described earlier, in high states of arousal, because individuals search less widely and deeply for scripts and retrieve the best connected scripts, aggressive behavior becomes even more likely in highly arousing situations for persons with predominately aggressive scripts. For the individual with a large, well-learned repertoire of simple, direct aggressive scripts for solving social problems and a smaller, less well-learned repertoire of complex, indirect scripts for prosocial solutions, the arousal associated with anger will make the selection of an aggressive script even more likely than priming from the anger would by itself. Furthermore, one can expect similar effects for script evaluation. A person in a highly aroused state of rage because of a provocation will evaluate scripts less carefully and focus on retaliation beliefs in evaluating scripts. At the other extreme, individuals who are very hard to arouse may evaluate scripts accurately but misevaluate societal responses to their behaviors and perceive the outcome of their aggressive behavior as more desirable than it really will be.

ACQUIRING AND MAINTAINING
AGGRESSIVE SCRIPTS AND SCHEMAS

So far we have examined how existing scripts may be accessed and used to guide behavior, and how certain individual and environmental factors might promote the use of aggressive scripts. Within this framework a habitually aggressive person is presumed to be someone who regularly retrieves and employs aggressive scripts for social behavior. A number of factors have been noted that might promote the retrieval and utilization of aggressive scripts. It may be, for example, that the cues present in the environment trigger the recall only of aggressive scripts. However, the regular retrieval and use of aggressive scripts would suggest above all that a large number of aggressive scripts have been stored in memory. Similarly, the regular execution of such scripts would suggest that normative beliefs and other schemas supporting aggression have been acquired and encoded. Thus, we must examine how schemas and scripts are acquired.

Huesmann (1982b, 1986, 1988) has argued that while a variety of preexisting neurophysiological factors can predispose individuals toward particular modes of cognitive processing or toward particular schemas and scripts, the child's early learning experiences play a critical role in the acquisition of scripts and schemas for social behavior just as early learning plays a key role in the acquisition of procedural and declarative knowledge relevant to intellectual life. Evolutionary forces and random variation create communalities and individual differences in the biological mechanisms underlying cognition and behavior. These individual differences in biology interact with individual differences in environment to mold the software and data structures directly controlling the child's cognitive processing and social behavior. As described earlier in the discussion on social learning theory, observational and enactive learning combine to shape the development of the child's scripts and schemas. A script is most likely to first be acquired by observing others and then more firmly established by having its use reinforced.

During the observational learning process the person's current emotional state and current memory contents influence which existing schemas are activated. The activated schemas in turn influence how well the observed script can be encoded and integrated into memory. If the activated schemas are discrepant with the observed script, encoding is difficult; if they are consistent it is easier. When highly aroused and angry, for example, persons may view a physically aggressive sequence of behaviors as more appropriate than they would otherwise. A young boy who can only recall seeing aggressive behaviors is more likely to encode a newly observed aggressive behavior than is a boy whose mind is filled with memories of prosocial solutions. A child with normative beliefs accepting of aggression is much more likely to encode new aggressive scripts for behavior.

The maintenance of a script in memory will be influenced by the extent to which its use produces desired consequences, i.e., by instrumental learning. One might think that because aggressive behavior very often produces negative consequences for the aggressor, the retrieval of aggressive scripts would extinguish. However, the unified information processing theory asserts that such instrumental learning depends on how the individual interprets society's response to the behavior. As described earlier, very often, because of the schemas activated, the aggressor does not attribute the negative reaction of society to the specific script that the aggressor employed, and no learning takes place. The boy who is harshly punished by a teacher for taking another child's toy will not unlearn the behavior if he interprets the cause of his punishment as dislike by the teacher.

As with all learned information, in order to maintain a script in memory, a child would probably need to rehearse it from time to time. The rehearsal may take several different forms, from simple recall of the original scene, to fantasizing about it, to play acting. The more elaborative, ruminative type of rehearsal characteristic of children's fantasizing is likely to generate greater connectedness for the script, thereby increasing its accessibility in memory. Also, through such elaborative rehearsal the child may abstract higher-order scripts representing more general strategies for behavior than the ones initially stored. Of course, rehearsal also provides another opportunity for reevaluation of any script. It may be that some scripts initially accepted as appropriate (under specific emotional and memory states) may be judged as inappropriate during rehearsal.

EMPIRICAL DATA ON INFORMATION PROCESSING AND AGGRESSION

This unified information processing model for the development of aggressive behavior has grown out of an accumulating body of empirical data linking a variety of cognitive processes to social behavior in general and aggressive behavior in particular. The model is based on the presumption that predisposing personal factors and environmental context interact through observational and enactive learning to lead to the emergence of cognitive processes (including emotional processes) and cognitive schemas that promote aggression. Cue attention and evaluation, script and schema acquisition and retrieval, script evaluation, and evaluation of the environment's responses to one's actions are the four key parts of the social/cognitive performance model as outlined in Figure 4.2. In this section a subset of key studies will be reviewed that provide evidence about the variety of cognitive processes implicated within this model.

CUE ATTENTION AND EVALUATION

An extensive literature has grown up addressing the extent to which more aggressive individuals tend to perceive hostility in others where there actually is no hostility, i.e., display a hostile attributional bias. Dodge and Newman (1981) have reported evidence that aggressive boys attend to fewer social cues in their environment, and Gouze (1987) reports that they tend to focus on cues more suggestive of aggression. Equally important, there is good evidence that aggressive children are more likely to interpret an ambiguous act by another as indicating hostility (Dodge, 1980; Dodge & Coie, 1987; Dodge & Frame, 1982; Dodge, Price, Bachorowski, & Newman, 1990; Graham & Hudley, 1994; Nasby, Hayden & DePaulo, 1979; Slaby & Guerra, 1988; Steinberg & Dodge, 1983). Longitudinal analyses have suggested that a propensity toward hostile attributional bias mediates the relation between early childhood aggression and later antisocial behavior (Dodge, Pettit, Bates & Valente, 1995). Although this relation between aggression and hostile attributional bias can sometimes be difficult to detect (e.g., Pettit, Dodge, & Brown, 1988; Zelli & Huesmann, 1993), one should not be surprised by the lack of large effects given the multidetermined nature of aggressive behavior. Furthermore, experiments with random assignment of subjects have shown that improving the accuracy of intent attributions decreases the likelihood of aggressive behavior in children (Hudley & Graham, 1993).

The fact that one's interpretations of potentially hostile social cues are affected by the schemas one has encoded and activated is not only supported by a long history of research on social perception (e.g., see Fiske & Taylor, 1991; Schneider, 1991) but is also supported by a variety of research on aggression. Dodge and Tomlin (1987) reported evidence that aggressive children rely on their own encoded aggressive self-schemas and stereotypes in making intent attributions. Zelli and Huesmann (1993) have found that college students with greater ingrained persecution beliefs are more likely to perceive hostility when none is there. There is also strong evidence that these hostile cue interpretations become an automatic cognitive process. Bargh (1989) and Winter and Uleman (1984) have shown that inferences about the dispositions of others occur automatically without conscious awareness. More recently, Zelli, Huesmann, and Cervone (1995) have shown that more aggressive individuals automatically encode ambiguous sentences with an aggressive interpretation and then are more likely to recall them when prompted with an aggressive cue. Along these lines the "cultivation" effects data on media exposure reported by Gerbner and colleagues (Gerbner & Gross, 1980) suggest that high exposure to media violence in adults makes them see the world as a more hostile place and thus primes them for hostile attributional bias. Finally, Dodge and Somberg (1987) have shown that hostile attributional bias, as predicted by information processing theory, is more likely to occur under conditions of high emotional arousal.

ACQUISITION, MAINTENANCE, AND RETRIEVAL OF SCRIPTS AND SCHEMAS

Although it is methodologically more difficult to assess the kinds of scripts that individuals have encoded, one can assess the kinds of scripts they are most likely to retrieve and make inferences from those data. Available evidence suggests that, in fact, the more accessible scripts for more aggressive children are more aggressive. The scripts retrieved by more aggressive children to solve hypothetical problems tend to incorporate more physical aggression and manipulation actions (Rubin, Bream & Rose-Krasnor, 1991; Rubin, Moller, & Emptage, 1987; Waas, 1988). Priming by negative intent cues is more likely to activate an aggressive script in aggressive children (Graham & Hudley, 1994). Aggressive children are less likely to generate more subtle prosocial scripts to solve social problems (Deluty, 1981; Taylor & Gabriel, 1989), and there is some evidence that, as hypothesized, a narrower search process for a script is associated with more aggressive behavior (Shure & Spivack, 1980).

There is also extensive evidence that, as predicted, the observation of aggressive scripts in real life or in the mass visual media leads to the encoding of such scripts. Of course, children growing up observing violence around them behave more violently (e.g., Guerra, Huesmann, Tolan, VanAcker & Eron, 1995), and children whose parents physically aggress against them are more likely to aggress physically against their own children later in life (Widom, 1989). Nevertheless, it is hard to show that such effects are due to the acquisition of specific scripts through observation. Research on media violence and aggression provides more compelling evidence of that process. Copycat crimes and the well-known contagion of suicide (Berkowitz, 1993) provide some of the clearest examples of specific aggressive scripts being acquired by adults through observation from the media. More importantly from a scientific standpoint perhaps, numerous laboratory and field experiments (see Paik & Comstock, 1994; Huesmann, 1982b; Huesmann, Moise, & Podolski, in press) have demonstrated the encoding of specific scripts from such observations. It is also clear that new aggressive scripts are abstracted out of the elements of specific scripts being observed. Thus, the aggressive scripts that children display after being exposed to violent scenes are not exactly the same as the scripts observed (Bjorkqvist, 1985). These observational learning studies have also confirmed the validity of the encoding specificity principle with regard to aggressive scripts. Even a neutral cue that is present in an observed aggressive script may trigger the retrieval of that script. For example, Josephenson (1987) showed that a walkie-talkie present in an aggressive video could trigger aggressive behavior in boys who had watched that video.

A substantial body of research in cognitive psychology has shown that re-hearsal of information enhances its connectedness in the memory network and makes it more accessible (Klatzky, 1980). Thus, as argued earlier, a child's re-hearsal of an aggressive script should make its retrieval more likely in the future. One common type of rehearsal of social behavior is fantasizing, and empirical ev-idence shows that fantasizing about aggressive behaviors is positively related to behaving aggressively. Early studies clearly showed that more aggressive adults scored higher on projective tests of hostility imagery (Eron, 1959). More recently, direct measures of children's fantasizing have been related to children's aggres-sive behavior (Rosenfeld, Huesmann, Eron, & Torney-Purta, 1982). For example, in a longitudinal study of early elementary school children conducted in five dif-ferent countries, Huesmann and Eron (1984) reported that self-reported fantasiz-ing about aggression was correlated with peer-nominated aggressive behavior in all five countries. Both Viemero (Viemero & Paajanen, 1992) and Huesmann (1986) have also found in field studies that TV violence viewing predicts fanta-sizing about aggression, which in turn predicts later aggressive behavior.

There is also significant empirical support for the premise that even quite dif-ferent specific aggressive scripts and schemas are linked together in one's mem-ory network by a common "hostility" node and thus can be primed by other aggressive ideas or cues, even if they have no substantive connection. The classic example of such an effect is the Berkowitz and LePage (1967) "gun" experiment. In this study, subjects gave larger shocks to punish a partner who was not learning if there was a gun in the experimental room. The gun cues the hostility node, which leads to the utilization of a more aggressive script for behaving in the ex-periment. The priming cue need not be a tangible object; the same effect can be obtained when the cue activating the "hostility" node is anger or another negative emotion (Berkowitz, Cochran, & Embree, 1981). In addition, the observation of violence in the mass media or environment has been shown to prime a wide vari-ety of hostile thoughts (Bushman & Geen, 1990).

Actually, according to the information processing model, violent cues, bad moods, irritability, and arousal affect all four aspects of social information pro-cessing: cue attention and interpretation, script retrieval, script evaluation, and evaluation of environmental response. The dysphoric valence of the emotion acti-vates schemas related to hostility, and the arousal narrows memory activation. Thus, it is not surprising that high temperatures (Anderson & Anderson, 1984), crowding (Matthews, Paulus, & Baron, 1979), and other irritators and stressors (Guerra, Huesmann, Tolan, Eron, & VanAcker, 1995) increase aggression. Also, as predicted from the social/cognitive model, reflection on the cause of the irrita-tion that would reduce the activation of a general hostility node reduces aggres-sion at unrelated targets (Berkowitz & Troccoli, 1990).

EVALUATION OF SCRIPTS

Once a script has been activated, it still may not be employed if it is evaluated negatively. The behaviors involved may be evaluated as inappropriate when fil-

tered through an individual's normative beliefs about aggression; its expected outcome may be evaluated as undesirable when filtered through beliefs about environmental responses; or it may be evaluated as undoable when filtered through
conceptions of self-efficacy. Huesmann and associates (Huesmann and Guerra,
1997; Guerra, Huesmann, & Hanish, 1994; Huesmann, Guerra, Zelli, & Miller,
1992; Huesmann, Zelli, Fraczek, & Upmeyer, 1993) have developed a reliable
measure of normative beliefs about general aggression (e.g., "It is usually okay to
push and shove other people around?") and retaliation (e.g., "If a girl screams at
you, is it okay to hit her?") and have shown that children and adults who are more
aggressive have normative beliefs that are more approving of aggression. More important, longitudinal studies have shown that normative beliefs about aggression
seem to crystalize during early childhood (Huesmann & Guerra, 1997). For children aged 6 or 7, such beliefs are very unstable and do not predict much about subsequent aggressive behavior. However, such beliefs are predicted by the child's
own previous behavior. For children aged 10 and 11, the picture changes. Normative beliefs are now stable and predict subsequent aggressive behavior. Thus, ages
6 to 9 seem to be a period during which normative beliefs and other schemas relating to aggressive social behavior are being developed through interactions with the
environment. According to the unified information processing model of aggression, normative beliefs exert effects not just on the filtering of scripts, but on the activation of schemas relevant to cue interpretation and script retrieval. So far no
studies have been undertaken to discriminate between these different effects.

Normative beliefs are not the only schemas relevant to script selection and
evaluation. Self-schemas provide an internal context within which scripts must be
evaluated as well. Heightened activation of self-schemas decrease the likelihood
of aggression when the self-schema is nonaggressive (Carver, 1974), probably by
filtering out potential aggressive scripts. However, as Baumeister (Baumeister,
Smart, & Boden, 1996) has shown, a self-schema that includes an extremely positive evaluation of oneself can promote the selection of aggressive scripts when a
person threatens that self-evaluation. Perceptions of self-efficacy for executing the
script in question would also be expected to be important in the evaluation of a
script (Bandura, 1986; McFall, 1982). The implication for aggressive behavior
would seem to be that those with high self-efficacy for prosocial behavior would
be less likely to behave aggressively. Unfortunately, data have not born this out. In
at least two studies, children who scored higher on self-efficacy for prosocial or
competent behavior actually behaved more aggressively (Crick & Dodge, 1989;
Huesmann, Guerra, Eron, Miller, Zelli, Wroblewska, & Adami, 1991). One possible explanation may be that the high self-esteem associated with general feelings
of self-efficacy marks individuals who, when threatened, are particularly prone to
anger (Baumeister, Smart, & Boden, 1996).

Not only are self-schemas relevant to script evaluation, schemas about others
are relevant too. Schemas about others that promote deindividuation allow the utilization of aggressive scripts that might otherwise be unacceptable (Diener, 1976;
Prentice-Dunn & Rogers, 1983). Schemas about others' beliefs and attitudes, e.g.,
what others respect or disrespect, may make some scripts more acceptable than

others. In this unified information processing model, outcome expectancies are viewed as mostly an inherent part of social scripts rather than a separate component of behavior evaluation as Crick and Dodge (1994) suggested. Each script represents a sequence of behaviors and expected outcomes or responses of the environment. However, the meaning and value of objectively similar outcomes may change depending on one's schemas about the world. Thus, the evaluation process for a generated script includes an assessment of outcome "desirability." In fact, there is accumulating evidence that more aggressive children tend to believe that aggressive behavior will have more desirable outcomes (Crick & Ladd, 1990; Deluty, 1983; Dodge, Pettit, McClaskey, & Brown, 1986; Perry, Perry, & Rasmussen, 1986; Quiggle, Panak, Garber, & Dodge, 1992) and that prosocial behavior will have less favorable outcomes (Quiggle et al., 1992).

These studies have shown that aggressive youth differ from other youth in the beliefs and schemas they use to evaluate the appropriateness and effectiveness of potential scripts. However, there is also evidence that some youth are more aggressive because they do not devote much cognitive effort to this filtering step. For example, empirical data suggest that certain children, e.g., attention deficit hyperactivity disorder (ADHD) children, are neurophysiologically predisposed toward minimizing this evaluation step. The result is what many observers would call impulsive behavior (Barkley, 1995; Kendall & Braswell, 1985). If the first scripts activated are aggressive scripts, the result is aggressive behavior even if the child "knows" upon reflection that the behavior was inappropriate.

INFORMATION PROCESSING: HOSTILE
AND INSTRUMENTAL AGGRESSION

Evidence reviewed to this point has not addressed the issue of how cognitive processes differ between instrumental (proactive) and hostile (reactive) aggression. However, the predictions of this information processing theory of aggression are clear. Both kinds of aggression depend on the person having aggressive scripts along with normative beliefs and schemas supporting the positive evaluation of aggression. On the one hand, individuals most at risk for hostile (reactive) aggression should also display higher emotional reactivity in response to provocation and greater hostile attributional bias, which would lead to more impulsive, immediate responses to provocation. On the other hand, instrumental aggression should be more a function of having encoded a large repertoire of aggressive scripts for solving social problems and of having acquired normative beliefs approving of aggression. Instrumentally aggressive individuals do not need to be particularly reactive to provocation and should not display much anxiety in response to thoughts of aggression. In fact, empirical studies on arousability suggest that difficult to arouse individuals may indeed be more at risk for instrumentally aggressive behavior (Raine & Venables, 1981; Raine, Venables, & Wilson, in press). However, more easily arousable individuals seem to be more at risk for hostile aggression (Baker et al., 1984) and violent crimes (Hare & McPherson,

1984). In fact, Crick and Dodge (in press; Craven & Lochman, 1997; Dodge, 1997) have reported empirical data with children that seem to be consistent with these predictions, i.e., more arousable children display more hostile attributional bias and hostile aggression.

CONCLUSIONS

Over the past several decades it has become clear that an understanding of how human cognitive processes operate is necessary for an understanding of human social behavior in general and aggressive behavior in particular. Extensive empirical research on social information processing coupled with theoretical elaborations of cognitive science constructs has led to the emergence of a unified model of social information processing in aggressive behavior. The model identifies four processes in social problem solving where emotional arousal, activated schemas, and situational cues interact to affect aggression: (1) cue attention and interpretation, (2) script retrieval, (3) script evaluation and selection, and (4) evaluation of society's response to one's behavior. Although these processes may first require cognitive control in the developing child, they eventually seem to operate as relatively automatic cognitive processes.

Evidence suggests that humans attend to environmental cues differentially and interpret the cues differently as a function of predisposing neurophysiological factors, their emotional arousal, the kinds of cognitive schemas they have acquired, and which schemas are activated. More aggressive individuals tend to focus on fewer cues and cues that are more frequently symptomatic of hostility, tend to interpret ambiguous cues more readily as symptomatic of hostility, and tend to believe that the world is more hostile. This is particularly true when the individual is angry, either because of situational factors or a predisposition toward more general hostility. More aggressive individuals also have a greater proportion of aggressive scripts encoded in memory with more accessible links to everyday cues. They have been found to rehearse their aggressive scripts more through aggressive fantasizing and to recall more aggressive scripts from ambiguous cues. It has been shown that while young children do not have well-defined or stable normative beliefs about the appropriateness of aggression, older children do have well-formed beliefs, and those beliefs influence how they evaluate retrieved scripts. Finally, aggressive individuals often do not expect their own aggressive behaviors to have bad consequences for them.

Within this framework, what causes one child to become more aggressive than another? Clearly, we need to explore further the role of genetics, neurophysiology, and evolutionary forces in predisposing individuals to process information in ways that promote aggression. But we already have a pretty good idea of what causes one child to learn more aggressive scripts than another. Certainly instrumental conditioning plays a role. If a specific aggressive behavior is reinforced, the script that suggested that response is more likely to be retrieved and to be employed in the future. Furthermore, the effect of the reinforcement may generalize to scripts that are abstractions of the specific script, promoting a generalized disinhibition of aggression. The boy who solves a social problem successfully by hitting will be more likely in the future not just to hit, but to kick, punch, or push. Nevertheless, it is difficult to believe that the complex scripts for social behavior that children rapidly acquire are the result of random emission and selective reinforcement. Laboratory and field evidence suggests that, on the contrary, scripts for social behavior are often encoded from patterns of behaviors observed in others. Just as a boy may encode a motor program for throwing a football from observing others throw, a boy may encode a script for hitting those who victimize him from observing others hit those who victimize them. Children are constantly observing others, encoding what they see that seems salient, and integrating these observations into encoded scripts for behavior. Not every aggressive behavior they observe is encoded or stimulates the encoding of an aggressive script. Not every aggressive script is retained or remains accessible for long. The more salient an observed aggressive scene is to the child initially, and the more the child ruminates upon, fantasizes about, and rehearses the observed scene, the more likely it is that an aggressive script based on that scene is recalled and followed in a social problem-solving situation. The more the aggressive scene is consistent with the scripts for behavior that the child has already acquired, the more easily it is integrated into memory. The more the aggressive scene is perceived as consistent with the child's own normative beliefs about the appropriateness of social behavior, the more likely it is to be integrated into memory. The child encodes scripts for behavior that have subjective utility as potential strategies for social problem solving. The child encodes these scripts in the context of the situational cues, and the likelihood that a child will access a script for specific aggressive behaviors is dependent on how many relevant cues are reproduced in the environment at recall time.

In summary, from the social/cognitive perspective it is easy to see that once a child begins to perceive the world as hostile, to acquire scripts and schemas emphasizing aggression, and to believe that aggression is acceptable, the child enters a vicious cycle that will be difficult to stop. Cognitions, behavior, observations of others, and the responses of others all combine to promote aggression. If not interrupted, the cycle can be expected to continue into adulthood, maintaining aggressive behavior throughout the life span.

ACKNOWLEDGMENTS

The preparation of this manuscript was supported in part by grants from the National Institute for Mental Health and the Centers for Disease Control. The content of the manuscript has been greatly influenced by discussions I have had with David Buss, Ken Dodge, Leonard Eron, Nancy Guerra, George Levinger, Neil Malamuth, Jessica Moise, Meredith Reynolds, Arnaldo Zelli, and Eileen Zurbriggen. Requests for reprints should be sent to L. Rowell Huesmann, Research Center for Group Dynamics, Institute for Social Research, the University of Michigan, Ann Arbor, Michigan 48106.

REFERENCES

Abelson, R. P. (1968). Computer simulation of behavior. In G. Lindzey & E. Aronson (Eds.), *Handbook of social psychology* (Vol. II). Reading, MA: Addison-Wesley.

Abelson, R. P. (1976). Script processing in attitude formation and decision making. In J. S. Carroll & J. W. Payne (Eds.), *Cognition and social behavior.* Hillsdale, NJ: Erlbaum.

Abelson, R. P. (1981). The psychological status of the script concept. *American Psychologist, 36,* 715–729.

Anderson, C., & Anderson, D. (1984). Ambient temperature and violence crime: Tests of the linear and curvilinear hypotheses. *Journal of Personality and Social Psychology, 46,* 91–97.

Anderson, J. R. (1980). *Cognitive psychology.* San Francisco: Freeman.

Anderson, J. R. (1983). *The architecture of cognition.* Cambridge, MA: Harvard University Press.

Anderson, K. L. (1990). Arousal and the inverted-U hypothesis: A critique of Neiss's "reconceptualizing arousal." *Psychological Bulletin, 107,* 96–100.

Baker, L., Hastings, J., & Hart, J. (1984). Enhanced psychophysiological responses of type A coronary patients during type A-relevant imagery. *Journal of Behavioral Medicine, 7,* 287–306.

Bandura, A. (1973). *Aggression: A social learning analysis.* Englewood Cliffs, NJ: Prentice-Hall.

Bandura, A. (1977). *Social learning theory.* Englewood Cliffs, NJ: Prentice Hall.

Bandura, A. (1986). *Social foundations of thought and action: A social-cognitive theory.* Englewood Cliffs, NJ: Prentice-Hall.

Bandura, A., Ross, D., & Ross, S. A. (1963). Imitation of aggression through imitation of film-mediated aggressive models. *Journal of Abnormal and Social Psychology, 66,* 3–11.

Bargh, J. A. (1982). Attention and automaticity in the processing of self-relevant information. *Journal of Personality and Social Psychology, 43*(3), 425–436.

Bargh, J. A. (1989). Conditional automaticity: Varieties of automatic influence in social perception and cognition. In J. S. Uleman & J. A. Bargh (Eds.), *Unintended thought.* New York: Guilford Press.

Bargh, J. A., & Pietromonaco, P. (1982). Automatic information processing and social perception: The influence of trait information presented outside of conscious awareness on impression formation. *Journal of Personality and Social Psychology, 43*(3), 437–449.

Barkley, R. A. (1995). Response inhibition and attention-deficit hyperactivity disorder: A potential unified theory. Unpublished manuscript.

Baumeister, R. F., Smart, L., & Boden, J. M. (1996). Relation of threatened egotism to violence and aggression: The dark side of high self-esteem. *Psychological Review, 103,* 5–33.

Berkowitz, L. (1974). Some determinants of impulsive aggression: The role of mediated associations with reinforcements for aggression. *Psychological Review, 81,* 165–176.

Berkowitz, L. (1990). On the formation and regulation of anger and aggression: A cognitive-neoassociationistic analysis. *American Psychologist, 45*(4), 494–503.

Berkowitz, L. (1993). Pain and aggression: Some findings and implications. Special issue: The pain system: A multilevel model for the study of motivation and emotion. *Motivation and Emotion, 17,* 277–293.

Berkowitz, L., & LePage, A. (1967). Weapons as aggression-eliciting stimuli. *Journal of Personality and Social Psychology, 7,* 202–207.

Berkowitz, L., & Troccoli, B. T. (1990). Feelings, direction of attention, and expressed evaluations of others. *Cognition and Emotion, 4,* 305–325.

Berkowitz, L., Cochran, S., & Embree, M. (1981). Physical pain and the goal of aversively stimulated aggression. *Journal of Personality and Social Psychology, 40,* 687–700.

Bjorkqvist, K. (1985). *Violent films, anxiety and aggression.* Helsinki: Finnish Society of Sciences and Letters.

Broadbent, D. E. (1971). *Decision and stress.* London: Academic Press.

Bushman, B. J., & Geen, R. (1990). Role of cognitive-emotional mediators and individual differences in the effects of media violence on aggression. *Journal of Personality and Social Psychology, 58*(1), 156–163.

Carroll, J. S., & Payne, J. W. (1976). *Cognitive and social behavior.* Hillsdale, NJ: Erlbaum.

Carver, C. S. (1974). Facilitation of physical aggression through objective self-awareness. *Journal of Experimental Social Psychology, 10,* 365–370.

Chase, W. G., & Simon, H. A. (1973). Perception in chess. *Cognitive Psychology, 4,* 55–81.

Coie, J. D., & Dodge, K. A. (1997). Aggression and antisocial behavior. In N. Eisenberg (Ed.), *Handbook of child psychology* (Vol. 3), 779–862. New York: John Wiley & Sons.

Cloninger, C. R., & Gottesman, A. (1987). Genetic and environmental factors in antisocial behavior disorders. In S. A. Mednick, T. E. Moffitt, & S. A. Stack (Eds.), *The causes of crime: New biological approaches.* New York: Cambridge University Press.

Colby, K. M., Hilf, F. D., Weber, S., & Kraemer, H. C. (1972). Turing-like indistinguishability tests for the validation of a computer simulation of paranoid processes. *Artificial Intelligence, 3,* 199–221.

Craven, S. V., & Lochman, J. E. (1997). A study of boys' physiological, emotional, and attributional processes in response to peer provocation at three levels of aggression. *Society for Research in Child Development,* Washington, DC.

Crick, N. R., & Dodge, K. A. (1989). Children's perceptions of peer entry and conflict situations: Social strategies, goals, and outcome expectations. In B. Schneider, J. Nadel, G. Attili, & R. Weissberg (Eds.), *Social competence developmental perspective* (pp. 396–399). Boston: Kluwer-Nijhoff.

Crick, N. R., & Dodge, K. A. (1994). A review and reformulation of social information processing mechanisms in children's adjustment. *Psychological Bulletin, 115,* 74–101.

Crick, N. R., & Dodge, K. A. (1996). Social information-processing mechanisms in reactive and proactive aggression. *Child Development, 67(3),* 993–1002.

Crick, N. R., & Ladd, F. W. (1990). Children's perceptions of the outcomes of aggressive strategies: Do the ends justify being mean? *Developmental Psychology, 26,* 612–620.

Deluty, R. H. (1981). Alternative thinking ability of aggressive, assertive, and submissive children. *Cognitive Therapy and Research, 5,* 309–312.

Deluty, R. H. (1983). Children's evaluation of aggressive, assertive, and submissive responses. *Journal of Clinical Child Psychology, 12,* 124–129.

Diener, E. (1976). Effects of prior destructive behavior, anonymity, and group presence on deindividuation and aggression. *Journal of Personality and Social Psychology, 33,* 497–507.

Dodge, K. A. (1980). Social cognition and children's aggressive behavior. *Child Development, 53,* 620–635.

Dodge, K. A. (1986). A social information processing model of social competence in children. In M. Perlmutter (Ed.), *The Minnesota symposium on child psychology* (pp. 77–125). Hillsdale, NJ: Erlbaum.

Dodge, K. A. (1993). Social cognitive mechanisms in the development of conduct disorder and depression. *Annual Review of Psychology, 44,* 559–584.

Dodge, K. A. (1997). How early peer rejection and acquired autonomic sensitivity to peer conflicts influence each other to produce conduct problems in adolescence. *Society for Research in Child Development,* Washington, DC.

Dodge, K. A., & Coie, J. D. (1987). Social information processing factors in reactive and proactive aggression in children's peer groups. *Journal of Personality and Social Psychology, 53,* 1146–1158.

Dodge, K. A., & Frame, C. L. (1982). Social cognitive biases and deficits in aggressive boys. *Child Development, 53,* 620–635.

Dodge, K. A., & Newman, P. J. (1981). Biased decision making processes in aggressive boys. *Journal of Abnormal Psychology, 90,* 375–379.

Dodge, K. A., Pettit, G. S., Bates, J. E., & Valente, E. (1995). Social information-processing patterns partially mediate the effect of early physical abuse on later conduct problems. *Journal of Abnormal Psychology, 104,* 632–643.

Dodge, K. A., Pettit, G. S., McClaskey, C. L., & Brown, M. M. (1986). Social competence in children. *Monographs of the Society for Research in Child Development, 51*(2, Serial No. 213).

Dodge, K. A., Price, J. M., Bachorowski, J. A., & Newman, J. P. (1990). Hostile attributional biases in severely aggressive adolescents. *Journal of Abnormal Psychology, 99,* 385–392.

Dodge, K. A., & Somberg, D. A. (1987). Hostile attributional biases among aggressive boys are exacerbated under conditions of threats to the self. *Child Development, 58(1),* 213–224.

Dodge, K. A., & Tomlin, A. (1987). Utilization of self-schemas as a mechanism of attributional bias in aggressive children. *Social Cognition, 5(3),* 280–300.

Easterbrook, J. A. (1959). The effect of emotion on cue utilization and the organization of behavior. *Psychological Review, 66,* 183–201.

Eron, L. D. (1959). Thematic apperception test. In O. K. Buros (Ed.), *Fifth mental measurement year book* (pp. 306–310). Highland Park, NJ: Gryphon Press.

Eron, L. D., Walder, L. O., & Lefkowitz, M. M. (1971). *The learning of aggression in children.* Boston: Little Brown.

Farrington, D. P. (1982). Longitudinal analyses of criminal violence. In M. E. Wolfgang & N. A. Weiner (Eds.), *Criminal violence.* Beverly Hills, CA: Sage.

Farrington, D. P. (1985). The development of offending and antisocial behavior from childhood: Key findings from the Cambridge study in delinquent development. *Journal of Child Psychology and Psychiatry, 36,* 1–36.

Feigenbaum, E. A., & Feldman, J. (1963). *Computers and thought.* New York: McGraw-Hill.

Feldman, J. A., & Ballard, D. H. (1982). Connectionist models and their properties. *Cognitive Science, 6,* 205–254.

Feshbach, S. (1964). The function of aggression and the regulation of aggressive drive. *Psychological Review, 71,* 257–272.

Fiske, S. T. (1982). Schema-triggered affect: Applications to social perception. In M. S. Clark & S. T. Fiske (Eds.), *Affect and cognition: The 17th Annual Carnegie Symposium on Cognition.* Hillsdale, NJ: Erlbaum.

Fiske, S. T., & Taylor, S. E. (1984). *Social cognition.* Reading, MA: Addison-Wesley.

Fiske, S. T., & Taylor, S. E. (1991). *Social cognition.* New York: McGraw Hill.

Gerbner, G., & Gross, L. P. (1980). The violence face of television and its lessons. In E. L. Palmer & A. Dorr (Eds.), *Children and the faces of television: Teaching, violence, selling* (pp. 149–162). New York: Academic Press.

Gouze, K. R. (1987). Attention and social problem solving as correlates of aggression in preschool males. *Journal of Abnormal Child Psychology, 15,* 181–197.

Graham, S., & Hudley, C. (1994). Attributions of aggressive and nonaggressive African-American male early adolescents: A study of construct accessibility. *Developmental Psychology, 30(3),* 365–373.

Gregg, L. W., & Simon, H. A. (1967). Process models and stochastic theories of simple concept formation. *Journal of Mathematical Psychology, 4,* 246–276.

Guerra, N. G., Huesmann, L. R., & Hanish, L. (1994). The role of normative beliefs in children's social behavior. N. Eisenberg (Ed.), *Review of personality and social psychology, development and social psychology: The interface.* London: Sage.

Guerra, N. G., Huesmann, L. R., Tolan, P. H., VanAcker, R., & Eron, L. D. (1995). Stressful events and individual beliefs as correlates of economic disadvantage and aggression among urban children. *Journal of Consulting and Clinical Psychology, 63(4),* 518–528.

Gullahorn, J. T., & Gullahorn, J. E. (1963). A computer model of elementary social behavior. In E. Feigenbaum & J. Feldman (Eds.), *Computers and thought* (pp. 375–386). New York: McGraw-Hill.

Hare, R. D., & McPherson, L. M. (1984). Violent and aggressive behavior by criminal psychopaths. *International Journal of Law and Psychiatry, 7,* 35–50.

Hastie, R., & Carlston, D. (1980). Theoretical issues in person memory. In R. Hastie, T. M. Ostrom, E. B. Ebbesen, R. S. Wyer, D. L. Hamilton, & D. E. Carlston (Eds.), *Person memory: The cognitive basis of social perception.* Hillsdale, NJ: Lawrence Erlbaum Associates.

Hudley, C., & Graham, S. (1993). An attributional intervention to reduce peer-directed aggression among African-American boys. *Child Development, 64,* 124–138.

Huesmann, L. R. (1977). Formal models in social psychology. *Meetings of Society for Experimental Social Psychology,* Austin, Texas.

Huesmann, L. R. (1978). Cognitive processes and models of depression. *Journal of Abnormal Psychology, 87(1),* 194–198.

Huesmann, L. R. (1980). Toward a predictive model of romantic behavior. In K. S. Pope (Ed.), *On love and loving.* New York: Jossey-Bass.

Huesmann, L. R. (1982a). Information processing models of behavior. In N. Hirschberg & L. Humphreys (Eds.), *Multivariate applications in the social sciences* (pp. 261–288). Hillsdale, NJ: Lawrence Erlbaum Associates.

Huesmann, L. R. (1982b). Television violence and aggressive behavior. In D. Pearl, L. Bouthilet, & J. Lazar (Eds.), *Television and behavior: Ten years of scientific programs and implications for the 80's.* Washington, DC: U.S. Government Printing Office.

Huesmann, L. R. (1986). Psychological processes promoting the relation between exposure to media violence and aggressive behavior by the viewer. *Journal of Social Issues, 42,* 3, 125–139.

Huesmann, L. R. (1988). An information processing model for the development of aggression. *Aggressive Behavior, 14,* 13–24.

Huesmann, L. R., & Eron, L. D. (1984). Cognitive processes and the persistence of aggressive behavior. *Aggressive Behavior, 10,* 243–251.

Huesmann, L. R., Eron, L. D., Lefkowitz, M. M., & Walder, L. O. (1984). The stability of aggression over time and generations. *Developmental Psychology, 20,* 1120–1134.

Huesmann, L. R., & Guerra, N. G. (1997). Childrens' normative beliefs about aggression and aggressive behavior. *Journal of Personality and Social Psychology, 72(2),* 408–419.

Huesmann, L. R., Guerra, N. G., Eron, L. D., Miller, L., Zelli, A., Wroblewska, J., & Adami, P. (1991). Mitigating the development of aggression in young children by changing their cognitions. *Aggressive Behavior, 17,* 75–76.

Huesmann, L. R., Guerra, N. G., Zelli, A., & Miller, L. (1992). Differing normative beliefs about aggression for boys and girls. In K. Bjorkqvist & P. Niemela (Eds.), *Of mice and women: Aspects of female aggression.* Orlando, FL: Academic Press.

Huesmann, L. R., & Levinger, G. (1976). Incremental exchange theory: A formal model for progression in dyadic social interaction. In L. Berkowitz (Ed.), *Advances in experimental social psychology (Vol. 9). Journal of Consulting and Clinical Psychology, 46,* 1071–1078.

Huesmann, L. R., Moise, J., & Podolski, C. P. (1997). The effects of media violence on the development of antisocial behavior (pp. 181–193). In D. Stoff, J. Breiling, & J. Masser (Eds.), *Handbook of antisocial behavior.* New York: John Wiley & Sons.

Huesmann, L. R., & Woocher, F. D. (1976). Probe similarity and recognition of set membership: A parallel-processing serial-feature-matching model. *Cognitive Psychology, 8(1),* 124–162.

Huesmann, L. R., Zelli, A., Fraczek, A., & Upmeyer, A. (1993). Normative attitudes about aggression in American, German, and Polish college students. *Third European Congress of Psychology,* Tampere, Finland.

Jones, E. E., & Davis, K. E. (1965). From acts to dispositions: The attribution process in person perception. In L. Berkowitz (Ed.), *Advances in experimental social psychology (Vol. 2).* New York: Academic Press.

Josephson, W. L. (1987). Television violence and children's aggression: Testing the priming, social script, and disinhibition predictions. *Journal of Personality and Social Psychology, 53(5),* 882–890.

Kagan, J. (1988). Temperamental contributions to social behavior. *American Psychologists, 44,* 668–674.

Kelley, H. H. (1967). Attribution theory in social psychology. In D. Levine (Ed.), *Nebraska Symposium on Motivation, 15.* Lincoln, NE: University of Nebraska Press.

Kendall, P. C., & Braswell, L. (1985). *Cognitive-behavioral therapy for impulsive children.* New York: Guilford Press.

Kintsch, W. (1977). *Memory and cognition.* New York: Wiley.

Klatzky, R. L. (1980). *Human memory.* San Francisco: Freeman.

Lagerspetz, K., & Lagerspetz, K. M. J. (1971). Changes in aggressiveness of mice resulting from selective breeding, learning and social isolation. *Scandinavian Journal of Psychology, 12,* 241–278.

Lagerspetz, K., & Sandnabba, K. (1982). The decline of aggression in mice during group caging as determined by punishment delivered by cagemates. *Aggressive Behavior, 8,* 319–334.

Lindsay, P., & Norman, D. (1977). *Human information processing.* New York: Academic Press.
Loeber, R., & Dishion, T. J. (1983). Early predictors of male delinquency: A review. *Psychological Bulletin, 94,* 68–94.
Loehlin, J. C. (1969). Machines with personality. *Science Journal, 4(10),* 97–101.
Luria, A. R. (1973). *The working brain.* London: Penguin.
Magnusson, D., Duner, A., & Zetterblom, G. (1975). *Adjustment: A longitudinal study.* Stockholm: Almqvist & Wiksell.
Matthews, R., Paulus, P., & Baron, R. A. (1979). Physical aggression after being crowded. *Journal of Nonverbal Behavior, 4,* 5–17.
McCulloch, W. S., & Pitts, W. (1943). A logical calculus of the ideas immanent in neural nets. *Bulletin of Mathematical Biophysics, 5,* 115–137.
McFall, R. M. (1982). A review and reformulation of the concept of social skills. *Behavioral Assessment, 4,* 1–35.
Mednick, S. A., Gabrielli, W. F., & Hutchings, B. (1984). Genetic influences in criminal convictions: Evidence from an adoption cohort. *Science, 224,* 891–894.
Miller, G. A., Galanter, E., & Pribram, K. (1960). *Plans and the structure of behavior.* New York: Holt.
Minsky, M., & Papert, S. (1969). *Perceptrons.* Cambridge, MA: MIT Press.
Moffitt, T. E. (1990). Juvenile delinquency and attention-deficit disorder: Developmental trajectories from age 3 to 15. *Child Development, 61,* 893–910.
Moyer, K. E. (1976). *The psychobiology of aggression.* New York: Harper & Row.
Nachson, I., & Denno, D. (1987). Violent behavior and cerebral hemisphere dysfunctions. In S. A. Mednick, T. E. Moffitt, S. A. Stack (Eds.), *The causes of crime: New biological approaches.* New York: Cambridge University Press.
Nasby, H., Hayden, B., & DePaulo, B. M. (1979). Attributional bias among aggressive boys to interpret unambiguous social stimuli as displays of hostility. *Journal of Abnormal Psychology, 89,* 459–468.
Neisser, U. (1967). *Cognitive Psychology.* New York: Appleton.
Newell, A., & Simon, H. A. (1972). *Human problem solving.* Englewood Cliffs, NJ: Prentice-Hall.
Newell, A., Shaw, J. C., & Simon, H. A. (1958). Elements of a theory of human problem solving. *Psychological Review, 65,* 151–166.
Nilsson, N. J. (1965). *Learning machines.* New York: McGraw-Hill.
Olweus, D. (1979). The stability of aggressive reaction patterns in males: A review. *Psychological Bulletin, 86,* 852–875.
Olweus, D., Mattsson, A., Schalling, D., & Low, H. (1988). Circulating testosterone levels and aggression in adolescent males: A causal analysis. *Psychosomatic Medicine, 50,* 261–272.
Paik, H., & Comstock, G. A. (1994). The effects of television violence on antisocial behavior: A meta-analysis. *Communication Research, 21,* 516–546.
Patterson, G. R. (1995). Coercion: A basis for early age of onset for arrest. In J. McCord (Ed.), *Coercion and punishment in long-term perspective.* New York: Cambridge University Press.
Patterson, G. R., Capaldi, D. M., & Bank, L. (1991). An early starter model for predicting delinquency. In D. J. Pepler & K. H. Rubin (Eds.), *Systems and development: Symposia on child psychology.* Hillsdale, NJ: Lawrence Erlbaum.
Perry, D. G., Perry, L. C., & Rasmussen, P. (1986). Cognitive social learning mediators of aggression. *Child Development, 57,* 700–711.
Pettit, G. S., Dodge, K. A., & Brown, M. M. (1988). Early family experience, social problem solving, and children's social competence. *Child Development, 59(1),* 107–120.
Pontius, A. A. (1984). Specific stimulus-evoked violent action in psychotic trigger reaction: A seizure-like imbalance between frontal lobe and limbic system? *Perceptual and Motor Skills, 59,* 299–333.
Prentice-Dunn, S., & Rogers, R. (1983). Deindividuation in aggression. In R. G. Geen & E. Donnerstein (Eds.), *Aggression: Theoretical and empirical reviews* (Vol. 2, pp. 155–171). New York: Academic Press.
Quiggle, N., Garber, J., Panak, W., & Dodge, K. A. (1992). Social-information processing in aggressive and depressed children. *Child Development, 63,* 1305–1320.

Quattrone, G. A. (1982). Over-attribution and unit formation: When behavior engulfs the person. *Journal of Personality and Social Psychology, 42*, 593–607.

Raine, A., & Jones, F. (1987). Attention, autonomic arousal, and personality in behaviorally disordered children. *Journal of Abnormal Child Psychology, 15*, 583–599.

Raine, A., & Venables, P. H. (1981). Classical conditioning and socialization: A biosocial interaction. *Personality and Individual Differences, 2*, 273–283.

Raine, A., Venables, P. H., & Williams, M. (1996). Better autonomic conditioning and faster electrodermal harl-recovery times at age 15 as possible protective factors against crime at age 29 years. *Developmental Psychology, 32(4)*, 624–630.

Rosenblatt, F. (1960). Perceptual generalization over transformation groups. In M. C. Yovits & S. Cameron (Eds.), *Self-organizing systems* (pp. 63–96). New York: Pergamon Press.

Rosenfeld, E., Huesmann, L. R., Eron, L. D., & Torney-Purta, J. V. (1982). Measuring patterns of fantasy behavior in children. *Journal of Personality and Social Psychology, 42*, 347–366.

Rubin, K. H., Bream, L. A., & Rose-Krasnor, L. (1991). Social problem solving and aggression in childhood. In D. J. Pepler & K. H. Rubin (Eds.), *The development and treatment of childhood aggression.* Hillsdale, NJ: Lawrence Erlbaum.

Rubin, K. H., Moller, L., & Emptage, A. (1987). The preschool behavior questionnaire: A useful index of behavior problems in elementary school-age children. *Canadian Journal of Behavioral Science, 19*, 86–100.

Rumelhart, D. E., Lindsay, P. H., & Norman, D. A. (1972). A process model for long-term memory. In E. Tulving & W. Donaldson (Eds.), *Organization of memory.* New York: Academic Press.

Rumelhart, D. E., & McClelland, J. L. (1986). *Parallel distributed processing: Exploration in the microstructure of cognition* (Vol. 1). Cambridge, MA: MIT Press/Bradford Books.

Rushton, J. P., Fulker, D. W., Neale, M. C., Nias, D. K. B., & Eysenck, H. J. (1986). Altruism and aggression: The heritability of individual differences. *Journal of Personality and Social Psychology, 50*, 1192–1198.

Schneider, D. J. (1991). Social cognition. *Annual Review of Psychology, 4*, 527–561.

Schneider, W., & Shiffrin, R. M. (1977). Controlled and automatic human information processing. I. Detection, search, and attention. *Psychological Review, 84*, 1–66.

Shiffrin, R. M., & Schneider, W. (1977). Controlled and automatic human information processing. II. Perceptual learning, automatic attending, and general theory. *Psychological Review, 84*, 127–190.

Shure, M. B., & Spivack, G. (1980). Interpersonal problem-solving as a mediator of behavioral adjustment in preschool and kindergarten children. *Journal of Applied Developmental Psychology, 1(1)*, 45–57.

Simon, H. A. (1957). *Models of men.* New York: Wiley.

Simon, H. A. (1967). Motivational and emotional controls of cognition. *Psychological Review, 74*, 29–39.

Simon, H. A. (1969). *The sciences of the artificial.* Cambridge, MA: MIT Press.

Simon, H. A. (1978). Information processing theory of human problem-solving. In W. K. Estes (Ed.), *Handbook of learning and cognitive processes,* Hillsdale, NJ: Lawrence Erlbaum.

Simon, H. A. (1979). *Models of thought.* New Haven, CT: Yale University Press.

Slaby, R. G., & Guerra, N. G. (1988). Cognitive mediators of aggression in adolescent offenders. I. Assessment. *Developmental Psychology, 24*, 580–588.

Smith, C. A. (1989). Dimensions of appraisal and physiological response in emotion. *Journal of Personality and Social Psychology, 56*, 339–353.

Smith, C. A., & Ellsworth, P. C. (1985). Patterns of cognitive appraisal in emotion. *Journal of Personality and Social Psychology, 48*, 813–838.

Smolensky, P. (1988). On the proper treatment of connectionism. *Behavioral Brain Sciences, 11*, 1–74.

Spivack, G. (1983). *High risk early behaviors indicating vulnerability to delinquency in the community and school.* Washington, DC: NIMH.

Staub, E. (1996). Cultural-societal roots of violence: The examples of genocidal violence and of contemporary youth violence in the United States. *American Psychologist, 51(2)*, 117–132.

Stenberg, C. R., & Campos, J. J. (1990). The development of anger and expressions in infancy. In N. Stein, B. Leventhal, & T. Trabasso (Eds.), *Psychological and biological approaches to emotion.* Hillsdale, NJ: Lawrence Erlbaum Associates.

Steinberg, M. D., & Dodge, K. A. (1983). Attributional bias in aggressive boys and girls. *Journal of Social and Clinical Psychology, 1,* 312–321.

Taylor, A. R., & Gabriel, S. W. (1989). Cooperative versus competitive game-playing strategies of peer accepted and peer rejected children in a goal conflict situation. Paper presented at the biennial meeting of the Society for Research in Child Development, Kansas City, MO.

Townsend, J. T. (1976). Serial and within-stage independent parallel model equivalence on the minimum completion time. *Journal of Mathematical Psychology, 14(3),* 219–238.

Tulving, E., & Thompson, D. M. (1973). Encoding specificity and retrieval processes in episodic memory. *Psychological Review, 80(5),* 359–380.

Viemero, V., & Paajanen, S. (1992). The role of fantasies and dreams in the TV viewing-aggression relationship. *Aggressive Behavior, 18(2),* 109–116.

Waas, G. A. (1988). Social attributional biases of peer-rejected and aggressive children. *Child Development, 59,* 969–992.

Weiner, B. (1986). *An attributional theory of motivation and emotion.* New York: Springer-Verlag.

Widom, C. S. (1989). Does violence beget violence? A critical examination of the literature. *Psychological Bulletin, 106(1),* 3–28.

Winter, L., & Uleman, J. S. (1984). When are social judgements made? Evidence for the spontaneousness of trait inference. *Journal of Personality and Social Psychology, 4,* 904–917.

Wyer, R. S., Jr. (1974). *Cognitive organization and change: An information-processing approach.* Potomac, MD: Lawrence Erlbaum Associates.

Wyer, R. S., Jr., & Carlston, D. E. (1979). *Social cognition, inference, and attribution.* Hillsdale, NJ: Erlbaum.

Wyer, R. S., Jr., & Srull, T. K. (1980). The processing of social stimulus information: A conceptual integration. In R. Hastie, T. M. Ostrom, E. B. Ebbesen, R. S. Wyer, D. L. Hamilton, & D. E. Carlston (Eds.), *Person memory: The cognitive basis of social perception.* Hillsdale, NJ: Lawrence Erlbaum Associates.

Zelli, A., & Huesmann, L. R. (1993). *Accuracy of social information processing by those who are aggressive: The role of beliefs about a hostile world.* Prevention Research Center, University of Illinois at Chicago.

Zelli, A., Huesmann, L. R., & Cervone, D. P. (1995). Social inferences in aggressive individuals: Evidence for automatic processing in the expression of hostile biases. *Aggressive Behavior, 21(6),* 405–417.

5

AGGRESSION AND THE SELF: HIGH SELF-ESTEEM, LOW SELF-CONTROL, AND EGO THREAT

Roy F. Baumeister and Joseph M. Boden

Case Western Reserve University

INTRODUCTION

Two of the most heavily investigated topics in social and personality psychology are aggression and the self (for reviews, see Baumeister, in press; Geen, 1990; Tedeschi, & Felson, 1994). Despite the immense interest in these two, the interface between them has received surprisingly little attention. It seems more likely that the lack of such research reflects more the different backgrounds of the respective groups of researchers than any lack of relationship between self-processes and aggressive acts.

This chapter examines two important links between self and aggression. First, we shall discuss the link between self-esteem and violence. Although this particular link has been discussed and invoked, it is widely misunderstood, and a proper examination of research findings suggests a conclusion opposite to what is generally assumed. More precisely, we shall argue that it is high rather than low self-esteem that is most likely to lead to violent, aggressive acts. Second, we shall explore the role of self-control and self-regulation in aggression. The main thrust of that argument will be that breakdowns in self-control processes are the proximate causes of the majority of violent and aggressive actions that occur spontaneously in peacetime society.

Our comments have implications for some of the seeming ironies and paradoxes in the psychology of aggression. The first part will address the obvious problem in the widespread assumption that low self-esteem causes violence: If

111

that is correct, then why is there so much violence in a society that has devoted so much effort (with some apparent success) to raising everyone's self-esteem? The second will address an even more fundamental problem in the psychology of aggression, namely its embarrassment of riches. Researchers have identified a great many causes of aggression, and these causes (such as anger, frustration, provocation, or opportunity) are extremely common, and so one must wonder: Why is there not more aggression or violence than there is? In other words, the very success of aggression research in identifying so many causes of violence has raised a further theoretical problem of explaining why aggression so often fails to ensue when its known causes are present. Our response will be that people generally have a powerful and important set of internal restraints that inhibit aggressive behavior, and so the failure of these internal restraints is often final, proximate cause of aggression and violence.

We hasten to add that we are not trying to offer a general, exhaustive, or definitive theory of aggression. The views and evidence proposed in this chapter can easily be integrated with many other contributions to the psychology of aggression, including social learning, hereditary or genetic predispositions, cognitive patterns, and more. It is also plausible that there are other patterns of aggression to which the psychology of self is entirely irrelevant. We are simply trying to elucidate some of the ways that the self is involved in aggression, when it is.

THREATENED EGOTISM AND AGGRESSIVE BEHAVIOR

Our first link between self and aggression concerns the role of self-appraisals. As we shall see, there is a long tradition of asserting that low self-esteem causes aggression and violence, but empirical evidence contradicts this view. Instead, it may be more correct to say that a form of high self-esteem—more precisely, a highly favorable and possibly inflated view of self that is confronted with an external threat—leads to violence. A more thorough and detailed version of this position is available in Baumeister, Smart, and Boden (1996).

DOES LOW SELF-ESTEEM CAUSE VIOLENCE?

Low self-esteem has long been asserted to be one of the most important determinants of violent behavior. For example, Anderson (1994) cited low self-esteem as a cause of violent behavior among members of youth gangs. Jankowski (1991) also referred to gang members as possessing a strong sense of "self-contempt." Renzetti (1992) reported that negative feelings which result in domestic violence are often a result of low self-esteem. Long (1990) stated that terrorists suffer from low self-esteem and feelings of inadequacy which motivate their behavior. Mac-Donald (1975) suggested that armed robbers were low in self-esteem. Levin and McDevitt (1993) cited low self-esteem as an important contributor to the occurrence of hate crimes. These are but a few of the examples of researchers asserting that the lack of self-esteem leads in some way to violent behavior, thus creating the assumption that a causal link exists between low self-esteem and aggression.

The assumption that low self-esteem is a cause of violent behavior is a powerful one, but it is also one that is adhered to despite a lack of evidence, even in the face of contrary evidence. That is, the assumption that low self-esteem leads to violence may be at best overstated, at worst incorrect. The articles cited earlier were found by Baumeister, Smart, and Boden (1996) to contain almost no evidence to support the view that low self-esteem is a causal factor in violent behavior. Also, Baumeister et al. (1996) repeatedly encountered examples of research findings in which violent offenders were referred to with terms such as *egotistical* and *arrogant,* terms which connote high self-esteem rather than low. Yet the researchers would often then describe these same individuals as suffering from low self-esteem. For example, Toch (1993) alluded repeatedly to a strong relationship between low self-esteem and violent behavior, yet he also described violent offenders as being arrogant and having "exaggerated self-esteem" (p. 136). Furthermore, Toch's analysis lacked any direct evidence that linked low self-esteem and violence. In another example, Oates and Forrest (1985) referred to abusive mothers as having low self-esteem. Their assertion was based on the administration of a single-item questionnaire which purported to measure self-esteem. The question was, "Would you like your child to grow up to be like you?" As these mothers had been included in the study following a court referral for child abuse, one might assume that they would show a certain amount of self-deprecation and indicate that indeed they did not wish their children to grow up to be like them. Thus the assertion that this item measures self-esteem would seem to be at best misleading. The dearth of evidence relating low self-esteem to violent or aggressive behavior led Baumeister et al. (1996) to conclude that the prevailing assumption of the causal link between self-esteem and violent behavior is not well founded and urgently needs reappraisal.

There are several subgroups of aggressive people who have been specifically hypothesized to have low self-esteem, but researchers have explicitly rejected those views. Thus, Olweus (1994) concluded that childhood bullies do not suffer from low self-esteem. Jankowski (1991) said the belief in hidden insecurities among gang members is mistaken.

Our own reasoning led to the hypothesis that if low self-esteem should lead to any form of violence, it would most likely be found in domestic violence, because such violence is often marked by beating up on weak, helpless targets who pose no risk of retaliation. The view that domestic abusers have low self-esteem has been promoted by studies relying on victim reports (e.g., Walker, 1979), possibly because battered wives would rather believe they have chosen a romantic partner who suffers from low self-esteem instead of one who is a psychopathic sadist or cruel egomaniac. The few findings that have suggested low self-esteem have generally relied on people who referred themselves for therapy as abusers, which is methodologically problematic and risky, as critics have pointed out (e.g., Holtzworth-Munroe,

1992). That is, people who turn themselves in as spouse abusers are atypical and are presumably motivated to be contrite and self-deprecating. Prospective studies with proper samples have generally failed to find any link between self-esteem and domestic violence (Christensen et al., 1994).

THREATENED EGOTISM AS CAUSE OF AGGRESSION

Contrary to the low self-esteem view, Baumeister, Smart, and Boden (1996) suggested that favorable self-appraisals may be more likely to lead to violence. The term *high self-esteem* has acquired a very favorable connotation and people are reluctant to acknowledge that it may have an undesirable side, but the terms *arrogance, conceitedness, egotism,* and *narcissism* have less favorable connotations while carrying the same denotative meaning of a favorable self-appraisal.[1] The first point in our argument is therefore to propose that violent, aggressive people tend to be arrogant, conceited, egotistical, narcissistic, or otherwise enamored of themselves.

There are some ways in which favorable self-appraisals can lead directly to aggression. Regarding oneself as a superior being allows one to disregard the rights and well-being of others, and so a self-styled superior being might harm other people just as one swats a fly. Still, such cases are relatively rare. The main focus of our theory is threatened egotism.

By threatened egotism we mean favorable views of self that are disputed or that in some other way encounter an external appraisal that is far less favorable. Thus, we are not suggesting that high self-esteem leads directly to aggression. Rather, the point is that the combination of a highly favorable view of self and an external, unfavorable appraisal is the main cause of aggression.

There is already ample precedent in the empirical literature for suggesting that threatened egotism can lead to dangerous or irrational behavior. Schlenker, Soraci, and McCarthy (1976) showed that people with high self-esteem react poorly to criticism in general. McFarlin and Blascovich (1981) found that people high in self-esteem respond to failure by irrationally raising their predictions for future performance. Baumeister, Heatherton, and Tice (1993) showed that people with high self-esteem make excessive and self-defeating commitments in an irrational response to ego threat. Thus, after exposure to some negative self-relevant information in the laboratory, high self-esteem people seem to react in a manner that is often problematic and irrational, yet which seems to suggest a strong impulse to erase the threat by affirming one's superiority.

---

[1]Researchers interested in conducting direct tests of the link between self-appraisals and behavior may wish to keep in mind that the connotative biases may be implicit in the construction of some scales. That is, people who make up self-esteem measures may share the bias that high self-esteem is good, and so there may be some gratuitous intrusion of positivity in the scales; meanwhile, those who make up scales to measure narcissism may be equally biased against narcissism and this negativity may show up in the scale items. We recommend using multiple scales.

People with low self-esteem, however, do not display these tendencies in the laboratory. Instead, they become more conservative or cautious in their behavior. For example, in the study by Baumeister et al. (1993) in which subjects played a video game, high self-esteem people reacted to a threat to their sense of mastery and competence by wagering a greater amount of money that they would perform well in the future. Low self-esteem people, however, reacted to the same threat by making a smaller wager, seeming to doubt their ability to succeed at the task.

Thus, people who hold high opinions of themselves tend to react irrationally, impulsively, and emotionally when someone else presents a serious challenge to those favorable views. The core of our theory is that such reactions may often lead to violence and aggression.

SELF-APPRAISALS AND VIOLENCE: EVIDENCE

We have proposed that aggression follows from an explosive combination of favorable self-appraisals and external threat. We begin by examining evidence about the former. The next section will move on to consider evidence about threat.

The relationship between self-esteem and aggressive or violent behavior has been examined in a number of studies and in differing contexts. For example, group differences in self-esteem seem to be associated with group differences in aggression and hostility, but these patterns run directly opposite to the traditional view that low self-esteem produces violence. Instead, groups whose members demonstrate higher levels of self-esteem also demonstrate higher levels of hostility and violence. Males tend to have higher levels of self-esteem than females (Harter, 1993), although that difference is relatively small and may be growing even smaller (Crocker & Major, 1989). Males are also more aggressive and violent than females, and are from 5 to 50 times more likely to be arrested for violent crimes (Wilson & Herrnstein, 1985). Depressed people are known to have low self-esteem (e.g., Tennen & Affleck, 1993), but depression is one of the few forms of mental illness associated with lower levels of aggression and violence. Racial differences in self-esteem have shifted over time, as have racial differences in violence, and the covariation patterns run directly opposite to the view that low self-esteem breeds violence (Baumeister et al., 1996). Thus, group differences tend to link violence to favorable rather than unfavorable self-appraisals.

Another method for examining the relationship between high self-esteem and violent behavior is to examine whether people who commit violent crimes possess high or low self-esteem. Most such studies have not included standard self-esteem measures or systematic samples. Still, some studies have examined the self-esteem of participants either directly or indirectly, or do at least make mention of the self-opinions of people convicted of violent crimes. These studies find that violent criminals tend to have favorable opinions of themselves. Thus, a long series of studies with the Minnesota Multiphasic Personality Inventory (MMPI) found that the scales relevant to low self-esteem (especially 2, depression, which includes self-deprecation; and 7, introversion, which includes insecurity and shyness) have been negatively correlated with criminality (for review, see Wilson & Herrnstein, 1985). Thus, depressed, self-deprecating, shy, and insecure people are underrepresented among populations of violent offenders. Likewise, Berkowitz (1978) depicted a sample of British violent offenders as confident and egotistical. An astonishing level of egotism among rapists was documented by Scully (1990), who said that many of the convicted rapists she interviewed in prison spontaneously bragged to her about their sexual prowess and occupational accomplishments, often depicting themselves as "multitalented superachievers" (p. 112).

Collective violence tends to be linked to explicit beliefs in the superiority of the violent group. Chirot's (1994) study of modern tyrannies found that nearly all of them held a strong belief in their own cultural superiority. Most famously, perhaps, the German Nazis regarded themselves as a "master race" and often derogated their victims as subhuman. The ongoing importance of beliefs in white supremacy in violent groups such as the Ku Klux Klan is well-known (e.g., Wade, 1987; also Hamm, 1993). Accounts of life in organized crime emphasize that Mafia members regard themselves as almost god-like superior beings (Anastasia, 1991; Arlacchi, 1992). Accounts of life in modern violent youth gangs have stressed the central importance of highly favorable self-views, to the point at which one promotes oneself and one's group by putting down rivals and by responding with lethal violence to any sign of disrespect by others (Bing, 1991; Currie, 1991; McCall, 1994).

The lack of direct experimental tests of how self-appraisals affect aggression is surprising, given the long-standing interests in both topics. In an investigation conducted by Bushman and Baumeister (in press), self-appraisals were measured, participants were insulted or not (in ostensible evaluation of a brief essay they wrote on abortion), and then they were given an opportunity to aggress against the confederate who had or had not insulted them. In study 2, some participants were given an opportunity to aggress against a third person. In both studies, the highest levels of aggression were found to result from the combination of high narcissism and ego threat (i.e., the insult), consistent with the threatened egotism model. Self-esteem had no significant effects, either alone or interacting with ego threat. Aggression against the innocent third person was also unaffected; aggression was only increased toward the source of the bad evaluation.

Thus, a broad assortment of evidence from different disciplines contradicts the view that low self-esteem causes violence. Violent offenders and other aggressive individuals seem to be people who hold quite favorable views of themselves. This is not to say that all people with high self-esteem are aggressive or violent, and indeed there is some evidence contradicting any direct or simple link between any level of self-esteem and aggression. It does, however, suggest that the widespread belief in low self-esteem as a cause of violence should be rejected.

EGO THREATS AS AGGRESSIVE PROVOCATIONS

Our main view is not that high self-esteem leads directly to violence. Rather, it is that threatened egotism, i.e., the combination of favorable self-appraisal and external, unfavorable evaluation, is the decisive cause. The previous section noted that aggression seems to be linked to favorable self-appraisals. This section examines the second part, namely that external ego threats lead to aggression.

The role of ego threats seems indisputable. There is after all a long tradition of laboratory studies devoted to studying many different causes of aggression, but a great many of them only found aggression in the condition in which anger was manipulated, usually by administering an ego threat. For example, the classic study of film violence by Berkowitz and Geen (1966) focused on the role of aggressive modeling and the presence of aggressive cues that linked the film to one's own situation. Yet the presence of both aggressive film and connecting cues yielded no more aggression than the control conditions unless the confederate insulted and provoked the subject by delivering an aversive, highly derogatory evaluation of the subject's performance on a creativity test. More generally, we think that the importance of ego threats for generating violence became so commonplace that researchers tended to use them without even devoting much comment or analysis to that aspect of their procedures.

Ego threats have also been implicated in nonlaboratory violence. Toch (1993) found that many of the men included in his study committed violent crimes to avenge insults or, more generally, to prove their superiority to anyone who doubted them. Similarly, Berkowitz (1978) studied men imprisoned for assault and found that in most cases they had been attempting to retaliate against others who had made threatening or belittling remarks. A study of homicide by Polk (1993) found two major types, one of which occurs in connection with instrumental crime (e.g., robbery) and the other being in response to an insult. Katz (1988) likewise concluded that murder and other violent crimes tend to be responses to some threat to the person's public image, such as an insult, humiliation, or show of disrespect. Ego threat also appears to be a precursor to rape, although the evidence is weaker. Groth (1979) found that many rapes were preceded by some sort of blow to the rapist's ego.

Literature on domestic violence provides evidence that threats to the self-esteem of one partner in a relationship may lead to that partner aggressing toward the other partner. Goldstein and Rosenbaum (1985) found that what distinguished abusive husbands was a tendency to interpret a wife's behavior as threatening or damaging to the husband's favorable image of self. Gelles and Strauss (1988) found that one major cause of domestic violence was status inconsistency (generally occupational status). That is, when the wife's status was equal to or greater than her husband's, the husband was much more likely to beat his wife. In such cases, presumably, the husband felt threatened by his wife's success and thus acted aggressively to counter the threat to his self-esteem and reassert his superior position. Hornung, McCullough, and Sugimoto (1981) found that women who were beaten by their husbands were more likely to be employed outside the home rather than being homemakers, possibly because homemakers represent less of a threat (than employed wives) to their husbands' superior status. Hornung et al. (1981) also found that men who had been highly educated but had a low-status position (i.e., underachievers) were especially violent, whereas men whose achievements at work exceeded their education or expectation were especially nonviolent.

At times, cultures have formalized the link between violence and a blow to one's pride. Dueling, for example, was for the most part a specific pattern of ritualized violence precipitated by some ego threat, such as an insulting remark about the individual or his family, and of course it was mainly practiced by the upper classes who maintained a strong sense of superiority (see Kiernan, 1989).

Ego threats also play a role in collective violence. As noted earlier, tyrannies tend to arise in nations that nurture a sense of cultural superiority, but these tyrannies also tend to be characterized by a sense of grievance, especially the perception that other nations and groups fail to acknowledge this respect (Chirot, 1994). This can readily be seen in several of the most violent tyrannies of this century. Russia felt that its moral and cultural superiority over western Europe had been unfairly submerged by accidents of technology and geography, so that the western Europeans looked down on instead of up to Russia. Germany felt that it had been systematically deprived of its rightful place among (indeed, at the head of) the great powers of Europe. Cambodia blamed inept government and foreign influence for the downfall of their nation from a great power and cultural icon.

By the same token, collective violence in the United States has also tended to be marked by ego threat. For example, belief in white supremacy was centuries old, but the Ku Klux Klan only emerged and became violent when the emancipation of slaves and other trends eroded the institutionalized superiority of whites. Indeed, even today the skinheads and other white supremacist groups tend to be made up of white males whose sense of superiority and entitlement is felt to be jeopardized by the gains made by minorities (Hamm, 1993; Levin & McDevitt, 1993).

Thus, it seems clear that ego threats play an important role in causing aggression and violence. Probably the most common and effective violent provocation is some form of ego threat, whether a mere verbal insult or a more elaborate and substantive affront.

VIOLENCE-PRONE VERSIONS OF HIGH SELF-ESTEEM

The previous sections have asserted that threatened egotism is a main cause of aggression. We turn now to the problem of identifying what sorts of favorable self-appraisals are most prone to lead to aggression. That is, not all individuals with high self-esteem act violently, so which individuals might be more likely to act violently, and under what circumstances? Or, more precisely, what defines the subset(s) of people with high self-esteem who tend to act violently?

To answer that, we return to the basic point that violence results from threatened egotism. Favorable views of self should tend to lead to violence to the extent that they encounter external threats. Hence any factors that increase the frequency or subjective impact of ego threats will increase the likelihood of violent response.

One such factor is that excessive or inflated self-esteem will tend to lead to violence. The reasoning is as follows. One major determinant of the evaluative feedback that people receive from others will be accuracy. That is, attractive people will gradually find out that they are attractive, competent people will hear that they are competent, those who are not will gradually find this out, and so forth. To the extent that self-appraisals are accurate, interpersonal feedback may merely confirm them, and so ego threats may be relatively rare. But whenever an unrealistically inflated self-appraisal encounters accurate feedback, the result will be an ego threat. In other words, people who overestimate themselves will be constantly at high risk of receiving evaluations that they are not as good as they think (because, in fact, they are not).

A number of research findings support the notion that individuals with inflated self-opinions may be prone to violent or aggressive behavior. One relevant measure of inflated self-appraisals is *narcissism,* particularly the component involving grandiosity and exhibitionism, which denotes excessively favorable views of self. Wink (1991) found that narcissism in general was linked to disregard for other people, which is one factor that contributes to aggression. In particular, he found that grandiosity as a component of narcissism was an important predictor of aggressiveness. Raskin, Novacek, and Hogan (1991) likewise found that narcissism (particularly grandiosity) was linked to hostility. As noted earlier, Bushman and Baumeister (in press) found that narcissists responded to an ego threat with exceptionally high aggression, even when self-esteem failed to predict any such responses.

Another group known for inflated self-appraisals is psychopaths. Hare (1993) described psychopaths as having a "narcissistic and grossly inflated view of their self-worth and importance (p. 38; see also Meloy, 1988). They are also unusually aggressive. Indeed, Hare (1993) estimated that psychopaths make up less than 1% of the population but commit over half the serious crimes.

Another example might include people under the influence of alcohol, the consumption of which tends to raise the favorability of one's self-appraisals (Banaji & Steele, 1989; Diamond & Wilsnack, 1978). After consuming alcohol, individuals tend to rate themselves higher across a number of traits, thus demonstrating an artificial increase in their level of self-esteem. The consumption of alcohol is also known to increase hostile and violent behavior (Bushman & Cooper, 1990). In fact, the majority of violent crimes are committed by people under the influence of alcohol (National Research Council, 1993; Gottfredson & Hirschi, 1990). In this manner the consumption of a substance that seems to temporarily inflate self-esteem also seems to increase aggressive behavior, an assertion that lends support to the current model.

Alongside inflated self-appraisals, uncertain or unstable ones may be especially vulnerable to threat (and hence prone to violence). People with such views may well be quite sensitive to external evaluations. Uncertainty about one's positive worth may make the person extra desirous of external validation that could confirm those positive views. Thus, for example, Wicklund and Gollwitzer (1982) provided several laboratory studies to show that people who are uncertain about their positive traits become unusually sensitive to the evaluative feedback of others as well as becoming strongly motivated to induce others to confirm their positive identity claims. By the same token, people whose self-esteem fluctuates often or widely might be especially sensitive to external evaluations because these evaluations carry the power to deflate their self-esteem, which is presumably quite aversive.

Adolescence is one period in life when one's identity and self-esteem tend to be uncertain. Adolescents tend to rely more on external evaluations made by others, and they seem to lack their own internal standards for judging their behavior (e.g., Hauser, 1991; Sebald, 1984). Adolescents may therefore be a relevant group with which to study the link between uncertain self-esteem and aggression. As is well known, aggression tends to be high among adolescents, and indeed criminality tends to reach a peak during the late teen years, declining through adulthood (e.g., Gurr, 1979; Ianni, 1989).

Good evidence about the stability of self-esteem has been provided in studies by Kernis (1993) and various colleagues, which are based on taking multiple measures of self-esteem at different times and computing within-subject variations. Kernis, Granneman, and Barclay (1989) found that self-reported levels of angry and hostile responses were highest among people with high but unstable self-esteem, a pattern that precisely fits the threatened egotism hypothesis. Indeed, these researchers found that people with high but stable self-esteem scored the lowest in hostility: Thus, a favorable view of self that is immune to external threat tends to be nonviolent. Subsequent work has confirmed that defensive sensitivity to ego threats is highest among people with high, unstable self-esteem (Kernis, Cornell, Sun, Berry, & Harlow, 1993). The implication is that favorable but unstable views of the self are especially sensitive and hence prone to produce hostile responses to perceived threats.

Some of the evidence reviewed earlier may also be relevant here. In the subsection on ego threats, we did not distinguish between recent and chronic threats, and indeed both were implicated. It is possible, however, to assume that a chronically threatened self-esteem would be an unstable or uncertain one. Thus, men whose wives have outranked or surpassed them may tend toward violence because they are frequently subjected to specific threats, but it may also be that the constant awareness of their wives' superior status puts the men in a state of uncertainty regarding their belief in male superiority, and so they become extra sensitive to everyday remarks or other slights. The chronicity of the situation was likewise particularly apparent in Renzetti's (1992) studies of battering in lesbian relationships. She found that batterers wanted to be powerful, independent, autonomous decision-makers, but they found themselves in situations of chronic dependency (e.g., for financial reasons) on their partners. By the same token, nations that believe in their own superiority but believe that other nations have unfairly outperformed them may feel chronically threatened and may have uncertainty about their claims to superiority.

The parallel between unstable high self-esteem and narcissism may reflect a fundamental unity. Rhodewalt, Madrian, and Cheney (1997) found that narcissism is correlated with the stability of self-esteem, such that narcissists have high but unstable self-esteem. These results suggest that there may indeed be one variety or subset of high self-esteem that makes one especially prone to highly aggressive responding.

Thus, it seems that individuals with overly inflated, uncertain, or unstable self-appraisals might be at highest risk for experiencing the discrepancy between a favorable self-appraisal and an unfavorable external appraisal. This discrepancy often serves as the impetus for violent and aggressive behavior, yet it seems unlikely that the mere perception of discrepancy would lead to violent behavior. We suggest that the presence of negative affect may be vital in determining whether a person will respond to perceived slights with violence.

THE ROLE OF NEGATIVE AFFECT

It is hardly controversial to assert that negative affect is relevant to aggression. Early theories about aggression emphasize feelings of frustration (Dollard, Doob, Miller, Mowrer, & Sears, 1939). As already noted, many laboratory studies have included an anger manipulation, although it usually took the form of an ego threat. Ego threats do produce negative affect. Indeed, changes to state self-esteem show strong links to mood and aversive emotion (Heatherton & Polivy, 1991).

A general statement was offered by Berkowitz (1989). He proposed replacing the old emphasis on frustration with a broad view that any negative affect can lead to aggression. In our view, the evidence is inadequate to assert that all negative affect states increase aggression, and indeed there is evidence that some such states, such as guilt or empathic distress, can have the opposite effect (Baron, 1976). Still, the existence of exceptions should not detract from the importance of Berkowitz's central point that a broad range of negative affect has been implicated in aggression.

We propose that an external unfavorable evaluation presents the individual with a choice, and the choice one makes will dictate the affective (and other) responses. One option is to accept the evaluation and revise one's self-appraisal downward accordingly. This is likely to produce depression, sadness, and other negative affects, and it is not likely to lead to violence.

The other option is to reject the unfavorable evaluation and maintain one's favorable view of self. In this case the evaluation will be seen as an unfair, unwarranted threat, and so it is likely that the affective response will be anger or some similar affect directed outward toward the source of the evaluation. Because people are generally reluctant to revise their self-appraisals downward (e.g., Baumeister, 1993; Greenwald, 1980; Sullivan, 1953; Swann, 1987), this should tend to be the most common response, and it does increase the likelihood of aggression.

Studies of anger fit the view that it is particularly unjustified attacks that cause it (e.g., Averill, 1982; Baumeister, Stillwell, & Wotman, 1990). The implication is that if people consider another's criticism (or whatever) to be justified, it is less likely to elicit anger. This is not to say that people are always universally fair-minded and objective about whether another person's negative evaluation of them is justified. But that is irrelevant. If the person chooses not to revise his or her self-appraisal in response to a bad evaluation, then he or she is likely to see the evaluation as unjustified, which will cause aggression.

Relevant evidence is provided by studies of shame proneness. Shame is a highly aversive emotion marked by a global condemnation of self (Lewis, 1971; Tangney, 1992). Shame-prone people are also prone to become angry and hostile (Tangney, Wagner, Fletcher, & Gramzow, 1992). At first glance, this finding is counterintuitive because why should an emotion that involves a global condemnation of self lead to an attack on others? It may well be, however, that the anger is a defensive response. Shame-prone people are sensitive to the highly aversive state of feeling that the self is all bad and so they become angry at anyone who tries to make them feel that way. Directing anger outward prevents the person from having to make a downward revision in his or her global self-appraisal.

This analysis is consistent with Katz's (1988) observations on violent street crime. He emphasized that humiliating experiences trigger a defensive rage toward the source of the humiliation, often resulting in a violent attack on that source. This analysis is also consistent with Meloy's (1988) observation that psychopaths feel rage toward others in order to avoid a broad range of (other) unpleasant emotional states, particularly ones that might be directed toward the self.

Research on envy is also relevant. Envy is a form of negative affect based on unfavorable comparisons between the self and others (Salovey, 1991). Smith, Parrott, Ozer, and Moniz (1994) showed that responses to envy depended on whether the other person's advantage was seen as unjustified. Anger and hostility followed mainly when the envious person believed that the other's advantage was indeed unfair. If it was seen as justified, the person tended to feel sad or disappointed, but hostile responses were less likely. The implication is that perceiving another's advantage presents one with the same choice point already discussed. One may see it as justified, conclude that the self is relatively undeserving or unworthy, and sadly accept the situation. Alternatively, one may see it as unjustified, preserve the view of the self as worthy and deserving, and then feel anger toward the source (and perhaps beneficiary) of the unfairness. This path thus maintains the favorable view of self and increases the likelihood of aggression.

THE INTERPERSONAL ASPECT

It is important to recognize that violence is commonly an interpersonal act rather than a random venting of aggressive impulses. Implicit in our discussion thus far has been the point that aggression is often directed specifically at the source of an ego threat. To be sure, there is some evidence that aggression can be displaced toward innocent, unsuspecting other people or even toward inanimate targets such as furniture, but the very concept of displacement implies that there was a very specific target of the original impulse. (Furthermore, evidence for displacement is not strong and is subject to alternative explanations such as mere persistence of negative affect; see Baumeister, Dale, & Sommer, in press.) In a laboratory study, Bushman and Baumeister (in press) found that people showed increased aggression toward someone who had insulted them, but they failed to show increased aggression toward another person, even if they had been insulted.

Hence the final component of our theory is that threatened egotism specifically elicits aggressive impulses directed toward the source of the threat. Insulted individuals strike or abuse the person who insulted them. Threatened groups tend to attack the group who (they think) is encroaching on their privileges.

The specificity of the target suggests a communicative function of aggression. In a sense, the aggression is a form of rebuttal. It is, of course, a remarkably lame one, at least on the surface. Thus, assaulting someone who has derogated your intelligence or insulted your mother does not prove anything about your intelligence or your mother. It may, however, discourage that person (and others) from expressing similar derogatory views in the future. In that sense, aggression can be understood as a coercive action designed to influence the behavior of others, even when there is no direct instrumental gain (see Tedeschi & Felson, 1994). Aggression is one way of inducing others to treat one with respect.

A second interpersonal purpose of aggression following ego threat may be that violent acts (especially successful ones) serve to restore one's esteem in the sense of feeling superior to the victim. Aggression is one means of achieving dominance over another, and dominance may boost self-esteem. People will often respond to threats to their esteem by asserting other positive qualities (Baumeister & Jones, 1978; Steele, 1988), and aggressive dominance may be one such positive quality. Dominating someone who has derogated you may be especially satisfying in this regard. If you are superior to this person, then his or her derogation of you is passed right back.

Research on rape has provided some evidence that aggressive acts can boost a sense of superiority by dominating another person. Groth (1979) concluded that rapists often seem to enjoy the sense of superiority over the victim, and Scully and Marolla (1985) likewise concluded that the desire to feel powerful and superior is one of the main motives to commit rape. Groth also noted that some rapes are precipitated when the man believes that the woman has slighted or offended him, and by raping her he feels he proves her wrong and establishes his superiority. Likewise, marital rape appears to be often motivated by a husband's desire to prove his ownership and superior position over the wife, as well as in some cases to enable him to claim victory during a specific marital conflict (Finkelhor & Yllo, 1985). Martial rape sometimes features particular and unusual sex acts, such as anal sex and public fellatio, that seem best understood in the context of the husband's intention to prove dominance over his wife.

Yet another interpersonal aspect of the relationship between self-esteem and aggressive behavior is the notion that esteem is a scarce resource. In certain groups or areas, esteem may be negotiated in a zero-sum manner (Anderson, 1994); in order for one to gain esteem, another must lose esteem. Thus, any action that can be construed as self-aggrandizing will also be perceived as an ego threat by others in the group or area. One does not have to directly criticize another to initiate a threat to another's ego, thus expanding the range of actions that might be perceived as an ego threat. This notion is similar to that of the "tall poppy" effect (Feather, 1994), in which people tend to take pleasure at the downfall of a highly successful or powerful other. Among certain groups or under certain circumstances, then, esteem may be a precious resource, and any claims to esteem may serve as ego threats for others connected with the group or situation.

Relatively little research has been focused directly on the zero-sum hypothesis of esteem. Undoubtedly there are certain hierarchies in which one person can only rise if another falls, but it is not clear how pervasive these considerations are in most human violence. Indeed, Feather (1994) found the tall poppy effect to be limited to small effects under highly conducive circumstances. Still, there are some observations consistent with this view. Scully (1990) noted that some rapists had selected their victims on the basis of apparent self-esteem, using the rape to bring her down from a position of seeming superiority to one of inferiority.

SUMMARY

Self-appraisals are important to a broad range of human behavior and they play a role in the causation of aggression as well. A large body of evidence contradicts the conventional view that low self-esteem causes violence. Instead, violence and aggression seem to derive most commonly from a highly favorable view of self that encounters an external ego threat. The ego threat often seems to set off a defensive pattern in which the person refuses to accept it and insists on maintaining the favorable self-appraisal. The negative affect (a common result of ego threats) is directed outward, toward the source of the threat, especially insofar as the evaluation is seen as false and unjustified. The negative affect paves the way for an aggressive response, which is also usually directed toward the source of the ego threat. By attacking the source of the threat, the person (or group) symbolically rejects and refutes the threat, discourages further threats of the same kind, and establishes dominance over the person (or group) who had expressed the unfavorable evaluation.

Although we have rejected the view that low self-esteem causes violence, it would be misleading to say simply that high self-esteem causes it. Violent and aggressive acts are perpetrated by a small subset of people who hold favorable views of themselves. We proposed that the likelihood of aggression is increased by anything that can increase the frequency or power of ego threats. In particular, unrealistically positive views of self seem especially likely to encounter ego threats, if only because feedback is sometimes realistic and hence less favorable than an inflated self-appraisal. Also, positive views of self that are unstable or uncertain may make the person especially sensitive to evaluations by others, and so ego threats may be extra powerful—and so all the more likely to produce aggression—when they involve such self-views. Individual differences in narcissism may be the best predictor of violent responses to ego threats. High narcissism is characterized by an inflated or unrealistic, unstable, highly favorable view of self. Narcissism may in short be the nasty, obnoxious form of high self-esteem that leads to aggression.

The threatened egotism model does not purport to explain all acts of aggression and violence. It may, however, explain why certain acts of aggression, which at first glance might seem pointless and damaging to the self, are actually forms of protection of the self from outside threats. To certain individuals and in certain situations, aggression may seem a perfectly appropriate response to threats to one's view of self.

SELF-CONTROL AND AGGRESSION

Our second focus is on the link between self-regulation (more colloquially known as self-control) and aggression. We propose that self-control failure is a pervasive and underappreciated cause of violence.

If one were to list all the factors that have been shown to cause aggression, one would have a long list: anger, frustration, deprivation, opportunity for instrumental gain, desire for power, modeling and media violence, heat, and scapegoating only begin to cover this list. The length of this list is an impressive tribute to the energies of aggression researchers as well as a testimony to the multiplicity of factors that can cause aggression. But it also raises its own theoretical challenge: If so many factors cause aggression, why is aggression not far more common than it is?

To put this another way, it is clear that many people encounter many of the causes of aggression quite frequently without becoming aggressive. It is probably safe to say that during the past week most Americans have been angered or frustrated, have been exposed to media violence, have wanted something that someone else had, or experienced one of the other causes of aggression. Why do most Americans not aggress on that occasion? Why do the causes of aggression so often fail to cause aggression?

Thus, aggression research has perhaps succeeded too well in its initial challenge of identifying the causes of aggression. This success presents a second challenge, which is to explain why aggression is less frequent and pervasive than its causes.

We propose that a crucial answer to this second challenge is that most aggressive impulses or potential responses are prevented by internal restraints. That is, most people have internal blocks and inhibitions that prevent them from acting in a violent or aggressive fashion even when they experience states or situations that might otherwise lead to a violent response (see Baumeister, 1997; Baumeister, Heatherton, & Tice, 1994).

If this analysis is correct, then causal theories about aggression should include a place for the failure of these inner restraints. Indeed, the final proximate cause of aggression may generally be self-regulation failure. This is not to question the evidence that provocation, anger, frustration, high temperature, and many other factors cause aggression. Rather, it proposes that those causes are not a full explanation because many people experience them without becoming aggressive, insofar as people are held back by their internal restraints. Aggression results when provocation, anger, frustration, or other factors create aggressive impulses *and* the internal restraints are defeated.

There is thus another important and central role that self-theory may deserve in the psychology of aggression. One of the crucial functions of the self is its *executive function,* which makes choices and decisions and which exerts control over the self's responses. People are able to override and inhibit many responses or tendencies, and the self consists partly of a structure to accomplish that. Normally, the self will inhibit and prevent violent action even when one is provoked. The failure or abandonment of such self-control is an important link in the causal chain leading to aggression.

SELF-CONTROL FAILURE AND VIOLENCE

We begin with the issue of whether self-control is indeed central to aggression. Ironically, the strongest statement regarding the importance of this psychological variable has not been made by psychologists. A 1990 work by Gottfredson and Hirschi called *A General Theory of Crime* argued that lack of self-control may be the broadest and most important cause of crime. Because of the importance of their argument, we shall summarize it here.

Gottfredson and Hirschi (1990) contend that the research effort to explain specific crimes misses some crucial points that become apparent when one focuses on understanding criminality in general. In their view, certain people are characterized by chronic deficits in self-control, and these people are the ones most likely to commit crimes. To support their position, they provide considerable evidence contradicting the popular view that criminals specialize in only one type of crime and are in other respects similar to everyone else. Gottfredson and Hirschi's review shows repeatedly that most people who are arrested for some crime are later arrested for a different kind of crime. Therefore it is misleading to try to explain why someone becomes a thief or a rapist. Instead, one must understand that most such crimes occur in the context of a broad criminal life-style, in which laws are generally not respected.

Specific crimes are therefore often the result of chance, opportunity, and impulse. Gottfredson and Hirschi argue quite plausibly that the reason convenience stores are relative frequent targets of robbery is that they are, in fact, convenient. By the same token, many criminals who rationalize their violent deeds as the result of oppression by a different social or racial group often do not direct their violence at their supposed oppressors but instead at their supposedly fellow victims (e.g., McCall, 1994; Shakur, 1993), again because they tend to come into contact more easily and readily with other people like themselves. Indeed, there is an irony in the view that poverty causes crime because poor people are also most frequently victimized by crime. Gottfredson and Hirschi note that in the majority of burglaries, the burglar walked to the place he (or, less often, she) robbed, which again is an indication of the convenience aspect.

The impulsive, unplanned, and unskilled nature of crime is also a reflection of low self-control, according to Gottfredson and Hirschi. Unlike movie villains who develop exceptional skills and make detailed plans, most crimes occur on the spur of the moment and involve almost no skill. Gottfredson and Hirschi cite cases in which passengers in the car were not even aware that the driver had robbed the store at which they stopped, at least not until someone ran out of the store and fired shots at them while they sped off. Meanwhile, Gottfredson and Hirschi contrast the discipline and education needed to make a decent living by honest means with the relative ease of pointing a gun at someone and demanding cash.

The final piece in their argument is the evidence that criminals tend to show patterns of poor self-control even in legal activities. Gottfredson and Hirschi review multiple studies showing that criminals are more likely than other people to smoke cigarettes, drink alcohol to excess, be involved in unplanned pregnancies, have unstable romantic relationships, gamble, and so forth. Moreover, even the rare big score does not produce a lasting change for the typical criminal in the way it might for someone with self-control. Few criminals invest the proceeds in stocks or bonds or other long-term sources of income. Instead, they tend to spend all the money in a short time on sources of immediate gratification, such as drinking or drug binges, shopping sprees, gambling, and brief romantic liaisons (see also Katz, 1988). Such liberal spending enhances their status among their acquaintances but quickly leaves them in a position of needing more money in order to sustain this prestige and life-style.

Thus, there is a convincing argument to be made for the central role of self-control in the causation of crime. Committing crimes is the opposite of delaying gratification and controlling one's impulses: It offers immediate rewards, requires no planning or skill, and is exciting. The view of crime as the result of a specialized career choice is misleading. Rather, most criminals commit many different kinds of crimes, as the opportunities arise, and they also tend to exhibit poor self-control in other spheres of life.

WHY SELF-CONTROL?

The importance of self-control to crime can be appreciated by understanding just what self-control (or self-regulation) does. According to Baumeister, Heatherton, and Tice (1994), the essence of self-regulation is the overriding of responses or tendencies that would otherwise occur. Self-control can in large part be understood as the capacity to prevent oneself from responding in a certain way.

The application to violence and aggression is obvious: Self-control allows people to refrain from lashing out at someone who has provoked or frustrated them. People may be prepared by nature to respond aggressively in some situations, and in addition they learn to feel and act violently on many occasions. But they also learn how to inhibit and prevent these violent responses. Successful socialization should teach individuals to endure frustrations, provocations, and other aggressive instigations without becoming aggressive in response. The psychology of aggression thus has an important overlap with the psychology of self-regulation failure. Put another way, aggression occurs when people fail to exert control over their feelings and responses.

Why does self-regulation fail? Clearly there are multiple causes (for review, see Baumeister, Heatherton, & Tice, 1994; also Baumeister & Heatherton, 1996). Self-regulation fails when people lack clear, consistent internal standards or when they hold conflicting standards. It fails when people fail to monitor their actions. It also fails when they lack the strength needed to override their undesirable impulses. Let us comment on each of these briefly.

The problem of standards is probably not as important for aggression as the others, but there are circumstances in which standards may conflict. Most people find it difficult to aggress even when they are supposed to do so. For example, Keegan (1976) cites evidence that the majority of soldiers in wartime find themselves unable to bring themselves to aim at and shoot the enemy, at least at first. Most societies and cultures condemn violence by and large, but there are circumstances when it may be considered appropriate to act aggressively to defend oneself, one's honor, one's family, or others. Borderline cases may indeed invoke conflicting standards and make self-regulation difficult.

The failure to monitor one's actions is a more important cause than inadequate standards of self-regulation failure. Indeed, without attending to (monitoring) what one is doing, it is difficult to control it or bring it up to relevant standards (see Carver & Scheier, 1981). Loss of self-awareness, which prevents the meaningful monitoring of one's own actions, is relevant to a variety of aggressive patterns.

Alcohol, for example, reduces self-awareness and inhibits the thoughtful monitoring of one's own actions (see Hull, 1981), and alcohol abuse has been widely implicated in the majority of forms of self-regulation failure, ranging from poor emotional control to gambling (for review, see Baumeister, Heatherton, & Tice, 1994). Alcohol is also commonly implicated in a broad range of crimes (National Research Council, 1993; see also Bushman & Cooper, 1990). Indeed, Gelles (1974) suggested that alcohol may be used intentionally by people intending to commit a violent act. Alcohol is also used deliberately in noncriminal violence. For example, Keegan (1976) has described the common practice of preparing soldiers for battle by giving them special alcohol rations. Also, Browning (1992) described the Nazi officers in charge of killing Jews during the Holocaust as being chronically drunk, especially when on duty. In these cases, drinking may have decreased the person's self-awareness and reduced the extent to which he monitored his behavior, thus allowing the violent behavior to occur.

Likewise, anonymity and deindividuation increase aggressive activity, in laboratory studies as well as in actual crime (Zimbardo, 1970; also Mullen, 1986). Deindividuation involves loss of individual self-awareness, allowing a broader range of uninhibited behavior to occur, and aggression seems to be one such behavior that is thereby facilitated. In particular, Mullen (1986) suggested that when individuals in a lynch mob tended to lose self-awareness to the furthest extent (i.e., when the ratio of group size to number of victims was greatest), the lynchings were especially violent and atrocious. The loss of self-awareness, then, may be an important step in the reduction of the ability to monitor behavior. When one cannot monitor behavior to see how well it matches standards, it may be very difficult to control impulses toward violence and aggression.

The third cause of self-regulation failure, lack of strength, is less well understood than the others but probably no less important. If aggressive impulses have strength, then the capacity for self-control must have comparable strength in order to overcome them. When strength is depleted, aggression becomes more likely. A variety of observations fit these patterns. Thus, most violent crimes occur late at night, presumably when self-regulatory strength is depleted (Gottfredson & Hirschi, 1990). Emotional distress also appears to deplete regulatory strength, if only because people often try to cope by making themselves feel better (Isen, 1984; Muraven, Tice, & Baumeister, in press). Emotional distress is associated with a broad range of aggressive and criminal acts (e.g., Berkowitz, 1989). Moreover, some people seem chronically lacking in regulatory strength, as shown by the fact that failure to delay gratification at age 4 predicts social and academic success in high school and college (Mischel, Shoda, & Peake, 1988; Shoda, Mischel, & Peake, 1990), and such dispositional patterns may help explain why criminals seem to show such poor self-control in multiple spheres of life (Gottfredson & Hirschi, 1990).

ACQUIESCENCE

As noted earlier, failure or abandonment of self-control is an important cause of aggression. The distinction between failure and abandonment is an important one. It is therefore worth asking, does aggression occur because people are unable to restrain their violent impulses or do they somehow choose to act on them? This is more than a merely theoretical debate, although the theoretical issues are important and fascinating. Judgments and sentencing of many defendants often depend heavily on the issue of whether they could have refrained from perpetuating their violent acts. Defense lawyers are fond of notions of irresistible impulses and similar views that imply that no normal person could have held back from violent action under the circumstances, whereas prosecutors try to depict actions as deliberate and cold-blooded (i.e., done with full possession of one's faculties). Likewise, prisons and parole boards must face the question of whether a convicted violent offender will be likely to become violent again upon release, and if an inability to restrain one's aggression impulses was apparent in the crime then there is reason to think that rehabilitation must somehow increase the capacity for self-control before it is safe to release the individual.

The question of acquiescence versus being overwhelmed comes up in a great many spheres of self-regulation failure. After an extensive review of the research literature, Baumeister, Heatherton, and Tice (1994) concluded that there are relatively few impulses that are truly irresistible and that people generally acquiesce to some degree in their loss of control. For the most part, the notion of irresistible violent impulses seems to be a self-serving construction of defense lawyers and of perpetrators wishing for forgiveness rather than a psychological fact. Exceptions are possible, but they are just that: exceptions.

Research on aggression has provided some evidence relevant to the issue of acquiescence (i.e., choosing to abandon self-control). From self-reports of violent episodes, Berkowitz (1978) quoted a man who had been imprisoned for beating up his wife's lover. While beating the man, the perpetrator had broken a bottle to use as a weapon against the man, but he had not used the bottle in the fight. The perpetrator reported that he had thought at the time that if he used the bottle he might well kill the other man, which he did not want to do, so he set aside the bottle and continued the beating. That moment of rational thought suggests that he was capable of self-control because he stopped himself from exceeding a certain limit in his violent action. If his violent impulses had been truly uncontrollable, he certainly would not have been able to choose whether he wanted to use a particular weapon based on possible outcomes. Similar cases were reported by Tavris (1989). In one, a man who rationalized his beating his wife by saying that his anger became uncontrollable was asked by his therapist how he refrained from killing her. He too acknowledged that he stopped his violent actions at the point at which they would become too costly for him (see also Gelles, 1979).

Another relevant example concerns the highly disciplined aggression in professional football (see Baumeister et al., 1994). In particular, defensive players often use emotional stimuli and other techniques to make themselves highly aggressive in their efforts to knock the opposing quarterback roughly to the ground. Yet they wait motionless (well, most of the time) until the play begins, whereupon they set off on a ferocious attack directed at that quarterback. Once past the blockers, they may charge all out toward the hapless target with full intention of inflicting a bruising tackle on him. If the quarterback manages to throw the ball or step out of bounds, thereby ceasing to be a legal target for tackling, they must instantly stop their charge and not touch him. Occasionally they do inflict what is called a "late hit" on the quarterback, but these exceptions are to us less revealing than the general success of these combative young men at turning their aggression fully on and off on a second-by-second basis.

An important collective pattern involved the "running amok" among the Malay. The Malays believed that under some circumstances an individual would lose control and become wildly destructive. There was thus a strong cultural basis for the belief that some violent actions could not be restrained. During the period of British rule, however, severe penalties were instituted for running amok, and the practice decreased dramatically (Carr & Tan, 1976). Apparently the individuals could control themselves after all.

The latter pattern is particularly relevant to the issue of cultural and subcultural supports for violence. Tedeschi and Felson (1994) have furnished a compelling account and critique of the notion that *subcultures of violence* exist. This notion emerged in the 1960s to explain high crime rates among disadvantaged urban minorities: It held that certain subcultures place a positive value on violence and so people act aggressively to suit their cultural prescriptions and to gain prestige and respect for doing so. The theory gradually was discredited as researchers were unable to show that any subcultures placed a positive value on violence or that people performed violent acts in the belief that these would gain them respect for conforming to subcultural ideals (see also Berkowitz, 1978).

The role of self-control may, however, suggest a way to salvage part of the theory that certain subcultures promote violence, as argued by Baumeister, Heatherton, and Tice (1994). As stated earlier, there are plenty of causes of violence, and so to get more violence it is not at all necessary to provide further positive causes of it: It is merely necessary to weaken the restraints. A culture or subculture may get high levels of violence simply by promoting the belief that it is appropriate to lose control under certain circumstances.

This, after all, is what the traditional Malays had done. They did not hold that running amok was a desirable, commendable experience that should be rewarded. They merely believed that certain frustrations or provocations were sufficient to cause people to run amok. By the same token, urban gangs often have a finely honed sense of which insults can be ignored, which ones must be reciprocated, and which ones may and ought to elicit violent response. In short, subcultures of violence can exist by promoting norms that legitimize losing control under certain circumstances.

There is after all a long continuum of minor to severe provocations, and there is also a continuum of aggressive response ranging from verbal riposte to grisly homicide. Culture and socialization can exert considerable control over where people draw the lines beyond which the internal restraints against aggression are set aside, and to what extent they are. This is not to say that people are evil because they allow themselves to lose control and commit violent acts. Rather, it says that people learn from their culture at what point they are entitled or even expected to become violent.

To round out this analysis, it must be emphasized that self-control is often difficult and strenuous. Swallowing one's rage may take considerable effort and may also be aversive, whereas expressing it may offer at least an intense satisfaction, even if it is brief. Like dieters, recovering alcoholics, sexually abstinent people, or people trying to quit smoking, many an individual may find it takes frequent effort to refrain from indulging the temptation to lash out at some source of provocation. The prospect of letting go of that control and indulging one's impulses may therefore be appealing. Socialization and culture help define the points at which it is considered acceptable to do so. A subculture of violence may simply be one in which this permission to give in is granted more freely, i.e., at lower levels of exertion and of provocation, than others.

SUMMARY

The preceding discussion has attempted to demonstrate that one of the primary causes of aggressive and violent behavior is the failure to control or regulate violent impulses. The ability to control behavior is subject to a number of factors, including standards for behavior, the ability to monitor one's behavior, and the strength to control or change behavior. The commission of violent actions may be a result of a failure to monitor behavior or a lack of adequate strength to control violent impulses. Also, violent and aggressive behavior may also be the result of failing to transcend the immediate moment, which may disrupt a person's ability to regulate behavior. Finally, violent acts may often occur when a person chooses not to control their aggressive and violent impulses.

Thus violent and aggressive behavior may be viewed as one important type of failure to regulate behavior. As Baumeister et al. (1994) pointed out, many of the problems that plague individuals in modern society may be traced to the failure to control behavior adequately. Aggression and violence are among the major problems facing society today; the view of violence as stemming from the failure to control behavior would suggest that the cultivation of the ability to control our own behavior might be one way to alleviate some of our most pressing problems.

CONCLUDING REMARKS

Violence is one of the most important social problems facing modern society. Evidence presented in this chapter suggests that two important aspects of the self, self-esteem and self-control, may be related in important ways to aggressive behavior. Although behaving aggressively is subject to sanctions and other difficulties for the self, people continue to behave violently. It may be that under certain circumstances, aggression may serve the self by protecting the self against attacks that seem arbitrary or unwarranted. Furthermore, one's ability to exercise control over violent and aggressive impulses may also play an important role in the overt expression of such impulses. As such, important processes of the self may be closely linked to the occurrence of violent behavior.

Although we have emphasized the theoretical links between self and aggression, there are certainly some potentially important practical applications. The United States has for at least a decade been involved in a broad effort to boost self-esteem in the hope that it will (among other benefits) reduce violence (e.g., Adler, 1992; California Task Force, 1990). Our analysis suggests that this hope may have been quite fundamentally misguided. Raising self-esteem—in other words, making people generally more egotistical—is a questionable strategy for making them more pacific. Indeed, boosting self-esteem by itself might even increase violence, insofar as it creates favorable self-views that are inflated or uncertain. Certainly the poor record of the self-esteem movement, as well as the weight of empirical evidence we have reviewed, suggests that modesty and humility deserve to be tried as antidotes to violence.

In our view, however, the most promising and likely candidate for a psychological antidote to violence is self-control. Our reading of the evidence leads us to recommend that parents, schools, and others forget about raising self-esteem and concentrate instead on instilling self-control (which in fact seems to confer a broad range of advantages beyond stifling aggression). If we are correct in our analysis that the causes of aggression are legion and the inner workings of self-control are the most important restraining factor, then conceivably self-control is relevant to the vast majority of aggression and violence. We are not naive enough to expect that our nation can become a Utopian society in which every person can always exert full control over all his or her responses. Still, we think a 10% improvement in self-control would have a much more desirable effect on the crime rate than a 10% increase in self-esteem.

Self-control and self-esteem are not likely to be the only aspects of self theory that have implications for the psychology of aggression. We encourage other researchers to develop some of the others. Still, self-control failure and threatened egotism appear to be common, important causes of aggression. A greater exchange of ideas and findings between self researchers and aggression researchers seems likely to enrich both fields.

ACKNOWLEDGMENT

Preparation of this chapter was aided by a grant from the National Institutes of Health, MH 51482.

REFERENCES

Adler, J. (1992). Hey, I'm terrific! *Newsweek,* February 17, 46–51.

Anastasia, G. (1991). *Blood and honor: Inside the Scarfo mob—the Mafia's most violent family.* New York: Morrow.

Anderson, E. (1994). The code of the streets. *Atlantic Monthly, 273* (#5: May), 81–94.

Arlacchi, P. (1992). *Men of dishonor: Inside the Sicilian mafia.* (M. Romano, trans.). New York: Morrow.

Averill, J. (1982). *Anger and aggression: An essay on emotion.* New York: Springer-Verlag.

Banaji, M. R., & Steele, C. M. (1989). Alcohol and self-evaluation: Is a social cognition approach beneficial? *Social Cognition, 7,* 137–151.

Baron, R. A. (1976). The reduction of human aggression: A field study on the influence of incompatible responses. *Journal of Applied Social Psychology, 6,* 95–104.

Baumeister, R. F. (1993). Understanding the inner nature of low self-esteem: Uncertain, fragile, protective, and conflicted. In R. Baumeister (Ed.), *Self-esteem: The puzzle of low self-regard* (pp. 201–218). New York: Plenum.

Baumeister, R. F. (1997). *Evil: Inside human violence and cruelty.* New York: Freeman.

Baumeister, R. F. (in press). The self. In G. Lindzey, S. Fiske, & D. Gilbert (Eds.), *Handbook of social psychology* (4th ed.). New York: McGraw-Hill.

Baumeister, R. F., Dale, K., & Sommer, K. L. (in press). Defense mechanisms in modern personality and social psychology. *Journal of Personality.*

Baumeister, R. F., & Heatherton, T. F. (1996). Self-regulation failure: An overview. *Psychological Inquiry, 7,* 1–15.

Baumeister, R. F., Heatherton, T. F., & Tice, D. M. (1993). When ego threats lead to self-regulation failure: Negative consequences of high self-esteem. *Journal of Personality and Social Psychology, 64,* 141–156.

Baumeister, R. F., Heatherton, T. F., & Tice, D. M. (1994). *Losing control: How and why people fail at self-regulation.* San Diego, CA: Academic Press.

Baumeister, R. F., & Jones, E. E. (1978). When self-presentation is constrained by the target's knowledge: Consistency and compensation, *Journal of Personality and Social Psychology, 36,* 608–618.

Baumeister, R. F., Smart, L., & Boden, J. M. (1996). Relation of threatened egotism to violence and aggression: The dark side of high self-esteem. *Psychological Review, 103,* 5–33.

Baumeister, R. F., Stillwell, A., & Wotman, S. R. (1990). Victim and perpetrator accounts of interpersonal conflict: Autobiographical narratives about anger. *Journal of Personality and Social Psychology, 59,* 994–1005.

Berkowitz, L. (1978). Is criminal violence normative behavior? Hostile and instrumental aggression in violent incidents. *Journal of Research in Crime and Delinquency, 15,* 148–161.

Berkowitz, L. (1989). Frustration-aggression hypothesis: Examination and reformulation. *Psychological Bulletin, 106,* 59–73.

Berkowitz, L., & Geen, R. G. (1966). Film violence and the cue properties of available targets. *Journal of Personality and Social Psychology, 3,* 525–530.

Bing, L. (1991). *Do or die.* New York: HarperCollins.

Browning, C. R. (1992). *Ordinary men: Reserve police battalion 101 and the final solution in Poland.* New York: HarperCollins.

Bushman, B. M., & Baumeister, R. F. (in press). Threatened egotism, narcissism, self-esteem, and direct and displaced aggression: Does self-love or self-hate lead to violence? *Journal of Personality and Social Psychology.*

Bushman, B. J., & Cooper, H. M. (1990). Effects of alcohol on human aggression: An integrative research review. *Psychological Bulletin, 107,* 341–354.

California Task Force to Promote Self-esteem and Personal and Social Responsibility (1990). *Toward a state of self-esteem.* Sacramento, CA: California State Department of Education.

Carr, J. E., & Tan, E. K. (1976). In search of the true Amok: Amok as viewed within the Malay culture. *American Journal of Psychiatry, 133,* 1295–1299.

Carver, C. S., & Scheier, M. F. (1981). *Attention and self-regulation: A control theory approach to human behavior.* New York: Springer-Verlag.

Chirot, D. (1994). *Modern tyrants: The power and prevalence of evil in our age.* New York: Free Press.

Christensen, M. J., Brayden, R. M., Dietrich, M. S., McLaughlin, F. J., Sherrod, K. B., & Altemeier, W. A. (1994). The prospective assessment of self-concept in neglectful and physically abusive low-income mothers. *Child Abuse and Neglect, 18,* 225–232.

Crocker, J., & Major, B. (1989). Social stigma and self-esteem: The self-protective properties of stigma. *Psychological Review, 96,* 608–630.

Currie, E. (1991). *Dope and trouble: Portraits of delinquent youth.* New York: Pantheon.

Diamond, D. L., & Wilsnack, S. C. (1978). Alcohol abuse among lesbians: A descriptive study. *Journal of Homosexuality, 4,* 205–216.

Dollard, J., Doob, L., Miller, N., Mowrer, O., & Sears, R. (1939). *Frustration and aggression.* New Haven, CT: Yale University Press.

Feather, N. T. (1994). Attitudes toward high achievers and reactions to their fall: Theory and research concerning tall poppies. In M. Zanna (Ed.), *Advances in experimental social psychology* (Vol. 26, pp. 1–73). San Diego, CA: Academic Press.

Finkelhor, D., & Yllo, K. (1985). *License to rape: Sexual abuse of wives.* New York: Free Press.

Geen, R. G. (1990). *Human aggression.* Pacific Grove, CA: Brooks/Cole.

Gelles, R. J. (1974). *The violent home.* Beverly Hills, CA: Sage.

Gelles, R. J. (1979). *Family violence.* Beverly Hills, CA: Sage.

Gelles, R. J., & Straus, M. A. (1988). *Intimate violence: The causes and consequences of abuse in the American family.* New York: Simon & Schuster/Touchstone.

Goldstein, D., & Rosenbaum, A. (1985). An evaluation of the self-esteem of maritally violent men. *Family Relations, 34,* 425–428.

Gottfredson, M. R., & Hirschi, T. (1990). *A general theory of crime.* Stanford, CA: Stanford University Press.

Greenwald, A. G. (1980). The totalitarian ego: Fabrication and revision of personal history. *American Psychologist, 35,* 603–618.

Groth, A. N. (1979). *Men who rape: The psychology of the offender.* New York: Plenum.

Gurr, T. R. (1979). On the history of violent crimes in Europe and America: In H. D. Graham & T. R. Gurr (Eds.), *Violence in America: Historical and comparative perspectives* (pp. 353–374). Beverly Hills, CA: Sage.

Hamm, M. S. (1993). *American skinheads: The criminology and control of hate crime.* Westport, CT: Praeger.

Hare, R. D. (1993). *Without conscience: The disturbing world of the psychopaths among us.* New York: Simon & Schuster/Pocket.

Harter, S. (1993). Causes and consequences of low self-esteem in children and adolescents. In R. Baumeister (Ed.), *Self-esteem: The puzzle of low self-regard* (pp. 87–116). New York: Plenum.

Hauser, S. T. (1991). *Adolescents and their families.* New York: Free Press.

Heatherton, T. F., & Polivy, J. (1991). Development and validation of a scale for measuring state self-esteem. *Journal of Personality and Social Psychology, 60,* 895–910.

Holtzworth-Munroe, A. (1992). Attributions and maritally violent men: The role of cognitions in marital violence. In J. Harvey, T. Orbuch, & A. Weber (Eds.), *Attributions, accounts, and close relationships.* New York: Springer-Verlag.

Hornung, C. A., McCullough, B. C., & Sugimoto, T. (1981). Status relationships in marriage: Risk factors in spouse abuse. *Journal of Marriage and the Family, 43,* 675–692.

Hull, J. G. (1981). A self-awareness model of the causes and effects of alcohol consumption. *Journal of Abnormal Psychology, 90,* 586–600.

Ianni, F. A. J. (1989). *The search for structure.* New York: Free Press.

Isen, A. M. (1984). Toward understanding the role of affect in cognition. In J. R. S. Wyer & T. S. Srull (Eds.), *Handbook of social cognition* (Vol. 3). Hillsdale, NJ: Erlbaum.

Jankowski, M. S. (1991). *Islands in the street: Gangs and American urban society.* Berkeley, CA: University of California Press.

Katz, J. (1988). *Seductions of crime: Moral and sensual attractions in doing evil.* New York: Basic Books.

Keegan, J. (1976). *The face of battle.* New York: Military Heritage Press.

Kernis, M. H. (1993). The roles of stability and level of self-esteem in psychological functioning. In R. Baumeister (Ed.), *Self-esteem: The puzzle of low self-regard* (pp. 167–182). New York: Plenum.

Kernis, M. H., Cornell, D. P., Sun, C. R., Berry, A., & Harlow, T. (1993). There's more to self-esteem than whether it's high or low: The importance of stability of self-esteem. *Journal of Personality and Social Psychology, 65,* 1190–1204.

Kernis, M. H., Grannemann, B. D., & Barclay, L. C. (1989). Stability and level of self-esteem as predictors of anger arousal and hostility. *Journal of Personality and Social Psychology, 56,* 1013–1022.

Kiernan, V. G. (1989). *The duel in European history.* Oxford, England: Oxford University Press.

Levin, J., & McDevitt, J. (1993). *Hate crimes: The rising tide of bigotry and bloodshed.* New York: Plenum.

Lewis, H. B. (1971). *Shame and guilt in neurosis.* New York: International Universities Press.

Long, D. E. (1990). *The anatomy of terrorism.* New York: Free Press.

MacDonald, J. M. (1975). *Armed robbery: Offenders and their victims.* Springfield, IL: Thomas.

McCall, N. (1994). *Makes me wanna holler: A young black man in America.* New York: Random House.

McFarlin, D. B., & Blascovich, J. (1981). Effects of self-esteem and performance feedback on future affective preferences and cognitive expectations. *Journal of Personality and Social Psychology, 40,* 521–531.

Meloy, J. R. (1988). *The psychopathic mind: Origins, dynamics, and treatment.* Northvale, NJ: Aronson.

Mischel, W., Shoda, Y., & Peake, P. K. (1988). The nature of adolescent competencies predicted by preschool delay of gratification. *Journal of Personality and Social Psychology, 54,* 687–696.

Mullen, B. (1986). Atrocity as a function of lynch mob composition. *Personality and Social Psychology Bulletin, 12,* 187–197.

Muraven, M., Tice, D. M., & Baumeister, R. F. (in press). Self-control as limited resource: Regulatory depletion patterns. *Journal of Personality and Social Psychology.*

National Research Council (1993). *Understanding and preventing violence.* Washington, DC: National Academy Press.

Oates, R. K., & Forrest, D. (1985). Self-esteem and early background of abusive mothers. *Child Abuse and Neglect, 9,* 89–93.

Olweus, D. (1994). Bullying at school: Long-term outcomes for the victims and an effective school-based intervention program. In R. Huesmann (Ed.), *Aggressive behavior: Current perspectives* (pp. 97–130). New York: Plenum.

Polk, K. (1993). Observations on stranger homicide. *Journal of Criminal Justice, 21,* 573–582.

Raskin, R., Novacek, J., & Hogan, R. (1991). Narcissistic self-esteem management. *Journal of Personality and Social Psychology, 60,* 911–918.

Renzetti, C. M. (1992). *Violent betrayal: Partner abuse in lesbian relationships.* Newbury Park, CA: Sage.

Rhodewalt, F., Madrian, J. C., & Cheney, S. (1997). Narcissism and self-esteem instability: The effects of self-knowledge organization and daily social interaction on self-esteem and affect. Manuscript submitted for publication.

Salovey, P. (1991). Social comparison processes in envy and jealousy. In J. Suls & T. A. Wills (Eds.), *Social comparison: Contemporary theory and research.* Hillsdale, NJ: Erlbaum.

Schlenker, B. R., Soraci, S., & McCarthy, B. (1976). Self-esteem and group performance as determinants of egocentric perceptions in cooperative groups. *Human Relations, 29,* 1163–1176.

Scully, D. (1990). *Understanding sexual violence: A study of convicted rapists.* New York: HarperCollins.

Scully, D., & Marolla, J. (1985). "Riding the bull at Gilley's:" Convicted rapists describe the rewards of rape. *Social Problems, 32,* 251–263.

Sebald, J. (1984). *Adolescence: A social psychological analysis.* Englewood Cliffs, NJ: Prentice-Hall.

Shakur, S. (1993). *Monster: The autobiography of an L.A. gang member.* New York: Atlantic Monthly Press.

Shoda, Y., Mischel, W., & Peake, P. K. (1990). Predicting adolescent cognitive and self-regulatory competencies from preschool delay of gratification: Identifying diagnostic conditions. *Developmental Psychology, 26,* 978–986.

Smith, R. H., Parrott, W. G., Ozer, D., & Moniz, A. (1994). Subjective injustice and inferiority as predictors of hostile and depressive feelings in envy. *Personality and Social Psychology Bulletin, 20,* 717–723.

Steele, C. M. (1988). The psychology of self-affirmation: Sustaining the integrity of the self. In L. Berkowitz (Ed.), *Advances in experimental social psychology* (Vol. 21, pp. 261–302). New York: Academic Press.

Sullivan, H. S. (1953). *The interpersonal theory of psychiatry.* New York: Norton.

Swann, W. B. (1987). Identity negotiation: Where two roads meet. *Journal of Personality and Social Psychology, 53,* 1038–1051.

Tangney, J. P. (1992). Situational determinants of shame and guilt in young adulthood. *Personality and Social Psychology Bulletin, 18,* 199–206.

Tangney, J. P., Wagner, P. E., Fletcher, C., & Gramzow, R. (1992). Shamed into anger? The relation of shame and guilt to anger and self-reported aggression. *Journal of Personality and Social Psychology, 62,* 669–675.

Tavris, C. (1989). *Anger: The misunderstood emotion.* New York: Simon & Shuster (Touchstone).

Tedeschi, J. T., & Felson, R. B. (1994). *Aggression and coercive actions: A social interactionist perspective.* Washington, DC: American Psychological Association.

Tennen, H., & Affleck, G. (1993). The puzzles of low self-esteem: A clinical perspective. In R. Baumeister (Ed.), *Self-esteem: The puzzle of low self-regard* (pp. 241–262). New York: Plenum.

Toch, H. (1993). *Violent men: An inquiry into the psychology of violence.* Washington, DC: American Psychological Association. Original work published in 1969.

Wade, W. C. (1987). *The fiery cross: The Ku Klux Klan in America.* New York: Touchstone/Simon & Schuster.

Walker, L. E. (1979). *The battered woman.* New York: Harper and Row.

Wicklund, R. A., & Gollwitzer, P. M. (1982). *Symbolic self-completion.* Hillsdale, NJ: Erlbaum.

Wilson, J. Q., & Herrnstein, R. J. (1985). *Crime and human nature.* New York: Simon & Schuster.

Wink, P. (1991). Two faces of narcissism. *Journal of Personality and Social Psychology, 61,* 590–597.

Zimbardo, P. G. (1970). The human choice: Individuation, reason, and order versus deindividuation, impulse and chaos. In W. J. Arnold & D. Levine (Eds.), *Nebraska symposium on motivation* (pp. 237–307). Lincoln, NE: University of Nebraska Press.

6

PSYCHOACTIVE DRUGS
AND HUMAN AGGRESSION[1]

STUART P. TAYLOR AND MICHAEL R. HULSIZER

Kent State University

A wide variety of drugs are presumed to be related to aggressive behavior. In an earlier review (Taylor & Leonard, 1983), the evidence concerning the effect of alcohol on human aggressive behavior was scrutinized. The authors concluded, "Alcohol does appear to be a potent causal antecedent of aggressive behavior" (p. 97). This conclusion was confirmed in a more recent review (Taylor & Chermack, 1993). The purpose of this chapter is to critically examine the effects of several other commonly used psychoactive drugs on human aggression: marijuana, amphetamines, benzodiazepines, and morphine. This chapter describes the classification of major psychoactive drugs, discusses the traditional empirical and theoretical perspectives concerning the relationship between psychoactive drugs and aggression, reviews the results of a series of experiments designed to examine the instigating effects of psychoactive drugs, and considers the theoretical and policy implications of the empirical evidence.

CLASSIFICATION OF PSYCHOACTIVE DRUGS

One of the most traditional methods of classifying psychoactive drugs is in terms of their characteristic behavioral or clinical effects. Less typical drug classification schemes involve molecular structure and biochemical actions. Some of the major categories of drugs that alter behavior or mood are stimulants, depressants, opiates, hallucinogens/psychedelics, and marijuana.

[1]Correspondence concerning this chapter should be addressed to Stuart P. Taylor, Department of Psychology, Kent State University, Kent, OH 44242, or to Michael R. Hulsizer, who is now at the Department of Behavioral and Social Sciences, Webster University, St. Louis, MO 63119.

Stimulants consist of compounds that excite the central nervous system (CNS). It is widely accepted that while stimulants increase arousal, alertness, and euphoria, they also decrease fatigue and depression. Commonly consumed stimulants are cocaine, amphetamine, caffeine, and nicotine. Stimulants have been used to treat hyperkinetic and affective disorders.

Depressants include a wide variety of drugs with diverse chemical structures that are capable of inducing progressive depression of the CNS. There appears to be a general consensus that the depressant effects vary along a continuum from anxiety relief to sedation, sleep, and, finally, coma and death. The basic category includes alcohol, barbiturates, antihistamines, and benzodiazepines. Depressants have been used as anesthetics and for the treatment of epilepsy, insomnia, and anxiety.

Opiates, often called narcotic analgesics or opioids, refer to natural or synthetic drugs that have morphine-like actions. This category includes drugs such as morphine and codeine, which are purified from crude opium, and compounds such as heroin, derived from alterations of morphine, and synthetic analgesics. The major psychological effects of drugs such as morphine are euphoria and analgesia. Clinically, opiates are mainly used as painkillers. In fact, there appears to be a consensus in the medical literature that there is no class of drugs superior to opiates for analgesia.

The most commonly used products derived from cannabis sativa in this country are marijuana and hashish. Marijuana is a smoking preparation and consists of a mixture of crushed leaves and flowers. The active compound, Δ^9-tetrahydrocannabinol (THC), is concentrated in the resin obtained from the flowers of the plant. While marijuana effects vary widely from person to person, THC users often report enhanced taste, smell, and touch, an alteration in time perception, an increased sense of well-being, relaxation, and mild euphoria. Nonmedicinal use of marijuana is illegal in the United States. However, there is some indication that it is efficacious in the treatment of glaucoma, epilepsy, chronic pain, and nausea.

Hallucinogens, or psychedelics, cause distortions in perception, cognition, and mood. They tend to alter time and space perception, sense of body image, and sensitivity to sounds, shapes, and textures. Some of the compounds typically included in this category are lysergic acid diethylamide (LSD), phencyclidine (PCP), psilocybin, MDNA (also known as "Ecstasy"), and mescaline. Generally, hallucinogens have no recognized clinical use.

Contemporary psychopharmacologists often categorize drugs in terms of their full dose–response curves (Leccese, 1991). This approach allows for the creation of categories that include drugs that produce similar effects despite differences in basic pharmacology. Thus, certain drugs would be categorized as stimulants if they result in increased attention, heart rate, and wakefulness at low doses; insomnia, stereotypical motor movements, tremors, and highly elevated cardiac activity at moderate doses, and confusion, paranoia, and possible convulsions at very high doses. This category would include such drugs as caffeine, nicotine, amphetamine, and cocaine. A number of other drugs would be categorized as depressants if they tended to reduce motor coordination at low doses; produced loss of coordination, sleepiness, and depressed breathing at moderate doses; and caused coma and death at very high doses. This category would include antihistamines, benzodiazepines, opiates, and alcohol. Leccese (1991), who advocates this categorization system, also includes a separate category for hallucinogens. These drugs produce slight alteration in perception at low doses, hallucinations and sympathetic nervous system stimulation at moderate doses, and profound delusions as well as loss of contact with reality at very high doses.

TRADITIONAL PERSPECTIVES

The use, possession, and sale of some psychoactive drugs are illegal. It is a crime in this country to use, possess, buy, or sell such controlled substances as LSD, heroin, cocaine, and marijuana. However, many commonly used psychoactive drugs are legal or can be acquired legally. Psychoactive substances can be found in over-the-counter remedies (e.g., Dexatrim, No-Doz), in legally purchased products (e.g., tea, cola, cigarettes, alcoholic beverages), and in prescription drugs.

It is estimated that in any particular year, 15% of the U.S. population experience some form of psychological disorder (Klerman, 1983). Another 15% of the population seek clinical advice for symptoms that do not meet specific diagnostic criteria for a psychiatric disorder (e.g., anxiety). Psychoactive drugs are often prescribed to alleviate or control the symptoms of these disorders. According to Ray and Ksir (1990), there are over 300,000 physicians legally writing prescriptions in the United States, and 150,000 pharmacists at 60,000 locations selling the prescribed drugs.

There is a paucity of research on the direct effects of illicit as well as licit psychoactive drugs on human aggressive behavior. The medical establishment has certainly not concentrated its attention on studying the effects of psychoactive substances on aggression. Instead, they have been concerned with adverse medical effects. There are the infrequent letters to the editors of medical journals and surveys of drug-related affective states (e.g., Cole & Kando, 1993). However, a perusal of the *Physicians Desk Reference* clearly demonstrates the lack of interest in drug-induced interpersonal conflict.

Psychologists and psychopharmacologists have also devoted little attention to studying the direct relationship between drugs and human aggression. The best illustration of this problem is the relative lack of attention to drug-elicited aggression in the major psychological texts on aggressive behavior. In Baron and Richardson's (1994) comprehensive review of the psychological literature on aggression, literature is cited on the effects of only two drugs: alcohol and marijuana. The effects of marijuana are discussed for approximately two paragraphs. In his text entitled *Aggression: Its Causes, Consequences, and Control*, Berkowitz (1993), a leading authority on aggressive behavior, made only one reference to the possible instigating effects of drugs. He concluded, ". . . much of the growth in homicides seems to be independent of drugs" (p. 278). Berkowitz adds, "A better case can be made for the role of weapons" (p. 279).

Law enforcement and social science professionals also do not appear to be preoccupied with the possibility that prescription, over-the-counter, or illegal drugs might facilitate aggressive behavior. Instead, the assumption appears to be that violence is an indirect result of the illegal drug trade (e.g., Watters, Reinarman, & Fagan, 1985). A popular view that appears to be advocated by many contemporary social scientists (e.g., Goldstein, Bellucci, Spunt, & Miller, 1991) is that addicts will harm others to acquire drugs ("economic violence") and drug gangs will use violence to acquire and maintain territory ("systemic violence"). In an article concerning substance use in forensic psychiatry, Kermani and Castaneda (1996) argued, "Most violence associated with drugs other than alcohol is related to the business of selling them" (p. 2). Thus, there appears to be considerable skepticism concerning "psychopharmacological violence," i.e., the direct effects of drugs on aggression, among many contemporary investigators in the medical, psychological, psychopharmacological, legal, and sociological fields (Wish & Johnson, 1986).

Not withstanding the skeptics, a modest body of literature pertaining to the relationship between drug consumption and aggressive responding among humans has evolved. This endeavor has been sustained by a small minority of investigators who have steadfastly supported the possibility of drug-induced violence. These investigators have been influenced to a considerable extent by the numerous, impelling case studies and clinical reports of the facilitation of violence following drug consumption. Goode (1993) observed, for example, "To many of us, the linkage seems as clear, as strong, as direct as morning and the rising sun" (p. 120).

STIMULANTS

Traditionally, there has been a pronounced expectation, based on meager empirical evidence, that stimulants facilitate aggression. Mayfield (1983) presented this view in a typical fashion: "The amphetamines would seem to be a likely group of drugs to be implicated in aggressive physical assaults" (p. 147). He added, "Not only do these drugs enhance noradrenergic activity and general level of arousal, they produce paranoid psychosis with some regularity" (p. 147). Cohen (1981), the former director of the Division of Narcotic Addiction and Drug Abuse, the National Institute of Mental Health, was even more convinced of the instigating effects of stimulants. He professed, "It can be predicted that stimulants in large doses with their capacity to cause hyperactivity, paranoid suspiciousness and impulsivity will be productive of violence" (p. 362). More dramatically, Cohen described how "instances of interminable stabbing or clubbing of a victim long since dead are well known" (p. 362). Powers and Kutash (1978) argued that "aggression and violence due to amphetamine use are particularly likely in individuals with premorbid aggressive tendencies and problems of impulse control" (p. 327). They also indicated that "many individuals, however, with no apparent personality abnormalities have evidenced aggression or violence during amphetamine use" (p. 327). This perspective tends to be shared by numerous contemporary investigators. For example, Meloy (1987) noted, "Anecdotal clinical experience also suggests that certain psychostimulants, such as methamphetamine and cocaine, may precipitate violence that is characterized by both intense rage and paranoia" (p. 40). In a more recent article, Miller and Gold (1994) argued, "The link between stimulants and criminal activity has been known for some time" (p. 1070).

The belief that amphetamines instigate aggressive behavior may have been derived from two sources: the pervasive assumption that drugs which enhance arousal states increase aggression potential and early clinical reports of the adverse effects of amphetamines. One of the most influential studies on the effects of stimulants on aggression was conducted by Ellinwood (1971). In accordance with traditional assumptions, Ellinwood's rationale for the study was based on the following observation: "Reports from law-enforcement personnel and psychiatrists, as well as from drug abusers themselves, have indicated that amphetamines may also be related to aggressive behavior" (p. 1170). The author added, "Perhaps more specifically than any other group of drugs" (p. 1170). Ellinwood examined case histories of 13 persons who committed homicide, presumably under the influence of large dosages of amphetamines. Ellinwood concluded that "homicide was clearly related to an amphetamine-induced delusional process and/or state of emotional lability" (p. 1175). Of course, given the nature of the study, there is no way to assess the role played by the amphetamine presumably ingested by the subjects. For example, it is difficult, based on the self-report data, to determine the time that elapsed between the amphetamine ingestion and the murderous act, the dosages actually consumed by the subjects, or the independent effects of the many other factors involved in each case. Most telling, the assailants were polydrug users. While noting that, "At the present time, we have no basis for an estimate of the relative importance of amphetamine abuse in violent behavior," Mednick, Pollock, Volavka, and Gabrielli (1982) concluded that "Ellinwood's suggestion that every person arrested for a violent crime have a urine test for drugs of abuse is certainly worthwhile" (p. 60).

A few authors have questioned the widespread belief that stimulants are potent, independent instigators of aggressive behavior. Allen, Safer, and Covi (1975) concluded, following their review of the literature, that stimulants only instigate aggression in doses that produce "amphetamine psychoses." Moss, Salloum, and Fisher (1994) argued that amphetamines may lead to aggressive behavior only in presence of chronic use, paranoid psychosis, or sociopathy.

Allen et al. (1975) pointed out that amphetamines may actually reduce the likelihood of aggressive acts. They noted the efficacy of stimulants to reduce aggressive tendencies in hyperactive children, brain-damaged adults, and delinquent adolescents. A more recent review by Connor and Steingard (1996) confirmed the possibility that stimulants may actually reduce the aggressive acts of children and adolescents referred for psychiatric treatment.

Cocaine, a psychomotor stimulant, has often been associated with aggression in the literature (Honer, Gewirtz, & Turey, 1987; Rivinus & Larimer, 1993; Wetli

& Fishbain, 1985). There are many proposed theoretical explanations for this presumed association. Many investigators assume that the loss of control following
cocaine consumption is due to the neuroanatomical locations effected by the drug
(Burrows, Hales, & Arington, 1988; Sheard, 1988). It is conjectured that cocaine
exerts its influence in the frontal lobe and limbic system, where aggressive motivational states are suspected of being regulated. As with amphetamines, other investigators argue that aggressive behavior only occurs when the consumer in
intensely intoxicated (e.g., Brody, 1990).

While there is a great deal of speculation concerning the relationship between
aggression and cocaine, there is little empirical evidence regarding cocaine-
induced aggression. Miller, Gold, and Mahler (1991) asserted, "While violence
has been associated with many drugs of abuse and addiction, no quantitative assessment of violence associated with cocaine use . . . has been reported" (p.
1078). In an attempt to rectify this problem, these authors interviewed, on the telephone, cocaine addicts who were attempting to obtain information about cocaine.
They found that 26% of the participants admitted to committing a crime while
using crack cocaine, the majority violent. Of course, this study has the limitation
of being retrospective and the results are based on telephone interviews conducted
with a very selective sample of addicts. Furthermore, a number of correlational
studies have not found a relationship between cocaine use and violent behavior
(e.g., Kozel & DuPont, 1977).

A common interpretation of the presumed relationship between cocaine and
aggression, generally accepted by contemporary drug experts, is that the observed violence is due to systemic or economic influences (Fagan & Ko-Lin,
1990; Goldstein, 1989). In a review article appearing in the *Journal of the American Medical Association,* Hatsukami and Fischman (1996) asserted that "violence
and crime associated with cocaine are considered to be in large part related to either the system of drug distribution (systemic crime) and/or economically or fi-
nancially driven" (p. 1585). The authors went on to say that "in fact, violence
directly induced by the pharmacological effects of cocaine hydrochloride or crack
is considered uncommon" (p. 1585).

DEPRESSANTS

Depressants, sometimes labeled sedative hypnotics, decrease CNS activity. At
low doses, depressants are often called anxiolytics or sedatives, and they are prescribed to reduce anxiety. At higher doses, they are labeled hypnotics and are used
to induce sleep. Alcohol is one of the most commonly used sedative drugs. However, it is rarely used therapeutically. Two depressant drugs that have fallen out of
favor recently in the medical community due to their addiction potential and adverse side effects are barbiturates and methaqualone. These depressants have been
replaced, therapeutically, by benzodiazepines (minor tranquilizers).

Depressant drugs, such as barbiturates and benzodiazepines, are not generally
considered to be facilitators of aggressive behavior. In fact, these drugs are commonly presumed to decrease aggression. Corrigan, Yudofsky, and Silver (1993) de-

cided that "the greatest effects of these drugs on aggression is the sedation of patients who are currently assaultive . . ." (p. 127). The authors concluded, "We recommend use of these drugs during periods of current assaultive outbursts" (p. 127). Gunn (1979) argued that barbiturates and aggression may be associated under only two conditions: when consumed with amphetamines and when used for suicide. While recognizing the remote possibility that benzodiazepines may enhance hostility, Gunn concluded, "Nevertheless, these drugs are useful sedatives and we do use them . . . in the violence clinic" (p. 189). Some clinical literature tends to support the perspective that benzodiazepines have calming, antiaggressive effects (e.g., Bond, Mandos, & Kurtz, 1989; Pilowsky, Ring, Shine, Battersby, & Lader, 1992; Rickels & Downing, 1974).

Although the clinical literature advocates the use of benzodiazepines for the acutely agitated patient, there have been reports of antisocial behavior following benzodiazepine ingestion. Increased anger, hostility, and aggression have been associated with benzodiazepines since they made their commercial appearance with the introduction of chlordiazepoxide in 1960 (DeMascio, Shader, & Giller, 1970; Tobin & Lewis, 1960). Numerous case reports and clinical studies have documented aggressive responses in some patients consuming benzodiazepines (Hall & Zisook, 1981; Rosenbaum, Woods, Groves, & Klerman, 1984; Salzman, Kochansky, Shader, Porrino, Harmatz, & Swett, 1974). The medical community has traditionally downplayed the importance of these case reports, labeling the observed hostile responses to benzodiazepine ingestion "paradoxical rage."

Medical incident reports tend to support the claim that aggression occurs infrequently in patients taking benzodiazepines. Svenson and Hamilton (1966) reported that only .24% of approximately 18,000 patients who had received chlordiazepoxide developed irritability as a side effect. The authors concluded that troublesome reactions were rare and their occurrence was due to excessive dosages. Miller (1973) reported that a combined total of approximately 1% of patients receiving chlordiazepoxide or diazepam developed excitement and agitation reactions. In a study of approximately 11,717 patients who received alprazolam, only 4 patients reported hostile reactions and 13 irritability (Dietch & Jennings, 1988). These authors concluded, "In most surveys the incidence of aggressive dyscontrol after benzodiazepines are administered is quite low (less than 1%) and is comparable to the effects produced by a placebo" (p. 186).

Contemporary investigators have begun to express their concern that benzodiazepines may facilitate aggression. For example, Ratey and Gordon (1993) stated, "The disinhibiting effects of benzodiazepines may lead to the precipitation of hostility or aggression, and are, therefore, a potential adverse effect of their use" (p. 66).

OPIATES

There appears to be minimal controversy concerning the direct effect of opiates on aggressive behavior. Most investigators assume that opiates decrease aggressive behavior. Powers and Kutash (1978) argued that the consumption of an opiate creates "euphoria, relaxation, drowsiness, and lethargy." These effects, according to the authors, "reduce aggression rather than increase it" (p. 330). Goode (1993) recognized that the traditional view of the aggression-instigating properties of opiates has been based on the assumption that "since heroin sedates and tranquilizes, its effects incline the user *away* from aggressive, violent acts" (p. 137). Blue and Griffith (1995) stated, quite unequivocally, that "heroin intoxication has not been shown to induce violence" (p. 576). Goldstein (1989) concluded that "early reports, which sought to employ a psychopharmacological model to attribute violent behavior to the use of opiates and marijuana, have now been largely discredited" (p. 25). He assumed, instead, that violence associated with heroin is perpetrated to acquire money to secure more drugs and is an inherent risk of the drug trade.

The traditional perspective concerning the antiaggressive effects of opiates was based on the informal reports of opiate addicts. However, more controlled questionnaire studies have found evidence that opiates may facilitate aggressive behavior. For example, opiate-experienced participants often evidence higher, rather than lower, hostility scores on self-report or observer-reported measures (Babor, Meyer, Mirin, Davies, Valentine, & Rawlins, 1976; Lindquist, Lindsay, & White, 1979).

Miczek (1987) observed that "the evidence on opiates and human aggression ranges from the earlier practice of using acute morphine as an antiaggressive drug to the increasing concern with the high incidence of aggression and criminal behavior in narcotics addicts" (p. 253). He concluded, "It is surprising that the effects of acute and chronic opiates on aggression and violent behavior in humans have not been directly assessed in controlled experiments" (p. 253).

MARIJUANA

There has been a great deal of controversy concerning the relationship between marijuana and aggressive behavior. In the past, marijuana was suspected of instigating a wide variety of aggressive behaviors. In fact, these allegations had been used to support the position that marijuana should be prohibited. In the 1930s and 1940s, Harry Anslinger, the Commissioner of Narcotics, observed, "How many murders, suicides, robberies, criminal assaults, holdups, burglaries, and deeds of maniacal insanity it causes . . . can only be conjectured" (Kaplan, 1970, p. 89).

During the mid-1960s and 1970s the image of marijuana as the "killer weed" was modified. Investigators began to argue that, if anything, marijuana inhibits aggression. The National Commission on Marihuana and Drug Abuse, formed in response to the Comprehensive Drug Abuse Prevention and Control Act of 1970, conducted a study to determine whether marijuana caused violence. The survey of marijuana users suggested that marijuana was unlikely to cause violent crime (Goode, 1972). In 1977, Abel determined, after an extensive review of the literature, that marijuana was not an antecedent of aggression. Following a review of the literature, Mednick et al. (1982) argued, "Feelings of hostility or overt aggression are not caused by marijuana under either experimental or 'real-life' conditions" (p. 61). Mayfield (1983) observed, "It is generally agreed that cannabis use is associated with quiescence and passivity more than vigor and aggressivity" (p. 148).

In a study of 268 incarcerated participants, Spunt, Goldstein, Brownstein, and Fendrich (1994) found that a large percentage of homicide offenders had used marijuana in their lifetime (86%) and a number (32%) even used it on the day of the killing. However, the authors concluded that "marijuana rarely played a determining role in the homicides that were committed" (p. 209). Thus, there appears to be a consensus among investigators that marijuana is not an antecedent of aggression.

HALLUCINOGENS

The two drugs most commonly referred to as hallucinogens or psychedelics are LSD and PCP. LSD is one of the most common hallucinogenic drugs used in the United States. It appears to induce visual hallucinations and feelings of depersonalization. Consumers can suffer a number of untoward reactions, including panic reactions or "bad trips," over psychotic reactions and "flashbacks," or the reappearance of drug symptoms without further consumption. PCP tends to be mistakenly classified as a hallucinogen because it occasionally elicits hallucinations. However, following PCP ingestion, consumers do not experience vivid or unusual colors in their hallucinations or many of the other symptoms characteristic of LSD use. In fact, many of the subjective reactions are similar to those produced by sedative hypnotics. At large doses, however, some users have been observed to experience psychotic episodes, hallucinations, and convulsions.

From the early 1940s until the early 1960s, LSD was used extensively in psychotherapy. Few adverse reactions were reported. A survey was conducted by Cohen and Ditman (1963) of 44 therapists who provided LSD or mescaline to approximately 5000 patients. The most common problems associated with the use of LSD were psychotic reactions and suicide attempts. The authors reported that aggression was rare and consisted mainly of paranoid reactions. During the late 1960s, there was a rapid growth in the illicit use of LSD. Many instances of "bad trips" were documented, in which users experienced panic reactions.

There are many reports in the literature of aggressive responding associated with hallucinogen use (e.g., Fauman & Fauman, 1980; Reid, 1986; Siegel, 1980). However, the consensus in the literature appears to be that LSD is not a potent antecedent of aggressive behavior. It is assumed that aggression may occur as a result of disorganized responding during a panic reaction (Hurlbut, 1991). Mayfield (1983) concluded that hallucinogen-instigated aggression occurs "in the context of 'bad trips,' and the amount of assaultiveness relative to the use of these drugs is difficult to ascertain but is probably low" (p. 148). Powers and Kutash (1978) observed, "It is relatively uncommon for aggression and violence to occur under the influence of LSD . . ." (p. 337). According to Cohen (1981), "The most frequent cause of lethality during an LSD experience is accidental death" (p. 362).

There appears to be greater concordance concerning the instigating affects of PCP. Cohen (1981), for example, commented that "with the exception of phencyclidine, violent or criminal activities during the hallucinogenic state are infrequent" (p. 362). Blue and Griffith (1995) concluded that PCP has been "associated with increased aggression" (p. 576). There is controversy, however, concerning the nature of the relationship between PCP and aggression. Some investigators contend that the violence is due to psychotic reactions (Fauman, Aldinger, & Fauman, 1976; Luisada & Brown, 1976). Others assert that violence associated with PCP is economically motivated. Wish (1986) examined a sample of 4847 arrestees and found that "many PCP users are apprehended for goal-oriented, income-generating crimes" (p. 187). The author indicated, "We did not find a preponderance of the types of offenses one might expect from persons committing the bizarre, irrational acts ascribed to PCP users" (p. 187).

The literature that suggests a relationship between hallucinogens and violence has been criticized methodologically. Sbordone, Gorelick, and Elliott (1981) observed, "Phencyclidine has recently been associated with pathological aggressive behavior in humans." The authors charged, "Its reputation, however, is based largely on anecdotal case reports of the bizarre behavior induced in PCP users, rather than on epidemiological or experimental data." Miczek (1987) also observed that "dramatic episodes of seemingly inexplicable violent behavior in hallucinogen-using individuals have led to frequent allegations that these drugs provoke violence" (p. 261). The author acknowledged, however, that "the empirical evidence is mostly limited to statistics from apprehended delinquents, clients of drug abuse clinics, case reports, or uncontrolled, open trials" (p. 261). Furthermore, he correctly recognized that the reports are based on the behaviors of polydrug users. Wilkens (1989) suggested that "despite reports of violence associated with PCP use by humans . . . a causal relationship between PCP and aggressive behavior remains unclear" (p. 277).

EXPERIMENTAL INVESTIGATION

Enormous quantities of licit as well as illicit drugs are consumed in our society. It has been speculated that one presumed consequence of this consumption is aggressive behavior, yet there is relatively little experimental evidence concerning the direct effects of acute drug use on human aggression. Experimentalists within the scientific community have devoted attention to the influence of psychoactive drugs on addiction and adverse medical effects. However, they have paid minimal attention to the possible disruptive influence of drugs on complex human social behavior. The American Psychological Association has intermittently expressed concern about the apparent relationship between substance abuse and aggression. For example, they conducted a "mini-convention" on the effects of substance abuse on aggressive behavior at the 1990 American Psychological Convention. Although many hours of programming were devoted to this critical issue, there was a paucity of controlled, experimental research on drug-elicited aggression in humans. The American Association for the Advancement of Science held a conference entitled, "Drugs, Crime and Violence: What Do We Know?" Once again, few researchers at the conference acknowledged utilizing experimental methodology to investigate the influence of drug consumption on human aggressive responding. In fact, there appeared to be a startling animosity toward the use of experimental methodology in the investigation of the relationship between drugs and human aggression.

There are conventional methods used to study the effects of drugs on aggression that are considered to be "acceptable." These methods rarely provoke hostile criticism. One popular method involves correlating subjects' descriptions of their drug use with self-reported aggressive behaviors. While potentially providing useful information, there are significant problems associated with this fashionable methodology. Many people are reluctant to reveal such personal and potentially incriminating information. Furthermore, it is difficult to ascertain causal relationships from such data. A second method that has been fiercely promoted by critics of experimental methodology involves naturalistic observation. This approach has been especially advocated by a small group of animal researchers (ethopharmacologists). This research approach is especially difficult with human subjects, as aggression has a low base rate in natural settings and it is a laborious task to control such important variables as dose in a natural environment. For example, it is difficult to assess how much of a drug a subject had ingested prior to a "natural" observation. The use of crime statistics, another common approach, can be troublesome due to sampling biases, unreliable police observations, and underreporting.

Our laboratory has been involved for a number of years in a program of research designed to experimentally investigate the effects of commonly used drugs on human aggressive behavior. The paradigm used in these controlled, laboratory experiments provides a subject with the opportunity to aggress against a bogus opponent while competing in a reaction time task. Prior to each competitive trial, the subject receives a signal to select the intensity of shock he wishes to administer to his competitor. The subject and his competitor then compete on a reaction time trial. The person with the slower reaction time receives the shock that had presumably been selected by the competitor. The person with a faster reaction time does not receive a shock. However, he is informed, by means of feedback lights, of the intensity of shock his competitor had set for him. Thus, the subject realizes that either he or his opponent will receive a shock, depending on the outcome of the trial, and that each can select the intensity of shock the other will receive. The measure of aggression used in this paradigm is the intensity of electric shock the subject selects for his opponent.

In comparison to case study and correctional designs, the experimental paradigm randomly assigns subjects to conditions, disguises the true nature of the experiments by telling the subjects that the purpose of the study is to examine the effects of drugs on performance variables, controls the dosage of the drug, obtains a direct, behavioral measure of the propensity to harm under controlled conditions, uses a normal, nondrug-using sample, and assesses the effects of an acute dose.

The reaction time paradigm provides a valid measure of aggressive behavior. The paradigm discriminates between groups of subjects theoretically expected to differ in aggression (e.g., Dengerink, 1971; Genthner & Taylor, 1973) and is sensitive to situational variables expected to influence aggressive responding, such as social pressure and gender of target. In their review of contemporary paradigms, Baron and Richardson (1994) concluded, "The Taylor procedures do in fact yield a useful and valid measure of physical aggression" (p. 81). Bernstein, Richardson, and Hammock (1987) examined the convergent and discriminate validity of the Taylor paradigm and reported that the procedure provided a valid measure of aggressive behavior.

In a review of the literature on "drugs and violent crime," Goldstein (1989) concluded that "the need for better data to elaborate on these relationships is clear and pressing" (p. 41). He added, "It is important that we move beyond simple correlations between drug use and violent crime to achieve a real understanding of how drugs contribute to the process of violence" (p. 41). It is the authors' belief that the utilization of methodologies that actually manipulate the ingestion of a variety of drugs and monitor acts with a potential for physical harm or injury can most optimally contribute to this objective.

During the first stage of the research program, attention was focused on the potential instigative effects of alcohol on aggression. Prior to the initiation of this research, there was a paucity of controlled, experimental research concerning the effects of alcohol consumption on aggressive interactions. The research involved administering varying doses of alcohol to subjects in the reaction time paradigm. The results indicated that alcohol was a potent causal antecedent of aggressive behavior (Taylor & Leonard, 1983).

MARIJUANA

Following the successful attempt to study the effects of alcohol on aggression, an effort was made to investigate the effects of other commonly used psychoactive drugs. Studies were initially conducted to explore the effects of marijuana on aggressive responding. There appeared to be a consensus among investigators that marijuana was not a potent antecedent of aggression. The research that had been done, however, relied on retrospective case studies, anecdotal evidence, and correlational studies of the relation between marijuana and violent crime. These methodologies rely on unreliable self-reports of witnesses and cannot substantiate the presence of marijuana in an aggressor. Our research provided empirical support for the conviction that marijuana did not instigate aggressive responding. In the first study (Taylor, Vordaris, Rawtich, Gammon, Cranston, & Lubetkin, 1976), subjects were provoked by the confederate following their ingestion of high or low dosages of either alcohol or THC. As expected, aggression was found to be related to the quantity of alcohol ingested. The high dose of alcohol facilitated more intense aggression (higher shock settings) than the low dose. The high dose of THC, however, did not increase aggressive responding. In fact, it tended to suppress aggressive behavior. In the second study, conducted by Myerscough and Taylor (1985), subjects received intense provocation following their ingestion of one of three doses of THC. Subjects in the low dose condition responded in a more aggressive manner than subjects in the moderate and high dose conditions. Subjects in the high dose condition tended to respond in a relatively nonaggressive manner throughout the experimental session. The authors concluded that the results were "congruent with a growing consensus among drug investigators that marijuana does not instigate, precipitate, or enhance aggressive behavior" (p. 1555).

Cherek, Roache, Egli, Davis, Spiga, and Cowan (1993) challenged the revisionist position that marijuana decreases aggression. These authors investigated the effects of smoking marijuana on a behavioral measure of aggression. The participants in this study were eight "inner-city males with extensive drug use histories and self-reported "anti-social" behavior patterns" (p. 167). The study demonstrated that aggressive responding increased during the first hour after marijuana smoking. Given the small number and characteristics of the participants, the authors included the following caveat: "Determining the effects of marijuana smoking on aggressive responding among marijuana smokers with no other drug use history and not meeting criteria for anti-social personality disorder would be essential in interpreting the present data" (p. 167).

STIMULANTS

Our research, using an experimental approach, provided support for the traditional assumptions concerning the effects of both alcohol and marijuana on aggressive behavior. We next turned our attention to the possible instigating effects of CNS stimulants. As discussed earlier, there has been considerable disagreement concerning the instigating effects of stimulants. While arousal theories assume that acute amphetamine consumption may enhance aggression, there has been little evidence to support this perspective. In fact, there is some indication that amphetamines may actually decrease aggressive tendencies.

Three studies were conducted in our laboratory in an attempt to examine the direct effects of stimulants on aggressive behavior (Beezley, Gantner, Bailey, & Taylor, 1987). In these studies, subjects consumed varying dosages of dextroamphetamine prior to competing in the reaction time task. The results of the three studies were very consistent. While the high doses of amphetamine increased systolic and diastolic blood pressure, aggressive behavior was not found to increase as a function of amphetamine dosage. These findings are congruent with clinical evidence and demonstrate that amphetamines in acute, moderate doses do not appear to facilitate aggressive behavior. Following a review of the experimental literature, Bushman (1993) concluded that "CNS stimulants do not consistently facilitate or inhibit aggression" (p. 150).

Findings on the relationship between amphetamines and aggression have important theoretical as well as practical implications. It has traditionally been assumed that "arousal" is one of the major facilitators of aggression. Although amphetamines enhanced physiological arousal, they had a minimal impact on aggression. These findings indicate that researchers must reconsider the role of arousal in regulating aggressive behavior.

Cocaine has become a major drug of abuse. It has been estimated that approximately 30 million people have used cocaine in the United States. Many researchers believe that cocaine facilitates aggressive behavior (Honer et al., 1987; Miller et al., 1991; Siegal, 1982), whereas others tend to question this belief (Kozel & DuPont, 1977).

Licata, Taylor, Berman, and Cranston (1993) attempted to experimentally investigate the propensity of cocaine to facilitate aggression. Participants received a placebo, a low dose (1 mg/kg), or a high dose (2 mg/kg) of orally administered cocaine prior to competing in the competitive reaction-time task. Results indicated that subjects in the high dose condition behaved more aggressively than placebo subjects under all levels of provocation.

It has been suggested that the route of administration may influence cocaine-induced violence (Giannini, Miller, Loiselle, & Turner, 1993). One proposal is that the route which provides the quickest onset of intoxication would be most likely to enhance aggression. Findings reported by Licata et al. (1993) are not congruent with this proposition. Orally ingested cocaine does not provide direct entry of cocaine into the central nervous system, yet subjects who received the high dose of orally ingested cocaine selected higher levels of shock than the placebo subjects during each block of trials.

Cocaine and dextroamphetamine are central nervous system stimulants. However, research cited earlier suggests that moderate doses of cocaine may enhance aggression, whereas moderate doses of dextroamphetamine may have no appreciable influence on aggressive behavior. Future research must determine whether the variation in aggression observed was due to pharmacological differences between these drugs or the particular dosages used in the studies. The findings do underscore the possibility that two drugs within the same drug category may produce very different levels of aggressive responding.

DEPRESSANTS

There appears to be a consensus that opiates reduce aggressive responding. It is assumed that opiates decrease aggressive behavior by inducing a positive affective experience (Khantzian, 1974, 1985). Unfortunately, these beliefs of the antiaggressive properties of opiates tend to be based on informal, self-reports of opiate addicts.

As discussed earlier, Powers and Kutash (1978), who argued that opiates reduced aggression, believed that opiates produced "euphoria, relaxation, drowsiness, and lethargy" (p. 330). These adjectives quite accurately describe the subjective effects of other commonly used depressants. Given the fact that the effects of opiates such as morphine are similar to other depressants and that depressants such as alcohol tend to facilitate aggression, it is not unreasonable to argue that morphine might also increase aggressive behavior.

Berman, Taylor, and Marged (1993) attempted to examine the effects of an acute dose of morphine, a prototypical opiate, on a behavioral measure of aggression. Subjects were randomly assigned to either a morphine or an inactive placebo condition. They were then given the opportunity to aggress against an increasingly provocative opponent in the competitive reaction time task. Subjects in the morphine condition received 45 mg of immediate-release oral morphine sulfate placed in a gelatin capsule. Subjects in the placebo condition received an inactive placebo.

Subjects in the morphine condition initiated attacks against the opponent prior to receiving information about the opponent's aggressive intentions and responded more aggressively than the subjects in the placebo condition under all provocation levels. The results suggest the possibility that violent acts of opiate users might not be solely determined by economics (acquisition of drugs) and involvement in drug trafficking. It is very plausible to assume that the consumption of opiates itself facilitates aggressive behaviors. The authors concluded, "The results of this study suggest that the traditional view that opiates reduce aggressive behavior requires re-examination" (p. 267).

A similar controversy exists concerning the effect of benzodiazepines, the drug class of choice for the treatment of anxiety, on aggressive behavior. Since their introduction, numerous case studies have reported that benzodiazepines, such as diazepam and chlordiazepoxide, may facilitate hostility in psychiatric patients (e.g., Gardos, DiMascio, Salzman, & Shader, 1968). However, the medical community has continued to label the instances of aggressive behavior following benzodiazepine ingestion as "paradoxical rage reactions" as the response is contrary to their expectation of how a patient should respond to these agents. For example, in an article on the use of benzodiazepines in the treatment of anxiety disorders, Shader and Greenblatt (1993) concluded, "There is no evidence that benzodiazepines directly impair impulse control or conscience or lead to aggressive or self-destructive acts" (p. 1402).

Earlier reports of aggressive behavior following the ingestion of benzodiazepines were based on clinical descriptions using single-case designs, uncontrolled studies, and self-report measures of aggression. The first attempt to study the effect of a benzodiazepine on a direct measure of physical aggressive behavior, in a controlled laboratory setting, occurred in the early 1980s. Pagano (1981) monitored the aggressive behavior of male subjects in the reaction time paradigm after they had ingested a placebo, a 5-mg, or a 10-mg dose of diazepam. The subjects in the 10-mg condition were observed to display significantly higher levels of aggression as compared to subjects in the other groups. Furthermore, under high provocation, when the bogus opponent was setting high shocks, the 5-mg diazepam group behaved as aggressively as the 10-mg group.

The results of the Pagano study were quite surprising. We did not anticipate that a tranquilizer would increase the subjects' tendencies to administer intense noxious stimuli to peers, especially when the peers could retaliate. We have naively accepted the conventional belief that a "tranquilizer" produces a calm, peaceful state. The findings instigated a series of studies designed to explore the relationship between benzodiazepine consumption and aggressive behavior.

In a subsequent study, Wilkinson (1985) assessed the acute effects of diazepam on the aggressive behavior of subjects varying in trait anxiety. High, moderate, and low trait anxiety groups were administered either 10 mg of diazepam or a placebo capsule. Wilkinson reported that under conditions of high provocation, all anxiety trait groups who received diazepam had significantly higher levels of aggressive behavior than those who received a placebo. However, she also found that under minimal provocation conditions, in which the opponent set low intensity shocks, low anxious subjects administered diazepam were more aggressive than highly anxious subjects who received the drug. Thus, subjects who came into the laboratory with low anxiety levels were more aggressive under nonthreatening conditions than subjects who were anxious. Wilkinson concluded, "The results are consistent with reports of the ability of antianxiety drugs to disinhibit suppressed behaviors" (p. 101).

There is considerable evidence that a larger proportion of females than males use benzodiazepines. Yet there is a paucity of research investigating the interactive effects of diazepam and the sex of the aggressor on aggressive responding. Gantner and Taylor (1988) randomly administered diazepam (10 mg) or a placebo to male and female subjects prior to their participating in the paradigm. Results were similar to earlier studies: the aggression-enhancing effects of diazepam occurred for both male and female competitors.

A number of studies have related triazolam (Halcion), a benzodiazepine used to treat insomnia, with acts of aggression. For example, van der Kroef (1979) observed hostile responses in several patients who received triazolam. Regestein and Reich (1985) reported a series of cases in which agitation and anger were associated with triazolam. These behaviors were observed in patients with and without psychiatric histories.

To investigate the effects of triazolam on aggressive behavior, Berman and Taylor (1995) provided subjects with either a placebo or 0.25 mg of triazolam prior to their participation in the reaction time paradigm. The 0.25-mg dose was used in the study because it is the highest dose marketed in the United States and has been reported to produce greater cognitive effects than the only other available dose, 0.125 mg (Greenblatt, 1992).

The results of the study demonstrated, very convincingly, that triazolam enhanced aggressive behavior. Participants who received triazolam set more intense shock for the opponent than participants who received a placebo, prior to knowledge of the opponent's aggressive intent as well as during the competitive trials and selected the most extreme shock response for the opponent more frequently than the placebo subjects.

Bond and Lader (1988) examined the differential effects of two other benzodiazepines, oxazepam and lorazepam, on aggressive behavior. Subjects were administered these drugs or a placebo in a modification of the Taylor competitive paradigm (noise intensity was used instead of electric shock). The higher dose of lorazepam was reported to have increased aggressive behavior more than the oxazepam or placebo. Weisman (1991) conducted a study to compare the effects of diazepam and oxazepam on aggression using the traditional paradigm. He observed that diazepam produced a higher level of aggression than oxazepam. Thus, in neither study did oxazepam, a less potent benzodiazepine, facilitate aggressive responding.

A major implication of this series of experiments is that the ingestion of depressants, such as benzodiazepines, may result in an escalation in aggressive behavior. Following a meta-analysis of the available evidence, Bushman (1993) concluded that "there is strong evidence to suggest that low doses of CNS depressants cause aggressive behavior in humans" (p. 150).

Depressant drugs that sedate but do not have potent anxiolytic properties may be less apt to instigate aggressive responding. Chermack and Taylor (1993) reported that neither secobarbital nor pentobarbital, potent sedatives with relatively weak anxiolytic attributes, had an appreciable impact on aggressive responding.

DISCUSSION

There is a great deal of controversy in the literature concerning the direct effects of psychoactive drugs on the expression of aggressive behavior. Traditional literature suggests that stimulants instigate and depressants inhibit aggressive acts. Recent experimental evidence suggests that these conventional assumptions are in need of revision.

The dissension in the field is partly due to the traditional methodologies used to study the relationships between drugs and aggression. Due to the multiple threats to validity inherent in these methodologies, the evidence generated by traditional research strategies must be interpreted with considerable caution.

In an attempt to rectify this problem, we have been conducting a program of research that involves administering a variety of psychoactive drugs to nonaddicted subjects in a controlled laboratory situation designed to monitor interpersonal physical aggression. The methodology assures the random assignment of subjects, provides placebo comparisons, disguises the true purpose of the experiments, and enables investigators to manipulate important experimental conditions.

The results of these experiments are consistent with traditional perspectives in three major respects. First, alcohol is a potent antecedent of aggressive responding. Second, marijuana does not appear to facilitate aggressive behavior. Finally, there is tentative evidence of a relationship between cocaine consumption and physical aggression. Many investigators have suggested that violence by cocaine users may simply be the by-product of the activities necessary to procure the drugs. Results of the study conducted by Licata et al. (1993) suggest that this perspective needs to be revised. One may recall that the authors found that subjects in the high dose condition reacted more aggressively than placebo subjects under all levels of provocation.

Our research findings are not congruent with conventional "wisdom" pertaining to the instigating effects of amphetamines, opiates, and benzodiazepines. First, no appreciable evidence has been found that amphetamine consumption, at least in moderate doses, enhances aggression. Subjects who consumed moderate doses of dextroamphetamine were no more willing to harm their opponent than subjects who consumed a low dose of dextroamphetamine or a placebo. Subjects who received dextroamphetamine evidenced no affective or behavioral tendency that could be interpreted as offensive. This was decidedly the case in the experimental paradigm as well as in their interactions with the experimenters. Of course, future studies must investigate the effects of higher doses, chronic use, and divergent subject populations. Furthermore, researchers must attempt to delineate the factors responsible for the differential effects of amphetamine and cocaine on aggressive responding. Second, there is strong evidence of a relationship between morphine consumption and aggressive responding. Many studies have demonstrated a significant relationship between opiate use and violence. However, they have not been able to explain the nature of the relationship. Usually, the violence is attributed to the procurement of the drug. The study conducted by Berman et al. (1993) suggests that aggression can result from the psychopharmacological effects of morphine. Finally, traditional literature suggests that benzodiazepines reduce aggressive behavior. Our research has clearly and convincingly demonstrated that benzodiazepines can increase aggressive responding.

Given our understanding of the traditional literature, the experimenters were surprised to observe the aggressive responding of the subjects who consumed morphine and benzodiazepines and the nonaggressiveness of the subjects who consumed amphetamine. How can we account for the apparent discrepancies between our observations and the traditional literature on drugs and aggression? One possibility is that drug investigators and practitioners have been biased by traditional theories and opinions concerning the effects of CNS activity on affective processes.

One of the most pervasive beliefs in the biomedical and psychological communities is that a direct relationship exists between the activity of the CNS and both anxiety and aggression. Presumably, as the activity of the CNS increases, the probability of the occurrence of fear and aggression is elevated. Kirov (1989), a representative proponent of this established perspective, argues that anxiety can turn to fighting and vice versa due to the fact that both affective states have a similar origin: the "basic activity of the nervous system," the "normal functioning of the neuron itself" (p. 846). Due to the presumed parallel relationship between anxiety and aggression, it is posited that a drug which decreases anxiety would also decrease aggression and a drug which decreases aggression would also decrease anxiety. Thus, Kirov advocates a "rule of thumb" for medical professionals concerning the dispensing of drugs. He proposes that any drug which stimulates the CNS, such as amphetamine, would be expected to facilitate both aggression and anxiety and any drug which depresses the CNS would be expected to decrease both aggression and anxiety. Although fear and aggression would appear to be very different symptoms, they could both be treated with the same psychoactive substances. For example, if benzodiazepines decreased anxiety, they would also be expected to decrease aggression. What if this anticipated relationship is not observed and a patient experienced an increase in aggression after being treated for anxiety with a benzodiazepine? Advocates of this "rule of thumb" would argue that this "rare" observation is due to an exceptionally high dosage of the substance or an "idiosyncratic" characteristic of the consumer. Anxiety and aggression are assumed to have a common origin and are positively correlated. Thus, aggressive behavior would not be expected from a drug that is suppose to decrease anxiety. The presence of aggression subsequent to the ingestion of a moderate dose of a tranquilizer would be considered "paradoxical." The resultant affective state would be interpreted as being due to some unspecified characteristic of the consumer, not the drug.

One major consequence of this pervasive view is that adverse clinical or behavioral drug reactions, such as hostility, may not be monitored or reported by physicians and drug investigators. Expectancies concerning drug effects may strongly bias the medical community against observing disruptive behavior. Manufacturers rely on physicians' reports of adverse drug reactions. Spontaneous reporting occurs when a physician reports that a particular patient has suffered an adverse reaction following the consumption of a drug. It is recognized that only a small proportion of adverse drug reactions are actually reported by doctors (Inman, 1972). Given the small proportion of serious side effects reported, it is not unreasonable to assume that an even smaller proportion of aggressive acts would be reported. Because of prevalent expectancies, a physician may fail to recognize that aggressive behaviors are drug related, a physician might not question patients about aggressive events, a patient may be reluctant to report interpersonal behaviors, and reports of incidents of aggression would most likely be interpreted as "idiosyncratic."

The psychological establishment envisions the dynamics of aggression in a similar manner. The most common conceptualization concerning the etiology of aggression in the psychological literature is that aggression is mediated by enhanced arousal. In a review of the aggression literature, Baron and Richardson (1994) stated, "Several formal theories of aggression (Berkowitz, 1981, 1988; Zillman, 1988) and some explanations for effects of other variables (e.g., noise) are based on the notion that aggression and arousal are closely related" (p. 263). Most traditional explanations of aggression theorize that there are certain antecedent conditions, such as frustration or noxious cues, that reliably elevate arousal states. The heightened arousal increases the probability that aggressive behavior will eventuate. An important implication of this pervasive model is that any drug that enhances arousal states facilitates hostile acts and any drug that decreases arousal states reduces aggression. Thus, stimulants, such as amphetamine, would be expected to increase aggressive behavior, whereas sedative hypnotics, such as minor tranquilizers, would be expected to decrease aggression. The prototypical impressions in the psychological literature are that of the crazed amphetamine addict or agitated patient who is subdued with a sedative. This picture fits the traditional conceptualization of a direct relationship between aggression and CNS arousal.

A second related reason for the failure to appreciate the aggression-enhancing potential of certain psychoactive drugs is justifiable apprehension concerning their potentially life-threatening medical side effects. The biomedical community concedes that psychoactive substances, licit and illicit, can produce adverse drug reactions. Most drugs affect many neurotransmitter systems and their effects are not localized to the CNS. The use of psychoactive substances, including psychotherapeutic drugs, can result in a wide range of adverse effects. A large number of drugs antagonize dopaminergic, adrenergic, acetylcholine, and histaminergic neuronal systems. Therefore, medical practitioners routinely monitor such symptoms as postural hypotension, weight gain, allergic reactions, cardiac conduction abnormalities, seizures, vomiting, menstrual dysfunction, dystonia, blurred vision, and hyperthermia. More specifically, there is serious concern in the medical community that stimulants, such as cocaine, could result in heart failure or a convulsion-induced halt in breathing. Depressants, such as ethyl alcohol and barbiturates, are acknowledged to produce life-threatening emergencies, such as respiratory depression, as well as vomiting, blurred vision, muscle weakness, anterograde amnesia, and circulatory collapse. Adverse medical effects of opiates, such as morphine and methadone, include respiratory and circulatory depression, leading to possible cardiac arrest as well as seizures, delirium, pruritus, and urticaria.

Because of the obvious seriousness of the aforementioned problems, the medical/pharmacological community tends to limit its focus to serious medical complications resulting from the pharmacodynamic effects of drugs. Insufficient attention is paid to adverse clinical or behavioral events. When describing the psychological side effects of a drug, there is a tendency to concentrate on the drug's immediate impact on the CNS (e.g., memory deficits) rather than on complex, interpersonal behavior.

Pre- and postmarketing surveillance of most drugs focuses on identifying adverse drug reactions that involve serious medical complications. It has been argued that by focusing attention on adverse drug reactions, the medical/pharmacological community may fail to observe important adverse clinical events (e.g., aggressive behavior). Fisher (1995) has argued that the types of postmarketing surveillance used by the FDA may compromise its ability to delineate and resolve side effects of psychoactive drugs. The system used by the FDA relies almost exclusively on judgments of physicians to identify serious medical reactions with little focus on clinical reactions. The FDA appears to have little interest in gathering information directly from patients who consume drugs. The approaches currently used to detect adverse drug reactions involve spontaneous physician reporting, physician case reports, consolidation of medical records on particular patients, and postmarketing studies initiated by drug manufacturers. Although these approaches may be useful for detection of medical events, they are relatively ineffective in detecting less serious drug reactions (e.g., alterations in interpersonal behavior).

There is a third possible reason for the failure of drug researchers to detect the instigating effects of widely used psychoactive drugs. Given the traditional training of experimental psychologists and psychopharmacologists, they have felt more comfortable utilizing animal models. They have been reluctant to use controlled, experimental methods to examine the effects of drugs on human aggressive behavior. This has led to many complications. For example, these researchers sometimes fail to appreciate that the effects of drugs on human aggressive behavior are mediated by complex social and cognitive processes. Furthermore, because of their inherent biases, they have a tendency to disregard the experimental evidence concerning the relationship between psychoactive substances and human aggression. These biases are clearly manifested in the material selected for inclusion in contemporary biopsychology textbooks (Carlson, 1994, 1995; Kalat, 1995; Pinel, 1997). These textbooks are devoid of experimental research pertaining to the relationship between psychoactive drugs and human aggression.

POLICY IMPLICATIONS

The Panel on the Understanding and Control of Violent Behavior was established, in 1989, in response to requests from a number of federal agencies (e.g., the National Science Foundation) to conduct a comprehensive analysis of violent behavior. The panel admitted that it was not possible to design a comprehensive national policy for preventing drug-induced aggression. This was based on the realistic appraisal that our understanding of the instigating effects of drugs was deficient. The panel, nevertheless, recommended the following policies: developing tactics to disrupt illegal drug market, monitoring drug usage of pretrial releases, implementing drug abuse treatment for criminals, designing drug abuse prevention projects, and the development of pharmacological therapies to reduce the craving for psychoactive drugs (Reiss & Roth, 1993).

Based on the evidence presented in this chapter, a very different list of recommendations could be generated. First of all, we should not be influenced by the artificial distinction between licit and illicit drugs. A wide variety of drugs, some provided by means of prescriptions, have the potential to facilitate aggressive behavior. There is mounting evidence that drugs which depress the CNS, such as minor tranquilizers, alcohol, and morphine, have the potential to enhance aggression. Some of these drugs are obtained legally, others are acquired illegally. Texts and journal articles on the relationship between drug use and aggression all too often deal exclusively with illicitly acquired drugs.

Second, we must stimulate and promote experimental as well as correlational research on the effects of psychoactive drugs on human aggression. This will require financial support from federal and state agencies, interdisciplinary cooperation among a wide variety of disciplines, and the development of alternative experimental methodologies. Of even greater importance is the need for supportive, enlightened attitudes in the scientific establishment. It is acceptable to study the instigating effects of drugs on animal aggression by means of experimental paradigms. However, due to ethical concerns, intransigent negative perspectives concerning social psychological research, and the misguided belief that the only viable means of studying human behavior is through self-report, some investi-gators question the credibility of experimental paradigms. Thus, Leccese (1991) argued that "controlled experiments may be difficult to conduct in an ethical man-ner . . . [because] . . . it may be that violent behavior can only be induced by doses that are sufficient to cause organ damage or other behavioral toxicities" (p. 200). This position is unfortunate as controlled laboratory experiments are not only fea-sible, but crucial for delineating the complex relationships between drug use and aggression. The National Institute on Drug Abuse published a monograph enti-tled, "Drugs and Violence: Causes, Correlates, and Consequences." The manu-script, edited by De La Rosa, Lambert, and Gropper (1990), covered such topics as distribution of crack, gangs, mental illness, and drug sales. Not one paper even alluded to human experimental research.

Third, the biomedical establishment must appreciate that psychoactive drugs have interpersonal consequences. This requires pre- and postmarketing assess-ments of drug-induced behavioral dysfunction, routine monitoring by physicians of the aggressive behaviors of patients consuming psychoactive drugs, enhanced interest by the FDA in gathering behavioral information directly from patients who consume drugs, and educational programs to inform the public of the behav-ioral consequences of drug use.

Fourth, while recognizing the importance of social, economic, and develop-mental factors, it is essential that we acknowledge that psychopharmacological factors play a decisive role in determining whether a particular drug will facilitate aggressive behavior. Efforts to understand the role of these underlying biological mechanisms will eventually provide us with the knowledge to prevent and control drug-induced aggressive behavior.

Following a review of the literature concerning the effects of alcohol on ag-gression, Taylor and Leonard (1983) concluded that alcohol was a potent an-tecedent of aggression. The authors recommended that researchers attempt to delineate the variables that interact with alcohol to produce aggressive responding and strive to understand the processes that mediate the relationship. In the years following this review, researchers have expended considerable energy investigat-ing the dynamics of the alcohol–aggression relationship. In 1993, Taylor and Chermack reviewed the evidence concerning the relationship between alcohol/ drugs and aggression. They confirmed the earlier conclusion that aggressive be-havior is related to alcohol consumption. The authors also indicated that there was sufficient evidence to suggest that certain prescription medications could facilitate hostile behavior. Taylor and Chermack counseled, "While depressants such as di-azepam may reduce anxiety and be helpful in the treatment of insomnia, they may also result in impaired judgment and a propensity to behave aggressively" (p. 80). The current authors reaffirm this position and recommend that contemporary in-vestigators reconsider their beliefs concerning the potential instigating effects of licit as well as illicit psychoactive drugs. Collins (1991) concluded, "There is vir-tually no evidence that the pharmacological effects of drugs (alcohol excepted) ac-count for a substantial proportion of drug-related violence" (p. 265). Due to the lack of epidemiological data, it is impossible to currently estimate the degree of violence instigated by the consumption of prescription drugs. However, there is sufficient anecdotal, case study, and experimental evidence to contradict this unsophisticated and intransigent position. Given the current empirical evidence suggesting the presence of pharmacological-induced aggression, it is sobering to reflect on the fact that "during the last 25 years it has been estimated that over 500 million people worldwide have taken a course of benzodiazepine treatment" (Leonard, 1993, p. 99).

REFERENCES

Abel, E. (1977). The relationship between cannabis and violence: A review. *Psychological Bulletin, 84,* 193–211.

Allen, R. P., Safer, D., & Covi, L. (1975). Effects of psychostimulants on aggression. *The Journal of Nervous and Mental Diseases, 160(2),* 138–145.

Babor, T. F., Meyer, R. E., Mirin, S. M., Davies, M., Valentine, N., & Rawlins, M. (1976). Interpersonal behavior in a small group setting during the heroin addiction cycle. *The International Journal of the Addictions, 11,* 513–523.

Baron, R. A., & Richardson, D. R. (1994). *Human aggression* (2nd ed.). New York: Plenum Press.

Beezley, D. A., Gantner, A. B., Bailey, D. S., & Taylor, S. P. (1987). Amphetamines and human physical aggression. *Journal of Research in Personality, 21,* 52–60.

Berkowitz, L. (1993). *Aggression: Its causes, consequences, and control.* New York: McGraw-Hill.

Berman, M., & Taylor, S. (1995). The effects of triazolam on aggression in men. *Experimental and Clinical Psychopharmacology, 3,* 411–416.

Berman, M., Taylor, S., & Marged, B. (1993). Morphine and human aggression. *Addictive Behaviors, 18,* 263–268.

Bernstein, S., Richardson, D., & Hammock, G. (1987). Convergent and discriminate validity of the Taylor and Buss measures of physical aggression. *Aggressive Behavior, 13,* 15–24.

Blue, H. C., & Griffith, E. E. H. (1995). Sociocultural and therapeutic perspectives on violence. *The Psychiatric Clinics of North America, 18,* 571–587.

Bond, A., & Lader, M. (1988). Differential effects of oxazepam and lorazepam on aggressive responding. *Psychopharmacology, 95,* 369–373.

Bond, W. S., Mandos, L. A., & Kurtz, M. B. (1989). Midazolam for aggressivity and violence in three mentally retarded patients. *American Journal of Psychiatry, 146,* 925–926.

Brody, S. L. (1990). Violence associated with acute cocaine use in patients admitted to a medical emergency department. In M. De La Rosa, E. Y. Lambert, & B. Gropper (Eds.), *Drugs and violence: Causes, correlates, and consequences* (NIDA Research Monograph No. 103, pp. 44–59). Washington, DC: U.S. Government Printing Office.

Burrows, K. L., Hales, R. E., & Arington, E. (1988). Research on the biological aspects of violence. *The Psychiatric Clinics of North America, 11,* 499–509.

Bushman, B. (1993). Human aggression while under the influence of alcohol and other drugs: An integrative research review. *Current Directions in Psychological Science, 2,* 148–152.

Carlson, N. R. (1994). *Physiology of behavior* (5th ed.). Boston: Allyn and Bacon.

Carlson, N. R. (1995). *Foundations of Physiological Psychology* (3rd ed.). Boston: Allyn and Bacon.

Cherek, D. R., Roache, J. D., Egli, M., Davis, C., Spiga, R., & Cowan, K. (1993). Acute effects of marijuana smoking on aggressive, escape and point-maintained responding of male drug users. *Psychopharmacology, 111,* 163–168.

Chermack, S., & Taylor, S. P. (1993). Barbiturates and human physical aggression. *Journal of Research in Personality, 27,* 315–327.

Cohen, S. (1981). *The substance abuse problems.* New York: The Hawthorne Press.

Cohen, S., and Ditman, K. (1963). Prolonged adverse reactions to lysergic acid diethylamide. *Archives of General Psychiatry, 8,* 475–480.

Cole, J. O., & Kando, J. C. (1993). Adverse behavioral events reported in patients taking alprazolam and other benzodiazepines. *Journal of Clinical Psychiatry, 54(Suppl. 10),* 49–61.

Collins, J. J. (1990). Summary thoughts about drugs and violence. In M. De La Rosa, E. Y. Lambert, & B. Gropper (Eds.), *Drugs and violence: Causes, correlates, and consequences* (NIDA Research Monograph No. 103, pp. 265–275). Washington, DC: U.S. Government Printing Office.

Connor, D. F., & Steingard, R. J. (1996). A clinical approach to the pharmacotherapy of aggression in children and adolescents. *Annals of the New York Academy of Sciences, 794,* 290–307.

Corrigan, P. W., Yudofsky, S. C., and Silver, J. M. (1993). Pharmacological and behavioral treatments for aggressive psychiatric inpatients. *Hospital and Community Psychiatry, 44,* 125–133.

De La Rosa, M., Lambert, E. Y., & Gropper, B. (Eds.) (1990). *Drugs and violence: Causes, correlates, and consequences* (NIDA Research Monograph No. 103). Washington, DC: U.S. Government Printing Office.

Dengerink, H. A. (1971). Anxiety, aggression, and physiological arousal. *Journal of Experimental Research in Personality, 5,* 223–232.

Dietch, J. T., & Jennings, R. K. (1988). Aggressive dyscontrol in patients treated with benzodiazepines. *Journal of Clinical Psychiatry, 49,* 184–188.

DiMascio, A., Shader, R. I., and Giller, D. R. (1970). Behavior toxicity. In R. I. Shader & A. DiMascio (Eds.), *Psychotropic drug side effects: Clinical and theoretical perspectives* (pp. 132–141). Baltimore: Williams & Wilkins Co.

Ellinwood, E. H. (1971). Assault and homicide associated with amphetamine abuse. *American Journal of Psychiatry, 127,* 1170–1175.

Fagan, J., & Ko-lin, C. (1990). Violence as regulation and social control in the distribution of crack. In M. De La Rosa, E. Y. Lambert, & B. Gropper (Eds.), *Drugs and violence: Causes, correlates, and consequences* (NIDA Research Monograph No. 103, pp. 8–43). Washington, DC: U.S. Government Printing Office.

Fauman, B. A., Aldinger, G., & Fauman, M. (1976). Psychiatric sequelae of phencyclidine abuse. *Clinical Toxicology, 9,* 529–538.

Fauman, M. A., & Fauman, B. J. (1980). Chronic phencyclidine (PCP) abuse: A psychiatric perspective. *Psychopharmacology Bulletin, 16,* 70–72.

Fisher, S. (1995). *Patient self-monitoring: A challenging approach to pharmacoepidemiology.* Pharmacoepidemiology and Drug Safety, 4, 359–378.

Gantner, A. B., & Taylor, S. P. (1988). Human physical aggression as a function of diazepam. *Personality and Social Psychology Bulletin, 14,* 479–484.

Gardos, G., DiMascio, A., Salzman, C., & Shader, R. (1968). Differential actions of chlordiazepoxide and oxazepam on hostility. *Archives of General Psychiatry, 18,* 757–760.

Genthner, R. W., & Taylor, S. P. (1973). Physical aggression as a function of racial prejudice and the race of the target. *Journal of Personality and Social Psychology, 27,* 207–210.

Giannini, A. J., Miller, N. S., Loiselle, R. H., & Turner, C. E. (1993). Cocaine-associated violence and relationship to route of administration. *Journal of Substance Abuse Treatment, 10,* 67–69.

Goldstein, P. J. (1989). Drugs and violent crime. In N. A. Weiner & M. E. Wolfgang (Eds.), *Pathways to criminal violence* (pp. 16–48). Newbury Park, CA: Sage.

Goldstein, P. J., Bellucci, P. A., Spunt, B. J., & Miller, T. (1991). In S. Schober & C. Schade (Eds.), *The epidemiology of cocaine use and abuse* (NIDA Research Monograph No. 110, pp. 113–138). Washington, DC: U.S. Government Printing Office.

Goode, E. (1972). Marijuana use and crime. In National Commission on Marihuana and Drug Abuse, *Marihuana: A signal of misunderstanding* (Vol. 1., pp. 447–469). Washington, DC: U.S. Government Printing Office.

Goode, E. (1993). *Drugs in american society* (4th ed.). New York: McGraw-Hill.

Greenblatt, D. (1992). Pharmacology of benzodiazepine hypnotics. *Journal of Clinical Psychiatry, 56(Suppl. 6),* 7–13.

Gunn, J. (1979). Drugs in the violence clinic. In M. Sandler (Ed.), *Psychopharmacology of aggression* (pp. 183–195). New York: Raven Press.

Hall, R. C. W., & Zisook, S. (1981). Paradoxical reactions to benzodiazepines. *British Journal of Clinical Pharmacology, 11*, 995–1045.

Hatsukami, D. K., & Fischman, M. W. (1996). Crack cocaine and cocaine hydrochloride: Are the differences myth or reality? *Journal of the American Medical Association, 276*, 1580–1588.

Honer, W. G., Gewirtz, G., & Turey, M. (1987). Psychosis and violence in cocaine smokers. *Lancet, 2*, 451.

Hurlbut, K. M. (1991). Drug-induced psychoses. *Emergency Medicine Clinics of North America, 9*, 31–52.

Inman, W. (1972). Monitoring by voluntary reporting at national level. In D. Richards & R. Rondell (Eds.), *Adverse drug reactions*. Baltimore: Williams & Wilkins, Co.

Kalat, J. W. (1995). *Biological Psychology* (5th ed.). Pacific Grove, CA: Brooks/Cole.

Kaplan, J. (1970). *Marijuana: The new prohibition*. New York: World.

Kermani, E. J., & Castaneda, R. (1996). Psychoactive substance use in forensic psychiatry. *American Journal of Drug and Alcohol Abuse, 22*, 1–27.

Khantzian, E. J. (1974). Opiate addiction: A critique of theory and some implications for treatment. *American Journal of Psychotherapy, 28*, 59–71.

Khantzian, E. J. (1985). The self-medication hypothesis of addictive disorders: Focus on heroin and cocaine dependence. *The American Journal of Psychiatry, 142*, 1259–1264.

Kirov, K. (1989). Aggressiveness, anxiety and drugs. *British Journal of Psychiatry, 155*, 846.

Klerman, G. (1983). The prevalence and impact of mental illness on society. In R. L. Habig (Ed.), *The brain, biochemistry, and behavior.* Washington, DC: American Association for Clinical Chemistry.

Kozel, N. J., & DuPont, R. L. (1977). Trends in drug use and crime and their relationship in an arrested population. *American Journal of Drug and Alcohol Abuse, 4*, 413–429.

Leccese, A. P. (1991). *Drugs and society: Behavioral medicines and abusable drugs*. Englewood Cliffs, NJ: Prentice Hall.

Leonard, B. E. (1992). *Fundamentals of psychopharmacology.* New York: John Wiley & Sons.

Licata, A., Taylor, S., Berman, M., & Cranston, J. (1993). Effects of cocaine on human aggression. *Pharmacology, Biochemistry and Behavior, 45*, 549–552.

Lindquist, C. U., Lindsay, J. S., & White, G. D. (1979). Assessment of assertiveness in drug abusers. *Journal of Clinical Psychology, 35*, 676–679.

Luisada, P. C., & Brown, B. I. (1976). Clinical management of the phencyclidine psychosis. *Clinical Toxicology, 9*, 539–545.

Mayfield, D. (1983). Substance abuse and aggression: A psychopharmacological perspective. In E. Gottheil, K. Druley, T. Skoloda, & H. Waxman (Eds.), *Alcohol, drug abuse and aggression* (pp. 139–149). Springfield: Charles Thomas.

Mednick, S., Pollock, V., Volavka, J., & Gabrielli, W., Jr. (1982). Biology and violence. In M. Wolfgang & N. Weiner (Eds.), *Criminal violence*. Beverly Hills, CA: Sage.

Meloy, J. R. (1987). The prediction of violence in outpatient psychotherapy. *American Journal of Psychotherapy, 41*, 38–45.

Miczek, K. (1987). The psychopharmacology of aggression. In L. Iversen, S. Iversen, & S. Snyder (Eds.), *Handbook of psychopharmacology* (pp. 183–328). New York: Plenum Press.

Miller, N. S., & Gold, M. S. (1994). Criminal activity and crack addiction. *The International Journal of the Addictions, 29*, 1069–1078.

Miller, N. S., Gold, M. S., & Mahler, J. C. (1991). Violent behaviors associated with cocaine use: Possible pharmacological mechanisms. *The International Journal of the Addictions, 26*, 1077–1088.

Miller, R. R. (1973). Drug surveillance utilizing epidemiologic methods: A report from the Boston Collaborative Surveillance Program. *American Journal of Hospital Pharmacology, 30*, 584–592.

Moss, H. B., Salloum, I. M., & Fisher, B. (1994). Psychoactive substance abuse. In M. Hershen, R. T. Ammerman, & L. A. Sisson (Eds.), *Handbook of aggressive and destructive behavior in psychiatric patients* (pp. 175–201). New York: Plenum Press.

Myerscough, R., & Taylor, S. P. (1985). The effects of marijuana on human physical aggression. *Journal of Personality and Social Psychology, 49,* 1541–1546.

Pagano, M. R. (1981). *The effects of diazepam (Valium) on human physical aggression.* Unpublished doctoral dissertation, Kent State University, Kent, OH.

Pilowsky, L. S., Ring, H., Shine, P. J., Battersby, M., & Lader, M. (1992). Rapid tranquillisation: A survey of emergency prescribing in a general psychiatric hospital. *British Journal of Psychiatry, 160,* 831–835.

Pinel, J. P. J. (1997). *Biopsychology* (3rd ed.). Boston: Allyn and Bacon.

Powers, R., & Kutash, I. (1978). Substance-induced aggression. In I. Kutash, S. Kutash, & L. Schlesinger (Eds.), *Violence: Perspectives on murder and aggression.* San Francisco: Jossey-Bass.

Ratey, J. J., & Gorden, A. (1993). The psychopharmacology of aggression: Toward a new day. *Psychopharmacology Bulletin, 29,* 65–73.

Ray, S., & Ksir, C. (1990). *Drugs, society and human behavior* (5th ed.). St. Louis: Times Mirror/ Mosby.

Regestein, Q. R., & Reich, P. (1985). Agitation observed during treatment with newer hypnotic drugs. *Journal of Clinical Psychiatry, 46,* 280–283.

Reid, G. W. (1986). Acute care for the violent patient. *The Journal of the Arkansas Medical Society, 82,* 541–543.

Reiss, A. J., Jr., & Roth, J. A. (Eds.) (1993). *Understanding and preventing violence.* Washington, DC: National Academy Press.

Rickels, K., & Downing, R. W. (1974). Chlordiazepoxide and hostility in anxious outpatients. *American Journal of Psychiatry, 131,* 442–444.

Rivinus, T. M., & Larimer, M. E. (1993). Violence, alcohol, other drugs, and the college student. *Journal of College Student Psychotherapy, 8,* 71–119.

Rosenbaum, J. F., Woods, S. W., Groves, J. E., & Klerman, G. L. (1984). Emergence of hostility during alprazolam treatment. *American Journal of Psychiatry, 141,* 792–793.

Salzman, C., Kochansky, G. E., Shader, R. I., Porrino, L. J., Harmatz, J. S., & Swett, C. P., Jr. (1974). Chlordiazepoxide-induced hostility in a small group setting. *Archives of General Psychiatry, 31,* 401–405.

Sbordone, R., Gorelick, D., & Elliott, M. (1981). An ethological analysis of drug-induced pathological aggression. In P. Brain & D. Benton (Eds.), *Multidisciplinary approaches to aggression research.* New York: Elsevier/North-Holland Biomedical Press.

Shader, R. I., & Greenblatt, D. J. (1993). Use of benzodiazepines in anxiety disorders. *The New England Journal of Medicine, 328,* 1398–1405.

Sheard, M. H. (1988). Clinical pharmacology of aggressive behavior. *Clinical Neuropharmacology, 11,* 483–492.

Siegal, R. K. (1980). PCP and violent crime: The people vs. peace. *Journal of Psychedelic Drugs, 12,* 317–330.

Siegal, R. K. (1982). Cocaine smoking. *Journal of Psychoactive Drugs, 14,* 272–341.

Spunt, B., Goldstein, P., Brownstein, H., & Fendrich, M. (1994). The role of marijuana in homicide. *The International Journal of the Addictions, 29,* 195–213.

Svenson, S. E., & Hamilton, R. G. (1966). A critique of overemphasis on side effects with the psychotropic drugs: An analysis of 18,000 chlordiazepoxide-treated cases. *Current Therapeutic Research, 8,* 455–464.

Taylor, S. P., & Chermack, S. T. (1993). Alcohol, drugs and human physical aggression. *Journal of Studies on Alcohol (Suppl. 11),* 78–88.

Taylor, S. P., & Leonard, K. E. (1983). Alcohol and human physical aggression. In R. G. Geen & E. I. Donnerstein (Eds.), *Aggression: Theoretical and empirical reviews* (2nd ed., pp. 77–101). San Diego, CA: Academic Press.

Taylor, S. P., Vardaris, R. M., Rawtich, A. B., Gammon, C. B., Cranston, J. W., & Lubetkin, A. I. (1976). The effects of alcohol and delta-9-tetrahydrocannabinol on human physical aggression. *Aggressive Behavior, 2,* 153–161.

Tobin, J. M., & Lewis, N. D. C. (1960). New psychotherapeutic agent, chlordiazepoxide: Use in treatment of anxiety states and related symptoms. *Journal of the American Medical Association, 174,* 1242–1249.

van der Kroef, C. (1979). Reactions to triazolam. *Lancet, 2,* 526.

Watters, J. K., Reinarman, C., & Fagan, J. (1985). Causality, context and contingency: Relationships between drug use and delinquency. *Contemporary Drug Problems, 15,* 351–373.

Weisman, A. M. (1991). *The effect of diazepam, clorazepate, and oxazepam on human physical aggression.* Unpublished doctoral dissertation, Kent State University, Kent, OH.

Wetli, C. V., & Fishbain, D. A. (1985). Cocaine-induced psychosis and sudden death in recreational cocaine users. *Journal of Forensic Science, 30,* 873–880.

Wilkens, J. (1989). Clinical implications of PCP, NMDA and opiate receptors. In L. S. Harris (Ed.), *Problems of drug dependence 1989: Proceedings of the 51st annual meeting of the Committee on Problems of Drug Dependence* (NIDA Research Monograph No. 95, pp. 275–281). Washington, DC: U.S. Government Printing Office.

Wilkinson, C. J. (1985). Effects of diazepam (Valium) and trait anxiety on human physical aggression and emotional state. *Journal of Behavioral Medicine, 8,* 101–114.

Wish, E. D. (1986). PCP and crime: Just another illicit drug? In D. H. Clovet (Ed.), *Phencyclidine: An update* (NIDA Research Monograph No. 64, pp. 174–189). Washington, DC: U.S. Government Printing Office.

Wish, E. D., & Johnson, B. D. (1986). The impact of substance abuse on criminal careers. In A. Blumstein, J. Cohen, J. A. Roth, & C. A. Visher (Eds.), *Criminal careers and career criminals* (pp. 52–88). Washington, DC: National Academy Press.

7

HARMFUL EFFECTS OF

EXPOSURE TO MEDIA

VIOLENCE: LEARNING OF

AGGRESSION, EMOTIONAL

DESENSITIZATION, AND FEAR

STACY L. SMITH AND EDWARD DONNERSTEIN

University of California, Santa Barbara

America is a violent country. The statistics on crime and violence in the United States are staggering, particularly regarding children and adolescents. For example, consider the following figures cited by the American Psychological Association (1993) and U. S. Department of Justice (1997):

- Every 5 min a child is arrested for a violent crime.
- Adolescents account for 24% of all violent crimes leading to arrest. This rate has increased over time for 12 to 19 year olds and is down for individuals 35 and older.
- Every day over 100,000 children carry guns to school.
- Nearly 9 million 12 to 17 year olds have seen someone being shot with a gun, knifed, sexually assaulted, mugged, robbed, or threatened with a weapon during their lifetime.
- Gun-related violence takes the life of an American child every 3 hr.
- Among individuals 15 to 24 years old, homicide is the second leading cause of death. For African-Americans in this age bracket, however, it is number one.
- A child growing up in Chicago is 15 times more likely to be murdered than a child growing up in Northern Ireland.

Human Aggression: Theories, Research, and
Implications for Social Policy

What accounts for these alarming trends? Violent and criminal behavior is the result of a multiplicity of factors such as gang membership, drug and alcohol use, gun availability, poverty, brain damage, impulsivity, and racism, among many others. Many of these variables may independently or interactively affect antisocial responding. Due to the complexity of these and many other contributory factors, groups such as the American Psychological Association, American Medical Association, National Academy of Science, and Centers for Disease Control have all examined extensively the multiple causes of aggression in society. Cutting across all these investigations was a profound realization that the mass media, particularly television and film violence, also contributes to antisocial behavior in our country.

We realize that media violence is not the sole cause of aggressive behavior. We also recognize that media violence is not the only or even the most important cause of antisocial actions. Furthermore, it is not every violent act on television or film that is of concern. Nor will every child or adult act aggressively after watching a violent media portrayal. However, as shown in this chapter, there is clear evidence that exposure to media violence contributes in significant ways to violence in our society.

The goal of this chapter is to review what is known about the harmful impact of exposure to media violence on children, adolescents, and adults. This chapter is divided into six major sections. The first section focuses on individuals' television viewing habits. Specifically, we examine just how much time adults and children spend watching TV. In the second section, the amount of violence on American television is examined. Understanding the prevalence of violence across both broadcast and cable channels illustrates the risk that television may be posing to viewers. The third section examines what the research community has concluded about the effects of exposure to media violence. As we will note, over 40 years of social science research reveals that viewing television violence contributes to a range of antisocial effects on the audience. We then turn to examine the theoretical mechanisms that account for the impact of exposure to violence on television in the fourth section. Research indicates that not all violent portrayals pose the same risk of harm to the audience, however. Therefore, the fifth section delineates all those contextual features of violence that have been found by empirical research to either increase or decrease the risk of harmful effects on both child and adult viewers. In the final section, the possible solutions to mitigating the harmful impact of exposure to television violence are considered. Specifically, research on the effectiveness of ratings and advisories, teaching critical viewing skills, and media-initiated educational campaigns is reviewed.

EXPOSURE TO TELEVISION

Americans are fascinated with television. Indeed, a full 98% of the homes in this country have one television set and nearly 66% have two or more (APA, 1993; Comstock, 1993; Comstock & Paik, 1991). Of those homes that own at least one television, over 65% subscribe to cable programming and approximately two-thirds own a VCR (NCTA, 1995; Comstock, 1993). In most U.S. households, the television set is "on" an average of 7 hr per day and over 8 hr per day for those households that subscribe to cable (Harris, 1994; Liebert & Sprakfin, 1988). These figures reveal that the television set in the "average" American home is "on" approximately 50–64 hr per week!

Given these statistics, how much time do individuals actually spend watching television? Nielsen ratings for the first quarter of the 1996 season revealed that individuals 18 and over are watching an average of 32 hr of television a week (Nielsen Media Research, 1997) with women (34 hr a week) viewing slightly more than men (30 hr a week). Thus, the average adult spends over 4 hr per day watching TV, which is more time spent on any one activity outside of working or sleeping (Kubey & Csikszentmihalyi, 1990).

Surprisingly, children spend slightly less time viewing television than do adults. Nielsen ratings for the first quarter of the 1996 viewing season revealed that 2 to 11 year olds spend an average of 22 hr per week watching television whereas 12 to 17 year olds spend an average of 20 hr per week viewing television (Nielsen Media Research, 1997). Even more conservative estimates suggest that children spend 2–3 hr viewing television per day (see Huston et al., 1992). Similar to adults, these statistics indicate that America's youth also spend a great deal of their leisure time in front of the TV. Indeed, a national survey of 1228 parents and their children reveals that after sleeping, 2 to 17 year olds spend more time watching television than doing homework, reading books, using a computer, playing video games, or reading magazines or newspapers (Stanger, 1997).

Viewing estimates for children from specific subgroups of the population are even higher. For instance, Tangey and Feshbach (1988) assessed the impact of several demographic variables on television viewing across three different samples of older elementary school-aged children. Across all three groups, results revealed that African-American children watch nearly twice as much television per week as Caucasian children, independent of parents' level of education. Other studies have revealed that children from low-income families watch substantially more television than do children from mid- to high-income families (Huston et al., 1992; Kubey & Csikszentmihalyi, 1990). Clearly, children who come from some of the most vulnerable subgroups of the population are the heaviest viewers of television (see Eron, Gentry, & Schlegel, 1994), presumably due to their lack of alternative activities.

In total, the research reviewed in this section reveals three major trends in Americans' television viewing habits. First, individuals in this country are heavy consumers of television programming. Second, adults spend a great deal of time watching television in general and they seem to be "modeling" their viewing habits to the children of this country. Third, children are also heavy viewers of television, particularly if they come from African-American or poor families.

VIOLENCE ON AMERICAN TELEVISION

With a steady viewing diet of 2–3 hr of television per day, how much violence are children being exposed to? Researchers have estimated that by the time a child finishes elementary school, he/she will have seen approximately 8000 murders and over 100,000 other acts of violence on TV (Huston et al., 1992). These figures are significantly higher for youngsters who are heavy viewers of television or who have access to premium cable programming or violent films they can rent or buy and watch on a VCR.

Several content analyses over the last three decades have been conducted to systematically assess the prevalence of violence on television (Gerbner, Gross, Morgan, & Signorielli, 1980; Gerbner, Gross, Signorielli, & Morgan, 1986; Mustonen & Pulkkinen, 1993; Potter & Ware, 1987; Potter et al., 1995; Signorielli, 1990; Williams, Zabrack, & Joy, 1982). The largest and most rigorous of these was undertaken by 10 researchers (i.e., Barbara Wilson, Dale Kunkel, Daniel Linz, Edward Donnerstein, James Potter, Stacy Smith, Eva Blumenthal, Tim Gray, Michael Berry, and Carolyn Colvin) at the University of California, Santa Barbara (see Kunkel et al., 1995, 1996; Wilson et al., 1997, 1998). Working under the auspices of the National Television Violence Study (NTVS), these scholars were funded by the National Cable Television Association to examine longitudinally the amount and context of violence on American television for 3 consecutive years. The focus of this section is to review (a) the foundations of this study, (b) several unique contributions this content analysis has made to social science research, and (c) some of the study's findings for the 1994–1995 and 1995–1996 viewing seasons.

The NTVS is grounded on two major assumptions: that exposure to television violence contributes to a range of antisocial effects on viewers and that not all violent portrayals pose the same risk of harm to viewers. Research indicates that some depictions of violence increase the risk of antisocial effects whereas others decrease such a risk. Simply put, the context or way in which violence is presented on television influences its impact on the audience. Based on these assumptions, there were two goals of the NTVS: to craft a unique content analysis framework (i.e., definition, units of analysis, coding scheme) sensitive to capturing both the amount and the context of violence on television and to analyze the nature and extent of violent depictions across the television landscape.

Of the several unique contributions NTVS has offered to the body of social science research, the first is the highly conservative definition of violence used in the study. The definition of violence is as follows:

> Violence is defined as any overt depiction of a credible threat of physical force, or the actual use of such force intended to physically harm an animate being or group of beings. Violence also includes certain depictions of physically harmful consequences against an animate being or group that occur as a result of unseen violent means. Thus, there are three primary types of violent depictions: credible threats, behavioral acts, and harmful consequences.

Three key components of this definition—intentionality, physical harm, and animate beings—warrant some further explication.

Intentionality is the most vital aspect of the definition. If intentionality was excluded, then a plethora of harmful behaviors not normally considered "aggressive" would qualify as violence. For example, all accidental harm (i.e., slips, mishaps) and practical jokes (i.e., pie in the face) would count as violence as well as many medical acts by surgeons and dentists, although none of these behaviors have been identified by research to contribute to psychological harm.

According to the definition, the use of force must be intended to *physically harm* an animate being or group of beings. One could argue that verbal threats that intimidate or physical acts meant to cause psychological or emotional harm (i.e., humiliation) should be violence. Such actions may be aggressive and in some instances may contribute to antisocial effects. For the NTVS definition, however, these researchers chose to draw the line at the point that is most strongly supported by research. Physical harm or the threat thereof is at the center of all conceptualizations of aggression and most of the operationalizations of past research (Baron & Richardson, 1994; Reiss & Roth, 1993). By using this approach, one can be assured that the findings from this study are conservative in nature.

Finally, the perpetrator of violence must be an *animate being.* Individuals can incur physical harm from many forces other than living beings on television. Acts of nature may range from a killer whale devouring a seal in the wild to natural disasters such as earthquakes, fires, and floods which can claim thousands of lives. Although these types of acts may cause fear (see Wilson & Smith, 1998; also Cantor, 1994), they do not contribute to the learning of aggressive thoughts, attitudes, and behaviors. Consistent with the previous point that intent to harm is the fundamental linchpin of the definition, an animate being must also be capable of evidencing intentionality as a perpetrator in order to have an instance of violence.

Another unique contribution of this content analysis is the multilevel approach to quantifying violence. Given the researchers' desire to examine the context of violence, it was imperative to evaluate more than each violent act in isolation, as many content analyses have done in the past. In explanation, violence incidents occur between characters in particular scenes. These violent scenes are situated in programs that may portray violence in very different ways. In order to capture the "meaning" of violence at each of these stages, aggressive acts were assessed at three distinct levels. The most novel and micro level was the violent interaction. A violent interaction is simply an aggressive exchange between a perpetrator (P) engaging in a particular type of act (A) against a target (T), yielding the convenient acronym, PAT. It was at this level that a myriad of contextual variables such as the type of act, the reason for the act, and the immediate consequences of violence (i.e., harm/pain) were assessed. Judgments were also made at the end of each violent scene. For example, coders assessed whether any rewards or punishments were present within a violent scene and how much blood and gore were featured. Finally, the narrative purpose or overall message about violence, the duration of harm/pain, and realism of violence were assessed at the end of each violent program.

Prior to developing the coding scheme, the NTVS researchers reviewed comprehensively the experimental research to ascertain what particular content attributes of violence have been found to increase the risk of learning aggression, emotional desensitization, or fear. Nine specific contextual variables were identified in this search, which will be fully reviewed later in this chapter. Those nine variables include nature of the perpetrator, nature of the target, justification, extensiveness and graphicness of violence, weapons, rewards/punishments, harm/pain, realism, and humor. Based on this review, over 40 variables were crafted to accurately "measure" the relative presence of each of these contextual features of violence on television.

The programs for NTVS were randomly sampled from 23 broadcast and cable channels over a 20-week period of time ranging from October to June during the 1994–1995 and 1995–1996 viewing seasons. Programs were selected randomly from 6:00 a.m. to 11:00 p.m. across all seven days of the week. A representative composite week was compiled for each programming source, yielding a sum of 119 hr per channel or 2500 hr of television programming assessed each year. Per contract parameters with the National Cable Television Association, all sports, news, game shows, infomercials, and religious programs were sampled but *not* examined for violence. In total then, 2693 programs were examined for violence during the 1994–1995 viewing season and 2757 for the 1995–1996 viewing season. To date, this is the largest and most representative sample of television programming in the history of social science research.

What is the prevalence of violence on American television? Results from the first-year NTVS report reveal that a full 57% of programs on television contain some violence. Over 8000 violent scenes and 18,000 violent interactions spanned the entire sample, with 66% of those interactions including behavioral acts of violence, 29% involving credible threats of violence, and 3% involving harmful consequences of unseen violence. Only 4% of all violent programs on television feature an "antiviolence" theme. Put in another way, 96% of all violent television programs use aggression as a narrative, cinematic device for simply entertaining the audience. These prevalence findings are incredibly consistent across two randomly sampled composite weeks of television from 2 different years.

When we take a look at the prevalence of violence across different channels and genre types, some significant differences emerge. Comparing channel types to the industry average (57%), premium cable (85%) features substantially more programs with violence than broadcast networks (44%) and PBS (18%). In terms of genre types, movies (90%) and drama series (72%) contain significantly more violence than reality-based shows (30%) and comedies (27%).

Although the aforementioned results are interesting, they only inform us about the prevalence of violence on television. What should be of greater concern is the context or way in which violence is portrayed on TV. When we look more closely at the context of violence, the results reveal that most aggression on television is glamorized. Nearly one-half (44%) of the violent interactions on television involve perpetrators who have some attractive qualities worthy of emulation. Nearly 40% of the scenes involve humor either directed at the violence or used by characters involved with violence. Furthermore, a full 74% of all violent scenes on television feature no immediate punishment or condemnation for violence. Almost 40% of the programs feature "bad" characters who are never or rarely punished for their aggressive actions. As Figure 7.1 illuminates, these findings are

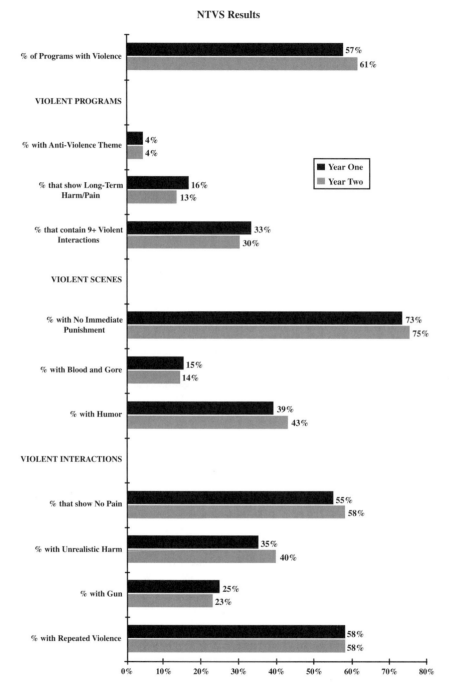

FIGURE 7.1   National Television Violence Study findings for the 1994–1995 and 1995–1996 television viewing seasons. From the Center for Communication and Social Policy, 1997, with permission.

also incredibly consistent across two composite weeks of television sampled over a 2-year period.

Much of the violence on television is also sanitized. For example, over half of the violent behavioral interactions on television feature no pain (55%) and 47% feature no harm. A full 40% of the violent behavioral interactions depict harm in an unrealistic fashion with the greatest prevalence of unrealistic harm appearing in children's programming, presumably due to cartoons. Of all violent scenes on television, 86% feature *no* blood or gore. This is surprising given that nearly 40% of all interactions involved conventional weapons such as guns, knives, bombs, or other heavy weaponry! Finally, only 16% of violent programs featured the long-term, realistic consequences of violence. As Figure 7.1 reveals, these findings are remarkably stable across a composite week of television randomly sampled from the 1994–1995 and 1995–1996 viewing seasons.

The NTVS is not without limitations, however. Perhaps one of the major draw-backs of this study was the decision to sample but *not* assess violence in news pro-grams. Empirical research indicates that much of news programming is filled with stories about crime and violence (Johnson, 1996; Lichter & Amundson, 1994; Slattery & Hanaken, 1994). Approximately 15% of the programs on the broadcast networks and 10% of the programs on the independent stations are news, not to mention the two CNN channels on basic cable (Wilson et al., 1997). Given that news stories often feature violence or its harmful aftermath, the prevalence of vi-olence on American television may be considerably higher than the NTVS find-ings reveal.

In total, the focus of this section was to examine the nature of violence on American television. The fundamental assumptions, definition of violence, levels of analysis, and contextual variables of the National Television Violence Study were reviewed. The findings from this massive study suggest two major trends in television programming: (a) violence is pervasive on television and (b) much of violence is glamorized and sanitized.

CONCLUSIONS ABOUT THE EFFECTS
OF MEDIA VIOLENCE

If individuals are exposed to television content that is filled with portrayals of violence, what effect is it having on children, adolescents, and adults? In a poll of 600 adults conducted by Time and CNN, many Americans believe that violence contributes to harmful effects on viewers (Lacayo, 1995). Three quarters of those surveyed said that violence in television, movies, and music videos inspires young people to act violently. Furthermore, a full 76% of those interviewed stated that it numbs individuals to violence so that they are insensitive or calloused to it (Lacayo, 1995, p. 26). These figures suggest that many Americans believe that ex-posure to media violence contributes to a range of antisocial effects on viewers.

Over the years, several governmental and professional organizations have con-ducted exhaustive reviews of the scientific literature to ascertain the relationship between exposure to media violence and aggressive behavior [American Medical Association (AMA), 1996; American Psychological Association (APA), 1993; Center for Disease Control and Prevention (CDCP), 1991; National Academy of Science (NAS), 1993; National Institute of Mental Health (NIMH), 1982; U.S. Surgeon General, 1972]. These investigations have documented consistently that exposure to media violence contributes to aggressive behaviors in viewers and may influence their perceptions and attitudes about violence in the real world.

The earliest of these investigations was conducted by the U.S. Surgeon General (1972). The Surgeon General funded several studies specifically designed to assess the impact of exposure to media violence on child and adolescent viewers. Research revealed that there was a significant correlation between viewing television violence and aggressive behavior. This finding emerged across several different measures of aggressive behavior (i.e., self-report, peer ratings) and across several different methodological approaches (i.e., correlational, cross-lagged longitudinal investigations) to studying the problem (for review, see Liebert & Sprafkin, 1988). Experimental evidence in the report also made it clear that there was a direct, causal link between exposure to television violence and subsequent aggressive behavior in child viewers.

Ten years later, the National Institute of Mental Health (1982) conducted a follow-up investigation to review and integrate research that had been undertaken since the Surgeon General's (1972) report. The NIMH (1982) report concluded that exposure to television violence contributes to aggressive behavior in children, completely supporting the conclusion reached in the Surgeon General's study. Only now, the relationship could be extended to also account for preschoolers and older adolescents, and was generalizable to both boys and girls. The NIMH (1982) report also revealed that there were other harmful effects associated with exposure to television violence. Studies had revealed that heavy exposure to television violence contributes to increased fear of becoming a victim of violence and exaggerated perceptions of how much aggression and criminal activity occur in the world.

Additional reports have lent further support to the mass media's harmful impact on the audience. For example, the CDCP (1991), the NAS (1993), the AMA (1996), and the APA (1992) all examined the relationship between exposure to media violence and antisocial behavior. Of all these reports, the most comprehensive came from the APA in 1992. Establishing a commission on youth and violence, the APA committee reviewed five decades of scientific research on the causes and prevention of violence in society. Like previous investigations into violence, the role of the mass media was considered and the conclusions reached were strikingly similar to the NIMH and Surgeon General's report.

After scouring hundreds of empirical studies, the commission arrived at several significant conclusions regarding the harmful effects of exposure to media violence. First, heavy viewing of media violence is correlated with aggressive behavior and increased aggressive attitudes (see Donnerstein, Slaby, & Eron, 1994). The correlation between viewing violence on television and exhibiting aggressive behavior is fairly stable over time, place, and demographics (Huesmann & Eron, 1986). Experimental and longitudinal studies also supported the position that viewing television violence is related causally to aggressive behavior (Huston et al., 1992). Even more important, naturalistic field studies and cross-national investigations reveal that viewing televised aggression leads to increases in subsequent aggression and that such behavior can become part of a lasting behavioral pattern (e.g., Huesmann & Eron, 1986).

The APA report stated that exposure to media violence at a young age can have lasting, long-life negative consequences. If aggressive habits are learned early in life, they may form the foundation for later antisocial behavior. For example, aggressive children who struggle academically and socially/ interpersonally tend to watch more television. Viewing violence on television reinforces their aggressive tendencies, only increasing their social and academic failure (APA, 1993, p. 33). These effects may have both short- and long-term implications. Indeed, Huesmann and colleagues (e.g., Huesmann & Eron, 1986; Huesmann, Eron, Lefkowitz, & Walder, 1984) found a clear and significant relationship between early exposure to televised violence at age 8 and adult criminal behavior 22 years later.

The APA commission also concluded that exposure to television violence may alter individuals' attitudes and behaviors toward violence in two particular ways. First, prolonged viewing of media violence may emotionally desensitize viewers toward real world violence. As a result, individuals may develop calloused attitudes toward aggression directed at others and a decreased likelihood to take action on behalf of a victim when violence occurs (see Donnerstein, Slaby, & Eron, 1994).

Second, exposure to media violence can contribute to increased fear in viewers about becoming a victim of real world violence. As a result, individuals may become increasingly untrusting or suspicious of others and engage in a variety of self-protective behaviors. Research on the effects of cumulative exposure to television reveals that heavy viewers may develop attitudes and beliefs about the world that "match" or are very similar to the world presented on television (for review, see Gerbner, Gross, Morgan, & Signorielli, 1994). Because television is filled with stories about crime and violence, heavy viewing can contribute to developing exaggerated perceptions of how much violence occurs in this world or unrealistic fears and beliefs about becoming a victim of violence.

In total then, over four decades of social science research reveals that exposure to media violence contributes to many undesirable effects on the audience. As evidenced in this section, viewing television violence contributes to (a) learning aggressive thoughts, attitudes, and behaviors, (b) emotional desensitization to real world aggression and its victims, and (c) fear of becoming a victim of violence.

THEORETICAL PERSPECTIVES ON MEDIA VIOLENCE

What theoretical mechanisms can be used to explain each of the three aforementioned effects? Several theories have been offered to account for learning, desensitization, and fear. The goal of this section is to review some of those theories that have made significant contributions to our understanding of how exposure to media violence contributes to psychological harm.

LEARNING OF AGGRESSION

One of the early and most notable theoretical accounts of learning aggression is social learning theory (Bandura, 1965, 1971). Developed by Albert Bandura, social learning theory advances that individuals acquire social behaviors through direct experience and indirectly through the observation of models. Models may include a child's peers, siblings, parents, or even characters depicted in the mass media. By watching or observing models, a child comes to view what behaviors are socially sanctioned or rewarded in society on one hand and those actions that are reprehensible or punishable on the other. Surely, an assumption of social learning theory is that much of human behavior is directed toward achieving some particular goal or reward.

Several investigations have documented that individuals learn aggressive behaviors from being exposed to models (Bandura, 1965; Bandura, Ross, & Ross, 1961, 1963a,b; Berkowitz & Geen, 1967; Liebert & Baron, 1972). Perhaps the most renowned of these were the classic "Bobo doll" studies undertaken by Bandura and colleagues in the 1960s. In a series of experiments, Bandura and his research team found repeatedly that preschoolers exposed to an aggressive TV or live model who was rewarded were significantly more likely to engage in aggressive behavior than were those preschoolers exposed to the same aggressive TV or live model who was punished (Bandura, 1965; Bandura et al., 1963b).

Much of the experimental research investigating the causal relationship between viewing media violence and aggression has been criticized for being too artificial and contrived. More naturalistic field studies, however, also provide support for the social learning of aggression through exposure to violent mass media. For instance, Huesmann and Eron (1986) have argued that aggressive habits are learned early in life and become resistant to change over the course of a child's development. In an effort to assess the long-term impact of early exposure to television violence on later aggressive and criminal behavior, Huesmann, Eron, Lefkowitz, and Walder (1984) studied a group of youth originally from Columbia County, New York, across a 22-year time frame. Data on the subjects' television viewing and aggressive behavior were collected when they were 8, 18, and 30 years of age.

Results from structural modeling analyses revealed a longitudinal effect that bridged 22 years. Early viewing of television violence by boys was associated with self-reported aggressive behavior at age 30 and added a significant increment to the prediction of serious criminal arrests accrued by that age. These findings held up even after controlling for intellectual functioning, social class, and parenting variables. Based on these findings, Huesmann and Eron (1986) concluded that early viewing of violence on television stimulates aggression and that early aggression is a statistical precursor to later criminal behavior, leading to the longitudinal relation from habitual childhood exposure to television violence to adult crime. Their analyses indicate that approximately 10% of the variability in later criminal behavior can be attributed to television violence.

A social learning approach has been widely accepted and used by mass media scholars attempting to examine the relationship between exposure to media violence and aggressive behavior in both children and adults (see Comstock & Paik, 1991; Liebert & Sprafkin, 1988). A little over a decade ago, however, Bandura (1986) reformulated this theory to account for more of the cognitive processes involved in observational learning and thus reentitled his explanatory framework, social cognitive theory. As noted later, other media researchers have also turned to cognitive models and information processing perspectives to explain the relationship between viewing television violence and aggressive behavior.

One such cognitive theory, a priming effects perspective, was advanced by Leonard Berkowitz. Berkowitz and colleagues (Berkowitz, 1984; Berkowitz & Rogers, 1986; Jo & Berkowitz, 1994) offer an explanatory framework, grounded in cognitive neoassociation theory, for many of the short-term, transient effects of exposure to media violence. According to Jo and Berkowitz (1994), stimuli seen or heard in the mass media can activate or "prime," for a short time, other related thoughts in viewers. These thoughts, in turn, can activate other semantically associated ideas, feelings, and even action tendencies (see Jo & Berkowitz, 1994, p. 45). The process of thought activation has been labeled a "priming effect." To illustrate how the priming process is instantiated, watching a violent film can "prime" hostile or aggressive thoughts or ideas in viewers. These hostile thoughts may automatically trigger in the viewer other hostile thoughts, feelings, and possibly even behavioral action tendencies.

Several studies have documented that aggressive media content can "prime" aggressive thoughts in viewers (Bushman & Geen, 1990). For example, Bushman (in press) assessed the impact of exposure to either a 15-min violent video excerpt (i.e., *Karate Kid III*) or a nonviolent video excerpt (i.e., *Gorillas in the Mist*) on the priming of individuals' aggressive thoughts. Bushman (1996) found that undergraduates exposed to the violent film clip generated a greater number of aggressive associations to stimulus words than did undergraduates exposed to the nonviolent film clip. Research suggests that other forms of violent media can also evoke aggressive thoughts in viewers. Berkowitz, Parker, and West (cf., Berkowitz, 1973, pp. 125 and 126) found that children who had read a war comic book (i.e., *Adventures of the Green Berets*) were significantly more likely to choose words with aggressive meanings to complete sentences than were children who had read a neutral comic book (i.e., *Gidget*). These findings suggest that exposure to violence, independent of the medium, can evoke aggressive ideas and thoughts in viewers.

What impact does "priming" hostile thoughts have on individuals? Research reveals that activating aggressive thoughts can have significant social consequences. For instance, Carver, Ganellen, Froming, and Chambers (1983) found that subjects exposed to a hostile video clip of a businessman and his secretary rated a subsequent ambiguous person as significantly more hostile than those subjects exposed to a nonhostile version of the same video clip. Berkowitz (1970) found that undergraduate women exposed to a hostile comedic routine (e.g., Don Rickles) rated a job applicant significantly harsher than those subjects exposed to a nonhostile comedic routine (e.g., George Carlin), independent of whether they were previously angered by the job candidate or not. Other studies have revealed that individuals who have witnessed certain types of violent encounters via the mass media (i.e., portrayals of sexual violence) are more likely to favor violence in interpersonal settings (Malamuth & Check, 1981). These results suggest that priming aggressive thoughts can alter both individuals' interpretations of others and attitudes toward aggressive behavior.

Research evidence also points to the fact that priming aggressive thoughts may heighten the probability of acting aggressively. For example, Carver et al.'s (1983) results reveal that male subjects primed to have aggressive thoughts delivered significantly more intense electric shocks than those male subjects in the control (neutral prime) condition. Similar findings have been obtained by Worchel (1972).

Taken together, these studies provide support for explaining the short-term, instigational effects of exposure to media violence from a cognitive priming perspective. One limitation of Berkowitz' priming approach is that it only focuses on the immediate impact of viewing violent media on the audience. What about the long-term or cumulative effect of exposure to violence on television? Another information processing perspective, Rowell Huesmann's (1986) social developmental theory, offers an excellent explanatory framework that delineates how exposure to television violence, as well as several other intervening variables, contributes to a child's socialization to habitual aggressive behavior.

According to Huesmann (1986), social behavior is controlled to a great extent by cognitive "scripts" that are learned early in the course of a child's development. A script is simply a cognitive map stored in memory that serves as a guide for behavior. Scripts are developed either through direct experience or by observing models, such as those portrayed in the mass media. By watching a great deal of interpersonal or media violence, children can develop aggressive scripts or cognitive rules for dealing with problems that arise in social situations (Huesmann, 1986).

Not every violent scene on television is encoded and stored in memory, however. Huesmann (1988) indicates that certain factors heighten the probability of encoding. For example, violent scenes that are perceived as realistic by the viewer and that feature aggressive characters with whom the child can identify are particularly salient and thus increase the likelihood of encoding. Not only must aggressive scenes be encoded, but they must also be maintained in memory over time. Mentally rehearsing aggressive scenes viewed on television, by way of fantasizing about or cognitively ruminating over, increases the probability that an aggressive script will be stored in memory (Huesmann, 1988).

Not every aggressive script that is encoded and stored in memory will be retrieved when a child faces a problem-solving situation, however. Script retrieval is dependent on several factors, particularly the cues that are present at the time of recall. According to Huesmann (1988), "the most important cues are characteristics of the environment (even seemingly irrelevant ones) that are identical with those present when the script was encoded" (p. 21). Other cues, such as the presence of guns or other conventional weapons, may also trigger or instantiate aggressive scripts from memory even if they were not present when the script was initially encoded (Huesmann, 1988).

Huesmann's (1986, 1988) model can clearly account for both the short- and the long-term effects of viewing violent mass media content on aggressive behavior. Repeated exposure to violence on television contributes to a child's development and maintenance of aggressive scripts in memory for dealing with social problem solving. Such cumulative learning eventually leads a child to employ aggressive scripts and behaviors to solve interpersonal conflicts (Huesmann, 1988). Indeed, naturalistic studies reveal that a child's viewing of television violence is both correlated with aggressive behavior and is a precursor to later adult aggressiveness and criminality (Huesmann et al., 1984; Huesmann, Moise, Podolski, & Eron, 1997). Violent scenes on television may also function to trigger and strengthen already acquired aggressive scripts stored in memory. In fact, innumerable experiments have documented the immediate, short-term effect of viewing television violence on aggressive behavior across both child and adult viewers (see Wilson et al., 1997; Paik & Comstock, 1994).

Huesmann and colleagues have found that several intervening variables strengthen the relationship between viewing television violence and aggressive behavior, thereby heightening the likelihood that a child will adopt aggression as a characteristic way of solving social conflicts (see Huesmann, 1986, pp. 133–135). Longitudinal studies have documented that children (a) who identify with aggressive television characters, (b) who fantasize about aggression, (c) who believe that television is an accurate reflection of social reality, (d) who are unpopular with peers or classmates, and (e) who do poorly in school are particularly at risk for learning aggressive scripts, attitudes, and behaviors from exposure to television programming (see Huesmann, 1986 for complete review; Huesmann & Eron, 1986; Huesmann et al., 1984, 1997; Lefkowitz, Eron, Walder, & Huesmann, 1977).

DESENSITIZATION

One much more pervasive but less well-known harmful effect of exposure to media violence is emotional desensitization. Desensitization refers to the process whereby repeated exposure to a particular object or stimulus leads to decreases in emotional responsivity to that stimulus (Wilson, 1995, p. 12). In the same way, repeated exposure to television violence can "desensitize" viewers or make them less sensitive to, less aroused by, or less emotionally upset over violent acts they see on TV. Such effects have significant social consequences.

Several of the early desensitization studies were concerned primarily with the impact of exposure to media violence on viewers' physiological arousal. For example, Cline, Croft, and Courrier (1973) found that boys who were heavy viewers of television responded with significantly less physiological arousal to a short violent movie clip than boys who were light viewers of television. Other investigations have demonstrated decreases in adults' galvanic skin response (GSR) while viewing a 17-min violent film clip (Lazarus, Speisman, Mordkoff, & Davison, 1962). Desensitization to media violence has also been found to influence individuals' reactions to real life violence. In two experiments, Thomas, Horton, Lippencott, and Drabman (1977) had children and adults view either an 11-min excerpt from a violent program or nothing prior to watching videotaped scenes of "real life" violence. Physiological arousal was assessed via GSR. Results reveal that children and adult males who viewed the aggressive films were *less* responsive physiologically to scenes of "real life" violence than were those subjects in the control condition.

Other studies have demonstrated that viewing television violence can also impact individuals' behavioral responses to real life aggression. For example, Drabman and Thomas (1974) were interested in the impact that viewing television violence had on children's tolerance for "real life" aggression. These researchers exposed third graders to either an 8-min clip from a violent western or a no exposure control. Children were then asked to monitor two younger children at play, who end up getting physically aggressive with one another. Tolerance was operationalized as the time it took subjects to solicit adult help after the onset of the younger children's aggressive behavior. Results revealed that children who saw the violent television clip took significantly longer to seek help of an adult than those children in the no exposure control group. Several studies have replicated these findings (Hirsch & Molitor, 1994; Thomas & Drabman, 1975).

What impact does extended exposure to media violence have on viewers' affective and behavioral reactions to violence? Daniel Linz and colleagues have examined extensively the effects of viewing repeatedly more graphic and sexual forms of media violence (i.e., "slasher" films) on viewers' perceptions, attitudes, and emotional reactions. In one study, Linz, Donnerstein, and Penrod (1984) exposed male undergraduates to five films depicting violence against women across 5 consecutive days. Comparisons between first and last day measures revealed that subjects' initial levels of self-reported anxiety and depression decreased considerably with repeated exposure, and the films were perceived by subjects to be less violent and less degrading to women. After viewing the fifth and final film, subjects were asked to participate in an allegedly separate study, which involved watching a rape trial documentary and rating the target of a sexual assault on several measures such as victim responsibility, sympathy, injury, and worthlessness. Results revealed that subjects who were exposed to a diet of slasher films rated the rape victim as significantly less injured and less worthy than subjects in the no exposure control group.

In a follow-up study, Linz, Donnerstein, and Penrod (1988) had male undergraduates view up to five, full-length slasher films over a longer period of time, 2 full weeks. Similar to Linz et al. (1984), these researchers found that when comparing first and last day measures, participants' anxiety and depression decreased substantially, and the films were perceived by subjects to be less violent and less degrading to women over time. Subjects were exposed to the same videotaped rape trial and asked to respond to a series of measures 2 days after viewing their last film. Results revealed two additional significant findings. Subjects who were exposed to a diet of violent slasher films were less sympathetic to the rape victim in the trial and less able to empathize with rape victims in general than were subjects in a no exposure control group or who had been exposed to a diet of nonviolent, R-rated sex films. Linz et al. (1988) concluded that exposure to sexual violence over a longer period of time was necessary to affect subjects' general empathetic response.

Theoretically, Linz et al. (1984, 1988) suggested that viewers were becoming comfortable with anxiety-provoking situations. It was also suggested that self-awareness of reductions in anxiety and emotional arousal may be instrumental in the formation of other perceptions and attitudes about violence portrayed in the films which are then carried over to other contexts. This position is similar to that offered in the behavioral treatment of pathological fears from exposure therapy. This research demonstrates that simply exposing a patient to the situations or objects he/she is afraid of will significantly diminish the anxiety or negative affect that was once evoked by the objects or situations (Foa & Kozak, 1986).

Similar processes may operate when subjects are repeatedly exposed to graphic media violence. Once viewers are emotionally "comfortable" with the violent content of films, they may also evaluate the film more favorably in other domains. Material originally believed to be offensive or degrading to the victims of violence may be evaluated as less so with continued exposure. A reduction in the level of anxiety may also blunt viewers' awareness of the frequency and intensity of violence in the films. Reductions in anxiety may serve to decrease sensitivity to emotional cues associated with each violent episode, thereby reducing viewers' perceptions of the amount of violence in the films. Consequently, by the end of an extensive exposure period, viewers may perceive aggressive films as less violent than they had initially. These altered perceptual and affective reactions may then be carried over into judgments made about victims of violence in other more realistic settings.

FEAR

Another harmful effect of watching television violence is fear. Viewing of media violence can lead to unrealistic perceptions of how much violence occurs in this world and thus a general fear of becoming a victim of crime. These fright reactions can be quite stable over time. Exposure to certain types of media violence may also evoke immediate fear responses that are transitory and fleeting in nature, such as when one watches a scary or suspenseful violent film. Both of these effects have been documented across child and adult viewers.

One theoretical explication of individuals' long-term fear reactions to media violence is cultivation theory. Initially developed by George Gerbner and colleagues (i.e., Gerbner, 1969; Gerbner & Gross, 1976; Gerbner, Gross, Morgan & Signorielli, 1994), cultivation theory is based on the premise that heavy exposure to the mass media can shape or alter individuals' perceptions of social reality. Gerbner and his research team first tested this theory in terms of entertainment television messages about violence (e.g., Gerbner & Gross, 1976; Gerbner, Gross, Morgan, & Signorielli, 1980). These researchers argued that because violence permeates most of entertainment programming, repeated exposure should "cultivate" in heavy viewers perceptions about violence and crime that are similar to those displayed on television.

Research reveals that heavy viewers believe the world they live in is more violent and unsafe when compared to light viewers. This is suggested by heavy viewers' (a) fear of walking alone at night, (b) use of guns, locks, and dogs for protection, (c) mistrust of police, (d) estimations of the prevalence of violence, and (e) overall fear of crime (e.g., Gerbner & Gross, 1976). These results have been documented with both child and adult audiences.

Cultivation theory has been heavily criticized over the last two decades, however. One methodological criticism has been that all of the evidence for cultivation is correlational (see Doob & Macdonald, 1979; Hirsch, 1980). Experimental research, however, has found that heavy viewing of violence under more controlled conditions also increases fear and anxiety in viewers (Bryant, Carveth, & Brown, 1981; Ogles & Hoffner, 1987). Conceptually, there is a general belief that the theory is too simplistic and that a number of mediating factors may influence the cultivation process (see Wilson, 1995; Potter, 1993). For example, factors such as experience with crime (O'Keefe, 1984; O'Keefe & Reid-Nash, 1987), motivations for viewing television (Perse, 1990), and overall cognitive abilities (Van Evra, 1990) seem to be important components in determining the cultivation effect.

In addition, Gunter (1994) has noted that the effect may be program specific rather than an effect of total TV viewing. Content specific programs, such as crime-related shows, would be most influential in affecting perceptions of crime or the effects may be due to how the viewer perceives and interprets the content, particularly if they see the program as being more realistic (Potter, 1986). Finally, individuals may selectively attend to those programs that reinforce their perception of the world (Gunter, 1994).

In an overview of their theory, Gerbner and colleagues acknowledge these criticisms and note:

> The elements of cultivation do not originate with television or appear out of a void. Layers of social, personal, and cultural contexts also determine the shape, scope, and degree of the contribution television is likely to make. Yet, the meaning of those contexts and factors are in themselves aspects of the cultivation process. That is, although a viewer's gender, age, or class makes a difference in perspective, television viewing can make a similar and interacting difference. . . . The interaction is a continuous process (as is cultivation) beginning with infancy and going on from cradle to grave (Gerbner et al., 1994, p. 23).

For cultivation theory, viewing television is a lifelong process. Whether television shapes or maintains beliefs about the world is not as important as its role in a dynamic process that leads to enduring and stable assumptions about the world, particularly violence.

For children, however, the effect may not be so general, i.e., younger viewers may not believe that the world is a mean and scary place. Children's reactions may be more specific, immediate, and urgent. Fright reactions to violent forms of media can be instantaneous and dramatic. For example, a child may scream or hide his/her eyes from a frightening depiction. Later, nightmares and recurring thoughts may keep both children and their parents awake at night (Wilson & Cantor, 1985).

A growing body of research suggests that both younger and older children can experience strong emotional reactions, such as fear and anxiety, from viewing media depictions of criminal activities, violence, physical injury, or danger (see Wilson, 1995; Cantor, 1994; Cantor & Wilson, 1988; Wilson & Smith, 1998). However, research also indicates that children at different levels of cognitive development are frightened by different types of portrayals (see Cantor, 1994; also Wilson & Smith, 1998). Younger children, for example, respond with more fear to those fantastic depictions of threats that look scary or frightening (Cantor & Sparks, 1984; Sparks, 1986). Older children, however, respond with more fear to realistic and abstract portrayals of danger that could possibly occur in the real world (Cantor & Sparks, 1984; Sparks, 1986).

Although most of this research on children's emotional reactions has assessed immediate or short-term impact, research suggests that the effects of viewing scary or frightening media can last several days or weeks (see Cantor, 1994). Some of these longer lasting effects may be relatively mild whereas others may be acute and disabling, i.e., a child may experience a severe anxiety state after viewing violence that may last up to several weeks (Mathai, 1983). As Cantor notes, transitory fright reactions occur in a large proportion of children, with more enduring reactions affecting an "appreciable" minority of viewers.

To account for these fear reactions, it has been suggested that a process similar to stimulus generalization might be operating. Although the viewer is in no "real" danger from viewing a violent media depiction, portrayals that would lead to danger in the real world are capable of producing fear reactions, although of a less intense nature. Cantor and colleagues (Cantor, 1994; Cantor & Wilson, 1988; Wilson & Cantor, 1985) have suggested that three types of stimuli readily produce these reactions: (a) danger and injuries, (b) distortions of human characters, and (c) situations in which others are in fear or danger. Each of these are quite common elements in violent programming.

Further, there are three important factors that mediate a fear effect. First, the more similar the depiction to real life the stronger the reaction. Depictions of real life events would, according to Cantor (1994), be more influential than cartoons. A second factor is the motivations of the viewer for selecting particular media depictions. In particular, older children may select or seek out frightening media fare because of its arousal or entertaining properties. For many of these viewers, the emotional impact may be heightened as they attempt to minimize the mediated aspect of the depiction (i.e., Zillmann, 1982; Cantor, 1994). Likewise, viewers who self-select certain media to become more familiar with an issue (e.g., the Oklahoma City bombing) might be more emotionally impacted as they "pay particular attention to whether or not the events portrayed are real or fictional" (Cantor, 1994, p. 227). Finally, factors that generally contribute to emotional reactions, such as physiological arousal, will also increase fright reactions.

CONTEXTUAL FEATURES OF VIOLENCE

It has been noted throughout this chapter that exposure to media violence contributes to aggression, desensitization, and fear. Social science research also indicates, however, that not all violent portrayals pose the same risk to viewers (Wilson et al., 1997). For example, the violence in an action-adventure film like *The Terminator* may facilitate learning of aggressive thoughts and behaviors in viewers whereas the violence in a dramatic movie such as *Boyz in the Hood* may actually inhibit such learning. Clearly, this example illuminates that the context within which violence is presented can alter the "meaning" of aggression and thus viewers' affective and behavioral reactions.

What specific contextual factors increase or decrease the risk of harmful effects in viewers? Experimental research, longitudinal investigations, and correlational studies, as well as meta-analyses, reveal that nine different contextual cues can influence individuals' learning of aggression, fear, and/or emotional desensitization to media violence. Those nine features include (a) nature of the perpetrator, (b) nature of the target, (c) the justification of violence, (d) the presence of weapons, (e) the extent and graphicness of violence, (f) the degree of realism of violence, (g) whether violence is rewarded or punished, (h) the consequences of violence, and (i) whether humor accompanies violence. Each of these factors will be reviewed briefly in the section that follows. For a fuller and more detailed explication of each factor and its effects on both children and adults, see the scientific papers of the National Television Violence Study (Wilson et al., 1997, 1998).

NATURE OF THE PERPETRATOR

The first contextual feature is the nature of the perpetrator. Perpetrators vary considerably in violent programs from cultural heroes such as Arnold Schwarzenegger to anthropomorphized animals such as Bugs Bunny. Also, perpetrators use aggression very differently in violent programming. Some perpetrators may be portrayed as "good" and use violence to protect society whereas others may be "bad" and use physical force for means to a selfish end. What types of aggressive perpetrators have a harmful impact on the learning of aggression? Studies indicate that both children and adults are more likely to attend to, identify with, and learn from attractive role models significantly more than unattractive ones (Bandura, 1986, 1994). Attractive perpetrators, therefore, may be more potent role models for learning aggressive behaviors than unattractive perpetrators.

Two specific characteristics or attributive qualities can increase the attractiveness of violent perpetrators. Studies have found that viewers rate prosocial or benevolent characters more favorably than cruel and malevolent characters (Hoffner & Cantor, 1985; 1991; Zillmann & Cantor, 1977). One type of "good" or prosocial character is the superhero (i.e., Batman, Superman) who uses violence to oppose the forces of evil. Research reveals that exposure to "good" or identification with heroic violent perpetrators increases the risk of aggressive behavior in both child and adult viewers (Leyens & Picus, 1973; Liss et al., 1983; Perry & Perry, 1976; Turner & Berkowitz, 1972).

In addition to prosocial orientation, perceived similarity to the viewer can increase a violent character's attractiveness. Perceived similarity may be the result of shared demographics (i.e., age and sex) between the perpetrator and the viewer. For instance, boys are more likely to attend to and imitate male characters whereas girls are more likely to attend to and imitate female characters (Bandura, 1986; Bandura, Ross, & Ross, 1963a). Research also reveals that children are more likely to engage in aggressive behavior after viewing a violent child perpetrator than after watching a violent adult perpetrator (Hicks, 1965). Furthermore, studies have found that any "cue" in a violent depiction that is relevant to a viewer can evoke or elicit aggressive behavior in children and adults (Berkowitz & Geen, 1966; 1967; Geen & Berkowitz, 1966; Huesmann, 1986; Josephson, 1987). Collectively, the nature of the perpetrator seems to be an important factor in the learning of aggression with attractive perpetrators or perpetrators with whom the viewer can identify posing the most risk.

NATURE OF THE TARGET

The second contextual feature is the nature of the target or victim of violence. Targets of violence, just like perpetrators, vary greatly in terms of their demographics, motives, and attributive qualities. Similar to the attractiveness of the perpetrator, attractiveness of the target is also an important contextual cue that impacts viewers' responses to violence. Attractive targets, however, elicit a different reaction in viewers than do attractive perpetrators. When attractive characters fall prey to violence, it may evoke fear or anxiety in audience members (Wilson et al., 1997, p. 18). Studies have found that viewers often experience the same feelings and affective states that attractive characters experience (Comisky & Bryant, 1982; Feshbach & Roe, 1968; Zillmann, 1980, 1991; Zillmann & Cantor, 1977). Wilson and colleagues (1997, p. 19) have argued that when attractive characters become victimized by violence, viewers may empathetically share their anxiety and experience some level of fear and/or distress.

JUSTIFICATION OF VIOLENCE

The third contextual feature is the justification of violence. Violence may be used for a variety of reasons in television programming and some of those reasons may be justified or socially acceptable whereas others may not. Research has consistently documented that justified portrayals of violence increase aggressive responding in viewers (Berkowitz & Geen, 1967; Berkowitz & Powers, 1979; Geen & Stoner, 1973, 1974). This effect has been documented across both fictional and more realistic programming (Meyer, 1972) and with adults and child viewers (Liss et al., 1983). Scholars have theorized that viewing justified violence may reduce individuals' inhibitions toward aggression, thereby heightening the likelihood of engaging in antisocial behavior (Jo & Berkowitz, 1994). A meta-analysis of 217 experiments revealed that justified violence increases the risk of aggressive behavior in viewers (Paik & Comstock, 1994).

Does viewing unjustified acts of aggression have an influence on the audience? Unjustified acts of aggression have been found to affect both the learning of aggression and fear in viewers. In terms of learning aggression, studies reveal that exposure to unjustified violence has been found to decrease aggressive behavior in audience members (Berkowitz & Powers, 1979; Geen, 1981). Indirect experimental evidence suggests that exposure to unjustified acts of aggression can have a significant effect on adult viewers' fear of victimization as well. For example, Bryant, Carveth, and Brown (1981) had undergraduates watch a heavy diet of violent television programming for 6 weeks that featured either "just" or "unjust" endings. The "just" programs usually featured violence that was punished (i.e., personal vengeance, legal restitution) whereas "unjust" programs typically featured violence that was unpunished. A third group of subjects were assigned to a "light" viewing condition and asked to watch very little television. Results revealed that subjects exposed to the violent programs with "unjust" endings were significantly more anxious than were subjects in the two other groups.

THE PRESENCE OF WEAPONS

The fourth contextual feature is the presence of weapons. A variety of weapons may be used in violent portrayals. For example, a perpetrator of violence may use his/her natural means to overcome an enemy or a police officer may fire his gun to "protect and serve" society. Some characters involved with violence may use explosives or heavy weaponry to annihilate their enemies. Other portrayals may include the use unconventional weapons such as bats, ropes, or chains to inflict physical harm.

What impact do violent portrayals featuring weapons have on viewers? Studies show that the presence of conventional weapons such as guns or knives significantly increases viewers' aggressive responding (Berkowitz & LePage, 1967; Leyens & Parke, 1974; Page & O'Neal, 1977; Turner, Layton, & Simons, 1975). From a priming effects perspective, Berkowitz and others have argued that such weapons prompt or trigger aggressive thoughts and memories in viewers (Berkowitz, 1990; Huesmann, 1988; Leyens & Parke, 1974; Wilson et al., 1997). When these types of thoughts are primed, viewers may be more susceptible to acting or behaving aggressively. Indeed, a meta-analysis of 56 published experiments reveals that the presence of weapons in pictures or in the natural environment significantly increases aggressive behavior in both angered and nonangered adults (Carlson, Marcus-Newhall, & Miller, 1990).

EXTENT AND GRAPHICNESS OF VIOLENCE

The fifth contextual feature is the extent and graphicness of violence. Extent refers not only to the duration or amount of time devoted to violence but also the distance with which such actions are portrayed. For example, a perpetrator may fire a gun from a long camera shot that lasts only for a split second or a violent villain may engage in rapid fire that endures for several moments and encompasses the full frame of the TV screen. Graphicness of violence, however, refers to the amount of blood and carnage shown. Some violent scenes may not contain any blood or gore whereas others may be bathed with such viscera.

Most of the research on extensive or graphic violence has focused on individuals' emotional desensitization to such portrayals. Several studies have found that both adult and child viewers become physiologically desensitized during exposure to violent programs or films (Cline, Croft & Courrier, 1973; Lazarus & Alfert, 1964; Lazarus, Speisman, Mordkoff, & Davison, 1962; Speisman, Lazarus, Mordkoff, & Davison, 1964). Other studies have examined individuals' emotional desensitization to violent programming over several viewing sessions.

As mentioned earlier, Linz et al. (1988) exposed male subjects to five different "slasher films" over the course of 2 weeks. With repeated exposure, subjects perceived the films to be less violent. Similar findings have been replicated by Mullin and Linz (1995). Taken together, these investigations indicate that both short- and long-term exposure to repeated acts of violence may contribute to viewers becoming emotionally desensitized to real world aggression and its harmful physical, emotional, and psychological effects.

DEGREE OF REALISM OF VIOLENCE

The sixth contextual variable is the realism of the violence. Realism refers to the actuality of the characters, settings, and/or events in violent portrayals. Some violent acts are portrayed as very realistic whereas others are depicted as completely fictional or fantastic in nature. Comparing the violence in *ABC Nightly News* with those aggressive actions in a *Ninja Turtles* cartoon illustrates this difference.

Research indicates that the level of realism surrounding a violent portrayal influences both aggressive responding and fear. In terms of aggressive actions, several studies have found that more realistic portrayals of violence increase aggressive responding in children and adult males significantly more than do fictionalized or fantastic accounts of such behavior (Atkin, 1983; Berkowitz & Alioto, 1973; Feshbach, 1972; Geen, 1975; Hapkiewicz & Stone, 1974; Thomas & Tell, 1974). Many scholars have argued that realistic depictions increase aggressive responding for two reasons: (a) viewers can easily identify with realistic perpetrators of violence and (b) they may reduce viewers' inhibitions toward aggressive responding because they are so similar to real life (Wilson et al., 1997, p. 23; Huesmann, 1988; Jo & Berkowitz, 1994).

In terms of fear, several investigations have found realistic portrayals of violence to be more emotionally disturbing or frightening to viewers than fantastic depictions of aggression (Cantor & Sparks, 1984; Geen, 1975; Geen & Rakosky, 1975; Lazarus, Opton, Nomikos, & Rankin, 1965; Sparks, 1986). This effect has been documented with both children and adults.

REWARDED OR PUNISHED VIOLENCE

Rewards and punishments are the seventh contextual element of violent portrayals. Rewards are those positive reinforcements that are given to a perpetrator for acting violently. A perpetrator's reward for violence may be as extravagant as $1,000,000 or as simple as a congratulatory pat on the back. Punishments, however, are those negative reinforcements that are given to a perpetrator for acting aggressively. A perpetrator's punishment for violence may range from a disapproving frown to the death penalty.

What impact do these types of positive and negative reinforcements have on viewers? Studies have found consistently that violence that is rewarded increases the risk of learning aggressive thoughts and behaviors (Bandura, Ross, & Ross, 1961; 1993b; Lando & Donnerstein, 1978). More recently, Paik and Comstock's (1994) meta-analysis of 217 experiments reveals that rewarded violence increases the risk of learning in viewers of all ages. Violence does not have to be explicitly rewarded to increase the risk of a harmful effect, however. Social learning theory indicates that behavior that is not punished may also function as a tacit reward (Bandura, 1965; Walters & Parke, 1964). Thus, violence that is either rewarded or not punished may facilitate viewers' learning of aggressive thoughts and behaviors.

CONSEQUENCES OF VIOLENCE

The eighth contextual feature is the consequences of violence. Consequences refer to the harm and pain that occurs as a result of violence. For example, a victim could let out a blood-curdling scream while being stabbed with a knife. Such a reaction indicates that the person is experiencing excruciating pain. Another character, however, may get punched in the face and not even flinch. This response suggests that the character did not experience any pain or harm from the aggressive action.

Innumerable studies with adults have documented that intense harm and pain cues decrease aggressive responding in viewers (Baron, 1971a,b; Gorenson, 1969; Sanders & Baron, 1975; Schmutte & Taylor, 1980). Many have argued that these types of cues inhibit aggressive responding because they "sensitize" viewers to the physical, emotional, and psychological harm that results from violence. To date, only one study has been conducted on children's responses to violent portrayals featuring harm and pain. Wotring and Greenberg (1973) found that young boys who were exposed to a violent clip depicting serious injuries were significantly less aggressive than those boys who saw an excerpt without any such injuries. A handful of studies, however, have found harm/pain cues to increase aggressive behavior in viewers (Baron, 1979; Dubanoski & Kong, 1977; Swart & Berkowitz, 1976). These effects have been limited to either extremely angered subjects or subjects who were highly susceptible to aggression and then placed in settings with aggressive cues in the environment (Wilson et al., 1997). In sum, results from these studies suggest the depiction of physical pain or suffering functions as an inhibitor to aggressive responding for most viewers.

HUMOR ACCOMPANYING VIOLENCE

The last contextual feature is humor. Humor may be used in a myriad of ways in violent programming. For instance, a perpetrator may crack a joke immediately before, during, or after killing an innocent victim or a violent act may be depicted in a farcical fashion. Alternatively, the consequences of violence may be presented in a comical and mirth-provoking manner. Clearly, these examples illuminate the heterogeneity of humor used in violent programming.

Evidence suggests that humor may foster emotional desensitization to violence. In one experiment, Jablonski and Zillmann (1995) found that subjects rated film clips of violence juxtaposed with humor as significantly less distressing than subjects exposed to film clips of violence devoid of humorous overtones. Other studies have found that violent programs featuring high levels of humor are perceived as significantly less serious and less violent than those programs featuring low levels of humor (Gunter & Furnharm, 1984; Gunter, 1985). Surely, these findings suggest that humor may trivialize the seriousness of violence. Perhaps repeated exposure to such trivialized depictions may cause viewers to become calloused toward "real world" aggression and its harmful physical, social, and psychological consequences.

Research also suggests, however, that violent portrayals flavored with humor may facilitate aggressive responding. Two studies have found that humor, when presented in a hostile context, increases aggressive behavior (Baron, 1978; Berkowitz, 1970). Many scholars have argued that humor may function as a reward or positive reinforcement for violence (Berkowitz, 1970; Wilson et al., 1997). As noted earlier, rewarded violence increases the risk of aggressive responding (Bandura, Ross, & Ross, 1961, 1963b; Lando & Donnerstein, 1978). Other scholars have suggested that humor may increase a viewer's level of arousal over that attained by violence alone (Wilson et al., 1997). Increased arousal has been found to increase aggressive responding (Zillmann, 1979). Taken together, these studies suggest that violent portrayals featuring humor may increase the risk of desensitization and aggressive behavior in viewers.

In total, the research reviewed earlier indicates that nine different contextual features of violence either increase or decrease the risk of psychological harm. Summing across all the variables, it becomes obvious that the most "risky" violent depictions for learning aggression are those featuring attractive perpetrators engaging in justified and rewarded violence that fail to depict any pain/harm to their victims. In terms of desensitization, viewing extensive and repeated acts of violence juxtaposed with humor or blood and viscera heightens the risk of growing calloused or numb toward aggression. Finally, those depictions involving unjustified acts of aggression that are not punished increase the risk of long-term fear and anxiety in viewers.

ISSUES OF COGNITIVE DEVELOPMENT AND AGGRESSION

Viewer variables may also influence the impact of exposure to different types of violent depictions. One particular characteristic, age or level of cognitive development, has a significant impact on a child's learning of aggressive thoughts, attitudes, and behavior. Younger children (2 to 6 year olds) are a special audience and they bring different cognitive skills and capabilities to the viewing experience than do older children (7 to 12 year olds). As a result, younger children make sense of and interpret television programming in a slightly different way than their older counterparts (see Van Evra, 1990; also Wilson & Smith, 1998). Two specific developmental differences in cognitive skills or information processing capabilities make younger children more vulnerable to learning aggressive thoughts, attitudes, and behaviors from certain types of violent depictions than older children.

FANTASY AND REALITY

The first cognitive skill is the ability to ascertain the difference between reality and fantasy. Research reveals that understanding the distinction between reality and fantasy emerges slowly over the course of a child's development (Morison & Gardner, 1978). As a result, younger children have a tendency to believe "unrealistic" types of portrayals and events (i.e., monsters, creatures, ghosts) are "real" or "possible" more than their older counterparts (see Rosengren, Kalish, Hickling, & Gelman, 1994; Cantor, 1994).

What impact does this developmental difference have on children's learning of aggressive thoughts, attitudes, and behaviors from television? Much of the violence targeted to younger audiences is packaged in cartoon and animated programming. For the older child or adult, these types of portrayals are simply discounted as "unrealistic" and thus pose very little, if any, risk of harm. For the younger child, however, these types of depictions may be perceived as very "real" and thus may actually increase the risk of learning aggression. Indeed, several studies have documented that exposure to cartoon programming increases imitative aggressive behaviors in younger children (Bandura, Ross, & Ross, 1963a; Boyatzis, Matillo, & Nesbitt, 1995; Friedrich & Stein, 1973; Hapkiewicz, 1979; Paik & Comstock, 1994; Steuer, Applefield, & Smith, 1971).

DRAWING INFERENCES

The second cognitive skill involves the ability to draw inferences and connect scenes across a violent program. Research reveals that when compared to younger children, older children are better at (a) linking scenes in a story, (b) integrating pieces of a story together, and (c) drawing inferences from story information (Collins, 1979; 1983; Schmidt, Schmidt, & Tomalis, 1984; Thompson & Meyers, 1985). The ability to link scenes and integrate information across a violent program has important implications for the timing of "punishments" delivered to perpetrators for acting violently.

Much of violent programming features characters who act violently throughout an entire program but get caught, punished, or killed at the very end of the show. For the older child or adult, the punishment at the end of the program can easily be linked to the perpetrator's earlier aggressive acts and thus function as a negative reinforcement of aggression. For the younger child, however, the timing or placement of the punishment is much more crucial for it to actually serve as an inhibitor to aggressive behavior. Research reveals that for punishments to serve as negative reinforcements for younger children, they must be depicted contiguous with, and not temporally separated from, the aggressive actions being reprimanded (Collins, 1973).

POSSIBLE SOLUTIONS OF MITIGATING THE EFFECTS OF MEDIA VIOLENCE

Is there any way to potentially mediate the harmful impact of exposure to media violence? We take the position that the effects of viewing violence in the mass media can be mitigated. In an examination of the psychological research we find that educational efforts in terms of media literacy/critical viewing and programming designed with antiviolent messages can be effective. In this section we would like to note these alternatives to governmental regulation (V-chip, ratings) as a solution to the media violence problem.

CRITICAL VIEWING

Children can be taught "critical viewing skills" by parents and in schools so that they learn to better interpret what they see on television (e.g., Huston et al., 1992). For example, children can learn to distinguish between fictional portrayals and factual presentations. In addition, children can be taught to recognize ways in which violence is portrayed unrealistically (e.g., when it is portrayed without any negative consequences). Children can also learn to think about alternatives to the violence portrayed, a strategy that is particularly effective when an adult viewing the violence with the child expresses disapproval of violence as a means of solving problems and then offers alternatives.

For example, Huesmann, Eron, Klein, Brice, and Fischer (1983) attempted to motivate children not to encode and later enact aggressive behaviors they observed on television. They designed their intervention to take advantage of ideas from counterattitudinal advocacy research found effective in producing enduring behavioral changes in other domains. Specifically, the intervention was predicated on a notion contained in both dissonance and attribution theory—when a person finds himself or herself advocating a point of view that is either unfamiliar or even counter to an original belief he or she is motivated to shift attitudes into line with what is being advocated. Children in the Huesmann et al. experimental group were first credited with the antiviolence attitudes that the experimenters wished them to adopt and then were asked to make videotapes for other children who had been "fooled" by television and "got into trouble by imitating it" even though they themselves knew better. The children composed persuasive essays explaining how television is not like real life and why it would be harmful for other children to watch too much television and imitate the violent characters. Each child was videotaped reading his/her essay. Then, each child's taped presentation was played before the entire group. This gave the child an opportunity to see himself advocate an antiviolence position and also made the child's position public. The intervention was successful both in changing children's attitudes about television violence and in modifying aggressive behavior. Four months after the intervention there was a significant decline in peer-nominated aggression and attitudes about the acceptability of television violence for the experimental group.

In addition, a large number of professional organizations concerned with the well-being of children and families have recommended that professionals take a more active role in reducing the impact of violent media (American Academy of Pediatrics, American Medical Association, American Psychological Association, Group for the Advancement of Psychiatry, National Parent Teachers Association). Research on intervention programs has indicated that we can reduce some of the impact of media violence by "empowering" parents in their roles as monitors of children's television viewing. These studies indicate that parents who view programs with their children and discuss the realities of violence, as well as alternatives to aggressive behaviors in conflict situations, can actually reduce the negative impact (increased aggressiveness) of media violence (i.e., Donnerstein, et al., 1994). There are currently a number of programs being developed by researchers that can be used by parents in their interactions with children during the viewing of television (Strasburger, 1993).

MEDIA INITIATIVES

Another educational resource is the mass media itself. Professionally produced educational movies about violence that are also designed to be entertaining have great potential for informing the public and, under some conditions, might even change antisocial attitudes about violence. An example in this area is provided by a NBC made-for-television movie. In September of 1990, NBC aired a made-for-TV

movie about the trauma and aftermath of acquaintance rape. This program, entitled *She Said No*, was featured during prime-time hours and attracted a large
audience. *She Said No* also received critical acclaim, winning an award from
American Women in Radio and Television for its realistic portrayal of the plight
of a rape victim. An evaluation of the effectiveness of this movie was undertaken
by Wilson, Linz, Donnerstein, and Stipp (1992). The study measured whether exposure to this movie would decrease acceptance of rape myths and/or increase
awareness of date rape as a serious social problem.

The study employed a total of 1038 adults, randomly selected from four locations in the United States who were assigned to view or not to view *She Said No*
over a closed-circuit channel, prior to the network broadcast of the film. Individuals from this representative sample were randomly assigned to view or not view
the made-for-TV movie in their own home—a more naturalistic viewing environment than is achieved in most media experiments. The viewers and nonviewers
were contacted the next day and asked about acceptance of rape myths and perceptions of rape as a social problem.

The results of this study indicated that the television movie was a useful tool in
educating and altering perceptions about date rape. Specifically, exposure to the
movie increased awareness of date rape as a social problem across all viewers, independent of gender or age. The movie also had a prosocial effect on older females who were less likely to attribute blame to women in date rape situations
after exposure as compared to older women who did not view the movie.

SUMMARY AND CONCLUSIONS

It would be safe to conclude that the mass media is a contributor to a number
of antisocial behaviors and health-related problems in children, adolescents, and
adults. We must keep in mind, however, that the mass media is but one of a mul-
titude of factors that contribute and, in many cases, is not the most significant.
Nevertheless, it is one of those factors in which proper interventions can mitigate
its impact, which can be controlled with reasonable insight. As discussed in the
previous section, there are a number of ways in which media violence can be mitigated. As a conclusion to this chapter the authors would like to note that there are
a number of other suggestions that might also be effective.

In their report for the National Television Violence Study, Wilson et al. (1998)
suggested the following recommendations for the media industry, policy makers,
and parents as a means of confronting the problem of media violence. For the
media industry the following were recommended:

- Produce more programs that avoid violence; if a program does contain violence, keep the number of violent incidents low
- Be creative in showing
  —more violent acts being punished
  —more negative consequences, both short term and long term, for violence

—more alternatives to the use of violence in solving problems
—less justification for violent actions
* When violence is presented, consider greater emphasis on a strong antiviolence theme
* Ensure that ratings for violence take into account the context of the portrayals
* Ensure that cartoons featuring high-risk portrayals for young children are rated in a way that clearly warns parents

In considering those who recommend and make policy in the area of the mass media, the following were offered:

* Continue to monitor the nature and extent of violence on television
* Recognize that context is an essential aspect of television violence and rely on scientific evidence to identify the context features that pose the most risk
* Ensure that television program ratings accurately convey to parents the risks associated with different types of violent portrayals

Finally, for parents, the authors of the National Television Violence Study recommended the following:

* Be aware of the three risks associated with viewing television violence (learning of aggression, desensitization, and fear)
* Consider the context of violent depictions in making viewing decisions for children
* Consider a child's developmental level when making viewing decisions
* Recognize that certain types of violent cartoons pose a particularly high risk for young children's learning of aggression

These recommendations are considered to be viable and realistic because they are based on a knowledge base supported by scientific research discussed throughout this chapter. A stronger reliance needs to be placed on educational and media interventions specifically directed at changing beliefs about violence. The authors' solution then is to err on the side of education and self-regulation rather than on legal regulation. Research evidence to date is consistent with a call for more educational interventions. Our ever-increasing knowledge of media effects, attitude formation and change, child development, and human behavior positions researchers as a force in the solution of the problem of media violence.

REFERENCES

American Medical Association. (1996). *Physician guide to media violence*. Chicago, IL: Author.
American Psychological Association. (1993). *Violence and youth: Psychology's response*. Washington, DC: Author.
Atkin, C. (1983). Effects of realistic TV violence vs. fictional violence on aggression. *Journalism Quarterly, 60*, 615–621.

Bandura, A. (1965). Influence of models' reinforcement contingencies on the acquisition of imitative responses. *Journal of Personality and Social Psychology, 1(6),* 589–595.

Bandura, A. (1971). *Social learning theory.* New York: General Learning Press.

Bandura, A. (1986). *Social foundations of thought and action: A social cognitive theory.* Englewood Cliffs, NJ: Prentice-Hall.

Bandura, A. (1994). Social cognitive theory of mass communication. In J. Bryant & D. Zillmann (Eds.), *Media effects* (pp. 61–90). Hillsdale, NJ: Erlbaum.

Bandura, A., Ross, D., & Ross, S. A. (1961). Transmission of aggression through imitation of aggressive models. *Journal of Abnormal and Social Psychology, 63,* 575–582.

Bandura, A., Ross, D., & Ross, S. A. (1961). Transmission of aggression through imitation of aggressive models. *Journal of Abnormal and Social Psychology, 63,* 575–582.

Bandura, A., Ross, D., & Ross, S. A. (1963a). Imitation of film-mediated aggressive models. *Journal of Abnormal and Social Psychology, 66(1),* 3–11.

Bandura, A., Ross, D., & Ross, S. A. (1963b). Vicarious reinforcement and imitative learning. *Journal of Abnormal and Social Psychology 67(6),* 601–607.

Baron, R. A. (1971a). Aggression as a function of magnitude of victim's pain cues, level of prior anger arousal, and aggressor-victim similarity. *Journal of Personality and Social Psychology, 18(1),* 48–54.

Baron, R. A. (1971b). Magnitude of victim's pain cues and level of prior anger arousal as determinants of adult aggressive behavior. *Journal of Personality and Social Psychology, 17(3),* 236–243.

Baron, R. A. (1978). The influence of hostile and nonhostile humor upon physical aggression. *Personality and Social Psychology Bulletin, 4(1),* 77–80.

Baron, R. A. (1979). Effects of victim's pain cues, victim's race, and level of prior instigation upon physical aggression. *Journal of Applied Social Psychology, 9(2),* 103–114.

Baron, R. A., & Richardson, D. R. (1994). *Human Aggression* (2nd ed.), New York: Plenum Press.

Berkowitz, L. (1970). Aggressive humor as a stimulus to aggressive responses. *Journal of Personality and Social Psychology, 16(4),* 710–717.

Berkowitz, L. (1973). Words and symbols as stimuli to aggressive responses. In J. Knutson (Ed.), *Control of aggression: Implications from basic research.* Chicago, IL: Aldine-Atherton.

Berkowitz, L. (1984). Some effects of thoughts on anti- and prosocial influences of media events: A cognitive-neoassociation analysis. *Psychological Bulletin, 95(3),* 410–427.

Berkowitz, L. (1990). On the formation and regulation of anger and aggression: A cognitive neoassociationistic analysis. *American Psychologist, 45(4),* 494–503.

Berkowitz, L., & Alioto, J. T. (1973). The meaning of an observed event as a determinant of its aggressive consequences. *Journal of Personality and Social Psychology, 28(2),* 206–217.

Berkowitz, L., & Geen, R. G. (1966). Film violence and the cue properties of available targets. *Journal of Personality and Social Psychology, 3(5),* 525–530.

Berkowitz, L., & Geen, R. G. (1967). Stimulus qualities of the target of aggression: A further study. *Journal of Personality and Social Psychology, 5(3),* 364–368.

Berkowitz, L., & LePage, A. (1967). Weapons as aggression-eliciting stimuli. *Journal of Personality and Social Psychology, 7(2),* 202–207.

Berkowitz, L., & Powers, P. C. (1979). Effects of timing and justification of witnessed aggression on the observers' punitiveness. *Journal of Research in Personality, 13,* 71–80.

Berkowitz, L., & Rogers, K. H. (1986). A priming effect analysis of media influences. In J. Bryant and D. Zillmann (Eds.), *Perspectives on media effects* (pp. 57–82). Hillsdale, NJ: Erlbaum.

Boyatzis, C. J., Matillo, G. M., & Nesbitt, K. M. (1995). Effects of The Mighty Morphin Power Rangers on children's aggression with peers. *Child Study Journal, 25(1),* 45–55.

Bryant, J., Carveth, R. A., & Brown, D. (1981). Television viewing and anxiety: An experimental examination. *Journal of Communication, 31(1),* 106–119.

Bushman, B. (1996). Priming effects of violent media on aggressive thoughts. Unpublished manuscript.

Bushman, B., & Geen, R. (1990). Role of cognitive-emotional mediators and individual differences in the effects of media violence on aggression. *Journal of Personality and Social Psychology, 58,* 156–163.

Cantor, J. (1994). Fright reactions to mass media. In J. Bryant & D. Zillmann (Eds.), *Media effects* (pp. 213–245). Hillsdale, NJ: Lawrence Erlbaum Associates.

Cantor, J., & Sparks, G. G. (1984). Children's fear responses to mass media: Testing some Piagetian predictions. *Journal of Communication, 34(2),* 90–103.

Cantor, J., & Wilson, B. J. (1988). Helping children cope with frightening media presentations. *Current Psychology: Research & Reviews, 7,* 58–75.

Carlson, M., Marcus-Newhall, A., & Miller, N. (1990). Effects of situational aggression cues: A quantitative review. *Journal of Personality and Social Psychology, 58(4),* 622–633.

Carver, C. S., Ganellen, R. J., Froming, W. J., & Chambers, W. (1983). Modeling: An analysis in terms of category accessibility. *Journal of Experimental Social Psychology, 19,* 403–421.

Centers for Disease Control. (1991). *Position papers from the Third National Injury Conference: Setting the National Agenda for Injury Control in the 1990s.* Washington, DC: Department of Health and Human Services.

Cline, V. B., Croft, R. G., & Courrier, S. (1973). Desensitization of children to television violence. *Journal of Personality and Social Psychology, 27(3),* 360–365.

Collins, W. A. (1973). Effect of temporal separation between motivation, aggression and consequences: A developmental study. *Developmental Psychology, 8(2),* 215–221.

Collins, W. A. (1979). Children's comprehension of television content. In E. Wartella (Ed.), *Children communicating: Media and development of thought, speech, understanding* (pp. 21–52). Beverly Hills, CA: Sage.

Collins, W. A. (1983). Interpretation and inference in children's television viewing. In J. Bryant & D. R. Anderson (Eds.), *Children's understanding of television* (pp. 125–150). New York: Academic Press.

Comisky, P., & Bryant, J. (1982). Factors involved in generating suspense. *Human Communication Research, 9(1),* 49–58.

Comstock, G. (1993). The medium and the society: The role of television in American life. In G. L. Berry & J. K. Asamen (Eds.), *Children and television: Images in a changing sociocultural world.* Newbury Park, CA: Sage Publications.

Comstock, G., & Paik, H. (1991). *Television and the American child.* New York: Academic Press.

Donnerstein, E., Slaby, R., & Eron, L. (1994). The mass media and youth violence. In J. Murray, E. Rubinstein, & G. Comstock (Eds.), *Violence and youth: Psychology's response* (Vol. 2). Washington, DC: American Psychological Association.

Doob, A. N., & Macdonald, G. E. (1979). Television viewing and fear of victimization: Is the relationship causal? *Journal of Personality and Social Psychology, 37(2),* 170–179.

Drabman, R. S., & Thomas, M. H. (1974). Does media violence increase children's tolerance for real life aggression? *Developmental Psychology, 10,* 418–421.

Dubanoski, R. A., & Kong, C. (1977). The effects of pain cues on the behavior of high and low aggressive boys. *Social Behavior and Personality, 5(2),* 273–279.

Eron, L., Gentry, J. H., and Schlegel, P. (1994). *A reason to hope: A psychosocial perspective on violence and youth.* Washington, DC: American Psychological Association.

Feshbach, S. (1972). Reality and fantasy in filmed violence. In J. P. Murray, E. A. Rubinstein, & G. Comstock (Eds.), *Television and social behavior: Television and social learning* (Vol. 2, pp. 318–345). Washington, DC: US Government Publication.

Feshbach, N. D., & Roe, K. (1968). Empathy in six- and seven-year-olds. *Child Development, 39(1),* 133–145.

Foa, E. B., & Kozak, M. J. (1986). Emotional processing of fear: Exposure to corrective information. *Psychological Bulletin, 99,* 20–35.

Friedrich, L. K., & Stein, A. H. (1973). Aggressive and prosocial television programs and the natural behavior of preschool children. *Monographs of the Society for Research in Child Development, 38* (4, Serial No. 151).

Geen, R. G. (1975). The meaning of observed violence: Real vs. fictional violence and consequent effects on aggression and emotional arousal. *Journal of Research in Personality, 9,* 270–281.

Geen, R. G. (1981). Behavioral and physiological reactions to observed violence: Effects of prior exposure to aggressive stimuli. *Journal of Personality and Social Psychology, 40(5),* 868–875.

Geen, R. G., & Berkowitz, L. (1966). Name mediated aggressive cue properties. *Journal of Personality and Social Psychology, 34,* 456–465.

Geen, R. G., & Rakosky, J. J. (1975). Interpretations of observed violence and their effects on GSR. *Journal of Experimental Research in Personality, 6,* 289–292.

Geen, R. G., & Stonner, D. (1973). Context effects in observed violence. *Journal of Personality and Social Psychology, 25(1),* 145–150.

Geen, R. G., & Stonner, D. (1974). The meaning of observed violence: Effects on arousal and aggressive behavior. *Journal of Research in Personality, 8,* 55–63.

Gerbner, G. (1969). Dimensions of violence in television drama. In R. K. Baker & S. J. Ball (Eds.), *Violence in the media* (Staff Report to the National Commission on the Causes and Prevention of Violence, pp. 311–340). Washington, DC: U.S. Government Printing Office.

Gerbner, G., & Gross, L. (1976). Living with television: The violence profile. *Journal of Communication, 26(2),* 172–199.

Gerbner, G., Gross, L., Morgan, M., & Signorielli, N. (1980). The 'mainstreaming' of America: Violence profile No. 11. *Journal of Communication, 30(3),* 10–29.

Gerbner, G., Gross, L., Morgan, M., & Signorielli, N. (1994). Growing up with television: The cultivation perspective. In J. Bryant & D. Zillmann (Eds.), *Media effects* (pp. 17–41). Hillsdale, NJ: Lawrence Erlbaum.

Gerbner, G., Gross, L., Signorielli, N., & Morgan, M. (1986). Living with television: The dynamics of the cultivation process. In J. Bryant & D. Zillmann (Eds.), *Perspectives on media effects* (pp. 17–40). Hillsdale, NJ: Lawrence Erlbaum.

Goransen, R. E. (1969). Observed violence and aggressive behavior: The effects of negative outcomes to observed violence. *Dissertation Abstracts International, 31(01),* DAI-B. (University Microfilms No. AAC77 08286).

Gunter, B. (1985). *Dimensions of television violence.* Aldershots, England: Gower.

Gunter, B. (1994). The question of media violence. In J. Bryant & D. Zillmann (Eds.), *Media effects* (pp. 163–211). Hillsdale, NJ: Lawrence Erlbaum Associates.

Gunter, B., & Furnham, A. (1984). Perceptions of television violence: Effects of program genre and physical forms of violence. *British Journal of Social Psychology, 23,*155–184.

Hapkiewicz, W. G. (1979). Children's reactions to cartoon violence. *Journal of Clinical Child Psychology, 8,* 30–34.

Hapkiewicz, W. G., & Stone, R. D. (1974). The effect of realistic versus imaginary aggressive models on children's interpersonal play. *Child Study Journal, 4(2),* 47–58.

Harris, R. J. (1994). *A cognitive psychology of mass communication* (2nd ed.). Hillsdale, NJ: Lawrence Erlbaum.

Hicks, D. J. (1965). Imitation and retention of film-mediated aggressive peer and adult models. *Journal of Personality and Social Psychology, 2(1),* 97–100.

Hirsch, K., & Molitor, F. (1994). Children's toleration of real-life aggression after exposure to media violence: A replication of the Drabman and Thomas Studies. *Child Study Journal, 24(3),* 191–207.

Hirsch, P. M. (1980). The 'scary world' of the nonviewer and other anomalies: A reanalysis of Gerbner et al.'s findings of cultivation analysis, part I. *Communication Research, 7,* 403–456.

Hoffner, C., & Cantor, J. (1985). Developmental differences in responses to a television character's appearance and behavior. *Developmental Psychology, 21(6),* 1065–1074.

Hoffner, C., & Cantor, J. (1991). Perceiving and responding to mass media characters. In J. Bryant & D. Zillmann (Eds.), *Responding to the screen* (pp. 63–101). Hillsdale, NJ: Lawrence Erlbaum.

Huesmann, L. R. (1986). Psychological processes promoting the relation between exposure to media violence and aggressive behavior by the viewer. *Journal of Social Issues, 42(3),* 125–140.

Huesmann, L. R. (1988). An information processing model for the development of aggressive behavior. *Aggressive Behavior, 14(10),* 13–24.

Huesmann, L. R., & Eron, L. D. (Eds.) (1986). *Television and the aggressive child: A cross-national comparison.* Hillsdale, NJ: Lawrence Erlbaum Associates.

Huesmann, L. R., Eron, L. D., Klein, A., Brice, P., & Fischer, P. (1983). Mitigating the imitation of aggressive behaviors by changing children's attitudes about media violence. *Journal of Personality and Social Psychology, 44*, 899–910.

Huesmann, L. R., Eron, L. D., Lefkowitz, M. M., & Walder, L. O. (1984). The stability of aggression over time and generations. *Developmental Psychology, 20(6)*, 1120–1134.

Huesmann, L. R., Moise, J., Podolski, C. L., & Eron, L. (1997, April). *Longitudinal relations between early exposure to television violence viewing and young adult aggression: 1977–1992.* Paper presented at the biennial meeting for the Society for Research on Child Development, Washington, DC.

Huston, A. C., Donnerstein, E., Fairchild, H., Feshbach, N. D., Katz, P. A., Murray, J. P., Rubinstein, E. A., Wilcox, B. L., & Zuckerman, D. (1992). *Big world, small screen: The role of television in American society.* Lincoln, NE: University of Nebraska Press.

Jablonski, C., & Zillmann, D. (1995). Humor's role in the trivialization of violence. *Medienpsycholgie: Zeitschrift fur Individual und Massenkommunikation, 7(2)*, 122–133.

Jo, E., & Berkowitz, L. (1994). A priming effect analysis of media influences: An update. In J. Bryant & D. Zillmann (Eds.), *Media effects* (pp. 43–60). Hillsdale, NJ: Lawrence Erlbaum Associates.

Johnson, R. N. (1996). Bad news revisited: The portrayal of violence, conflict, and suffering on television news. *Peace and Conflict: Journal of Peace Psychology, 2(3)*, 201–216.

Jose, P. E., & Brewer, W. F. (1984). Development of story liking: Character identification, suspense, and outcome resolution. *Developmental Psychology, 20(5)*, 911–924.

Josephson, W. L. (1987). Television violence and children's aggression: Testing and priming, social script, and disinhibition predictions. *Journal of Personality and Social Psychology, 53(5)*, 882–890.

Kubey, R. W., & Csikszentmihalyi, M. (1990). *Television and the quality of life: How viewing shapes everyday experience.* Hillsdale, NJ: Lawrence Erlbaum.

Kunkel, D., Wilson, B. J., Donnerstein, E., Linz, D., Smith, S. L., Blumenthal, E., Gray, T., & Potter, W. J. (1995). Measuring television violence: The importance of context. *Journal of Broadcasting and Electronic Media, 39*, 284–291.

Kunkel, D., Wilson, B. J., Linz, D., Potter, W. J., Donnerstein, E., Smith, S. L., Blumenthal, E., and Gray, T. (1996). Violence in television programming overall: University of California, Santa Barbara. *Scientific Papers: National Television Violence Study* (pp. 1–172). Studio City, CA: Mediascope.

Lacayo, R. (1995). Violent reaction time. *Time Magazine*, June 12, 25–30.

Lando, H. A., & Donnerstein, E. I. (1978). The effects of a model's success or failure on subsequent aggressive behavior. *Journal of Research in Personality, 12*, 225–234.

Lazarus, R. S., & Alfert, E. (1964). Short-circuiting of threat by experimentally altering cognitive appraisal. *Journal of Abnormal and Social Psychology, 69(2)*, 195–205.

Lazarus, R. S., Opton, E. M., Nomikos, M. S., & Rankin, N. O. (1965). The principal of short-circuiting of threat: Further evidence. *Journal of Personality, 33*, 622–635.

Lazarus, R. S., Speisman, M., Mordkoff, A. M., & Davison, L. A. (1962). A laboratory study of psychological stress produced by a motion picture film. *Psychological Monographs: General and Applied, 76(34)*, Whole No. 553.

Lefkowitz, M. M., Eron, L. D., Walder, L. Q., & Huesmann, L. R. (1977). *Growing up to be violent: A longitudinal study of the development of aggression.* New York: Pergamon Press.

Leyens, J. P., & Parke, R. D. (1974). Aggressive slides can induce a weapons effect. *European Journal of Social Psychology, 5(2)*, 229–236.

Leyens, J. P., & Picus, S. (1973). Identification with the winner of a fight and name mediation: Their differential effects upon subsequent aggressive behavior. *British Journal of Social and Clinical Psychology, 12*, 374–377.

Lichter, S. R., & Amundson, D. (1994, August). *A day of TV violence 1992 vs 1994.* Washington, DC: Center for Media and Public Affairs.

Liebert, R. M., & Baron, R. A. (1972). Short-term effects of televised aggression on children's aggressive behavior. In J. P. Murray, E. A. Rubinstein, & G. A. Comstock (Eds.), *Television and social behavior: Television and social learning* (Vol. 2, pp. 181–201). Washington, DC: Government Printing Office.

Liebert, R. M., & Sprafkin, J. (1988). *The early window* (3rd ed.). New York: Pergamon Press.

Linz, D., Donnerstein, E., & Penrod, S. (1984). The effects of multiple exposures to filmed violence against women. *Journal of Communication, 34(3),* 130–147.

Linz, D. G., Donnerstein, E., & Penrod, S. (1988). Effects of long-term exposure to violent and sexually degrading depictions of women. *Journal of Personality and Social Psychology, 55(5),* 758–768.

Liss, M. B., Reinhardt, L. C., & Fredriksen, S. (1983). TV heroes: The impact of rhetoric and deeds. *Journal of Applied Developmental Psychology, 4,* 175–187.

Malamuth, N., & Check, J. V. P. (1981). The effects of mass media exposure on acceptance of violence against women: A field experiment. *Journal of Research in Personality, 15,* 436–446.

Mathai, J. (1983). An acute anxiety state in an adolescent precipitated by viewing a horror movie. *Journal of Adolescence, 6,* 197–200.

Meyer, T. P. (1972). Effects of viewing justified and unjustified real film violence on aggressive behavior. *Journal of Personality and Social Psychology, 23(1),* 21–29.

Morison, P., & Gardner, H. (1978). Dragons and dinosaurs: The child's capacity to differentiate fantasy from reality. *Child Development, 49,* 642–648.

Mullin, C. R., & Linz, D. (1995). Desensitization and resensitization to violence against women: Effects of exposure to sexually violent films on judgments of domestic violence victims. *Journal of Personality and Social Psychology, 69(3),* 449–459.

Mustonen, A., & Pulkkinen, L. (1993). Aggression in television programs in Finland. *Aggressive Behavior, 19,* 175–183.

National Academy of Science. (1993). *Understanding and preventing violence.* Washington, DC: National Academy Press.

National Cable Television Association. (1995). Cable television developments. *Research and Policy Analysis Department, 20(2),* 1–4.

National Institute of Mental Health (1982). *Television and behavior: Ten years of scientific progress and implications for the eighties (Vol. 1). Summary Report.* Washington, DC: U.S. Government Printing Office.

Nielsen Media Research. (1997). *Television audience 1996.* New York: author.

Ogles, R. M., & Hoffner, C. (1987). Film violence and perceptions of crime: The cultivation effect. In M. L. McLaughlin (Ed.), *Communication Yearbook* (Vol. 10, pp. 384–394). Newbury Park, CA: Sage.

O'Keefe, G. J. (1984). Public views on crime: Television exposure and media credibility. In R. N. Bostrom (Ed.), *Communication yearbook 8* (pp. 514–535). Beverly Hills, CA: Sage Publications.

O'Keefe, G. J., & Reid-Nash, K. (1987). Crime news and real-world blues: The effects of the media on social reality. *Communication Research, 14(2),* 147–163.

Page, D., & O'Neal, E. (1977). "Weapons effect" without demand characteristics. *Psychological Reports, 41,* 29–30.

Paik, H., & Comstock, G. (1994). The effects of television violence on antisocial behavior: A meta-analysis. *Communication Research, 21(4),* 516–546.

Perry, D. G., & Perry, L. C. (1976). Identification with film characters, covert aggressive verbalization, and reactions to film violence. *Journal of Research in Personality, 10,* 399–409.

Perse, E. M. (1990). Involvement with local television news: Cognitive and emotional dimensions. *Human Communication Research 16(4),* 556–581.

Potter, W. J. (1986). Perceived reality and the cultivation hypothesis. *Journal of Broadcasting and Electronic Media, 30(2),* 159–174.

Potter, W. J. (1993). Cultivation theory and research: A conceptual critique. *Human Communication Research, 19,* 564–601.

Potter, W. J., Vaughan, M., Warren, R., Howley, K., Land, A., & Hagemeyer, J. (1995). How real is the portrayal of aggression in television entertainment programming? *Journal of Broadcasting and Electronic Media, 39,* 496–516.

Potter, W. J., & Ware, W. (1987). An analysis of the contexts of antisocial acts on prime-time television. *Communication Research, 14(6),* 664–686.

Reiss, A. J., & Roth, J. A. (Eds.) (1993). *Understanding and preventing violence.* Washington, DC: National Academy Press.

Rosengren, K. S., Kalish, C. W., Hickling, A. K., and Gleman, S. A. (1994). Exploring the relationship between preschool children's magical beliefs and causal thinking. *British Journal of Developmental Psychology, 12(19),* 69–82.

Sanders, G. S., & Baron, R. S. (1975). Pain cues and uncertainty as determinants of aggression in a situation involving repeated instigation. *Journal of Personality and Social Psychology, 32(3),* 495–502.

Schmidt, C. R., Schmidt, S. R., & Tomalis, S. M. (1984). Children's constructive processing and monitoring of stories containing anomalous information. *Child Development, 55,* 2056–2071.

Schmutte, G. T., & Taylor, S. P. (1980). Physical aggression as a function of alcohol and pain feedback. *The Journal of Social Psychology, 110,* 235–244.

Signorielli, N. (1990). Televisions mean and dangerous world: A continuation of the cultural indicators perspective. In N. Signorielli & M. Morgan (Eds.), *Cultivation analysis: New directions in media effects research.* Newbury Park, CA: Sage.

Slattery, L. L., & Hakanen, E. A. (1994). Sensationalism versus public affairs content of local TV news: Pennsylvania revisited. *Journal of Broadcasting and Electronic Media, 30,* 309–323.

Sparks, G. G. (1986). Developmental differences in children's reports of fear induced by the mass media. *Child Study Journal, 16,* 55–66.

Speisman, J. C., Lazarus, R. S., Mordkoff, A., & Davison, L. (1964). Experimental reduction of stress based on ego-defense theory. *Journal of Abnormal and Social Psychology, 68(4),* 367–380.

Stanger, J. D. (1997). *Television in the home: The 1997 survey of parents and children.* University of Pennsylvania: Annenberg Public Policy Center.

Steuer, F. B., Applefield, J. M., & Smith, R. (1971). Televised aggression and the interpersonal aggression of preschool children. *Journal of Experimental Child Psychology, 11,* 442–447.

Strasburger, V. C. (1993). Children, adolescents, and the media: Five crucial issues. *Adolescent Medicine: State of the Art Reviews, 4,* 479–493, 1993.

Surgeon General's Scientific Advisory Committee on Television and Social Behavior. (1972). *Television and growing up: The impact of televised violence.* Washington, DC: U.S. Government Printing Office.

Swart, C., & Berkowitz, L. (1976). Effects of a stimulus associated with victim's pain on later aggression. *Journal of Personality and Social Psychology, 33(5),* 623–631.

Tangey, J. P., & Feshbach, S. (1988). Children's television-viewing frequency: Individual differences and demographic correlates. *Personality and Social Psychology Bulletin, 14,* 145–158.

Thomas, M. H., & Drabman, R. S. (1975). Toleration of real life aggression as a function of exposure to television violence. *Journal of Personality and Social Psychology, 35,* 450–458.

Thomas, M. H., Horton, R. W., Lippencott, E. C., & Drabman, R. S. (1977). Desensitization to portrayals of real-life aggression as a function of exposure to television violence. *Journal of Personality and Social Psychology, 35,* 450–458.

Thomas, M. H., & Tell, P. M. (1974). Effects of viewing real versus fantasy violence upon interpersonal aggression. *Journal of Research in Personality, 8,* 153–160.

Thompson, J. G., & Myers, N. A. (1985). Inferences and recall at ages four and seven. *Child Development, 56,* 1134–1144.

Turner, C. W., & Berkowitz, L. (1972). Identification with film aggressor (covert role taking) and reactions to film violence. *Journal of Personality and Social Psychology, 21(2),* 256–264.

Turner, C. W., Layton, J. F., & Simons, L. S. (1975). Naturalistic studies of aggressive behavior: Aggressive stimuli, victim visibility, and horn honking. *Journal of Personality and Social Psychology, 31(6),* 1098–1107.

U. S. Department of Justice. (1997). *The prevalence and consequences of child victimization.* [on-line]. Available: http://www.ncjrs.org/txtfils/fs000179.txt.

Van Evra, J. (1990). *Television and child development.* Hillsdale, NJ: Lawrence Erlbaum.

Walters, R. H., & Parke, R. D. (1964). Influence of response consequences to a social model on resistance to deviation. *Journal of Experimental Child Psychology, 1,* 269–280.

Williams, T. M., Zabrack, M. L., & Joy, L. A. (1982). The portrayal of aggression on North American television. *Journal of Applied Social Psychology, 12(5),* 360–380.

Wilson, B. J. (1995). Les recherches sur médias et violence: Aggressivité, désensibilisation, peur [Effects of media violence: Aggression, desensitization, and fear]. *Les Cahairs de la sécurité Intérieure, 20(2),* 21–37.

Wilson, B. J., & Cantor, J. (1985). Developmental differences in empathy with a television protagonist's fear: *Journal of Experimental Child Psychology, 39,* 284–299.

Wilson, B. J., Kunkel, D., Linz, D., Potter, W. J., Donnerstein, E., Smith, S. L., Blumenthal, E., & Berry, M. (1998). Violence in television programming overall: University of California, Santa Barbara. *National Television Violence Study 2: Scientific papers* (pp. 3–204). Newbury Park, CA: Sage.

Wilson, B. J., Kunkel, D., Linz, D., Potter, W. J., Donnerstein, E., Smith, S. L., Blumenthal, E., & Gray, T. E. (1997). Violence in television programming overall: University of California, Santa Barbara. *National Television Violence Study: Scientific papers* (pp. 1–172). Newbury Park, CA: Sage.

Wilson, B. J., Linz, D., Donnerstein, E., & Stipp, H. (1992). The impact of social issue television programming on attitudes toward rape. *Human Communication Research, 19,* 179–208.

Wilson, B. J., & Smith, S. L. (1998). Children responses to emotional portrayals on television. In P. Andersen & L. Guerrero (Eds.), *Handbook of communication and emotion: Theory, application, and contexts.* New York: Academic Press.

Worchel, S. (1972). The effect of films on the importance of behavioral freedom. *Journal of Personality, 40,* 417–435.

Wotring, C. E., & Greenberg, B. S. (1973). Experiments in televised violence and verbal aggression: Two exploratory studies. *The Journal of Communication, 23,* 446–460.

Zillmann, D. (1979). *Hostility and aggression.* Hillsdale, NJ: Lawrence Erlbaum.

Zillmann, D. (1980). Anatomy of suspense. In P. H. Tannenbaum (Ed.), *The entertainment functions of television* (pp. 133–163). Hillsdale, NJ: Lawrence Erlbaum.

Zillmann, D. (1982). Television viewing and arousal. In D. Pearl, L. Bouthilet, & J. Lazar (Eds.), *Television and behavior: Ten years of scientific progress and implications for the eighties* (Vol. 2, pp. 53–67). Washington, DC: U.S. Government Printing Office.

Zillmann, D. (1991). Empathy: Affect from bearing witness to the emotions of others. In J. Bryant & D. Zillmann (Eds.), *Responding to the screen* (pp. 135–167). Hillsdale, NJ: Lawrence Erlbaum.

Zillmann, D., & Cantor, J. R. (1977). Affective responses to the emotions of a protagonist. *Journal of Experimental Social Psychology, 13,* 155–165.

8

MALE VIOLENCE

TOWARD WOMEN:

AN INTEGRATED PERSPECTIVE

JACQUELYN W. WHITE

University of North Carolina at Greensboro

ROBIN M. KOWALSKI

Western Carolina University

Women are victimized by strangers, acquaintances, friends, and relatives, including fathers, brothers, and husbands. The aggression can be nonintimate (i.e., robbery, burglary, aggravated assault, forcible rape, and murder), as well as intimate [i.e., child abuse, incest, courtship violence, acquaintance rape (includes forcible rape), battering, marital rape, and sexual harassment]. It can take many forms, from psychological intimidation and coercion through name-calling and moderate physical violence (pushing, shoving, slapping) to severe physical violence (beating, using weapons), sexual assault, and murder.

The focus of this chapter is male intimate aggression/violence directed toward females because intimate victimization is significantly greater for women than men.[1]

---

[1] Because of space limitations, this chapter will focus primarily on incest, courtship violence, sexual assault including rape, and wife battering. Other forms of violence against women, such as nonfamilial childhood sexual abuse and stranger rape, will not be considered in depth. The discussion is limited to male violence against women, although the authors acknowledge the seriousness of violence in gay and lesbian relationships (see White & Bondurant, 1996) and of female aggression (White & Kowalski, 1994). However, the authors suggest that their analysis can be extended to include these other forms of relationship violence.

Human Aggression: Theories, Research, and
Implications for Social Policy

Even in instances where data suggest that women and men aggress against each other at comparable rates (e.g., dating violence and spousal aggression), consequences for women are considerably more severe. The consequences can be psychological and/or physical, short term and long term, with posttraumatic stress disorder being the most common diagnosis for the victims of many forms of intimate violence (Goodman, Koss, & Russo, 1993). An integrative contextual developmental perspective is adopted to emphasize that an individual's behavior can be best understood by considering the impact of historical, sociocultural, and social factors across time on cognitive and motivational processes that result in aggression and violence against women. Furthermore, we argue that understanding the gendered nature of aggression and violence is critical.

This chapter uses the terms aggression and violence, especially violence, because these terms, along with the term abuse, are the ones most frequently used in the literature when speaking of harm-doing directed by a man toward a woman. Researchers usually use either prevailing legal definitions (e.g., of incest, rape) or their own operational definitions. Even though there are no clear a priori criteria for deciding whether a behavior is aggressive, violent, or abusive, aggression is used to refer to a continuum of behaviors that are intended to harm a target; when physical force is used or when severe harm is intended and/or occurs the term violence is used. Abuse is reserved for violence that occurs in an ongoing relationship (i.e., child abuse, spouse abuse). We were also guided by Koss, Goodman, Browne, Fitzgerald, Keita, and Russo's (1994) working definition of male violence toward women:

> Male violence toward women encompasses physical, visual, verbal, or sexual acts that are experienced by a woman or girl as a threat, invasion, or assault and that have the effect of hurting her or degrading her and/or taking away her ability to control contact (intimate or otherwise) with another individual (p. xvi).

The next section describes single and multifactor theories that have been used to explain male violence against women. Although informative in their own right, each of these theories has certain shortcomings (i.e., focusing on a single type of male violence against women without examining common, as well as distinct, features of different types of violence) that have limited researchers' ability to completely understand the phenomenon of male violence against women.

Following this discussion, we present the integrative contextual developmental model we have adopted to organize information about violence against women. This model provides a metatheoretical framework within which more specific theories and hypotheses can be considered. This approach recognizes the importance of historical and sociocultural factors, along with social network, dyadic relationship, situational, and interpersonal factors that affect the psychological processes (cognitive and motivational) that underlie all types of male violence against women. We then summarize briefly the evidence concerning the various forms of violence against women, including prevalence and characteristics of the perpetrator, the victim, and the circumstances surrounding each of the various forms of aggression. These factors are organized according to our model. The chapter concludes by arguing that the integrative contextual developmental approach provides the best opportunity for understanding violence against women.

THEORETICAL CONCEPTUALIZATIONS

The earliest theories of violence against women borrowed heavily from basic theories of aggression and may be classified best as single factor theories of aggression. These single factor approaches can be categorized as biological/evolutionary, intrapsychic, victim-precipitated, social learning, social information processing, sociological, and feminist. Each of these theories focuses on one primary factor that precipitates violence against women, usually at one level of analysis. More recent theories are more independent of the earlier mainstream theories, are more complex, and have a more applied focus. In this sense they are more eclectic.

EVOLUTIONARY THEORIES

Early evolutionary theories argued that male violence was rooted in genetics and biology due to natural selection pressure (Deutsch, 1944) and that rape in particular was a reproductive strategy (Thornhill & Thornhill, 1992). More current efforts still invoke constructs such as genetic determinism and sexual selection to account for gendered patterns of behavior (Buss, 1987; Smuts, 1992). In one of the most recent attempts to develop an evolutionary theory, Ellis (1991) still relies primarily on biological assumptions, although acknowledging environmental factors. His assumptions include (1) aggression is an unlearned drive to possess and control, (2) natural selection results in men's stronger sex drives, and (3) variability among men's motivations to rape are due in part to the degree and type of exposure of their brains to androgens. Lang, Flor-Henry, and Frenzel's (1990) comparison of the hormonal profiles of pedophiles, incest offenders, and community controls exemplifies research efforts to identify biological sources of influence.

INTRAPSYCHIC THEORIES

These theories focus on acts of violence as manifestations of deviations in one's personality. Research from this perspective has focused on identifying personality profiles of child molesters (Duthie & McIvor, 1990), rapists (Groth & Birnbaum, 1979), batterers (Geffner & Rosenbaum, 1990), and sexually aggressive men (Abel, Rouleau, & Cunningham-Rathner, 1986). These personality-oriented theories search for individual difference variables that propel some men toward violence and increase the likelihood of only certain women being victimized. In accounting for incest, psychoanalytic theory has focused on the Oedipal complex (for a critique see Simon, 1992) and has viewed incest as a vengeful infanticidal derivative (Feder, 1980). Psychoanalytic theory has also argued that poor narcissistic development may underlie domestic violence (Rosen, 1991).

VICTIM-PRECIPITATION THEORIES

These theories similarly examined the behaviors of women that "caused" them (Amir, 1971), or their children (Schonberg, 1992), to be victimized. However, research has failed to identify specific personality and attitudinal characteristics that make certain women more vulnerable to battering (Rusbult & Martz, 1995) or sexual assault (Koss & Dinero, 1988). Rather, situational features of women's lives, not characterological facets, have been related to histories of physical, emotional, or sexual abuse (Pitman & Taylor, 1992).

SOCIAL LEARNING THEORIES

Developed primarily out of Bandura's (1973) research, these theories focus on the socialization experiences of men that lead them to be violent toward women. Work in this arena has focused on modeling influences, reinforcement for aggressive behavior, and attitudes and beliefs that mediate violence. For example, Peretti and Statum (1984) found evidence for father–son intergenerational transmission of authoritarian paternal attitudes. Similarly, White and Shuntich (1991) found that college men's perceptions of their fathers' sexual aggressiveness toward their mothers were correlated with their own self-reported sexual aggression. In general, the intergenerational transmission of violence model has been used to account for various forms of adult criminal behavior, including incest (Reginer & LeBoy, 1991), dating violence (Gwartney-Gibbs, Stockard, & Brohmer, 1983), child abuse (Kaufman & Zigler, 1987), and domestic violence (Kalmuss, 1984; Straus & Gelles, 1990).

SOCIAL INFORMATION PROCESSING THEORIES

These approaches to violence against women have focused on the cognitive processes involved in an aggressive episode. The focus is on how the perpetrator's perception of the situation, as well as preexisting schema and perceptions, result in aggression. These models give us details on how individuals' mental representations of cultural scripts develop and how they come to filter and bias the encoding and decoding of information. Perhaps one of the earliest efforts was that of McFall (1982) who examined three stages in the development of social skills: decoding, decision-making, and encoding. This basic model has been adapted in various ways, resulting in models of child abuse (Milner, 1993), sexual assault (Craig, 1990; Lipton, McDonel, & McFall, 1987), and spouse abuse (Holtzworth-Munroe, 1991). Noteworthy examples of this approach to aggression in general are Dodge's (1986) work with aggressive children and Berkowitz's (1994; this volume) cognitive neoassociationist model.

SOCIOCULTURAL THEORIES

Sociocultural theories tend to rely on macro-level analyses and examine structural features of a society that could account for differences in rates of violence against women in different social groups. Numerous studies have identified regional, racial, and/or class differences in reported incidents of all the various forms of violence against women. Explanations lie in examining the effects of racism, sexism, social disorganization, unemployment, economic inequality, and alienating conditions of urban life (for examples see Baron & Straus, 1989; Erea & Tontodonato, 1988; Hastrup & Elsass, 1988; Rozee, 1993; Stout, 1992; Yllo, 1983). These theories suggest that violence may serve a social function and/or be reflective of a culture of violence.

FEMINIST THEORIES

These theories integrate features of social learning theory and sociocultural theory by stressing the impact of sociocultural influences on the learning process. However, feminists argue that violence against women is primarily an act of domination created by social inequalities, motivated by a need for power, and fundamentally rooted in a patriarchal value system (Brownmiller, 1975; Riger & Gordon, 1981). Thus, violence against women is seen as a social mechanism for the control of women.

MULTIFACTOR THEORIES

Application of each of these single factor theories to diverse types of male violence against women has generated testable hypotheses and yielded data contributing to our understanding of the various phenomena. However, each has focused on a single contributing factor or a single level of analysis to the exclusion of alternative sources of influence. For example, understanding the personality characteristics of men who show a proclivity to commit sexual assault, or assessing biases in social information processing, ignores the cultural milieu in which these tendencies were developed and are enacted. Conversely, focusing on sociocultural factors predictive of violence against women tells us little about the mechanisms that lead these factors to affect the behavior of some men but not others.

In response to the shortcomings of single factor theories, multifactor theories have emerged that provide a more complex and integrated perspective on male violence against women. Whereas some of these multifactor theories have examined the numerous determinants of a particular type of violence against women (i.e., Berkowitz, 1992; Finkelhor & Browne, 1985; Riggs & O'Leary, 1996; White & Koss, 1991; Worell & Remer, 1992), others have attempted to examine precipitating factors common to more than one type of violence (Malamuth, Linz, Heavey, Barnes, & Acker, 1995; Malamuth, Sockloskie, Koss, & Tanaka, 1991; Shotland, 1992). These more recent theories are more appropriately considered models. They are less tied to traditional theories, are more descriptive, and rely on complex forms of data analysis (i.e., path analysis, structural equation modeling) to derive a representation of the relationship between variables predicting some forms of violence against women.

For example, Finkelhor (1984) identified individual and social/cultural variables in his model of childhood sexual abuse. Similarly, Berkowitz (1992) examined the role of culture, social situations, early learning and experiences, and individual difference variables as antecedents of acquaintance rape and sexual assault, as did White and Koss (1991). White and Koss (1991) extended work on acquaintance sexual assault by using a levels-of-analysis approach to organize the multiple determinants of sexual aggression. Their approach was based on Dutton's (1988) analysis of domestic violence. However, these efforts have not looked closely at the relationship between sexual assault, dating violence, and battering, although there is evidence of a connection (Deal & Wampler, 1986; Feld & Straus, 1989; Roscoe & Benaske, 1985). Also using a levels-of-analysis approach, Bondurant and White (1994) have presented a model of men who sexually harass. Fitzgerald (1993) too adopts a multicomponent model of sexual harassment.

Although comprehensive in their coverage, these analyses focus on a single type of male violence against women. Furthermore, these theories still fall short on three dimensions in our effort to understand violence against women in its myriad manifestations.

First, gender is not a core construct in these multifactor theories, nor is the gendered nature of aggression acknowledged. We suggest that aggression and violence cannot be fully understood without considering the central role gender plays in the construction of aggression. By this, we mean that aggression is seen as an inherent component of a culturally constructed masculinity; it is a characteristic associated with power and control, to be used to dominate (see Thompson, 1991; White & Bondurant, 1995; White & Kowalski, 1994). It is seen as an appropriate affective response to frustration and anger for men, but not for women. Whereas women are taught self-control, men are taught to control (Campbell, 1993). Male violence against women occurs in a social context that prescribes particular gender-based roles and patterns of cross-gender interaction. An integrative levels-of-analysis approach to male violence against women, discussed in detail later, acknowledges the gendered nature of social relationships, including family, work, and peer relationships (Unger & Crawford, 1995). In addition, such an analysis recognizes that personality and cognitive factors that contribute to the incidence of male violence against women "are embedded in gendered social structures that define and direct the gendered meaning of sexual and violent behaviors" (Koss et al., 1994, p. 6).

Second, among multifactor theories that recognize sociocultural influences, the research focus is at the level of the individual. For example, the individual's perspective, usually obtained via self-report, is used to acquire information about dyadic factors and sociocultural variables. This focus stems, in part, from the methodological limitations imposed by traditional types of psychological research. Research has fallen short in investigating the multiple determinants of intimate male violence against women. Research focusing on intrapersonal predictors of male violence against women has ignored the situational, dyadic, social network, and sociocultural variables that interact with individual difference variables. What is needed is a more interdisciplinary research approach in which independent sources of information are acquired from sociologists, anthropologists, criminologists, and epidemiologists, as well as psychologists. Interventions designed to stop male violence against women or to aid victims of such violence similarly must be developed from information gained from more than one independent source. More research that actually examines dyads is needed (for examples, see O'Leary, 1988; Malamuth et al., 1995). Also, exploring cultural influences on behavior requires study at the macro level.

Third, the majority of the multifactor theories focus on a single type of violence. This renders less visible the commonalities that underlie all types of violence toward women.[2] Because of the complexity of each form of violence, we certainly recognize that it would be beyond the scope of individual research projects to assess all possible variables or to include all types of violence against women. However, this leads to a tradition of different researchers, journals, readers, and ultimately theories for each type of violence against women.[3]

In light of this, a more integrative approach toward male violence against women is needed that addresses all possible types of violence at all levels of analysis. To this end, we argue that the integrative contextual developmental perspective described in the next section is necessary for a full understanding of violence against women. It recognizes that various influences are embedded within others. The model suggests where in the larger picture specific relationships between variables fit.

AN INTEGRATIVE CONTEXTUAL DEVELOPMENTAL MODEL

The integrative contextual developmental perspective presents a metatheoretical model within which substantive theories can be elaborated and hypotheses derived. The model assumes an embedded (or hierarchical) perspective to categorize variables as sociocultural, dyadic, situational, and intrapersonal (see Dutton, 1988; Lerner, 1991). This perspective examines individual behavior in relationship to

[2]Arguing that research on violence against women should be more integrated with an examination of underlying factors common to different types of violence against women is not to say that each individual form that the violence takes may not have unique characteristics worthy of investigation.

[3]However, some exceptions can be found. Malamuth (this volume; Malamuth et al., 1991, 1995) developed a confluence model that examines the relationship between sexual and physical assault of men's intimate female partners. Shotland (1992) examined the similarities between spouse abuse with and without rape and courtship violence with and without rape. Finally, White and Bondurant (1996), in a review article, used a developmental levels-of-analysis approach to examine the gendered nature of violence.

the specific situation in which it occurs (i.e., proximal influences), as well as in relation to more distal situational/contextual influences. The model assumes gender-
related phenomena at all levels. We assume that patriarchy is defined at the
historical/sociocultural level, in turn prescribing power dynamics in terms of gender, race, class, ethnicity and age. As a result, these power dynamics become enacted at the interpersonal level, affecting the internalization of gendered values,
expectations, and behaviors.

The model does not specify which factors are the most important in predicting
an instance of violence against women, nor does it predict how or which factors
might interact. Rather, the model serves the goal of integrating a wide range of
factors and guiding researchers in the generation of substantive hypotheses.

Contextual factors exist at the cultural level and reflect the shared patterns of
ideas and beliefs that exist across generations (Frayser, 1989). Within this level
are societal, community, and neighborhood factors that define expectations for behavior and assignment of roles by sex (Schlegal, 1989). In turn, these sociocultural factors define features of one's social networks (family, peer groups, school,
and employment relations). Further embedded in these social networks are characteristics of the dyadic relationship in which violence occurs. This embedded
perspective argues that recognition of factors at all these levels enhances understanding of variables at the intrapersonal level, including traits, attitudes, motivations, and past history. Specifically, social and cultural influences and attitudes
create the context within which men with certain personality characteristics and
behavioral tendencies will likely be violent given particular social situations and
dyadic relationships. Theories of aggression are most useful in explaining men's
aggression and violence toward women when factors at each level of analysis are
considered. Historical and sociocultural factors create an environment in which
the growing child learns rules and expectations, first in the family network and
later in peer, intimate, and work relationships. Early experiences define the context for later experiences (Huesmann & Eron, 1995; Olweus, 1993; White & Bondurant, 1995).

Figure 8.1 illustrates the embedded perspective and shows the interconnections
between the various levels of analysis. Time is also a critical component of the
model; time, demarked by the arrow going from left to right, indicates that effects
change across time and are cumulative. The most distal influences are historical
and sociocultural. Embedded in these is a number of interconnected relationships
a person has (or may have at different points across the lifespan) and includes
family, social, school, and work. Within each network is embedded a relationship
between two individuals, the potential perpetrator and potential victim, denoted
by the circles telescoped out from each social network. These two individuals
have an interaction history that will influence their behaviors in any given situation; this situation provides the proximal cues for aggression and violence. All
these factors also coalesce to determine the particular behavioral manifestation of
aggression (i.e., verbal, physical, sexual). Certain situational factors will increase
the likelihood of an aggressive encounter. Figure 8.2 presents a further elaboration

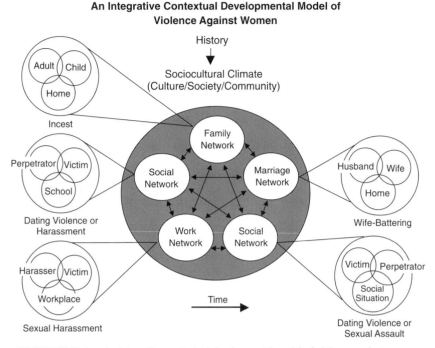

An Integrative Contextual Developmental Model of Violence Against Women

FIGURE 8.1   An integrative contextual developmental model of violence against women.

of the telescoped network components in Figure 8.1. This proximal confluence model indicates that the intrapersonal characteristics of the perpetrator and victim interact with each other, as well as with the situational context to result in an aggressive episode. The integrative contextual developmental perspective suggests that intrapersonal variables are expressed within a cultural and social context and reflect influences from one's genetic/biological makeup, personality, attitudes and beliefs, cognitive processes, and learning history. Thus, certain intrapersonal variables predict violence only in specific situations (White & Humphrey, 1997).

Using this model as a framework, various factors that distinguish violence against women can be conceptualized. As Figure 8.1 shows, the various types of violence against women are distinguished by the nature of the relationship, the ages of the perpetrator and victim, and the form the violence takes. The type of relationship between the perpetrator and victim provides the distinguishing features. For example, forcible sexual intercourse between a father and daughter is labeled incest, whereas forced sexual intercourse between a nonrelated male and female is labeled rape. Similarly, beating up one's wife is called spouse abuse, whereas beating up one's dating partner is called dating violence. In a work relationship, coerced sexual intercourse in exchange for job security is called quid pro quo sexual harassment, but in a dating relationship it is called acquaintance rape.

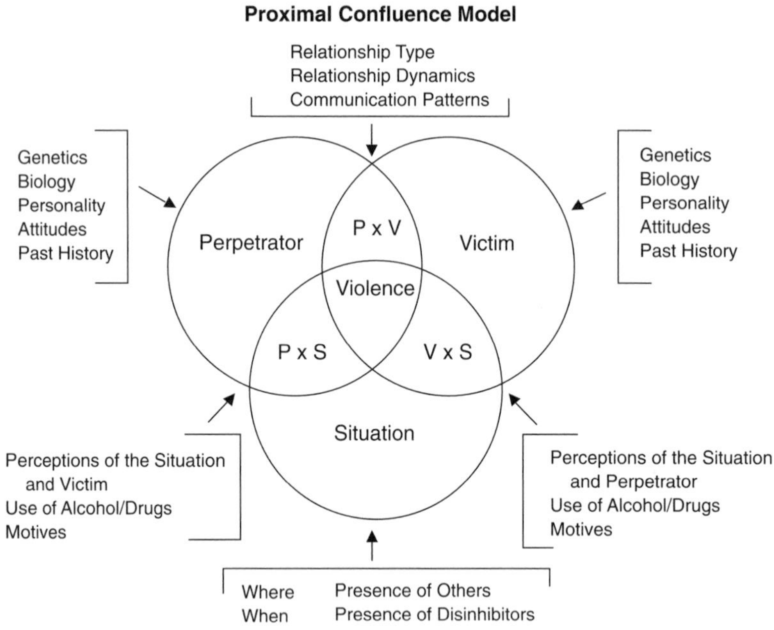

Proximal Confluence Model

Relationship Type
Relationship Dynamics
Communication Patterns

Genetics
Biology
Personality
Attitudes
Past History

Perpetrator   P x V   Victim

Genetics
Biology
Personality
Attitudes
Past History

Violence

P x S   V x S

Situation

Perceptions of the Situation
and Victim
Use of Alcohol/Drugs
Motives

Perceptions of the Situation
and Perpetrator
Use of Alcohol/Drugs
Motives

Where   Presence of Others
When   Presence of Disinhibitors

FIGURE 8.2   A proximal confluence model.

TYPES OF VIOLENCE AGAINST WOMEN: OVERVIEW OF COMMON AND UNIQUE CHARACTERISTICS

Dozens of books and hundreds of research articles have been published on the various forms of violence against women. Because a comprehensive review of this literature is beyond the scope of this chapter, we present an overview of a number of common as well as unique features that are characteristic of various forms of violence against women (for a more extensive description of various forms of violence against women, see Koss et al., 1994). Table 8.1 summarizes these characteristics for five types of violence against women (incest, dating violence, sexual assault, wife battering, and sexual harassment) and includes the best estimates of the prevalence of each.[4] At the top of Table 8.1 is a list of variables characteristic of all forms of violence against women, including patriarchal values and beliefs, power differences, experiences with family violence, need to dominate and control, physical isolation, and use of alcohol and/or drugs. Each type of violence is also

---

[4]Prevalence estimates are taken from Salter (1992) for incest; from White and Koss (1991) for dating violence; from Koss, Gidycz, and Wisniewski (1987) for acquaintance sexual assault; from Dutton (1988) for wife battering; and from Fitzgerald et al. (1988) for sexual harassment.

TABLE 8.1 Summary of Risk Factors for Perpetration

					Common risk factors		
					Patriarchal values and beliefs — Power (status) differences — Use of alcohol and/or drugs	Experiences with family violence — Physical isolation (due to time and/or location) — Need to dominate and control	
					Unique risk factors		
Manifestation of violence	Type of network	Prevalence	Risk factors sociocultural	Dyadic	Situational	Perpetrator characteristics	Victim characteristics
Incest	Parent/child	4.5%	Conservative family values; Belief in subordination of women and obedience of children	Familial	Dysfunctional marriage; Mother absent; Lower SES	Authoritarian, punitive, threatening; Low tolerance for conflict and anger; Believes in subordination of women and obedience of children	Vulnerable; Loyal; Trusting; Lacks other sources of love and support
Dating violence	Social/school	88% verbal; 32% physical	Dating script; Adolescents/young adults	Dating context; Committed relationship; Adolescents/young adults	Jealousy	Accepts interpersonal violence; Hostility toward women; Impulsive/aggressive personality; Quick to anger; Jealous	Believes violence means love; Uses interpersonal aggression to solve conflicts; Less traditionally feminine
Acquaintance sexual assault		53% (rape, 15%)	Sexual script	"Miscommunication"; Negative father–son relationship	Peer support; Denied sexual access; Organizational affiliation (sorority/fraternity/athletic team)	Delinquent; Accepts rape myths; Hedonistic and dominance as sexual motive; Hostility toward women; Self-centered; Insensitive to others; History of promiscuity	Previous history of sexual victimization; Higher use of alcohol/drugs than nonvictims; Earlier onset of sexual experiences
Wife or partner battering and rape	Marital	28–33%	Belief that women are property; Belief in sexual precedence	Cohabitating; Economic/social dependence; Assault is chronic	Stress (unemployment); Marital discord; Lower SES	Traditional gender role attitudes; Lacks coping skills; Need to dominate; Previous head injury; Younger; Depressive symptomology	Lacks alternatives; Fears for life of self and/or children
Sexual harassment	Work environment	42–53%	Belief that woman's place is in the home	Supervisor/supervisee; co-workers	Supportive; Male-dominated occupation or large percentage of female employees	Older, white, married; Quid pro quo type harasser is similar to sexually assaultive men	Younger, minority, single

characterized by the social network involved, along with unique sociocultural, dyadic, situational, perpetrator, and victim characteristics. Two criteria were used for determining if a factor was common or unique: (1) the factor was identified consistently across the various literatures on each type of violence against women, and (2) the factor was identified as a significant correlate in major studies. We suggest that it is the nature of the relationship that contributes to unique features of each type of violence. For example, belief in children's obedience is relevant in predicting incest, but not dating violence. Conversely, believing in sexual access beyond the first date would not be relevant to father–daughter incest but it is to date rape. However, in both cases a general belief in traditional gender roles and male entitlement is relevant. Similarly, sexual arousal is a component of acquaintance sexual assault but not of wife battering.

SOCIOCULTURAL LEVEL
(CULTURE/SOCIETY/COMMUNITY)

The sociocultural level of analysis includes cultural, social, community, and neighborhood influences on behavior (Lerner, 1991; for a complete review of cultural influences on male violence against women, see Koss et al., 1994). Thus, sociocultural is a broad descriptive term that includes sexual inequalities, gender role prescriptions (including dating and sexual scripts), and cultural norms and myths about women, men, children, family, sex, and violence. Cultural norms governing aggression as a tool of the powerful to subdue the weak, combined with cultural supports for the legitimacy of aggression as a form of self-defense, interact with gender inequalities to create a context conducive to violence against women.

Whether discussing incest, sexual harassment, courtship violence, or sexual assault, a common theme underlying all of these types of violence is gender inequality involving male dominance and female submissiveness. For example, power inequalities that underlie violence against women are evident in cases of father–daughter incest. Typically, fathers who sexually abuse their daughters maintain strict patriarchal family systems where they are the undisputed head of the household (Herman & Hirschman, 1993; Lesniak, 1993). Likewise, sexual harassment functions as a type of social control of women as evidenced by the preponderance of instances of sexual harassment in nontraditional employment settings where gender role expectations "spill-over" into the workplace, rendering women more vulnerable (Gutek, 1985).

> Just as women who hitchhike, dress provocatively, or go alone to bars are thought to be "asking for" rape (and women who argue with their partners, assert their own needs, or refuse to cook dinner are considered to be "asking for" physical violence), so women who venture into the dangerous (but challenging and lucrative) male worlds of firefighting, soldiering, mining, and so forth are expected to accept whatever harassment they receive (Fitzgerald, 1993, p. 1072).

Similarly, just as the dating script promotes the image of the man as the initiator of interactions (Rose & Frieze, 1993; Byers, 1996), the sexual script socializes

young men to be the initiators of sexual activity and women to be the passive re-
cipients. These scripts set the stage for many instances of dating violence and acquaintance rape. Although the link between sexual scripts and male violence
against women has been examined most thoroughly in the context of acquaintance
rape (Koss et al., 1994; Kowalski, 1992, 1993a,b; LaPlante, McCormick, & Brannigan, 1980; White & Koss, 1991), applications also have been made to the areas
of sexual harassment (Pryor, 1987), courtship violence (Bernard, Bernard, &
Bernard, 1985), and domestic violence (Koss & Gaines, 1993; Martin & Hummer,
1989; Sanday, 1981). Men who endorse traditional scripts are more likely than men
who do not to perceive force and coercion as acceptable means of obtaining desired
outcomes regardless of the particular situation or dyadic encounter involved.

Expectations about the appropriate roles for men and women are communi-
cated through various institutionalized practices of a society and include those of
the legal system, the church, schools, media, politics, and the military. All set the
stage for the evolution of cultural myths that perpetuate male violence against
women. Representative cultural myths underlying male violence against women
include women enjoy it or want it and women deserve it. According to Leidig
(1992, p. 199), the "linkage among all . . . acts of violence is the commonality of
the numerous myths attached to them." Thus, the cultural myth that women enjoy
male violence can be used to justify rape (women say no when they really mean
yes), courtship or domestic violence (some women are just attracted to violent
men), and sexual harassment (women invite sexual harassment and enjoy the attention) (Koss et al., 1994).

Thus, certain sociocultural variables are common to all types of male violence
against women. Cultures in which less traditional gender roles are prescribed and
in which male dominance and female subordination are not encouraged show
fewer instances of male violence against women, supporting the idea of sociocultural contributions to such violence (Rozee, 1993). Related to this, organizations
in which norms encourage sexual harassment obviously see more instances of harassment than organizations in which sexual harassment is clearly viewed as
counternormative (Pryor, La Vite, & Stoller, 1993).

However, although all men within a given culture are typically exposed to similar sociocultural pressures to behave in accordance with their assigned gender
roles, not all men commit violent acts against women. One reason all men are not
violent toward women lies in the multiply determined nature of male violence
against women. Embedded within one's culture are situational, dyadic, and intrapersonal influences that may either increase the likelihood of violence or mitigate against it. In part, this is because subcultural differences exist among men
within a particular culture (e.g., Western culture). Racial, ethnic, and class differences have been identified in all forms of violence against women (examples: for
incest, see Hernandez, 1993; for dating violence, see Miller & Simpson, 1991; for
sexual assault, see Fischer, 1987; Wyatt, 1992; for domestic violence, see Holzman, 1994; for sexual harassment, see Giuffre & Williams, 1994; Segura, 1992).
Hence, levels of analysis other than cultural are necessary.

SOCIAL NETWORK LEVEL

The gendered norms and expectations that contribute to male violence against women are transmitted through a number of different social institutions, including the family (Pagelow, 1984), peer relations (Ageton, 1983; Koss et al., 1994; Martin & Hummer, 1989), school (Ageton, 1983), church (Whipple, 1987), media (Donnerstein, this volume), and work settings (Fitzgerald, 1993). Variables such as family values, a history of family violence, peer group influences, exposure to media violence (including pornography), religiosity, and school-related functioning all play a critical role in influencing incidents of male violence against women.

Witnessing or experiencing family violence as a child is frequently related to various forms of violence toward women. Indeed, roughly one-third of individuals who witness or experience violence as children become violent as adults (Kaufman & Zigler, 1987). Many households in which violence occurs are characterized by patriarchal family structures where traditional sex roles are encouraged. Men raised in these households are more likely than men reared in less traditional households to become violent as adults (for incest, see Greenspun, 1994; for dating violence, see Gwartney-Gibbs et al., 1987; Riggs & O'Leary, 1986; for sexual aggression, see Fagot, Loeber, & Reid, 1988; Friedrich, Beilke, & Urquiza, 1988; Koss & Dinero, 1988; Malamuth et al., 1995; for domestic violence, see Hotaling & Sugarman, 1986; Kalmuss, 1984; Straus, Gelles, & Steinmetz, 1980).

Although the path from witnessing or experiencing violence as a child to later violence is neither direct nor simple, several factors determine its course. First, the experience of or exposure to violence as a child may lead to the development of attitudinal schema (i.e., adversarial sexual beliefs, acceptance of interpersonal violence, and the acceptance of rape myths) that pervade later social and sexual interactions as a parent and/or intimate partner (Friedrich et al., 1988; Malamuth et al., 1991; Wash & Knudson-Martin, 1994). Second, exposure to abuse may contribute to a threatened self-esteem, a factor also predictive of interpersonal violence (White & Humphrey, 1990). Third, exposure to interpersonal violence may constrain the behavioral options invoked when men are confronted with stressful situations (Herrenkohl, Herrenkohl, & Tiedter, 1983). Under conditions of ambiguity or stress, men may direct their behavior in accordance with the most cognitively accessible script, in this case, one reflecting traditional gender roles and violence against women (Kowalski, 1993).

As with the family social unit, other networks may promote a system of values that reflect sociocultural understandings of gender inequality. Within these networks, adversarial sexual relationships and the acceptance of interpersonal violence may be encouraged and rewarded. For example, exposure to delinquent peer groups, whether at school, work, or the community at large, has been shown to be related to dating violence (Gwartney-Gibbs et al., 1983), sexual assault (Ageton, 1983; White & Koss, 1991) and sexual harassment (Koss et al., 1994). Similarly, it has been suggested that fundamentalist clergy may inadvertently help perpetuate wife battering because of attitudes about gender roles and marriage (Whipple, 1987). Police officers, too, because of their attitudes and values concerning domestic violence, may help maintain it (Stith, 1990).

DYADIC LEVEL

Within each of the social networks just described, dyadic interactions play a major role in determining male violence against women. In almost all discussions of violence against women, the power, or status, differences between the perpetrator and the victim are noted. Stemming from historical and sociocultural traditions, women are regarded as weaker and more passive than men and, thus, rightfully should be dependent on men. Such culturally prescribed dependence increases women's vulnerability to abuse.

In cases of incest, the nature of the relationship between the perpetrator and the victim is particularly problematic because of the inherent intimate tie between the two individuals, particularly in the case of father–daughter incest. According to one survey (Herman & Hirschman, 1993), the fathers of many incest victims were relegated to a special status due to the frequent absence of the mother (usually due to disabilities requiring frequent hospitalizations). Because their father was frequently the only source of affection and because of their desire to maintain the intact nature of the family, the daughters reported feeling obligated to fulfill their father's sexual wishes.

In a model of courtship violence, Riggs and O'Leary (1986, 1996) map out a number of characteristics of relationships that have implications for aggressive interactions. These relate to relationship conflict and include relationship problems, problem-solving abilities, couple communication, relationship satisfaction, and intimacy. Malamuth et al. (1995) have shown that relationship distress predicts verbal and nonsexual physical violence.

Research on acquaintance rape has shown that the degree of acquaintanceship between the perpetrator and the victim influences whether a sexual assault will occur, the type of strategy the perpetrator will use, and the likelihood that the assault will end in rape (White & Koss, 1991). More sexual assaults occur among acquaintances than among strangers (Koss, 1988). Furthermore, acquaintance rape is more likely during initial dating encounters, especially first dates, than in long-term relationships (Muehlenhard & Linton, 1987). However, this finding may be confounded by the failure of many women involved in long-term relationships to recognize that they have been raped (Goodchilds, Zellman, Johnson, & Giarrusso, 1988). Shotland (1989, 1992) has proposed that relationship characteristics in conjunction with certain gender-role attitudes predict when sexual assault will occur. In particular, many people believe that sexual intercourse, even forced, is okay in relationships with a history of sexual intercourse (Shotland & Goodstein, 1992).

Similar dyadic relationship issues enter in cases of sexual harassment. Sexual harassment is more likely to occur among individuals who are involved in an unequal power relationship (i.e., between employer and employee), reflecting the role of power inequalities in promoting violence against women (Gutek, 1985). As in cases of incest, the unequal power relationships stem from dependency of the victim on the perpetrator for particular outcomes (i.e., employment, salary increase, promotion).

In some instances of male violence against women, especially courtship violence, acquaintance rape, wife abuse, and sexual harassment, nonverbal and verbal communication patterns between the members of the dyad may set the stage for violent interactions.[5] More specifically, men and women do not always perceive behaviors in exactly the same way. Some men interpret women's behavior in more sexualized ways than it was intended (Abbey, 1991; Kowalski, 1992, 1993a,b), do not take her verbal protestations seriously (Check & Malamuth, 1983), and perceive the woman's rejection of sexual advances as a threat to their manhood (Beneke, 1982). According to Kowalski (1993a), men who endorse adversarial sexual beliefs and interpersonal violence are more likely to misinterpret a woman's behavior as sexually connotative than men who do not hold such beliefs. Similarly, women may enter dating relationships with a cognitive set toward trust, companionship, and having a good time, and hence be less alert to the warning signs of assault (Norris, Nurius & Dimeff, 1996).

SITUATIONAL LEVEL

In order for male violence against women to occur, the situation must be conducive to the violence. A number of situational variables have been examined, including time, place, and the presence of social inhibitors or disinhibitors (i.e., the presence of others or the presence of alcohol). Regardless of the type of violence under investigation, features of the situation influence the likelihood that violence will occur by affecting the opportunity for the violent acts (i.e., times when privacy is available and detection minimal) and/or by contributing to the ambiguity of the situation (White & Koss, 1991).

The specific situational elements conducive to each type of violence examined in this chapter typically involve isolation to avoid detection: a child alone with a male family member for long periods of time or a woman alone with her dating partner, spouse, or colleague are more vulnerable to violence than those in situations in which others are around as potential witnesses to the violence. In one study of incest (Herman & Hirschman, 1993), over half of the respondents indicated that their mother had some sort of disability or other medical condition that necessitated absences from the home.

[5]However, the miscommunication approach to sexual assault has been criticized in part because it implies a failure on the woman's part to be clear about her intentions (Crawford, 1995; Donat & White, in press), but also because data suggest that sexually aggressive men tend to misperceive a woman's behavior independently of what she actually does (Bondurant, 1995; White & Humphrey, 1995).

Alcohol and drugs are also related to incidents of male violence against women (Pagelow, 1984). In an examination of a range of relationship-related homicides, Slade, Daniel, and Heisler (1991) found that alcohol and drug use was common and not dependent on the nature of the relationship between the suspect and the victim.

Alcohol acts as a disinhibitor for the man, as an excuse for the violence after it has occurred, and as a means of reducing the victim's resistance (Richardson & Hammock, 1991). Familial alcohol and drug problems have been associated with incest (Hernandez, 1992; Janikowski & Glover, 1994), as well as with domestic violence (Collins & Messerschmidt, 1993). In cases of dating violence, alcohol use is common (LeJeune & Follette, 1994; Williams & Smith, 1994). In addition, in cases of acquaintance rape, alcohol may enhance ambiguity by increasing the likelihood that men may misinterpret a woman's friendly behaviors as sexual (Abbey, 1991). Some men may interpret a woman's consumption of alcohol as an indication that she is "loose."

INTRAPERSONAL LEVEL

One of the earliest theories related to male violence against women suggested that men who perpetrate violent acts against women have some underlying deviant physiological arousal pattern or intrapsychic pathology. However, researchers find more similarities than differences between perpetrators and nonperpetrators. For example, no single "typical" profile of sex offenders has been found (Duthie & McIvor, 1990), and incestuous and pedophilic men resemble community volunteers in levels of some, although not all, sex hormones (Lange et al., 1990). Similarly, arousal patterns to rape depictions only inconsistently distinguish college-aged men who perpetrate acquaintance rape from those who do not (Rapaport & Posey, 1991). Also, these two groups are similar on numerous dimensions, just as men who sexually harass are similar to the typical employee on most dimensions (Gutek, 1985; Koss et al., 1994). Similarly, batterers do not differ from men in general on a number of psychological dimensions.

Although men who perpetrate violence against women may not differ in clearly observable ways from men who are not violent, certain intrapersonal variables have been identified that underlie instances of male violence toward women. The endorsement of traditional sex role stereotypes and cultural myths about violence is predictive of intimate male violence against women. For example, in cases of incest, particularly father–daughter incest, the perpetrator maintains very traditional attitudes toward the roles of men and women, and the family structure in which incest occurs is very patriarchal in nature (Herman & Hirschman, 1993). These men believe in male sexual privilege. They also believe that children are sexually motivated and are not seriously harmed by sexual abuse (Hanson, Gizzarelli, & Scott, 1994). Relative to nonsexually aggressive men, sexually aggressive men subscribe more strongly to traditional gender stereotypes (Burt, 1980; Malamuth, 1988; Mosher & Anderson, 1986; Rapaport & Burkhart, 1984). Similar findings have been obtained in studies examining the characteristics of men who abuse their dating partners or spouses (Dutton, 1988). In addition, men who sexually harass women typically feel that women should remain in their subordinate position within the home as opposed to venturing into fields traditionally dominated by men (Fitzgerald, 1993). These attitudinal underpinnings of male violence against women may stem, in part, from being reared in households where violence was considered normative. As noted, men who either witnessed or experienced violence as a child show a higher likelihood to be sexually aggressive than men who were not exposed to violence (Koss & Dinero, 1989) and to perpetrate courtship or domestic violence (Kalmuss, 1984; Straus et al., 1980). A history of promiscuous impersonal sex and hostile masculinity (distrust of women combined with gratification from dominating women) represent factors associated with sexual violence toward a female partner, whereas relationship distress and verbal nonsexual aggression are predictive of nonsexual physical aggression (Malamuth et al., 1995; Malamuth, this volume).

Furthermore, a man's need for power, dominance, and control over women appears to play a role in determining whether he will engage in violent acts against an intimate partner. Some researchers have suggested that all men have some biologically based need for power and dominance. However, "once that biological threshold is surpassed, the actual commission of the acts will be influenced by the strength of the drives and by various environmental factors, including opportunities and social sanctions. The stronger the drives, the less effective environmental restraints will be" (White & Koss, 1991, p. 195). Thus, a man who feels threatened by a loss of control, such as by being rejected sexually, may attempt to regain that control by behaving aggressively. A consideration of the components of the violent acts perpetrated against women (i.e., intimidation, coercion, belittlement) suggests that motives for power and dominance bear some relationship to the incidence of violence.

Certain personality and behavioral variables also seem to predict violence against women, including antisocial tendencies (Malamuth, 1986), nonconformity (Rapaport & Burkhart, 1987), impulsivity (Calhoun, 1990), low socialization and responsibility (Barnett & Hamberger, 1992; Rapaport & Burkhart, 1984), hypermasculinity, delinquent behavior, affective dysregulation (Hall & Hirschman, 1991; Murphy, Meyer, & O'Leary, 1991), and self-centeredness coupled with insensitivity to others (Dean & Malamuth, 1997). The extent to which these specific intrapersonal variables influence the incidence of violence against women depends on the degree to which cultural norms and the influence of social groups affect individual mental representations of the situation and the relationship with the woman.

POLICY IMPLICATIONS

Theoretical explanations for male violence against women have, until recently, typically focused on one type of violence at one level of analysis. Consistent with this, policies designed to prevent male violence against women have been implemented with a focus on identifying and reducing single factors contributing to a specific form of violence against women, such as characteristics of the offender or behaviors of the victim that put her at risk. For example, child abuse prevention has been considered separately from wife battering, neither of which were considered in conjunction with sexual assault.

However, as proposed in the integrative contextual developmental model of violence against women, male violence against women is multiply determined. Sociocultural variables, situational constraints, and the nature of dyadic interactions, as well as intrapersonal characteristics, collectively play a role in determining which men will aggress against which women in which situations. In light of this, policies oriented toward reducing male violence against women must take a more systematic, integrative, and multileveled approach with program interventions at community and institutional levels as well as specific programs designed for individual victims and perpetrators. These policies should recognize that although individual men perpetrate violence against individual female victims, social and cultural values and norms help maintain an atmosphere in which violence against women is condoned (Koss et al., 1994). In addition, the developmental perspective of the model suggests that the best intervention is prevention, which should begin at an early age.

Violence against women and children is increasingly recognized as a social, health, and political problem rather than the personal problem of a few individuals. Thus, policy initiatives should occur at societal, institutional, dyadic, and individual levels. A multipronged approach to intervention and prevention is necessary.

At the societal level, the Violence Against Women Act (Biden, 1993) is the first major national statement that violence against women will not be tolerated. The legislative, policy, and funding efforts that follow from this act must be supported. At the other levels of analysis, institutional, dyadic, and individual policy efforts to date remain piecemeal.

However, the commonalities among the various forms of violence against women also suggest the need for policies directed at changing traditional, patriarchal attitudes toward women, men, children, families, sex, and violence. Given the role of cultural support, various institutions must play a greater role in the attitude change process, including family, church, school, workplace, and criminal justice.

In addition to changing cultural attitudes, continued efforts are needed to expand our knowledge of prevalence, incidence, and consequences for victims of interpersonal violence through research and medical documentation. It is particularly important to better understand the manifestations of violence against women as a function of race, ethnicity, and class. Additional research is also needed on intervention and treatment programs, including how best to train mental health, medical, and judicial personnel to deal with victims of interpersonal violence. Koss et al. (1994) have presented a comprehensive set of suggestions directed toward psychologists in particular, as well as for educational and religious institutions. They have suggested strategies that the media and workplace can employ. Finally, they have suggested that "public policy initiatives cut across research, prevention, and intervention efforts, and include legal and legislative reform" (p. 249). This chapter concludes with Senator Joseph Biden's (1993) statement:

> If the leading newspapers were to announce tomorrow a new disease that, over the past year, had afflicted from 3 to 4 million citizens, few would fail to appreciate the seriousness of the illness. Yet, when it comes to the 3 to 4 million women who are victimized by violence each year, the alarms ring softly (p. 1059).

REFERENCES

Abbey, A. (1991). Misperceptions as an antecedent of acquaintance rape: A consequence of ambiguity in communication between men and women. In A. Parrot & L. Bechhofer (Eds.), *Acquaintance rape: The hidden crime* (pp. 96–112). New York: Wiley.

Abel, G. G., Rouleau, J. L., & Cunningham-Rathner, J. (1986). Sexually aggressive behavior. In W. J. Curran, A. L. McGarry, S. A. Shah (Eds.), *Forensic psychiatry and psychology: Perspectives and standards for interdisciplinary practice*. Philadelphia, PA: F. A. Davis.

Ageton, S. S. (1983). *Sexual assault among adolescents*. Lexington, MA: D. C. Heath.

Amir, M. (1971). *Patterns in forcible rape*. Chicago: University of Chicago Press.

Bandura, A. (1973). *Aggression: A social learning process*. Englewood Cliffs, NJ: Prentice-Hall.

Barnett, O., & Hamberger, L. K. (1992). The assessment of maritally violent men on the California Psychological Inventory. *Violence and Victims, 7,* 15–22.

Baron, L. & Straus, M. A. (1989). *Four theories of rape in American society: A state-level analysis*. New Haven, CT: Yale University Press.

Beneke, T. (1982). *Men who rape*. New York: St. Martin's Press.

Berkowitz, L. (1994). Is something missing? Some observations prompted by the cognitive-neoassociationistic view of anger and emotional aggression. In L. R. Huesmann (Ed.), *Aggressive behavior: Current perspectives*. New York: Plenum.

Berkowitz, A. (1992). College men as perpetrators of acquaintance rape and sexual assault: A review of recent research. *Journal of the American College Health Association, 40,* 175–181.

Bernard, J. L., Bernard, S. L., & Bernard, M. L. (1985). Courtship violence and sex-typing. *Family Relations, 34,* 573–576.

Biden, J. R. (1993). Violence against women: The congressional response. *American Psychologist, 48,* 1059–1061.

Bondurant, B. (1995). *Men's perceptions of women's sexual interest: Sexuality or sexual aggression*. Paper presented at 40th Annual Meeting of Southeastern Psychological Association, New Orleans, LA, March.

Bondurant, B., & White, J. W. (1995). Men who sexually harass. In D. K. Shrier (Ed.) *Sexual harassment in the workplace and academia: Psychiatric issues*. New York: American Psychiatric Press, Inc.

Borque, L. (1989). *Defining rape*. Durham, NC: Duke University Press.

Brownmiller, S. (1975). *Against our will: Men, women, and rape*. New York: Simon & Schuster.

Burt, M. R. (1980). Cultural myths and supports for rape. *Journal of Personality and Social Psychology, 38,* 217–230.

Buss, D. M. (1987). Sex differences in human mate selection criteria: An evolutionary perspective. In C. Crawford, M. Smith, & D. Krebs (Eds.), *Sociology and psychology*. Hillsdale, NJ: Erlbaum.

Byers, E. S. (1996). How well does the traditional sexual script explain sexual coercion? Review of a program of research. *Journal of Psychology and Human Sexuality, 8,* 7–26.

Calhoun, K. (1990). *Lies, sex, and videotapes: Studies in sexual aggression.* Presidential address, presented at the Southeastern Psychological Association, Atlanta, GA, March.

Campbell, A. (1992). *Men, women, and aggression.* New York: Basic Books.

Check, J. V. P., & Malamuth, N. M. (1983). Sex role stereotyping and reactions to depictions of stranger versus acquaintance rape. *Journal of Personality and Social Psychology, 45,* 344–356.

Collins, J. J., & Messerschmidt, P. M. (1993). Epidemiology of alcohol-related violence. *Alcohol Health and Research World, 17,* 93–100.

Craig, M. (1990). Coercive sexuality in dating relationships: A situational model. *Clinical Psychology Review, 10,* 395–423.

Crawford, M. (1995). *Talking differences: On gender and language.* Newbury Park, CA: Sage.

Deal, J. E., & Wampler, K. S. (1986). Dating violence: The primacy of previous experience. *Journal of Social and Personal Relationships, 33,* 457–471.

Dean, K. E., & Malamuth, N. (1997). Characteristics of men who aggress sexually and of men who imagine aggressing: Risk and moderating variables. *Journal of Personality and Social Psychology, 72,* 449–455.

Deutsch, H. (1944). *The psychology of women (Vol. 1).* New York: Bantam Books.

Dodge, K. A. (1986). A social information processing model of social competence in children. In M. Perlmutter (Ed.), *Minnesota Symposium on Child Psychology, 18* (pp. 77–125). Hillsdale, NJ: Erlbaum.

Donat, P. L. N., & White, J. W. (in press). The social construction of consent: Sexual scripts and acquaintance rape. In C. T. Travis & J. W. White (Eds.), *Sexuality, society, and feminism: Psychological perspectives on women.* Washington, DC: American Psychological Association.

Duthie, B., & McIvor, D. L. (1990). A new system for cluster-coding child molester MMPI profile types. *Criminal Justice and Behavior, 17,* 199–214.

Dutton, D. (1988). *The domestic assault of women: Psychological and criminal justice perspectives.* New York: Allyn & Bacon.

Ellis, L. (1991). A synthesized (biosocial) theory of rape. Special Section: theories of sexual aggression. *Journal of Consulting and Clinical Psychology, 59,* 631–642.

Erez, E., & Tontodonato, P. (1989). Patterns of reported parent–child abuse and police response. *Journal of Family Violence, 4,* 143–159.

Fagot, B. I., Loeber, R., & Reid, J. B. (1988). Developmental determinants of male-to-female aggression. In G. W. Russell (Ed.), *Violence in intimate relationships* (pp. 91–105). New York: PMA.

Feder, L. (1980). Preconceptive ambivalence and external reality. *International Journal of Psycho-Analysis, 61,* 161–178.

Feld, S. L., & Straus, M. A. (1989). Escalation and desistance of wife assault in marriage. *Criminology, 27,* 141–161.

Finkelhor, D. (1984). *Child sexual abuse: New theory and research.* New York: Free Press.

Finkelhor, D., & Browne, A. (1985). The traumatic impact of child sexual abuse: A conceptualization. *Orthopsychiatry, 55,* 530–541.

Fischer, G. J. (1987). Hispanic and majority student attitudes toward forcible date rape as a function of differences in attitudes toward women. *Sex Roles, 17,* 93–101.

Fitzgerald, L. F. (1993). Sexual harassment: Violence against women in the workplace. *American Psychologist, 48,* 1070–1076.

Fitzgerald, L. F., Shullman, S. L., Bailey, N., Richards, M., Swecker, J., Gold, A., Ormerod, A. J., & Weitzman, L. (1988). The incidence and dimensions of sexual harassment in academia and the workplace. *Journal of Vocational Behavior, 32,* 152–175.

Frayser, S. G. (1989). Sexual and reproductive relationships: Cross-cultural evidence and biosocial implications. *Medical Anthropology, 11,* 385–407.

Friedrich, W. N., Beilke, R. L., & Urquiza, A. J. (1988). Behavior problems in young sexually abused boys: A comparison study. *Journal of Interpersonal Violence, 3,* 21–28.

Geffner, R., & Rosenbaum, A. (1990). Characteristics and treatment of batterers. *Behavioral Sciences and the Law, 8,* 131–140.

George, L. K., Winfield, I., & Blazer, D. G. (1992). Sociocultural factors in sexual assault: Comparison of two representative samples of women. *Journal of Social Issues, 48,* 105–126.

Giuffre, P. A., & Williams, C. L. (1994). Boundary lines: Labeling sexual harassment in restaurants. *Gender and Society, 8,* 378–401.

Goodchilds, J. D., Zellman, G. L., Johnson, P. B., & Giarrusso, R. (1989). Adolescents and their perceptions of sexual interactions. In A. W. Burgess (Ed.), *Rape and sexual assault* (Vol. II). Garland: New York.

Goodman, L. A., Koss, M. P., & Russo, N. F. (1993). Violence against women: Physical and mental health effects: Part 2. Conceptualizations of posttraumatic stress. *Applied and Preventative Psychology, 2,* 123–130.

Greenspun, W. S. (1994). Internal and interpersonal: The family transmission of father–daughter incest. *Journal of Child Sexual Abuse, 3,* 1–14.

Groth, A. N., & Birnbaum, A. H. (1979). *Men who rape: The psychology of the offender.* New York: Plenum.

Gutek, B. (1985). *Sex in the workplace.* San Francisco: Jossey-Bass.

Gwartney-Gibbs, P. A., Stockard, J., & Brohmer, S. (1987). Learning courtship violence: The influence of parents, peers, and personal experiences. *Family Relations, 36,* 276–282.

Hall, G. C. N., & Hirschman, R. (1991). Toward a theory of sexual aggression: A quadripartite model. *Journal of Consulting and Clinical Psychology, 59,* 662–669.

Hanson, R. K., Gizzarelli, R., & Scott, H. (1994). The attitudes of incest offenders: Sexual entitlement and acceptance of sex with children. *Criminal Justice and Behavior, 21,* 187–202.

Hastrup, K., & Elsass, P. (1988). Incest in cross-cultural perspective. *Nordisk-Sexologi, 6,* 98–107.

Herman, J., & Hirschman, L. (1993). Father–daughter incest. In P. B. Bart & E. G. Moran (Eds.), *Violence against women: The bloody footprints* (pp. 47–56). Newbury Park, CA: Sage.

Hernandez, J. T. (1992). Substance abuse among sexually abused adolescents and their families. *Journal of Adolescent Health, 13,* 658–662.

Herrenkohl, E. C., Herrenkohl, R. C., & Tiedter, L. J. (1983). Perspectives on the intergenerational transmission of abuse. In D. Finkelhor, R. J. Gelles, G. T. Hotaling, & M. A. Straus (Eds.), *The dark side of families* (pp. 305–316). Beverly Hills, CA: Sage.

Holzman, C. G. (1994). Multicultural perspective on counseling survivors of rape. *Journal of Social Distress and the Homeless, 3,* 81–97.

Holtzworth-Munroe, A., & Hutchinson, G. (1993). Attributing negative intent to wife behavior: The attributions of maritally violent versus nonviolent men. *Journal of Abnormal Psychology, 102,* 206–211.

Hotaling, G. T., & Sugarman, D. B. (1986). An analysis of risk markers in husband to wife violence: The current state of knowledge. *Violence and Victims, 1,* 101–124.

Huesmann, L. R., & Eron, L. (1992). Childhood aggression and adult criminality. In J. McCord (Ed.), *Facts, frameworks, and forecasts: Advances in criminological theory* (Vol. 3). New Brunswick, NJ: Transaction Publishers.

Janikowski, T. P., & Glover, N. M. (1994). Incest and substance abuse: Implications for treatment professionals. *Journal of Substance Abuse Treatment, 11,* 177–183.

Kalmuss, D. S. (1984). The intergenerational transmission of marital aggression. *Journal of Marriage and the Family, 46,* 11–19.

Kaufman, J., & Zigler, E. (1987). Do abused children become abusive parents? *American Journal of Orthopsychiatry, 57,* 186–192.

Koss, M. P. (1985). The hidden rape victim: Personality, attitudinal, and situational characteristics. *Psychology of Women Quarterly, 9,* 193–212.

Koss, M. P., & Dinero, T. E. (1989). Discriminant analysis of risk factors for sexual victimization among a national sample of college women. *Journal of Consulting and Clinical Psychology, 57,* 242–250.

Koss, M. P., & Gaines, J. A. (1993). The prediction of sexual aggression by alcohol use, athletic participation, and fraternity affiliation. *Journal of Interpersonal Violence, 8,* 94–108.

Koss, M. P., Gidycz, C. A., & Wisniewski, N. (1987). The scope of rape: Incidence and prevalence of sexual aggression and victimization in a national sample of higher education students. *Journal of Consulting and Clinical Psychology, 55,* 162–170.

Koss, M. P., Goodman, L. A., Browne, A., Fitzgerald, L. F., Keita, G. P., & Russo, N. F. (1994). *No safe haven: Male violence against women at home, at work, and in the community.* Washington, DC: American Psychological Association.

Kowalski, R. M. (1992). Nonverbal behaviors and perceptions of sexual intentions: Effects of sexual connotativeness, verbal response, and rape outcome. *Basic and Applied Social Psychology, 13,* 427–445.

Kowalski, R. M. (1993a). Inferring sexual interest from behavioral cues: Effects of gender and sexually-relevant attitudes. *Sex Roles, 29,* 13–31.

Kowalski, R. M. (1993b). Interpreting behaviors in mixed gender encounters: Effects of social anxiety and gender. *Journal of Social and Clinical Psychology, 12,* 239–249.

Lang, R. A., Flor-Henry, P., & Frenzel, R. R. (1990). Sex hormone profiles in pedophilic and incestuous men. *Annals of Sex Research, 3,* 59–74.

LaPlante, M. N., McCormick, N., & Brannigan, G. G. (1980). Living the sexual script: college students' views of influence in sexual encounters. *Journal of Sex Research, 16,* 338–355.

Leidig, M. W. (1992). The continuum of violence against women: Psychological and physical consequences. *Journal of American College Health, 40,* 149–155.

LeJeune, C., & Follette, V. (1994). Taking responsibility: Sex differences in reporting dating violence. *Journal of Interpersonal Violence, 9,* 133–140.

Lerner, R. M. (1991). Changing organism-context relations as the basic process of development: A developmental-contextual perspective. *Developmental Psychology, 27,* 27–32.

Lesniak, L. P. (1993). Penetrating the conspiracy of silence: Identifying the family at risk for incest. *Family and Community Health, 16,* 66–76.

Lipton, D. N., McDonel, E. C., & McFall, R. M. (1987). Heterosocial perception in rapists. *Journal of Consulting and Clinical Psychology, 55,* 17–21.

Lundberg-Love, P., & Geffner, R. (1989). Date rape: Prevalence, risk factors, and a proposed model. In M. Pirog-Good & J. E. Stets (Eds.), *Violence in dating relationships* (pp. 169–184). New York: Praeger.

Malamuth, N. M. (1986). Predictors of naturalistic aggression. *Journal of Personality and Social Psychology, 50,* 953–962.

Malamuth, N. M. (1988). A multidimensional approach to sexual aggression: Combining measures of past behavior and present likelihood. *Human sexual aggression: Current perspectives. Annals of the New York Academy of Science, 528,* 113–146.

Malamuth, N. M., Linz, D., Heavey, C. L., Barnes, G., & Acker, M. (1995). Using the confluence model of sexual aggression to predict men's conflict with women: A 10-year follow-up study. *Journal of Personality and Social Psychology, 69,* 353–369.

Malamuth, N. M., Sockloskie, R. J., Koss, M. P., & Tanaka, J. S. (1991). Characteristics of aggressors against women: Testing a model using a national sample of college students. *Journal of Consulting and Clinical Psychology, 59,* 670–681.

Marsh, C. E. (1993). Sexual assault and domestic violence in the African American community. *Western Journal of Black Studies, 17,* 149–155.

Martin, P. Y., & Hummer, R. A. (1989). Fraternities and rape on campus. *Gender and Society, 3,* 457–473.

McFall, R. M. (1982). A review and reformulation of the concept of social skills. *Behavioral Assessment, 4,* 1–32.

Miller, S. L., & Simpson, S. S. (1991). Courtship violence and social control: Does gender matter? *Law and Society Review, 25,* 335–365.

Milner, J. S. (1993). Social information processing and physical child abuse. *Clinical Psychology Review, 13,* 275–294.

Mosher, D. L., & Anderson, R. D. (1986). Macho personality, sexual aggression, and reactions to guided imagery of realistic rape. *Journal of Research in Personality, 20,* 77–94.

Muehlenhard, C. L., & Linton, M. A. (1987). Date rape and sexual aggression in dating situations: Incidence and risk factors. *Journal of Counseling Psychology, 34,* 186–196.

Murphy, C. M, Myers, S., & O'Leary, K. D. (1991). Emotional vulnerability, psychopathology, and family of origin violence in men who assault female partners. Unpublished manuscript.

Norris, J., Nurius, P. S., & Dimeff, L. A. (1996). Expectations regarding sexual aggression among sorority and fraternity members. *Psychology of Women Quarterly, 35,* 427–444.

O'Keeffe, N. K., Brickopp, K., & Chew, E. (1986). Teen dating violence. *Social Work, 31,* 465–468.

O'Leary, K. D. (1988). Physical aggression between spouses: A social learning theory perspective. In V. B. Van Hasselt, R. L. Morrison, A. S. Bellak, & M. Herson (Eds.), *Handbook of family violence* (pp. 31–55). New York: Plenum.

Olweus, D. (1993). Victimization by peers: Antecedents and longterm outcomes. In K. H. Rubin & J. B. Asendorpf (Eds.), *Social withdrawal, inhibition, and shyness in childhood.* Hillsdale, NJ: Erlbaum.

Pagelow, M. D. (1984). *Family violence.* New York: Praeger.

Peretti, P. O., & Status, J. A. (1984). Father–son inter-generational transmission of authoritarian paternal attitudes. *Social Behavior and Personality, 12,* 85–89.

Pitman, N. E., & Taylor, R. G. (1992). MMPI profiles of partners of incestuous sexual offenders and partners of alcoholics. *Family Dynamics of Addiction Quarterly, 2,* 52–59.

Pryor, J. (1987). Sexual harassment proclivities in men. *Sex Roles, 17,* 269–290.

Pryor, J., LaVite, C. M., & Stoller, L. M. (1993). A social psychological analysis of sexual harassment: The person/situation interaction. *Journal of Vocational Behavior, 42,* 68–93.

Rapaport, K. R., & Burkhart, B. R. (1984). Personality and attitudinal characteristics of sexually coercive college males. *Journal of Abnormal Psychology, 93,* 216–221.

Rapaport, K. R., & Posey, D. D. (1991). Sexually coercive college males. In A. Parrot & L. Bechhofer (Eds.), *Acquaintance rape: The hidden crime* (pp. 217–228). New York: Wiley.

Regina, W. F., & LeBoy, S. (1991). Incest families: Integrating theory and practice. *Family Dynamics of Addiction Quarterly, 1,* 21–30.

Richardson, D., & Hammock, G. (1991). The role of alcohol in acquaintance rape. In A. Parrot & L. Bechhofer (Eds.), *Acquaintance rape: The hidden crime.* New York: Wiley.

Riger, S., & Gordon, M. T. (1988). The fear of rape: A study in social control. *Journal of Social Issues, 37,* 71–92.

Riggs, D. S., & O'Leary, K. D. (1989). A theoretical model of courtship aggression. In M. Pirog-Good & J. E. Stets (Eds.), *Violence in dating relationships* (pp. 53–71). New York: Praeger.

Riggs, D. S., & O'Leary, K. D. (1996). Aggression between dating partners: An examination of a causal model of courtship aggression. *Journal of Interpersonal Violence, 11,* 519–540.

Roscoe, B., & Benakse, N. (1985). Courtship violence experiences by abused wives: Similarities in patterns of abuse. *Family Relations, 34,* 419–424.

Rose, S., & Frieze, I. H. (1993). Young singles' contemporary dating scripts. *Sex Roles, 28,* 499–509.

Rosen, I. (1991). Self-esteem as a factor in social and domestic violence. *British Journal of Psychiatry, 158,* 18–23.

Rozee, P. D. (1993). Forbidden or forgiven? Rape in cross-cultural perspective. *Psychology of Women Quarterly, 17,* 499–514.

Rusbult, C., & Martz, J. (1995). The decision to remain in an abusive relationship: An investment model analysis. *Personality and Social Psychology Bulletin, 21,* 558–571.

Salter, A. C. (1992). The epidemiology of child sexual abuse. In W. O'Donohue & J. H. Geer (Eds.), *The sexual abuse of children* (Vol. 2). Hillsdale, NJ: Erlbaum.

Sanday, P. R. (1981). The socio-cultural context of rape: A cross-cultural study. *The Journal of Social Issues, 37,* 5–27.

Schlegal, A. (1989). Gender issues and cross-cultural research. *Behavior Science Research,* 265–280.

Schonberg, I. J. (1992). The distortion of the role of mother in child sexual abuse. *Journal of Child Sexual Abuse, 1,* 47–61.

Segura, T. A. (1992). Chicanas in white-collar jobs: "You have to prove yourself more." *Sociological Perspectives, 35,* 163–182.

Shotland, R. L. (1989). A model of the causes of date rape in developing and close relationships. In C. Hendrick (Ed.), *Close Relationships* (pp. 247–270). Newbury Park, CA: Sage.

Shotland, R. L. (1992). A theory of the causes of courtship rape: Part 2. *Journal of Social Issues, 48,* 127–143.

Shotland, R. L., & Goodstein, L. (1992). Sexual precedence reduces the perceived legitimacy of sexual refusal: An examination of attributions concerning date rape and consensual sex. *Personality and Social Psychology Bulletin, 18,* 756–764.

Simon, B. (1992). "Incest—see under Oedipus complex": The history of an error in psychoanalysis. *Journal of the American Psychoanalytic Association, 40,* 955–988.

Slade, M., Daniel, L. J., & Heisler, C. J. (1991). Application of forensic toxicology to the problem of domestic violence. *Journal of Forensic Sciences, 36,* 708–713.

Smuts, B. (1992). Male aggression against women: An evolutionary perspective. *Human Nature, 3,* 1–44.

Sorenson, S. B., & Siegel, J. M. (1991). Gender, ethnicity, and sexual assault: Findings from the Los Angeles epidemiological catchment area study. *Journal of Social Issues, 48,* 93–104.

Stith, S. M. (1990). Police response to domestic violence: The influence of individual and familial factors. *Violence and Victims, 5,* 37–49.

Straus, M. A., & Gelles, R. (1990). *Physical violence in American families: Risk factors and adaptations to violence in 8,145 families.* New Brunswick, NJ: Transaction.

Straus, M. A., Gelles, R. J., & Steinmetz, S. (1980). *Behind closed doors: Violence in the American family.* Garden City, NY: Anchor Press.

Stout, K. D. (1992). Intimate femicide: An ecological analysis. *Journal of Sociology and Social Welfare, 19,* 29–50.

Thompson, E. H. (1991). The maleness of violence in dating relationships: An appraisal of stereotypes. *Sex Roles, 24,* 261–278.

Thornhill, R., & Thornhill, N. W. (1992). The evolutionary psychology of men's coercive sexuality. *Behavioral and Brain Sciences, 15,* 363–421.

Unger, R., & Crawford, M. (1995). *Women and gender: A feminist analysis.* New York: McGraw-Hill.

Wash, G., & Knudson-Martin, C. (1994). Gender identity and family relationships: Perspectives from incestuous fathers. *Contemporary Family Therapy: An International Journal, 16,* 393–410.

Whipple, V. (1987). Counseling battered women from fundamentalist churches. *Journal of Marital and Family Therapy, 13,* 251–258.

White, J. W., & Bondurant, B. (1996). Gendered violence. In J. T. Wood (Ed.), *Gendered relationships* (pp. 197–210). Mountain View, CA: Mayfield Press.

White, J. W., & Humphrey, J. A. (1990). *A theoretical model of sexual assault: An empirical test.* Paper presented at the symposium on Sexual Assault: Research, Treatment, and Education. Southeastern Psychological Association meeting, Atlanta, GA, March.

White, J. W., & Humphrey, J. A. (1995). *The relationship between perceived justification for forced sexual intercourse and self-reported sexual aggression.* Paper presented at 40th Annual Meeting of Southeastern Psychological Association, New Orleans, LA, March.

White, J. W., & Humphrey, J. A. (1997). A longitudinal approach to the study of sexual aggression: Theoretical and methodological considerations. In M. D. Schwartz (Ed.), *Researching sexual violence against women: Methodological and personal perspectives.* Thousand Oaks, CA: Sage.

White, J. W., & Koss, M. P. (1991). Adolescent sexual aggression within heterosexual relationships: Prevalence, characteristics, and causes. In H. E. Barbarbee, W. L. Marshall, & D. R. Laws (Eds.), *The juvenile sexual offender.* New York: Guilford Press.

White, J. W., & Kowalski, R. M. (1994). Deconstructing the myth of the nonaggressive woman: A feminist analysis. *Psychology of Women Quarterly, 18,* 477–498.

White, S., & Shuntich, R. J. (1991). *Some home environment correlates of male sexual coerciveness/ aggressiveness.* Paper presented at 37th Annual Meeting of Southeastern Psychological Association, New Orleans, LA, March.

Widom, C. S. (1989). Does violence beget violence? A critical examination of the literature. *Psychological Bulletin, 106,* 3–28.

Williams, J. G., & Smith, J. P. (1994). Drinking patterns and dating violence among college students. *Psychology of Addictive Behaviors, 8,* 51–53.

Worell, J., & Remer, P. (1992). *Feminist perspectives in therapy: An empowerment model for women.* Chichester, England: John Wiley & Sons.

Wyatt, G. E. (1985). The sexual abuse of Afro-American and White-American women in childhood. *Child Abuse and Neglect, 9,* 507–519.

Wyatt, G. E. (1992). Sociocultural context of African American and White American women's rape. *Journal of Social Issues, 48,* 77–92.

Yllo, K. (1983). Sexual equality and violence against wives in American states. *Journal of Comparative Family Studies, 14,* 67–86.

9

THE CONFLUENCE MODEL AS AN ORGANIZING FRAMEWORK FOR RESEARCH ON SEXUALLY AGGRESSIVE MEN: RISK MODERATORS, IMAGINED AGGRESSION, AND PORNOGRAPHY CONSUMPTION

NEIL M. MALAMUTH

University of California, Los Angeles

This chapter describes recent developments in a research program studying the characteristics of sexually aggressive men identified in general population samples. This chapter has attempted to organize this line of research in a way that earlier studies are used to build upon and inform subsequent ones, with the goal of benefitting from the cumulative character of a systematic research program. The efforts of the recent studies highlighted here centered on three areas: (1) a dimension moderating the relationship between risk factors that could lead to aggression and manifested aggression, (2) the role of imagined sexual aggression, and (3) the association between use of pornographic material and sexual aggression in "real world" settings.

In order to present a cogent discussion of these developments, it is necessary to first describe theoretical and empirical underpinnings of our research. The confluence model of sexual aggression has been used as an organizing framework for the research to be described here and it can be similarly useful for addressing other questions in related areas. The analogy of a jigsaw puzzle may apply. Once certain key pieces have been identified, it is much easier to find the "right" positioning of the others. Similarly, it is suggested that the two major constellations of characteristics of sexually aggressive men identified in this model provide such key pieces, which can help position the role of other factors.

THE CONFLUENCE MODEL
OF SEXUAL AGGRESSION

Malamuth, Sockloskie, Koss, and Tanaka (1991) proposed a model of some key characteristics of sexual aggressors that includes developmental factors as well as features present at the time of aggression. This approach may be described as a "cumulative conditional probability" model (Belsky, Teinberg, & Draper, 1991). It suggests two interrelated aspects: (1) The likelihood for a certain factor to occur is affected by the presence/absence of other factors, although the presence of any one factor does not constitute a necessary condition for other factors to occur in a particular order nor is any one factor always necessary for the occurrence of the final outcome. (2) When a combination of certain antecedent factors in a sequence exists, the probability of a particular outcome is greater than when only some of these exist. Although each antecedent factor independently contributes to a higher probability of the outcome, the combination of certain factors has more than a simple additive effect on the likelihood of the outcome (e.g., a "synergistic" effect).

Malamuth et al.'s model suggests that coercive sex may reflect the convergence of two sets of characteristics or paths: The first consists of relatively high orientation to promiscuous/impersonal sex and the second of hostile, dominating personality features.

PROMISCUOUS/IMPERSONAL SEXUAL ORIENTATION

According to our model, early (e.g., home) exposure to certain conflicted and/or "harsh" environments can have important effects on increasing the likelihood of a promiscuous/impersonal sex orientation, mediated by various other "acting out" behaviors as the individual matures. Belsky et al. (1991) published a model of reproductive strategies that has clear parallels to this configuration. Both models stress the impact of early environments (e.g., family, home) on later development via the mediation of cognitive and emotional/attachment mechanisms. Following an evolutionary[1] paradigm, early experience may func-

---

[1]This chapter applies some recent ideas from evolutionary psychology theory to the topic of sexual aggression. For a general discussion of this theory, the reader is referred to Buss (1995). For applications to the area of sexual conflict and related topics, see Buss and Malamuth (1996).

tion as "switches" or "triggers" during a critical early formative period (e.g., the first 5 to 7 years) that shape an enduring reproductive strategy (Draper & Harpending, 1982). The environmental input, at this critical stage, informs the developing child whether the social circumstances (e.g., the trustworthiness of others and the stability of close personal relationships) and physical surroundings (e.g., the availability of resources) are relatively benign or harsh.[2] Evolutionary pressures would be expected to favor differing reproductive strategies in these contrasting environments: More benign environments favor a long-term "quality" strategy that involves high investment in relatively few offspring whereas harsh environments favor a short-term orientation, a high "quantity" of offspring, and relatively little investment in each (Belsky et al., 1991). Of particular relevance to the development of the promiscuous/impersonal sexual orientation[3] are "harsh" familial stressors such as marital discord, rejection, and violent/abusive parenting.

Both Malamuth et al. (1991) and Belsky et al. (1991) propose that harsh circumstances during early childhood may lead to "problem" behavior patterns involving nonconformity, impulsivity, and antisocial behaviors (labeled delinquency in one model and externalizing symptoms in the other). According to the Belsky et al. model, this oppositional behavior stimulates earlier biological maturation which fosters, among boys, indiscriminate and "opportunistic" sexuality, which increases the likelihood of becoming fathers before their peers. The biological mechanism mediating this process is not yet identified, but androgenic activity is hypothesized. Malamuth et al. also suggest that such nonconforming behaviors are likely to be expressed in various forms of sexual "acting out" involving short-term, promiscuous relationships.

HOSTILE MASCULINITY

Although the Belsky model did not address the topic of sexual coercion, Malamuth et al. contend that the "promiscuity/impersonal sex" orientation (reproductive strategy) is expressed in sexual aggression when a man also possesses

---

[2]Following an evolutionary perspective, such information would be important, if the environment in our ancestral history varied markedly in different geographical areas, but was relatively stable for any one person over the course of their life.

[3]The impersonal sex construct is similar to the concept of "sociosexuality," which refers to differences in the willingness to engage in sexual relations without intimacy or commitment (Gangestad & Simpson, 1990; Simpson & Gangestad, 1991). Individuals inclined to "unrestricted" sexuality report having engaged in sex earlier in relationships, to have more than one concurrent sexual partner, to have had many sexual partners in the past, to have had many sexual encounters, and to foresee many sexual partners in the future. In contrast, those ascribing to "restricted" sexuality report to seek intimacy and commitment before they engage in sex and appear, in general, to possess the opposite set of behavioral characteristics to those reported by the unrestricted individuals. These two profiles were supported by Simpson and Gangestad (1991) who gathered independent reports from sexual partners.

characteristics identified as comprising the "hostile masculinity" path. This path includes attitudes condoning aggression[4] toward women, contributing to the construct of hostile masculinity, which includes hostility toward women (e.g., feelings of rejection, hurt, anger) and gratification from dominating them (e.g., becoming sexually aroused by a sense of power over women).

From an evolutionary framework the mobilization of the type of attitudes and emotions encompassed in this path may increase the likelihood and effectiveness of aggressive behaviors used in a sexual context (Malamuth, in press). These characteristics may operate via several processes: They may decrease the impact of internal inhibitions and anxiety. For example, hostility may reduce sympathy for the victim and make the woman seem less powerful by denigrating her. Attitudes accepting of violence may nullify prohibitions against using aggression. Further, such characteristics may reduce the strength of external barriers or inhibitions. For instance, anger accompanying the hostility may increase the likelihood of overcoming a woman's resistance due to the vigor with which the act is carried out. Finally, the sexual arousal and gratification derived from dominating women may make high hostile masculine men less anxious about women's potential rejection of them (Malamuth, Feshbach, & Jaffe, 1977) and may reinforce the use of aggressive behaviors. In certain ancestral environments, such aggression may have increased some males' fitness by reducing women's choice and enabling sex with a woman who otherwise would have rejected the man.

EMPIRICAL TESTING OF THE MODEL

Belsky et al. (1991) review extensive data consistent with the links described in the promiscuity/impersonal sex path part of the confluence model. Malamuth et al. (1991, 1995) present data directly testing the confluence model of sexual aggression using structural equation modeling.[5]

An example of such analyses, shown in Figure 9.1, can be found in Malamuth et al. (1991). Data were gathered from a nation-wide representative sample of about 3000 males enrolled in any form of post high school education. Data consisted of subjects' responses to self-report measures and recollections of earlier experiences. The model was tested by using half of the sample for analysis and the second half for cross-validation purposes. The results produced by both "half"

---

[4]Because this chapter incorporates evolutionary theorizing, it is useful to note the general approach taken by this perspective regarding the topic of aggression. Nonevolutionary models tend to conceptualize aggression in pathological terms due to the pain and suffering it causes. From an evolutionary viewpoint, pathology involves the failure of a set of mechanisms to function in the way they were designed by evolutionary processes due to such factors as decay or subversion by competitive forms of life (e.g., viruses). Most aggressive acts (with some important exceptions) do not reveal such characteristics. Instead, aggression shows characteristics of functional design revealing an evolved adaptation that resulted in fitness promoting consequences for the aggressors, at least in some recurring ancestral environments (Daly & Wilson, 1994).

[5]These are tests of the developmental and current characteristics of sexual aggressors but not of the evolutionary-based explanations for the associations between variables.

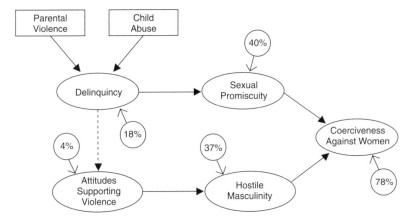

FIGURE 9.1 Structural model of the characteristics of sexual aggressors supported by the findings of Malamuth et al. (1991). Percentage in small circles indicates amount of variance of latent variance that was accounted for. Broken arrow between delinquency and attitudes supporting violence indicates hypothesized path that received only weak support.

samples generally fit the proposed model well. They showed that coming from a home with parental violence and/or child abuse was associated with a higher rate of delinquency in adolescence, which in turn was strongly predictive of greater sexual promiscuity. This path (labeled the sexual promiscuity/impersonal sex path) contributed to coerciveness against women, as did the other major constellation, which consisted of attitudes supporting violence and hostile masculinity.[6] Together, these two paths accounted for 78% of the latent variance of coerciveness against women, which was indicated by scales measuring sexual and nonsexual aggression against women.

Additional analyses presented by these investigators were designed to show mean differences between nonaggressive men and those displaying sexual and/or nonsexual aggression on the hostile masculinity and promiscuity/impersonal sex dimensions. Their sample consisted of 1713 men for whom data were available for both aggression measures. Subjects were divided into two levels (low vs high)

---

[6]In their original model, Malamuth et al. (1991) predicted that the experiences of "harsh" home environments and delinquency (i.e., acting out during adolescence) would contribute to attitudes supporting violence against women and hence to characteristics of the hostile masculinity path. This link was not supported well, being significant and quite weak in only one of the sample halves. This finding, consistent with data collected later, suggests that hostile masculinity and sexual promiscuity represent largely independent sets of characteristics, although they are both typically in many sexual aggressors' profiles. This pattern seems counterintuitive as one might expect that early exposure to violence would affect attitudes toward violence. The absence of a stronger link is also surprising because it predicts that sexual promiscuity could likely lead to more frequent rejection and hence to heightened hostile masculinity. Perhaps more refined analyses focusing on curvilinear relationships among variables will be sensitive to identifying conditions where links between the promiscuous/impersonal sex and hostile masculinity do exist (e.g., distinctions between successful vs unsuccessful promiscuous men).

Characteristics of Aggressors

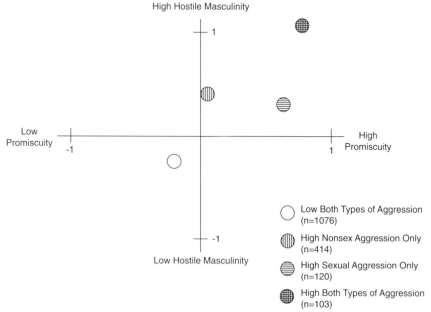

FIGURE 9.2   Means of hostile masculinity and sexual promiscuity dimensions (created by summing manifest indicators) for subjects classified as scoring high or low on sexual aggression and on nonsexual aggression. From Malamuth et al. (1991).

on the dimensions of sexual and of nonsexual aggression, thereby creating four groups: (1) Low on both sexual and nonsexual aggression ($n = 1076$), (2) high nonsexual aggression only ($n = 414$), (3) high sexual aggression only ($n = 120$), and (4) high on both types of coercion ($n = 103$).

A 2×2 MANOVA was performed using the sexual and nonsexual aggression groups as independent variables and scores on sexual promiscuity and hostile masculinity as dependent variables. The results revealed very strong multivariate and univariate main effects, except for the effect of nonsexual aggression on sexual promiscuity, which was much weaker. Means are shown in Figure 9.2, with one standard deviation from the mean as the marking point. Comparisons among means using Scheffé tests showed that on the dimension of sexual promiscuity, all groups differed from each other except for the group high on both sexual and nonsexual aggression vs the one high on sexual aggression only. On the hostile masculinity dimension, all groups differed significantly from each other save for one comparison: The group high on sexual aggression only did not differ from the group high on nonsexual aggression only. According to these data, men who are high on both types of aggression also evidence high (one standard deviation above the mean) levels of hostile masculinity and sexual promiscuity. Those high only on nonsexual aggression showed moderately elevated levels of hostile masculinity and were close to the average on the sexual promiscuity dimension. In contrast, men high only on sexual aggression were also relatively high on sexual promiscuity and moderately high on hostile masculinity. Finally, those low on both types of aggression were also relatively low on both promiscuity and hostile masculinity dimensions. Taken together, these data are consistent with the hypothesis that sexual aggression is associated with elevated levels of both sexual promiscuity and hostile masculinity, whereas nonsexual aggression is associated only with elevated hostile masculinity scores.

REPLICATING AND EXTENDING
THE CONFLUENCE MODEL

Efforts to refine and extend the confluence model were undertaken by Malamuth, Linz, Heavey, Barnes, and Acker (1995). In a longitudinal study, the model was used to predict difficulties in men's relationships with women. About 150 men were assessed twice, with an intervening period of about 10 years. The latter assessment focused on four behaviors that might have occurred during the 10 years since initial participation: (1) sexual aggression, (2) nonsexual physical aggression, (3) nonsexual verbal aggression, and (4) general relationship quality and distress. The researchers were able to secure, in many cases, collateral information from the men's partners as well as videotape some of the couples, thus lending further validity to the self-report measures.

Using cross-sectional data, Malamuth et al. (1995) replicated the findings that were obtained in the 1991 study. More importantly, in extending the model to make longitudinal predictions, it was argued that the two-path "causal structure" will be a useful predictor of sexual aggression assessed 10 years later as it is for current behavior. The results were indeed in accord with this prediction: Information about hostile masculinity and promiscuity/impersonal sex orientation enabled the prediction of later sexual aggression above and beyond that achieved based on knowing earlier sexual aggression only. Finally, Malamuth et al. used these data to successfully test a hierarchical model which suggests that some of the factors contributing to sexual aggression (e.g., proneness to general hostility) underlie various types of conflict and aggression in intimate relations, whereas other factors (e.g., hostility to women, sexual dominance) are more specific to sexual aggression itself.

ATTENUATING FACTORS
AND ACTING OUT OF AGGRESSION

Theorizing and research (e.g., Feshbach, 1970; Miller & Eisenberg, 1988) pertaining to the topic of aggression generally suggest that certain factors may attenuate the link between risk factors and actual aggression behavior. The hypothesis is that the effects of the risk factors on behavior may be blocked or reduced by counterinfluences. Empathy/sympathy levels, for example, were found in this literature to be inversely correlated with aggression and other antisocial behavior. Data in the area of sexual aggression also indicate inverse correlations between men's sexual aggression and empathic ability (Seto & Barbaree, 1993). However, studies testing the actual moderating function of such factors have not been conducted.

Dean and Malamuth (1997) sought to specifically examine the moderating role of a more general personality measure of which sensitivity to others' feelings is an important component. This personality measure is related to previous work showing correlations between Bem's (1974) scales designed to assess "masculinity" (M) and "femininity" (F) and various rape-related responses (e.g., attitudes, perceptions, proclivities, and behaviors) (Quakenbush, 1989; Ross & Allgeier, 1991; Tieger, 1981). Bem's (1974) scales were presented within the context of theory and research arguing that traditional gender roles prescribe a more dominant, self-centered orientation for males versus a more "connected to others" caring orientation for females. However, after Bem's original work, an extensive literature developed, indicating that femininity and masculinity labels are somewhat inappropriate. Wiggins and Holzmuller (1981), for example, concluded that Bem's scales are some of the best measures of the broad personality dimensions of dominance (agentic) and nurturance (communal). Others have similarly concluded that the scales measure personality dimensions that may be termed "self-directed" and "other-directed" (Ballard-Reisch & Elton, 1992).

Dean and Malamuth (1997) used the F and M scales to compute a score for each subject of the degree to which he was high on nurturance relative to dominance and tested whether this dimension moderated the relationship between proclivities to aggress sexually and actual behavior. The investigators proceeded as follows: First, the "two path" model developed by Malamuth et al. (1991) of the predictor "risk" characteristics of sexual aggressors was successfully replicated by Dean and Malamuth (1997). Second, analyses were conducted dividing this sample into two levels on the basis of the nurturance relative to dominance dimension. In both groups, the basic "two path" structure on the "predictor" side of the model remained essentially the same. However, in those men more oriented toward the "self" at the expense of "others" (e.g., little nurturance or compassion), linkages between risk characteristics and actual aggressive behavior were strong. In contrast, when the personality profile reflected higher levels of "other" orientation (e.g., greater compassion for others), relationships between "risk" characteristics and actual aggression were weak or not significant. These findings (and additional ANOVA analyses) supported the expected role of the nurturance relative to dominance orientation as a moderator of the relationship between "risk" predictor factors and actual aggression.

Additional support for the important role of nurturant characteristics such as empathy is provided by the findings of two studies focusing on sexual arousal and empathy. Malamuth, Linz, and Heavey (1996) evaluated the role of empathy as a moderator between the risk factor of sexual arousal to aggression (assessed by penile tumescence) and aggressive behavior in a 10-year longitudinal design. They found that when men's dispositional empathy was low, sexual arousal to aggression (measured 10 years earlier) was a successful predictor of later aggressive behavior (assessed by the reports of the wives or girlfriends of the men). However, when empathy was relatively high, there was not a significant relationship between sexual arousal to aggression and behavior. In a related study, Rice, Chaplin, Harris, and Coutts (1994) tested the explanation that differences in empathy may partially explain why rapists are more sexually aroused to rape depictions than men who are not sexually aggressive. According to this explanation, nonrapists' arousal is inhibited by empathy with the victim, but rapists' arousal is not similarly inhibited because they do not similarly empathize with the victim. Consistent with this explanation, it was found that rapists were less empathic than nonrapists and sexual arousal to rape was inversely related to self-reported empathy.

The findings of Dean and Malamuth and those of other research showing links between dimensions such as empathy levels and aggressive behavior may be viewed as providing support for treatment programs with sexual offenders that place a strong emphasis on empathy training (e.g., Pithers, 1993). However, it has not yet been established whether characteristics such as nurturance, compassion, or empathy reflect a "fixed" personality dimension or a trainable skill. This issue needs to be systematically examined in future research.

IMAGINED SEXUAL AGGRESSION

Although the behavioral manifestation of aggression may be inhibited in a man with relatively high nurturance relative to dominance, Dean and Malamuth (1997) hypothesized that the risk factors may be manifested in some nonbehavioral ways. Specifically, they also assessed imagined sexual aggression. Two lines of research have studied the characteristics of men who report imagining themselves being sexually aggressive. One has concentrated on assessing coercive sexual fantasies (e.g., Greendlinger, 1985; Greendlinger & Byrne, 1987) whereas the other has concentrated on attraction to sexual aggression (e.g., Malamuth, 1989a, 1989b). Dean and Malamuth (1997) sought to situate these lines of research within the confluence model framework. They created a single scale assessing imagined sexual aggression based on the measures of coercive sexual fantasies and of attraction to sexual aggression.

As expected, the nurturance relative to dominance orientation did not reveal a moderating role for imagined aggression, with several of the risk factors for actual aggression also showing a strong relationship to imagined aggression regardless of the levels of this orientation. These data contradict the view that imagined sexual aggression is an isolated response in no way related to a proclivity to aggress. Instead, they support the contention that such imagined aggression may provide important information pertaining to some of the underlying factors or mechanisms leading to actual aggression but which may not be displayed often in actual behavior. The importance of these findings may be considered within the context of studies reporting a low correlation between actual sexually aggressive behavior and either fantasies or attraction to sexual aggression (e.g., Malamuth, 1988). Such a correlation has been interpreted by some as questioning the value of assessing imagined sexual aggression as a basis for understanding the causes of actual sexually aggressive behavior, since in these researchers' view the strength of the relationship with the behavior is the critical criterion for evaluating its potential relevance to the causes of such behavior (e.g., Mould, 1988). As amplified next, this conclusion is challenged.

Both feminists (e.g., Brownmiller, 1975) and evolutionary psychologists (e.g., Symons, 1979) have suggested that there are psychological mechanisms (e.g., information processing rules or algorithms) in men in general and some men in particular that create considerable potential for sexual aggression. In this view, many men who have not committed any sexual aggression may have some motivation or desire to do so. As suggested by a number of investigators (e.g., Buss, 1990; Ellis & Symons, 1989), responses such as fantasies may actually provide more insight into the psychological mechanisms underpinning feelings, thoughts, and actions than do responses such as behaviors. This is because behaviors are often constrained by real life exigencies (e.g., potential punishment, reputation damage), whereas imagined acts are private and far less likely to be inhibited by fear of external consequences and, as suggested by the present findings, internalized inhibitors of actual aggression. In the area of sexual aggression, this may be particularly relevant as relatively few men in most societies admit to committing such acts, particularly if more severe behaviors are examined (e.g., physical coercion). However, in unusual circumstances such as war when certain external inhibitors are removed, it appears that a large percentage of the male population engages in such acts (e.g., Brownmiller, 1975). Studying men who imagine sexual aggression may help identify some of the mechanisms underlying sexual aggression, even if there is not observable aggression in current environments.

A similar argument has been made by Kenrick and Sheets (1993), who contend that many normal individuals have violent desires and inclinations that are not typically carried out in actual homicides but are reflected in homicidal fantasies. They conducted two studies which revealed that the majority of subjects reported having had at least one homicidal fantasy. In keeping with actual rates of murders, males recalled more homicidal fantasies than did females and reported longer and more detailed fantasies. However, these investigators did not examine whether the profile of men who fantasize more about homicide is similar in some respects to those who are more likely to commit such acts. The fact that Dean and Malamuth found that the profile of men who imagined sexual aggression was similar in certain key respects to that of those who actually commit such acts is critical to the argument that imagined sexual aggression can help identify some of the characteristics underlying actual behavior.

PORNOGRAPHY CONSUMPTION

Does exposure to pornography contribute to coerciveness against women, particularly sexual aggression? This question has been widely debated for many years in many countries. There has not been much consensus among researchers or national commissions (Linz & Malamuth, 1993).

Laboratory and some field experiments indicate that exposure to certain types of sexually explicit media, particularly those that combine sexual and violent images, can cause increases in attitudes accepting of violence against women and laboratory aggression (for a review, see Malamuth, 1993). However, one of the most frequently raised issues concerns the generalizability of such data to responses in naturalistic settings. Various commentators (e.g., Fisher & Barak, 1991) have emphasized that research has not shown that such connections actually exist "in the real world." Although it is ethically impossible to conduct an experimental study that would actually demonstrate such a causal connection, it is feasible to determine whether pornography consumption under certain circumstances is associated with a greater risk for sexual aggression after controlling for other known risk factors.

Malamuth, Koss, and Sockloskie (1993) conducted such a study by following up the Malamuth et al. (1991) findings. As described earlier, in the 1991 study the investigators had developed the confluence model and identified the risk factors of hostile masculinity and sexual promiscuity. In more recent analyses, the investigators used the same data base to conduct a series of structural equation modeling and risk analyses using the factors identified in the earlier research but also adding the variable of pornography consumption. For the purposes of this research, pornography consumption was operationally defined as the degree of exposure to sexually explicit magazines, which is the most widely consumed medium of the sexually explicit industry.

Researchers found that pornography consumption was significantly correlated with sexually aggressive behavior. However, the structural equation modeling indicated that this relationship might be equally well explained by a model suggesting that exposure to pornography causes a small increase in aggressive behavior once other relevant factors have been controlled for, as by a model indicating that sexual aggression causes greater pornography consumption. (Of course, "third variable" causation by some factor that was not measured in this research cannot be completely ruled out either.) Other analyses conducted by these investigators examined a "risk" approach that did not concern cause and effect but sought to determine whether knowledge about subjects' pornography consumption enables some greater statistical prediction of sexual aggression, once other variables have been taken into consideration. These data did indicate some greater statistical prediction, particularly at a relatively high risk for aggression. For example, Table 9.1 presents an analysis in which the risk factors used for predicting sexual aggression were hostile masculinity, sexual promiscuity, and pornography consumption. Each factor was divided into upper, middle,

TABLE 9.1   Predicting Self-Reports of Sexual Aggression against Women Based on the
Presence or Absence of High Scores on Hostile Masculinity, Sexual Promiscuity, and Pornography
Consumption

| Group | Presence of risk factor[a] | | | N | % aggression | Risk ratio | 95% confidence bounds | χ^2 | Difference between groups |
	High host.	High prom.	High porn.						
1.	Yes	Yes	Yes	18	72	3.9	2.5–6.2	33.5***	All
2.	Yes	Yes	No	139	44	2.5	2.0–3.1	59.5***	1,5,6,7,8
3.	Yes	No	Yes	22	32	1.7	0.9–3.3	2.4	1,8
4.	No	Yes	Yes	28	39	2.1	1.2–3.5	7.6**	1,8
5.	Yes	No	No	448	25	1.4	1.2–1.7	12.9***	1,2,8
6.	No	Yes	No	436	30	1.8	1.5–2.1	43.6***	1,2,8
7.	No	No	Yes	37	24	1.3	0.7–2.3	0.7	1,2,8
8.	No	No	No	1605	11	0.3	0.3–0.4	170.4***	All

Note: A subject was defined as sexually aggressive if scoring greater than 11 on the sexual
aggression measure. Approximately 19% of subjects in the total sample were defined as sexual
aggressors. $N = 2733$.
[a]Host., hostile masculinity; prom., sexual promiscuity; and porn., pornography consumption.
*$p < .05$; **$p < .01$; ***$p < .001$.

and lower thirds of the distributions. The existence of a risk factor was defined as
having a score in the top third of that variable's distribution.
   Table 9.1 presents an analysis of the number of sexually aggressive subjects as
a function of whether they had each of the three risk factors. The sample consists
of 2733 men constituting a representative national sample of those in some form
of post high school education. Sexual aggression was defined as having reported
some degree of such behavior on the revised Koss and Oros sexual aggression
measure (for more information, see Malamuth et al., 1991). For example, 1605
subjects were classified in the group that did not have any risk on all three variables. Of these individuals, 11% reported some level of sexual aggression.
   Table 9.1 also presents the risk ratio statistic. It is a descriptive statistic that
ranges from 0 to infinity and indicates the relative increase or decrease in risk of
one group from any one other group using a dichotomous-dependent variable. A
risk ratio of 1.00, for example, indicates that there is no difference in risk between
two chosen groups. In the analyses reported in this table, the risk ratio compares
subjects within each group (with its particular risk factor combination) to all other
subjects.[7] For example, the 1605 subjects who did not score high on any of the
risk factors have a risk ratio of 0.3. This indicates that these subjects are 0.3 times
as likely to be sexually aggressive as all other subjects combined. At the other ex-

[7]Differences in group sizes may render some of the comparisons less reliable than others.

treme, there were 18 subjects (out of the total of 2733) who were high in all three risk factors. The risk ratio of this group indicates that they are 3.9 times as likely to be sexually aggressive as compared to all other individuals combined.

Confidence bounds, which reflect the range of the "true" risk ratio for this population, are based on the 95% confidence level (Table 9.1). For example, the 95% confidence level for those subjects scoring high on all three risk factors suggests that the "true" risk ratio for this population probably ranges somewhere between 2.5 and 6.2.

To make comparisons in the levels of risk of one group compared to all the other subjects, the χ^2 statistic was used. For example, Table 9.1 indicates that in comparison to all others, a significant increase exists in sexual aggression for those high on all three risk factors. In contrast, Table 9.1 shows that those high in pornography consumption, but not high in hostility or sexual promiscuity, are not significantly greater in sexual aggression in comparison to all other groups in the sample. However, those who did not have any of the risk factors were significantly lower than all others in their aggression levels.

Finally, Table 9.1 presents a comparison of two groups at a time (in contrast to the statistic reported earlier that compared each group to all others). The numbers listed refer to the specific groups that were found to statistically differ at the .05 level. For example, Table 9.1 indicates that the risk ratio of subjects high on all of the three risk factors (group 1) differs significantly from subjects in each of the other groups (as indicated by the term "all").

Table 9.1 suggests that within the context of the variables studied, pornography consumption may indicate some increased likelihood for sexual aggression, but only when (1) neither of the other two other risk factors are present or (2) both of the other risk factors are present. This conclusion is indicated by focusing on comparisons between individual groups that do versus do not have pornography consumption as risk while the other two risk factors are "kept constant." First, the comparison is significant between those with only the "pornography" risk factor (group 7) as contrasted with those without any risk factors (group 8). Similarly, the comparison is also significant between those with all of the risk factors (group 1) to those with both hostility and promiscuity risk factors but not high on pornography consumption (group 2). In contrast, no difference exists between those high on the two risk factors of hostility and pornography but low on promiscuity (Group 3) to the group only high on hostility (group 5). Further, those high on promiscuity and pornography (group 4) do not differ in sexual aggression from those high on promiscuity alone (group 6).

Although there is some indication of pornography as a risk factor for those not showing any other risk and those showing a high risk on the two other factors, data shown here and other analyses conducted by Malamuth et al. (1993) indicate that the important increase is at the high risk end of the distribution. For example, at the low risk end of the distribution, Table 9.1 shows that although those with only the pornography risk factor differ from those without any risk factors, their sexual aggression is not significantly different in comparison to all others combined. Other comparisons using actual mean levels of sexual aggression (rather than classifying subjects as showing some aggression or none at all) indicated a very low level of aggression for this group.

However, 18 subjects who scored high on all risk factors showed a much higher level of aggression in comparison with all others combined and in comparison to all other individual groups. Although this group constitutes less than 1% of the sample, both the analyses illustrated here (e.g., 72% showing some aggression) and additional analyses focusing on the actual levels of aggression indicated that this group was much more aggressive than all other groups.

Additional results suggest that these findings are not consistent with a "general deviancy" explanation, which suggests that pornography consumption is simply an indicator of some general extremity or deviance. For example, Malamuth et al. (1993) also examined nonsexual aggression (e.g., yelling and hitting in a nonsexual context). Using the same risk factors, they found that pornography consumption did not increase the risk for this type of aggression. However, they did find that alcohol consumption was a contributor to the risk for nonsexual aggression. Correspondingly, levels of alcohol consumption were not found to contribute to the risk for sexual aggression in the context of the other two risk factors.

It is important to emphasize again that these data do not enable any causal conclusions but may only be useful as risk "markers" or indicators. However, they are consistent with some earlier experimental research showing that men who are relatively high in risk for sexual aggression are more likely to be attracted to and aroused by sexually violent media (e.g., Malamuth & Check, 1983) and may be more likely to be influenced by them (e.g., Malamuth & Check, 1985). This bidirectional relationship (i.e., higher proclivity to aggress resulting in more exposure to media violence, which in turn contributes to higher risk for aggression) is also consistent with research on media violence generally (Bushman, 1995).

SUMMARY

A model of the profile of sexual aggressors was presented, indicating that they may be characterized by certain developmental (early childhood and adolescent) and current personality and behavioral characteristics. These are well described by the confluence of impersonal sexuality and hostile masculinity constellations of characteristics. The first consists of a short-term, noncommittal orientation to sexual relations, the second of a dominant and hostile orientation to women. Evolutionary psychology theory was presented to help account for the particular set of characteristics associated with sexual aggression identified in this model. Both cross-sectional and longitudinal findings supporting the model were summarized. Within the framework provided by this model, findings were presented in three areas. First, a personality dimension labeled the nurturance relative to dominance orientation was shown to moderate the relationship between risk factors and actual aggression. Second, research focusing on imagined sexual aggression was integrated within the framework of the confluence model. It showed that while the actual acting out of aggression may not occur in some individuals, their aggressive tendencies may be expressed in imagined aggression. Third, research was described assessing whether information about a person's mass media usage adds to the ability to identify "risk" for committing sexual aggression. Using a nationwide representative sample, it was found that the added information of frequent use of sexually explicit media helped discriminate between "high risk" men (those scoring high on both hostile masculinity and impersonal sexual orientation) who actually aggressed against women and those "high risk" men who did not commit sexually aggressive acts. In contrast, knowledge of the degree of sexually explicit media consumption with "low risk" men was generally found to be of little predictive utility, although it was somewhat of an indicator for men not showing any other risk factors. It is suggested that the confluence model can serve as a useful framework for future research in examining the role of other factors potentially related to sexual aggression.

REFERENCES

Ballard-Reisch, D., & Elton, M. (1992). Gender orientation and the Bem Sex Role Inventory: A psychological construct revisited. *Sex Roles, 27,* 291–306.

Belsky, J., Steinberg, L., & Draper, P. (1991). Childhood experience, interpersonal development, and reproductive strategy: An evolutionary theory of socialization. *Child Development, 62,* 647–670.

Bem, S. L. (1974). The measurement of psychological androgyny. *Journal of Consulting and Clinical Psychology, 42,* 155–162.

Brownmiller, S. (1975). *Against our will: Men, women and rape.* New York: Simon & Schuster.

Bushman, B. J. (1995). Moderating role of trait aggressiveness in the effects of violent media on aggression. *Journal of Personality and Social Psychology, 69,* 950–960.

Buss, D. M. (1990). Evolutionary social psychology: Prospects and pitfalls. *Motivation and Emotion, 14,* 265–286.

Buss, D. M. (1991). Evolutionary personality psychology. *Annual Review of Psychology, 42,* 459–491.

Buss, D. M. (1995). Evolutionary psychology. *Psychological Inquiry, 6,* 1–30.

Buss, D. M., & Malamuth, N. M. (Eds.) (1996). *Sex, power, conflict: Evolutionary and feminist perspectives.* New York: Oxford University Press.

Christopher, F. S., Owens, L. A., & Stecker, H. L. (1993). Exploring the dark side of courtship: A test of a model of premarital sexual aggressiveness. *Journal of Marriage and the Family, 55,* 469–479.

Daly, M., & Wilson, M. (1994). Evolutionary psychology of male violence. In J. Archer (Ed.), *Male violence* (pp. 253–288). London: Routledge.

Dean, K., & Malamuth, N. M. (1997). Characteristics of men who aggress sexually and of men who imagine aggressing: Risk and moderating variables. *Journal of Personality and Social Psychology, 72,* 449–455.

Draper, P., & Harpending, H. (1982). Father absence and reproductive strategy: An evolutionary perspective. *Journal of Anthropological Research, 38,* 255–273.

Ellis, B., & Symons, D. (1989). Sex differences in sexual fantasy. *Journal of Sex Research, 27,* 527–555.

Feshbach, S. (1970). Aggression. In P. Mussen (Ed.), *Carmichael's manual of child psychology* (Vol. 2, pp. 159–259). New York: Wiley.

Fisher, W. A., & Barak, A. (1991). Pornography, erotica and behavior: More questions than answers. *International Journal of Law and Psychiatry, 14,* 65–83.

Gangestad, S. W., & Simpson, J. A. (1990). Toward an evolutionary history of female sociosexual variation. *Journal of Personality, 58,* 69–96.

Greendlinger, V. (1985). *Dispositional and situational variables as predictors of rape proclivity in college men.* Unpublished doctoral dissertation, State University of New York at Albany.

Greendlinger, V., & Byrne, D. (1987). Coercive sexual fantasies of college men as predictors of self-reported likelihood to rape and overt sexual aggression. *Journal of Sex Research, 23,* 1–11.

Kenrick, D. T., & Sheets, V. (1993). Homicidal fantasies. *Ethology and Sociobiology, 14,* 231–246.

Linz, D., & Malamuth, N. M. (1993). *Pornography.* Beverly Hills, CA: Sage.

Malamuth, N. (1988). A multidimensional approach to sexual aggression: Combining measures of past behavior and present likelihood. In R. Prentky & V. Quinsey (Eds.), *Human sexual aggression: Current perspectives* (Vol. 528, pp. 123–132). New York: The New York Academy of Sciences.

Malamuth, N. M. (1986). Predictors of naturalistic sexual aggression. *Journal of Personality and Social Psychology, 50,* 953–962.

Malamuth, N. (1989a). The Attraction to Sexual Aggression Scale: Part I. *Journal of Sex Research, 26,* 26–49.

Malamuth, N. (1989b). The Attraction to Sexual Aggression Scale: Part II. *Journal of Sex Research, 26,* 324–354.

Malamuth, N. (1993). Pornography's impact on male adolescents. *Adolescent Medicine: State of the Art Reviews, 4,* 563–576.

Malamuth, N. M. (in press). An evolutionary-based model integrating research on the characteristics of sexually coercive men. In J. Adair, K. Dion, & D. Belanger (Eds.). *Advances in Psychological Science (Vol. 2): Personal, Social and Developmental Aspects.* Hove, UK: Psychology Press.

Malamuth, N., & Check, J. (1983). Sexual arousal to rape depictions: Individual differences. *Journal of Abnormal Psychology, 92,* 55–67.

Malamuth, N. M., & Check, J. (1985). The effects of aggressive-pornography on beliefs in rape myths: Individual differences. *Journal of Research in Personality, 19,* 299–320.

Malamuth, N. M., Feshbach, S., & Jaffe, Y. (1977). Sexual arousal and aggression: Recent experiments and theoretical issues. *Journal of Social Issues, 33,* 110–133.

Malamuth, N. M., Heavey, C., & Linz, D. (1993). Predicting men's antisocial behavior against women: The "interaction model" of sexual aggression. In G. N. Hall, R. Hirschmann, J. R. Graham, & M. S. Zaragoza (Eds.), *Sexual aggression: Issues in etiology and assessment, and treatment* (pp. 63–97). New York: Hemisphere.

Malamuth, N. M., Koss, M., & Sockloskie, R. (1993). *Recent advances in research on the mass media and aggression against women.* Paper presented at the annual meetings of the Society of Experimental Social Psychology, Santa Barbara, CA.

Malamuth, N. M., Linz, D., & Heavey, C. (1996). *Sexual arousal to aggression, empathy levels and the prediction of sexual aggression: A 10-year follow-up study.* Manuscript in preparation.

Malamuth, N. M., Linz, D., Heavey, C., Barnes, G., & Acker, M. (1995). Using the confluence model of sexual aggression to predict men's conflict with women: A ten year follow-up study. *Journal of Personality and Social Psychology, 69,* 353–369.

Malamuth, N. M., Sockloskie, R., Koss, M. P., & Tanaka, J. (1991). The characteristics of aggressors against women: Testing a model using a national sample of college students. *Journal of Consulting and Clinical Psychology, 59,* 670–681.

Miller, P. A., & Eisenberg, N. (1988). The relation of empathy to aggressive and externalizing/antisocial behavior. *Psychological Bulletin, 103,* 324–344.

Mould, D. E. (1988). A critical analysis of recent research on violent erotica. *Journal of Sex Research, 24,* 326–340.

Pithers, W. D. (1993). Treatment of rapists: Reinterpretation of early outcome data and exploratory constructs to enhance therapeutic efficacy. In G. Nagayama Hall, R. Hirschman, J. Graham, & M. Zaragoza (Eds.), *Sexual aggression: Issues in etiology, assessment and treatment* (pp. 167–196). Washington, DC: Taylor & Francis.

Quakenbush, R. L. (1989). A comparison of androgynous, masculine sex-typed, and undifferentiated males on dimensions of attitudes toward rape. *Journal of Research in Personality, 23,* 318–342.

Rice, M. E., Chaplin, T. C. Harris, G. T., & Coutts, J. (1994). Empathy for the victim and sexual assault among rapists and nonrapists. *Journal of Interpersonal Violence, 10,* 435–449.

Ross, R. R., & Allgeier, E. (1991). *Correlate of males' feminine identification with sexually coercive attitudes and behaviors.* Unpublished manuscript, Bowling Green State University, Bowling Green, OH.

Seto, M. K., & Barbaree, H. E. (1993). Victim blame and sexual arousal to rape cues in rapists and nonoffenders. *Annals of Sex Research, 6,* 167–183.

Simpson, J. A., & Gangestad, S. W. (1991). Individual differences in sociosexuality: Evidence for convergent and discriminant validity. *Journal of Personality and Social Psychology, 60,* 870–883.

Symons, D. (1979). *The evolution of human sexuality.* New York: Oxford University Press.

Symons, D. (1992). On the use and misuse of Darwinism in the study of human behavior. In J. Barkow, L. Cosmides, & J. Tooby (Eds.), *The adapted mind* (pp. 137–162). New York: Oxford University Press.

Tieger, T. (1981). Self-rated likelihood of raping and the social perception of rape. *Journal of Research in Personality, 15,* 147–158.

Wiggins, J. S., & Holzmuller, A. (1981). Further evidence on androgyny and interpersonal flexibility. *Journal of Research in Personality, 15,* 67–80.

10

TEMPERATURE AND AGGRESSION: PARADOX, CONTROVERSY, AND A (FAIRLY) CLEAR PICTURE

CRAIG A. ANDERSON

University of Missouri

KATHRYN B. ANDERSON

Our Lady of the Lake University

> *I pray thee, good Mercutio, let's retire;*
> *The day is hot, the Capulets abroad,*
> *And, if we meet, we shall not 'scape a brawl,*
> *For now, these hot days, is the mad blood stirring.*
> Romeo and Juliet, *Shakespeare*

> *The day drags by like a wounded animal*
> *The approaching disease, 92°*
> *The blood in our veins and the brains in our head*
> *The approaching unease, 92°*
> 92° *by Siouxsie and the Banshees,* Tinderbox,
> *David Geffen Company, 1986*

Imagine the following scenario. You are in your overpriced hotel room, re-viewing your notes for an important presentation that you will be giving later in the day. The people next door have their television cranked to maximum volume. It is so loud that you can hear the dialogue as well as the gunfire and explosions; it is from Sylvester Stallone's movie *Judge Dredd*. Despite an earlier request to turn it down, the volume remains at an intolerable level. You pound on their door to explain your situation and make one more appeal. The appeal is met by laughter and a comment on the legitimacy of your birth. How do you respond? We would guess that most readers of this chapter would feel angry, but would not emit any aggressive behavior.

Now, imagine the same scenario, but with one additional stressful factor. The hotel air conditioning is off, and the rooms and hallways are at least 92°F. Now what is the likelihood that you would aggress? Most people would agree that the hot temperature would indeed increase the likelihood of an aggressive response of some kind. Even if it is merely a verbal insult, the probability of a violent encounter occurring also increases, perhaps as the end result of a series of escalating verbally abusive exchanges.

This chapter is structured to address theoretical, empirical, and practical issues surrounding the temperature–aggression hypothesis. First, a brief history of the temperature–aggression hypothesis is presented. Second, a paradox involving violence and lethargy is described and resolved. Third, the major issues and theories surrounding heat effects are outlined, and an integrated model of aggression is provided. Fourth, several epistemological issues concerning empirical tests of various theories are discussed. Fifth, modern empirical studies are reviewed, and new results that bear on issues of current concern are presented. Finally, the empirical data base is more specifically compared to the major theories, noting convergences and contradictions, and pointing out fruitful lines of inquiry for future research.

A BRIEF HISTORY OF THE
TEMPERATURE–AGGRESSION HYPOTHESIS

Social commentators have noted weather effects on human behavior and have used heat-related imagery for thousands of years. Cicero (106–43 B.C.) noted that "The minds of men do in the weather share, dark or serene as the day's foul or fair." Shakespeare noted (in *The Merchant of Venice*) that "the brain may devise laws for the blood, but a hot temper leaps o'er a cold decree." Shakespeare explicitly referenced what presumedly was a commonly held belief in the society of his day in *Romeo and Juliet,* as in the opening quote linking hot temperatures to violent behavior.

Social philosophers, social geographers, and other students of behavior began to apply empirical methods to this theory in the late 1800s. Even earlier, Montesquieu traveled extensively and drew upon his observations in various writings. Heat effects were included in his observations. In *The Spirit of the Laws* he stated that, "You will find in the northern climates peoples who have few vices, enough virtues, and much sincerity and frankness. As you move toward the countries of the south, you will believe you have moved away from morality itself: the liveliest passions will increase crime. . . ." (Montesquieu, 1748/1989, p. 234). In this work, Montesquieu even espoused a physiological theory for why hot temperatures produced such extreme emotionality in the peoples who lived in hot southern climates.

It was some time before this type of informal observation of and speculation about heat effects was supplemented with more objective empirical methods. The earliest such study located was by Leffingwell (1892), who examined quarter of the year effects on two broad categories of violent crime in England and Wales in 1878–1887. Other early studies of the heat effect include those by Lombroso in Italy (and elsewhere) (1899/1911), Guerry in France (as cited in Brearley, 1932), Dexter (1899) in the United States, and Aschaffenburg (1903/1913) in Germany and France. Although the empirical methods were somewhat crude by modern standards, these early studies supported the prevailing theory that uncomfortably hot temperatures produce increases in violent behavior (for a review of this work, see Anderson, 1989).

THE TEMPERATURE–AGGRESSION PARADOX

Some of the early writings concerning heat effects contained a paradox that to this day remains unresolved. Specifically, hot temperatures are seen as having two effects that seem opposite and contradictory. On the one hand, hot temperatures are seen as increasing aggression. On the other hand, hot temperatures are also seen as robbing people of motivation, alertness, and energy. Aggression usually requires considerable energy or effort, especially the aggression examined in studies focusing on violent crimes such as assault and murder. Thus, the paradox: How can lethargic people behave violently? If heat makes people reluctant to engage in energetic activities, how can it produce increases in aggression?

Before attempting to resolve this paradox, it is important to ask whether it truly exists. There are two parts to consider, the "increases aggressive behavior" part and the "decreases effort/energy" part. Much of this chapter is devoted to discovering whether hot temperatures directly increase aggressive behavior. As most readers will have guessed by now, the evidence of such direct effects is overwhelmingly positive. Assuming that we are right (and that the later sections of this chapter are convincing to you, the reader), then we are left with the second part, whether hot temperatures also make people lethargic. There has been surprisingly little research on this question, perhaps because it is somewhat vague.

There are several ways of thinking about lethargy, including at a simple affect level (e.g., How do you feel?), at a physiological level (e.g., Is heart rate decreased?), and at a task level (e.g., Is cognitive performance lowered?). In addition, we can ask whether modern citizens of western society (e.g., U.S. college students) believe there is a true heat effect. We begin by examining this "Do you believe?" question.

STUDY 1: SOCIAL THEORIES ABOUT HEAT EFFECTS

The goal of Study 1 was to assess the social theories of our subject population concerning the relation of temperature to the several variables of interest in this domain: affect, arousal, and aggression. A questionnaire was developed to measure subjects' social theories concerning the relation of both hot and cold temperatures to these variables.

Method

Procedures

Fifteen female and 7 male undergraduates at a large midwestern university participated in this experiment. Participants were given a two-page questionnaire, which was titled: "Beliefs about temperature, emotions, and behavior." They were instructed to "indicate your beliefs by circling a number for each item below." After completing the questionnaire, participants were thoroughly debriefed and thanked for their assistance.

Participants were asked six questions using the frame, "Compared to normal temperatures, what do you think the effect of (hot/cold) temperatures would be on (alertness and energy level, feelings of hostility and anger, aggression and violent behaviors)." Each question was answered on a five-point rating scale, with the lowest rating indicating a belief that the temperature (hot or cold) would decrease the target variable (i.e., alertness, hostility, or aggression), the midpoint indicating a belief in no heat effect, and the highest rating indicating a belief that the temperature would increase the target variable. The three questions concerning effects of hot temperatures and the corresponding three cold temperature questions were presented on separate pages. Participants were randomly assigned to completing the hot or the cold page first. This order manipulation allowed examination of the possibility that thinking about one type of heat effect (e.g., hot) would influence subjects' responses on the other (e.g., cold).

Results and Discussion

The six items and results are presented in Figure 10.1, in terms of average deviations from the scale midpoint of 3, which corresponded to a belief in no effect of temperature. There were no reliable effects of task order or of sex ($p > .05$), so subsequent tests ignored these factors. A t test was performed on each item mean to see whether it differed reliably from "no effect." As can be seen, hot temperatures were expected to have a very large impact on all three target variables. Compared to comfortable temperatures, participants believed that hot temperatures would produce a significant decrease in alertness and energy level [$M = 1.50$, $t(21) = -8.77$, $p < .001$], a significant increase in anger and hostility [$M = 4.64$, $t(21) = 13.24$, $p < .001$], and a significant increase in aggressive and violent behavior [$M = 4.45$, $t(21) = 10.14$, $p < .001$].

Participants also expected that cold temperatures (relative to comfortable ones) would have systematic effects on the target variables, but in every case the direction of the expected cold effect was opposite of the expected hot effect. Participants expected cold temperatures to produce a significant increase in alertness and energy level [$M = 3.64$, $t(21) = 2.32$, $p < .05$], a significant decrease in anger and hostility [$M = 2.45$, $t(21) = -2.83$, $p < .01$], and a significant decrease in aggressive and violent behavior [$M = 2.14$, $t(21) = -4.84$, $p < .001$].

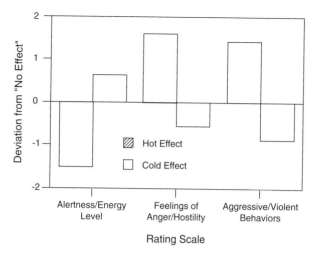

FIGURE 10.1 Social theories relating temperature to three dimensions.

Overall, these results confirm that people do have social theories relating temperature to a host of aggression-related variables.[1] The hot temperature paradox is also illustrated by these beliefs. Our participants believed that heat reduces alertness and energy levels, while simultaneously increasing aggressive behavior. The finding of opposite social theories for the effects of uncomfortably cold temperatures may prove useful in future research on the effects of temperature on aggression, especially in ruling out various alternative explanations that rely on suspicion or demand characteristics.

TEMPERATURE AND AROUSAL

A second part of the paradox question involves the actual effect of hot temperatures on arousal. Study 1 indicated that people believe that heat reduces alertness and energy, but what are its actual effects? This simple question turns out to have a complex answer. It depends on what one means by arousal.

In several experiments in our laboratories, we have shown that *subjective* perceptions of arousal, as measured by the self-report perceived arousal scale (Anderson, Anderson, & Deuser, 1996; Anderson, Deuser, & DeNeve, 1995), decrease at hot temperatures. Specifically, people assigned to play video games, perform a cognitive reaction time task, or do brief aerobic exercise in hot temperatures report feeling less aroused than people performing the same tasks in normal temperatures. Conversely, cold temperatures produce an increase in perceived arousal (Anderson et al., 1996).

[1]A larger study ($n = 55$) was also conducted using these same procedures and items. However, the order of hot versus cold questions was not varied. The result was a practically identical set of means, each of which differed significantly from the scale midpoint of "no effect."

Physiological arousal though, as assessed by changes in heart rate, complicates the picture. Hot temperatures systematically increase heart rate, relative to normal temperatures (Anderson et al., 1995, 1996). Interestingly, cold temperatures seem to produce decreases in heart rate under laboratory conditions (Anderson et al., 1996). Other research from a variety of laboratories produces heart rate results similar to ours (Bazett, 1927; Hardy, 1961; LeBlanc, 1975; Tromp, 1980).

TEMPERATURE AND PERFORMANCE

Performance on cognitive tasks seems to parallel the subjective arousal results. Hot temperatures reduce performance on various types of tasks. Tedious and repetitive tasks that involve a low level of physiological arousal are particularly susceptible to performance decrements in heat. Visual vigilance tasks are impaired when temperatures exceed 90°F (Mortagy & Ramsey, 1973; Pepler, 1958), sometimes as a result of perceptual distortions due to heat glare and shimmer (Kobrick & Johnson, 1991). Auditory vigilance decreases in temperatures above 100°F (Poulton, Edwards, & Colquhoun, 1974). Heat has been shown to impair performance in rifle marksmanship (Johnson & Kobrick, 1988, as cited in Kobrick & Johnson, 1991), flight simulations (Iampietro, Melton, Higgins, Vaughan, Hoffman, Funkhouser, & Saldivar, 1972), arithmetic tasks (Ramsey, Dayal, & Ghahramani, 1975), and short-term memory tasks (Wing & Touchstone, 1965, as cited in Kobrick & Johnson, 1991). Across tasks, those that are more interesting and arousing are less affected by increases in temperature as well as those that do not involve use of materials that become uncomfortable in heat such as metal surfaces and bulky protective clothing (Kobrick & Johnson, 1991). Few studies have been conducted on cold effects and performance, and the results do not warrant generalized summaries at this point in time. (For reviews of this literature, see Kobrick & Fine, 1983; Kobrick & Johnson, 1991).

PARADOX RESOLUTION

Although the effects of hot (and cold) temperatures on various kinds of variables are undoubtedly complex, no real paradox is seen in the position that hot temperatures can simultaneously decrease energy levels and increase aggressive behaviors. Although uncomfortable heat can decrease one's willingness to do a variety of things, it also increases one's irritability or state hostility (Anderson et al., 1995, 1996). Thus, any given provocation is received more negatively by a hot person than by a comfortable one. In other words, those kinds of aggression that are based on impulsive or affective reactions to provocation are likely to be increased by hot temperatures.

Although the focus of this chapter is on heat effects, it is important to consider another paradox. As will become apparent in our integrated model of aggression, discomfort appears to be the underlying factor in heat-induced aggression, suggesting that uncomfortably cold temperatures should also increase aggression.

However, real world violence does not appear to increase in cold temperatures. Doesn't this contradict the discomfort theory? Actually, it does not. The simple reason is that throughout most of human history and even in most modern societies, relief from cold discomfort is more available (via clothing, fire, heating systems) than relief is from heat discomfort. Thus, real world studies are not good sources of tests of cold effects. As seen in subsequent sections, cold discomfort does increase aggression in laboratory studies in much the same way as heat does.

MAJOR ISSUES IN THE STUDY
OF HEAT EFFECTS

There are three major issues in the study of heat effects on aggression. The first one concerns whether temperature has a direct impact on aggressive tendencies. The second concerns theoretical explanations for the various heat effects observed in a wide variety of contexts. The third concerns the practical significance of findings on the temperature–aggression hypothesis.

EXISTENCE OF THE HEAT EFFECT

It is clear from dozens of studies (e.g., Anderson, 1989) that hot temperatures are associated with increased violence. Of course, it is also clear that race in the United States is strongly associated with performance on standardized intelligence tests, but mere association is not the same as causation. The race/IQ association is hotly contested for both political and methodological reasons. The most obvious scientific reason for doubting that race is causally linked to these large test score effects is that there is a well-developed body of evidence linking a host of theoretically relevant variables to test performance and race. In other words, race in 20th century U.S. society is confounded with a number of truly causal variables such as poverty. Thus, there is good reason to doubt that race has a direct impact on standardized test performance.

Similarly, in correlational studies of the temperature–aggression hypothesis, there may be complexities that artificially give rise to strong heat effects. The existence question in this chapter refers to whether there is a true direct causal effect of hot temperatures on aggression. By direct impact we mean one that occurs at a psychological level, having its impact on aggression via the individual's affective state, way of thinking, or arousal level.

It is important to distinguish between two nondirect ways in which hot temperatures may be linked to aggressive behavior. The first way, which consists of indirect links, causally links temperature to some external factor, which in turn is causally linked to aggressive behavior. For example, hot temperatures may be associated with increases in violent crime rates because of the kinds of routine activities that people "do" in hot weather versus cooler weather. An analogous indirect effect in the race/IQ domain might be that skin color influences the expectations of teachers, whose behavior toward students of different races hinders the learning of certain racial groups while facilitating the learning of other racial groups.

The second nondirect way that temperature may be linked to aggressive behavior is via totally spurious links. For example, the common finding of higher violent crime rates in the "southern" cities of the United States may be a function of the higher proportion of impoverished and disadvantaged minorities in those cities, who typically have higher violent crime rates than other groups throughout the United States. Because temperature differences among cities do not "cause" the obtained socioeconomic and racial compositions of the cities, this temperature/violent crime link could be totally spurious. (However, as seen in a later section, controlling for socioeconomic and racial composition does not eliminate the heat effect in such studies, so it is not spurious.)

It is important to realize that the epistemological status of spurious links is not the same as that of indirect processes. Discovery that a particular heat effect disappears when spurious links are controlled weakens the temperature–aggression hypothesis by removing the spurious finding from the column of "successful predictions." However, discovery of indirect heat effects is largely irrelevant to the questions of whether there are true, causal direct effects of hot temperatures on aggressive behavior; surely there are many variables that influence the frequency and severity of aggression in modern society, some of which may correlate with temperature. The scholars' tasks in this area are to identify plausible causal influences on aggressive behavior, to develop testable hypotheses that allow for disconfirmation, to conduct tests of these hypotheses, and to refine the theories. Of course, if all the observed heat effects can be explained parsimoniously via an indirect route or are found to be spurious, then the answer to this first major issue, concerning the existence of direct heat effects, would be negative.

THEORETICAL POSITIONS

The second major issue asks, What are the major theories that might account for hot heat effects? Five such theories have been identified, and an integration of the most promising aspects of several of them has been provided in a broader model of affective aggression.

Biological Theories

Physiological theories of heat effects should be viewed on a different level of analysis from broader sociological, cognitive, and affective models. Biological theoretical explanations can be seen as complementing higher-level theories by suggesting the physiological mechanisms directly responsible for heat effects on emotions. This section briefly describes both a physiological theory of heat effects and the relation of thermoregulation to aggression.

Zajonc (1985, 1994; Zajonc, Murphy, & Inglhart, 1989) has proposed the innovative vascular theory of emotional efference, which focuses on the role of blood vessels in the cavernous sinus in cooling the blood that flows into the face and brain. The degree to which the blood is cooled or heated influences the stimulation of emotional centers in the brain. Zajonc's theory grew out of Waynbaum's (1907) work, which posited that the facial muscles (through constriction) regulate the amount of blood that flows to the cerebrum, which in turn influences subjective feelings. Zajonc clarifies that facial muscles are merely one of many regulators of cerebral blood flow but maintains that constriction or relaxation of certain facial muscles can affect the cooling of venous blood flow to the brain. The cooling of the brain is suggested to release certain neurotransmitters that increase the positive affect.

Zajonc et al. (1989) reported increases in forehead temperature in German and American participants as they utter the German phoneme "ü", which constricts air flow to veins in the cavernous sinus, while reading stories aloud or repeating a tape-recorded voice, compared to no utterance of the "ü" or to utterance of phonemes that open the sinuses (e.g., "ah" and "e"). Participants in these studies reported less liking for the ü sound and stated that producing the non-ü sounds put them in a better mood than did generation of the ü. Zajonc et al. (1989) further found that cool air, when blown into the nostrils, both decreased forehead temperature and increased positive subjective feelings. In line with the vascular theory of emotional efference, he concluded that when cool air is introduced to the nostrils, as occurs with the utterance of certain sounds, the blood flowing from the nostrils up to the forehead and the brain is cooled, thereby cooling the brain and increasing pleasant, positive feelings in the individual.

Another biological approach relates to thermoregulation, the process that the body undergoes to heat or cool itself in response to uncomfortable temperatures. Several of the physiological processes involved in thermoregulation have also been linked to emotion. The amygdala, hypothalamus, and hippocampus are all highly neuronally interconnected and are important brain centers for thermoregulation and the release of both hormones and neurotransmitters related to aggression. For example, the hypothalamus releases acetylcholine in response to ambient cold, which increases body temperature. Acetylcholine has been shown to increase aggression (Reis, 1974). The male and female sex hormones of testosterone and estrogen have also been associated with aggression. Increases in testosterone have been linked to aggressive behavior in men and women (Blanchard & Blanchard, 1984), and decreases in estrogen and progesterone (as in the premenstrual phase) have been associated with female aggression (Buchanan, Eccles, & Becker, 1992). The production of testosterone is influenced by corticosteroids, which are released from the adrenal cortex when the body sweats.

The amygdala acts as an emotional computer that assigns affective significance to incoming stimuli (LeDoux, 1993). Its neurons are also responsive to changes in heart rate and blood pressure, which can vary with ambient temperature. Therefore, the amygdala can create aggressive interpretations and reactions as a function of sympathetic and parasympathetic autonomic responses to temperature.

The relation between thermoregulation and emotion is far from understood due to the complex interrelation of relevant neuronal centers, hormones, and neurotransmitters. However, the interconnectedness of these systems suggests a relationship among ambient temperature, body temperature, and aggression.

Southern Culture of Violence

As evidenced in the earlier quote by Montesquieu (1748/1989), social theorists have long noticed an increase in violence in southern regions, which are closer to the equator. Theories of a U.S. southern culture of violence range from the sociological (e.g., Gastil, 1971; Hackney, 1970) to the evolutionary and economic (Nisbett, 1990, 1993).

Some sociological approaches focus on the relatively lengthy time period in which the South was an unsettled wilderness frontier (Gastil, 1971; Hackney, 1970). Others attribute the development of a southern culture of violence (SCV) to swashbuckling cavaliers who settled in the early South. The cavaliers held personal honor and virtue as ideals, which they combatively defended (Cash, 1941; Nisbett, 1993).

Of particular interest is Nisbett's theory of a southern culture of honor (Cohen & Nisbett, 1994; Nisbett, 1990, 1993). He posits that the livelihood of people who primarily settled in the South depended on a herding economy. In order to thrive in this economic system, male producers were required to be highly protective of their livestock from poachers. Because of the relative isolation that these men experienced, they alone defended their herds, their families, and their honor. These frontier people (adaptively) socialized their offspring to hold these aggressive defensive attitudes toward potential intruders as well as taught them the behaviors necessary to fight effectively (e.g., how to operate a gun).

Nisbett (1990, 1993) cites a variety of studies in support of this view and suggests that the culture of honor explains the regional differences in U.S. homicide rates. Of course this view also requires the assumption that once a culture of violence develops, it will persist even after the economic circumstances giving rise to it have shifted. Otherwise, the culture of honor would be irrelevant to aggression in urban environments.

Assumptions of some SCV theories have not been consistently supported by research. Bailey (1976), for example, reanalyzed Gastil's (1971) study of "southernness" effects on homicide rates and found that regional effects were greatly diminished when appropriate socioeconomic factors were controlled. Some studies have shown no differences in southern and nonsouthern samples in gun ownership (O'Connor & Lizotte, 1978) or violent attitudes (Erlanger, 1975). Nisbett (1993) provides the important caveat that southern violence is primarily linked to self-protection, so only homicides that occur in the interests of self-defense (or of personal honor) should (according to his theory) show regional differences. Similarly, southerners should not hold more general violent attitudes than northerners, rather southerners should endorse more violence for self-protection purposes.

In sum, the culture of honor view posits that the southern region of the United States has a socioeconomic history that has created a more violent culture than in northern regions. More specifically, this perspective predicts that the old south should have higher violent crime rates than other regions of the United States. Although both the culture of honor and the temperature–aggression hypotheses attempt to explain the high homicide rate often found in southern U.S. cities, they need not be viewed as mutually exclusive. A southern culture of violence (or culture of honor) could (a) have an effect on violence that is independent of temperature or (b) have partially (or wholly) evolved due to hot temperatures. Although the latter supposition is impossible to test, critical tests of the former will examine the relationships among SCV, temperature, and violence.

Routine Activity Theory

Cohen and Felson (1979) developed routine activity theory (RAT) to explain the link between increases in crime and increases in temperature. This sociological view states that opportunities to commit crimes increase in the summer because social behavior patterns change. In the summer, people (potential victims as well as perpetrators) are more likely to leave their homes and their families. Increases in alcohol consumption and a reduction in guardianship have also been posited as crime-related warm weather behaviors (Cohn, 1990; Landau & Fridman, 1993).

RAT has been supported by some archival studies of the temperature–aggression relation (Cohen & Felson, 1979; Field, 1992) and not by others (e.g., Michael & Zumpe, 1986). Although heat and changes in social behavior patterns co-occur, they can, and probably do, have independent effects on aggressive behavior. Some proponents of RAT propose that the temperature–aggression effect is at least mediated by, if not an artifact of, changes in routine activities.

Negative Affect Escape Theory

Baron and Bell's negative affect escape theory (NAE; Anderson & DeNeve, 1992; Baron, 1972; Bell, 1992; Bell & Baron, 1976) focuses on the current state of the individual and their behavioral motives. According to this theory, negative affect increases as temperatures become uncomfortably hot or cold. Both aggressive and escape motives are believed to increase as negative affect increases. At high levels of negative affect, if escape from the situation is possible then escape motives overcome aggressive motives and escape behavior is expressed (and aggressive behavior is not). If escape is not perceived as an option (as in many laboratory experiments), more aggressive behavior should result at uncomfortable temperatures.

Most laboratory studies of this theory have manipulated temperature and anger. Those that support the NAE have found a temperature × anger interaction in which hot temperatures led to decreases in aggression in angry conditions and increases in aggression in nonangry conditions (Anderson & DeNeve, 1992). This interaction has not been found in some studies (Baron, 1972; Bell & Baron, 1977) and has occurred in the reverse fashion in at least one (Bell, 1980). Overall, laboratory data testing the NAE as applied to the temperature–aggression hypothesis are inconsistent (Anderson, 1989). Further studies involving behavioral measures of aggression as well as those that pit aggressive and escape motives against each other are required to test the specific predictions of the theory.

Social/Cognitive Theories

Two theories that focus on the influence of environmental factors on aggressive cognitions and behaviors are (a) Bandura's (e.g., 1973) groundbreaking social learning theory (SLT) and (b) Berkowitz's (1984, 1993) contemporary cognitive neoassociation theory (CNT) of emotion. According to SLT, witnessing aggression leads to the acquisition, performance, and maintenance of aggressive behavior. An important aspect of this theory is that the aggressive behavior that is viewed can be encoded into memory and retrieved when the witness is faced with a similar situation (Geen, 1990). For example, a boy who grows up in an abusive household may well learn to use physical force as a means of coping with unpleasant situations. He may learn both the "how to hit" aspects and the "why hit" aspects, especially if the modeled aggression appears to work. As an adult he may well recreate this abusive pattern in his own family. Hot temperatures contribute to the unpleasantness of many situations and could therefore trigger the expression of the learned aggressive behavior patterns.

CNA, a more recent cognitive theory, is based on network models of memory that focus on the interconnectedness of related incidents or thoughts in memory. According to CNA, thoughts, feelings, and behavioral programs are stored together in memory such that when a particular thought or feeling emerges into consciousness, related thoughts, feelings, or behavioral propensities are activated (may be experienced). Central to CNA is the role of negative affect as the initiator of hostile thoughts, feelings, and behaviors. Berkowitz states that an increase in negative affect (as occurs in uncomfortable temperatures) can *automatically* bring aggressive thoughts and recollections to mind, as well as lead to the immediate experience of angry feelings and aggressive behavioral inclinations.

Dodge and colleagues (e.g., Dodge & Crick, 1990) and Huesmann and colleagues (e.g., Huesmann, 1984; Huesmann, Eron, Lefkowitz & Walder, 1984) have similarly shown that children learn aggressive scripts and apply them in many normal situations in everyday life. These scripts also bias the interpretation of ambiguous encounters in an aggression-related way. Presumedly, these scripts are learned in a variety of ways from many sources (including television) and can be linked to a variety of nodes in memory, such as negative affect.

A General Affective Aggression Model

A theory of affective aggression (Anderson et al., 1995, 1996) incorporates assumptions of some of the aforementioned theoretical perspectives. As the various perspectives address different aspects of the generation and maintenance of aggressive behavior, from the physiological to the social, the various theories are best considered as addressing different levels of analysis. Our goal is to integrate theoretical processes at different levels in order to more fully understand the processes by which social/environmental variables (e.g, temperature) operate via aggressive cognitions, feelings, and arousal to produce aggressive behaviors.

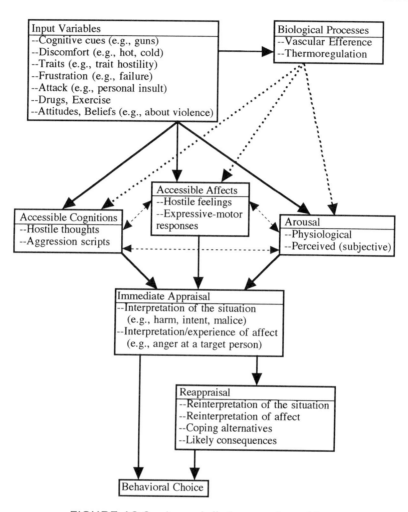

FIGURE 10.2   A general affective aggression model.

Our framework posits three main routes through which various input variables can influence aggressive behavior. Certain environmental factors (e.g., frustration) or individual differences (e.g., aggressive personality) can increase the accessibility of hostile thoughts, hostile feelings, or physiological arousal (see Figure 10.2). The automatic priming of aggressive thoughts and feelings may well come about, in part, because of the biological processes at work. For instance, Zajonc's vascular theory may account (in part or full) for increases in hostile affect in hot temperatures. Other thermoregulatory processes may also create specific aggression-related emotional and cognitive states via hormonal and neural links.

Consistent with CNA and various cognitive models, these initial priming effects may well spread to a variety of associated thoughts, feelings, scripts, and motor programs. All this sets the stage for subsequent aggressive behavior. When in such a state, people may feel more angry and may interpret ambiguous remarks as being more hostile than they normally would. In turn, this can influence how they behave. Under the right (or wrong) circumstances, an aggressive behavior may well result, which begins a reciprocal aggression cycle with another person that can spiral out of control.

In our model, situational factors such as hot temperatures as well as individual differences such as hot temperaments (aggressive personality) operate by making aggression-related thoughts and emotions readily accessible for application to the current situation. In other words, a variety of factors can increase the person's "preparedness" to aggress. Other factors may mitigate or exacerbate the aggressive impulse and its eventual expression in behavior. Such factors may influence the initial appraisal or the reappraisal processes. For instance, learning about mitigating circumstances may decrease a person's anger at someone who has thwarted their attempts at some task and may also decrease retaliative behaviors toward that person (e.g., Dill & Anderson, 1995).

PRACTICAL SIGNIFICANCE

The third and final major issue concerns practical implications. Although many implications follow directly from the work on the temperature–aggression hypothesis, others follow from the broader theoretical context concerning affective aggression. If the temperature–aggression hypothesis is correct, what can be done to reduce unwarranted aggressive behavior in society? In what situations or contexts would an intervention be likely to work? What type of interventions are likely to produce the desired effects? These issues will be examined at the end of the chapter, after empirical and theoretical issues have been presented and discussed in detail.

EPISTEMOLOGICAL STRATEGIES

This section specifies the epistemological strategies and assumptions used in examining the temperature–aggression literature. Definitions of key concepts used throughout this chapter are also spelled out in some detail.

TRIANGULATION

Triangulation is best illustrated by the following quote by Richard Cardinal Cushing (New York Times, 1964), commenting on the propriety of calling Fidel Castro a communist, "When I see a bird that walks like a duck and swims like duck and quacks like a duck, I call that bird a duck."

In other words, one extremely valuable way of examining a proposition is to test it from several different perspectives. If the results of tests from several perspectives converge on the same answer, confidence grows. This approach has a variety of names such as "multiple operationism" or "triangulation" (e.g., Anderson, 1987; Campbell & Fiske, 1959; Crano & Brewer, 1973; Feigl, 1958; McGrath, Martin, & Kukla, 1982).

In the temperature–aggression domain, three major perspectives have emerged: geographic region effects, time period effects, and concomitant heat effects (Anderson, 1989). Geographic region studies examine indices of aggression in regions that differ in climate or concurrent temperature. Do hotter cities have higher violent crime rates than cooler ones, for example? Time period studies examine aggression rates in one location (e.g., in one city, or one country) but in a number of different time periods that differ in temperature. Do hotter months produce higher violent crime rates than cooler ones? Concomitant studies assess aggression and temperature at the same time (i.e., concomitantly) and at several different times in which the temperature varies. For example, do subjects randomly assigned to a hot condition behave more aggressively toward a provoking confederate than subjects assigned to a comfortable temperature? In a sense, concomitant studies are really a subset of time period studies. The advantage of assessing temperature and aggression concomitantly is sufficiently important to warrant treating it as a separate perspective. These studies are typically performed in laboratory settings, although several impressive field studies of this type have also been conducted.

The main advantage of the triangulation approach is that weaknesses of a particular type of study usually do not apply to other types. Therefore, consistency of results across different types of studies allows us to triangulate or "home in" on a true causal factor. Thus, if the temperature–aggression hypothesis is supported in studies of geographic region effects, time period effects, and concomitant temperature aggression effects, we can be fairly sure that hot temperatures do have a direct effect on aggression.

META-ANALYSIS (IN SPIRIT, IF NOT IN METHOD)

The current popularity of meta-analytic techniques is often warranted and sometimes misplaced. On the one hand, using statistical procedures to combine the effect sizes of different studies examining the same hypothesis can be revealing, especially in literatures where there is considerable diversity of results and controversy in their interpretation. On the other hand, there is an unwarranted tendency to view the traditional narrative review approach as being vague and subjective. In actuality (at least, in our view) the traditional narrative review has many of the best features of a good meta-analysis. Both collect as many of the relevant studies as can be found. Both categorize the studies on the basis of potentially relevant features, such as type of dependent variable measure used, or the environmental setting of the research. Both test hypotheses about whether the underlying effect is consistent and whether certain features tend to increase, decrease, eliminate, or reverse the effect. Indeed, some "narrative" reviews of the past have statistically combined results from different studies to get a clearer view of the overall pattern of evidence (e.g., Anderson, 1989; Anderson, Miller, Riger, Dill, & Sedikides, 1994). This chapter has features of traditional narrative reviews and of meta-analytic approaches. The published literature was exhaustively searched for studies relevant to the temperature–aggression hypothesis. Unpublished material was excluded both because we are not particularly interested in establishing the exact effect size and because excluding unpublished work provides some quality control. In addition, a few of the published studies were excluded because their data were reported elsewhere, data were reported in so poor a fashion that we could not determine whether they really supported or contradicted a given position, or the methods used were so poor that any conclusions based on them would be misleading at best. Where possible, results of statistically combined sets of studies are presented. In most cases, officially sanctioned meta-analytic procedures were not used, either because they were not needed or because they seemed inappropriate. In essence, a meta-analytic approach as adopted in spirit, if not always in method.

DESTRUCTIVE TESTING

"Destructive testing" is a term borrowed from structural engineering and materials science (Timoshenko, 1953; Wilson, 1984). It is best illustrated by analogy. A new metal alloy has been developed. Initial tests have shown it to be fairly strong. To find out just how strong it is, a series of destructive tests are conducted, i.e., increasing stresses are applied to a sample of the new alloy until it breaks. There is no question about whether it can be broken, only how much stress it can take before it does break.

The initial test of strength is analogous to a zero-order correlation, perhaps between the hotness of U.S. cities and their violent crime rates. It is a simple test of the basic theoretical hypothesis. Adding increasing stresses is analogous to adding various statistical controls to the regression model, such as poverty rates in various cities. The relevant question about the obtained relation between heat and aggression is not, "Can it withstand all possible attempts to reduce it to nonsignificance?" What is of interest in destructive testing is how much stress the target relation can withstand. The ultimate judgment concerning the strength of the target relation (here, temperature and violent crime rate) is somewhat subjective and will therefore differ from scholar to scholar. However, there are reasonable rules of thumb that all scholars can apply. For instance, control variables with good theoretical grounding are more appropriate and more informative than post hoc variables of dubious relevance.

Destructive testing is a hybrid of the traditional "theory centered" approach to science, in which hypotheses are derived from a formal theory and then tested, and the "result centered" approach advocated by Greenwald, Pratkanis, Leippe, and Baumgardner (1986), in which one asks, "Under what conditions does x lead to y?" rather than "Does x lead to y?" This approach was applied in evaluating the current temperature–aggression hypothesis literature (for a more detailed presentation of destructive testing, see Anderson & Anderson, 1996).

DEFINITIONS

Some of the controversy in the temperature–aggression hypothesis literature stems from ambiguous definitions of key concepts. Definitions for several concepts are provided to reduce this problem.

Aggression, Affective Aggression, and Violence

"Aggression," "affective aggression," and "violence" are used interchangeably in this chapter, with the only distinction being that violence is restricted to the most extreme types of aggressive behavior. Our definition includes three components. First, these terms refer to behavioral acts, not to thoughts or feelings. We explicitly specify when we mean "aggressive cognitions" or "aggressive feelings." Second, the primary intent of these acts is to harm the victim. Third, there is a large anger/hostility component in the acts.

Some behaviors typically classified as violent do not meet this definition. For instance, robbery is classified by the FBI as a violent crime. However, in our view the primary intent in most robberies is not to harm the target, it is to gain some economic benefit. Thus, because of the motive ambiguity, robbery is not included as a measure of aggression or violence.

Another somewhat ambiguous case is rape. Although it is clear that rape is violent in its consequences to the victim, there is some debate about what portion of rapes are perpetrated with harm as the primary intent (e.g., Felson, 1993). We believe that a significant portion of rapes are intended to harm the victim, and that anger or hostility toward the victim is a part of many rapes. Thus, rape is included as a measure of aggression/violence. However, because of the mixed motives involved, one might expect weaker relationships between rape and aggression-instigating variables than between more purely aggressive acts (e.g., assault) and aggression-instigating variables. In sum, our definition of aggression includes most acts that typically have been labeled as spontaneous aggression, pain-induced aggression, and affective aggression.

Temperature Aggression Hypothesis vs Heat Effect

The *temperature aggression hypothesis* refers to the theoretical statement that uncomfortable temperatures cause increases in aggressive motivation and (under the right conditions) in aggressive behavior, and that they do so in a direct fashion. In most cases the temperature–aggression hypothesis refers to the "hot" side of this relation. On occasion, however, it also refers to the "cold" temperature side. As noted in earlier works (e.g., Anderson & Anderson, 1996), any theoretical hypothesis is protected from disconfirmation by multiple translation layers; the more abstract the theory, the more translation layers are necessary to get to the specific empirical realizations that can be subjected to testing.

The *heat effect* refers to an empirical observation that hot temperatures are positively associated with increased aggressive behavior. It is, essentially, a brief description of a specific type of empirical relation.

With these epistemological and definitional issues in hand, we now turn to the empirical literature. When possible, we will summarize findings presented in Anderson (1989). Newer results will be presented in greater detail.

GEOGRAPHIC REGION

Anderson's earlier reviews (1989; Anderson & DeNeve, 1992) revealed amazing levels of consistency in geographic region effects across countries and eras. Hotter locations have higher violent crime rates than cooler locations within the same country.

EARLY STUDIES

Some of the early studies of the temperature–aggression hypothesis do not present data in sufficient detail to allow statistical analysis. Nonetheless, the results are impressive in their consistency. For instance, Guerry (cited in Brearley, 1932) reported that in the years 1826–1830 crimes against people (e.g., assault) were twice as prevalent in southern France as in central or northern France, whereas crimes against property (e.g., burglary) were twice as prevalent in the north. Similarly, Lombroso (1911) reported that the homicide rate in the south of England was almost 10 times that of northern England.

Other studies did allow some form of statistical analysis. Lombroso (1911) reported several aggressive crime rates by degrees latitude of the region for both Spain and Italy. In both countries, of course, latitude is essentially a proxy measure of average temperature. Anderson (1989) found that in Lombroso's data violent crime rates correlated significantly and positively with latitude in both countries. Brearly (1932) reported the state-level homicide rates in the United States during the 1918–1929 time period. Anderson (1989) showed that in Brearly's data "the southern states had dramatically higher homicide rates ($M = 19.37$ per 100,000) than did the northern states [$M = 3.55$, $t(16) = 7.93$, $p < .001$]" (p. 79).

MODERN ERA STUDIES

None of the early studies included controls for other variables such as poverty rate, other than by restricting aggression rate comparisons to within country comparisons. Several modern era studies similarly focused primarily on the heat effect with minimal attention to possible third-variable controls. Lester (1986) compared the homicide rates of the 45 largest standard metropolitan statistical areas (SMSAs, i.e., cities) in the United States in 1970. Predictor variables included average temperature and precipitation (30-year averages), latitude, and longitude. Of most relevance here was the finding that temperature was strongly correlated with the homicide rate ($r = .54, p < .001$).

Two studies compared aggression rates as a function of climate across countries and cultures. The one by Robbins, DeWalt, and Pelto (1972) included measures of behavior that would meet our definition of aggression (homicide) as well as one that is less clearly an example of affective aggression (incidence of warfare). They found a significant positive relation between temperature and homicide ($p < .01$), but no relation with warfare. Schwartz (1968) similarly found no relation among the temperatures of 51 countries and frequency of political violence. In other words, the heat effect is by and large restricted to what we have termed affective aggression. More planful violence, such as wars and revolutions, does not appear to be related to temperature.

Other studies in the modern era have included various types of socioeconomic and social controls. deFronzo's (1984) study of crime rates in 142 SMSAs in the United States in 1970 included such controls. Although the results provided support for the temperature–aggression hypothesis at the level of zero-order correlations, statistical analysis shortcomings preclude any firm judgments about the strength of the heat effect when socioeconomic factors are controlled (for more details, see Anderson, 1989). Rosenfeld (1986) included some socioeconomic factors in two studies of crime rates in U.S. cities in 1970 and found significant region effects. Southern cities were especially higher than northern ones on murder and assault. Other region studies (Rotton, 1986; Rotton, Barry, & Kimble, 1985) have also found support for the temperature–aggression hypothesis, despite some conceptual and statistical ambiguities (for more details, see Anderson, 1989). The most extensive geographic region study is one on 1980 crime rates in 260 SMSAs (Anderson, 1987). That study included 14 "social" variables for each city such as unemployment, per capita income, education, age, and racial composition. The results were that hotter cities had higher violent crime rates even when other social variables were statistically controlled.

More recently, Anderson and Anderson (1996) recreated this data set with several modifications. The most important addition was a "southern culture of violence" index for each city. White arrest rate data were also gathered for these same cities in 1980, in response to Nisbett's (1993) suggestions that his "culture of honor" thesis can explain the higher incidence of violent crime in the south and that only white perpetrator data are relevant. The specific procedures and results are described in the following section.

Violent Crime Rates in U.S. Cities

Aggression

Two measures of violent crime were constructed. The first was a z-score composite of overall murder, rape, and assault rates. The second was a z-score composite of murder, rape, and assault arrest rates for the white population, as suggested by Nisbett's work.

Southernness

Each city's southernness was indexed by converting three indicators to z scores and summing them. One indicator was a simple south–nonsouth distinction based on U.S. Census Bureau classifications. Cities in southern states were assigned a score of 1, whereas nonsouth cities were given a score of 0. The second indicator was Gastil's (1971) southernness index, based on migration patterns from the old south. The third indicator was the percentage of voters who voted for George Wallace in the 1968 presidential election (Scammon, 1970). Preliminary analyses revealed that this SCV index was linearly and curvilinearly related to violent crime. We therefore converted the SCV index score to z scores and then created a quadratic term (SCV^2). This procedure allowed us to examine the linear SCV effect on violent crime independently of the curvilinear component.

Temperature

The hotness of each city was assessed with a four-item summed index of z scores. The items were (1) number of hot days ($\geq 32.2°C$, $90°F$), (2) number of cold days ($\leq 0°C$, $32°F$), (3) cooling degree days (amount of cooling needed to maintain a comfortable base temperature of $18.3°C$, $65°F$), and (4) heating degree days (amount of heating needed to maintain a comfortable base temperature of $18.3°C$, $65°F$). The number of cold days and heating degree days were multiplied by -1 so that larger scores meant warmer temperatures on all indicators.

Social Variables

The 12 social variables used were unemployment rate, per capita income, poverty rate, mobility (percentage living in a different home in 1975), high school education (percentage of the ≥ 25-year-old population that had graduated), college education (percentage of the ≥ 25-year-old population that had attended 4 or more years), population size, percentage Black, percentage Spanish, percentage less than 18 years old, percentage 18–64 years old, and median age.

Results: Heat Effect on Violence

Figure 10.3 presents the results from several regression analyses on the heat effect on violence. As can be seen, regardless of whether we examine overall crime rates, or the white arrest rate for violent crime, temperature significantly predicts violence rate differences in major U.S. cities. This is true even when all 12 social variables and the southernness index are partialled out first.

Results: Southernness Effect on Violence

Figure 10.4 presents the parallel results when the southernness index is the predictor of interest. As can be seen in Figure 10.4, the linear correlations between the southernness index and both violence measures are positive and statistically significant when the only other predictor in the model is the curvilinear term. However, controlling for temperature and other predictor variables eliminates the linear southernness effect on overall violent crime rate and appears to reverse its effect on the white arrest rate for violent crime.

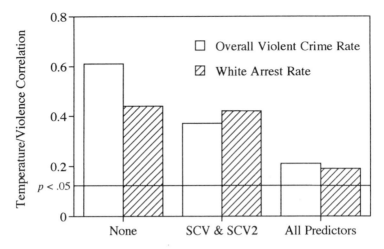

Variable(s) Partialled from the Temperature/Violence Relation

FIGURE 10.3   Zero-order and partial correlations between temperature and violence.

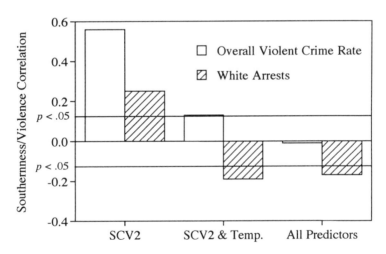

Variable(s) Partialled from the Linear SCV/Violence Relation

FIGURE 10.4   Partial correlations between southernness (SCV) and violence.

Results: Latent Variable Analysis

In the preceding regression analyses, all 12 social variables were used. A look at the list of variables reveals some redundancy in them. For instance, there are several measures of average wealth or poverty. To get a better picture of the relationship between temperature and the violent crime rate, a number of latent

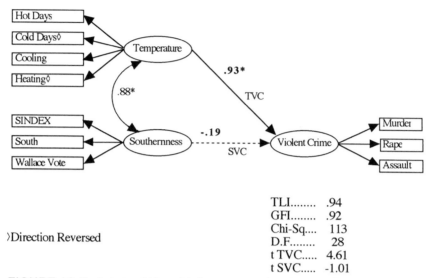

TLI........ .94
GFI........ .92
⟩Direction Reversed
Chi-Sq.... 113
D.F........ 28
t TVC..... 4.61
t SVC..... -1.01

FIGURE 10.5   Latent variable model of temperature and southernness effects on violent crime.

variable models were tested. Getting a model with a good overall fit and without serious statistical shortcomings proved to be a difficult task. Figure 10.5 presents a simple model that includes only violence, temperature, and southernness variables.[2] As can be seen from Figure 10.5, the overall fit was quite good according to the Tucker–Lewis index, the goodness-of-fit index, and the ratio of χ^2 to degrees of freedom (Church & Burke, 1994; Marsh, Balla, & McDonald, 1988; Marsh & Hocevar, 1985). Figure 10.5 also shows that the latent temperature factor is significantly related to the violent crime latent factor, whereas southernness is not. Indeed, the southernness relation to violent crime is even in the wrong direction.

Figure 10.6 adds the three social variables that produced the best fit, given theoretical constraints. The percentage of the city population that was classified as Black or Spanish (Census Bureau designations) and the poverty rate combined to produce a latent factor called low socioeconomic status (SES). Population size also proved to be a valuable predictor of violent crime rate, but it did not form a meaningful latent factor. The results of this analysis were very similar to the model that did not include any of the social variables. The various fit indices all yielded acceptable fits. The latent temperature factor was significantly related to the latent violent crime factor. Southernness was related to violent crime in the direction predicted by the southern culture of violence model, but not significantly so ($t < 1$). In addition, the low SES latent factor was positively related to violent crime. Cities

[2]Error terms and correlations among error terms in the final model are not displayed in Figures 10.5 and 10.6 to simplify the picture. We tested identical models with a quadratic southernness measure as well. The basic results shown in Figures 10.5 and 10.6 were replicated, but there were statistical shortcomings that led us to prefer the displayed models.

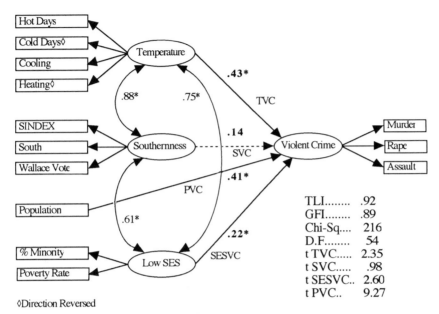

FIGURE 10.6 Latent variable model of temperature and southernness effects on violent crime, with three social variables.

with large, poor, minority populations had higher violent crime rates. Finally, population size was positively related to violent crime rates, even though this data set (restricted to SMSAs) contains only fairly large metropolitan areas.

SUMMARY OF GEOGRAPHIC REGION STUDIES

Across a wide range of years and countries, the geographic region studies produce a highly consistent picture of heat effects. Hotter regions in the United States and in several western European countries have higher violent crime rates than cooler regions. The more recent studies that have included statistical controls for various possible confounds and indirect effects show that the heat effect in region studies cannot be easily dismissed as artifactual.

Of course, by themselves these studies do not rule out all possible indirect effects. For instance, it is possible that better measures of southern culture of violence would yield somewhat different results. For example, it is possible that an attitude/value measure of adherence to the culture of honor, administered to a representative sample of residents of each city, would eliminate the heat effect when partialled out statistically. In other words, it could be that hot locations have tended to produce cultures of honor in which high violence is a part of being well socialized. If true, this temperature/culture of honor relationship would then need explaining. As noted elsewhere (Anderson & Anderson, 1996), the temperature–aggression hypothesis could easily handle such a state of affairs. If hot temperatures do tend to increase aggressive behaviors, cultures that develop and evolve in hot climates would tend to develop rationales (or rationalizations) for violent acts committed by its high status citizens. In other words, direct heat effects could, over time, lead to the development of a set of attitudes and values that encourage violence, at least under certain "honorable" conditions.

Several theories remain plausible as explanations for the obtained heat effect in these region studies. Routine activity theory could be playing a role, although certain versions of it cannot account for the findings. Perhaps the typical "routine" activities of people in warmer climates are those that promote aggressive behaviors. There may be more intermingling of people in general, increasing the potential for conflict and violence.

Although data argue against a strong version of southern culture of honor theory—the version that says all region-based heat effects are due to SCV and none are due to direct heat effects—a weaker version seems plausible and is not completely ruled out by extant findings. There may well be a southern culture of violence that has developed in the U.S. south, and it may continue to increase violence independently of direct heat effects. Nisbett's preliminary studies on his version of culture of honor (e.g., Nisbett, 1993) are quite interesting in this regard.

The general model of affective aggression is more strongly supported by these region data than are other theories. The temperature–aggression hypothesis aspect of the general model has survived a number of possible disconfirmations, and thus gains strength.

TIME PERIOD

Time period studies examine aggression rates across time periods that differ in temperature. Many such studies have been conducted using time periods of various lengths, with the unit of analysis being as short as a day or as long as a year. Because humans are skilled at carrying grudges and recreating earlier emotional states, time periods of less than 1 day are probably inappropriate except for studies in which the target aggressive behaviors can be carried out by the subject almost immediately. (Most laboratory studies of aggression have this characteristic, for example.) Anderson (1989) presents a detailed summary of many time period studies. This section mentions those studies briefly and focuses on more recent studies.

HOT DAYS

Anderson (1989) analyzed Dexter's (1899) New York City assault data and found both linear and curvilinear effects of temperature on the relative frequency of assaults (both $ps < .001$). The specific form of this relation was that at cool temperatures, slight increases in temperature had only a small impact on assault, whereas at uncomfortably warm temperatures, further increases in temperature yielded relatively large increases in assaults. Carlsmith and Anderson's (1979) study of riots in the United States in 1967–1971, Harries and Stadler's (1988) study of assault in Dallas, Rotton's (1982) study of rape in Dayton, Rotton and Frey's (1985) study of assaults and family disturbances in Dayton, Cotton's (1986) studies of violent crime in Des Moines and in Indianapolis, and Anderson and Anderson's (1984) studies of violent crime in Chicago and in Houston all produced similar findings of maximum aggression in the highest temperature ranges. Interestingly, several of these studies also examined heat effects on less aggressive crimes such as burglary. The heat effects were consistently weaker for these "less violent" crimes (Anderson & Anderson, 1984; Cotton, 1986).

More recent studies add to the consistency of the heat effect in daily time period studies. Three studies have used calls to police departments as criterion variables. LeBeau and Langworthy (1986) studied the frequency of "calls for service" to the Chicago Police Department during 1976–1979. They found (among other interesting effects) that temperature was the best predictor. As temperature went up, so did the frequency of calls. However, because calls for service include calls for relatively nonaggressive problems as well as aggression-related ones, the results must be interpreted with caution.

Walters (1991) examined temperature and pollen counts as predictors of frequency of 911 calls to the Kansas City, Kansas, police department in the years 1986–1989 from March 1 through October 31 in each year. Data for each year were broken down into three time periods: March 1–May 24, May 25–August 14, and August 15–October 31. Results were reported in the form of correlations in each time period in each of the 4 years. The temperature/police call correlations were averaged for each time period across years. For each time period the average temperature/police call correlation was significant (all p values < .01), $r = .57$, $r = .18$, and $r = .49$, for the first, second, and third time periods, respectively. Even though each was significant, it is obvious that the lowest correlations occurred in the second time period. We suspect that this is due to a relatively smaller range (or standard deviation) of temperatures in that late spring/early summer time period, although we cannot be certain of this. It is also interesting to note that partialling out the pollen count factor did not appreciably affect the temperature/police call correlations. Once again, these data support the temperature–aggression hypothesis, but caution in interpretation is warranted because not all 911 calls involve affective aggression. (Walters reports that about 85% of these calls are for police assistance of some kind.)

Another interesting study of the heat effect in daily time periods is Reifman, Larrick, and Fein's (1991) study of aggression in major league baseball. The criterion variable was the number of players hit by a pitch (HBP) in the 1986–1988 seasons. A regression analysis of the heat effect included statistical controls for walks, wild pitches, passed balls, errors, home runs, and attendance. The heat effect was still significant ($p < .002$), with relatively more HBPs in games played on hotter days. Other control procedures were used to rule out the possibility that some teams whose home games were played in hot climates were simply more likely to have high HBPs regardless of temperature. Finally, in a replication study, data from the 1962 season showed essentially the same heat effect correlation.

Cohn (1993) examined weather and temporal variables as predictors of police calls for service for rape and for domestic violence in Minneapolis for the years 1985, 1987, and 1988. Although the results are complex and occasionally difficult to interpret, the main findings of relevance to this chapter are (a) temperature was strongly related to both types of violence (p values < .001), (b) higher temperatures yielded higher violence rates, and (c) rape was less predictable by the whole set of variables than was domestic violence. Cohn (1993) discussed several possible reasons for the weaker results on the rape measure. Of particular interest is her discussion of other work showing that a significant portion of rapes are planned. This suggests, as noted earlier, that rape may well be a less pure exemplar of spontaneous affective aggression and thus should be examined separately from purer acts of affective aggression such as assault and murder. One alternative explanation of the weaker results for rape concerns the incidence rate. Domestic violence calls were about 40 times as frequent as rape calls, which would tend to make the domestic violence measure less susceptible to random fluctuations in frequency than rape.[3]

Cohn and Rotton (1997) conducted a time series analysis of the reported assaults in Minneapolis in 1987 and 1988 as a function of time of day, day of week, month, and temperature. (Many other "control" variables were also included, but are not particularly relevant to this chapter.) The study was performed to test (a) the NAE-inverted U shape prediction of the temperature–aggression relation and (b) the RAT assumption that time of day moderates the relation between temperature and assault rates. The authors found significant positive relations between temperature and assault for every time period (in 3-hr intervals) except between 6:00 and 11:59 a.m. This complex data set contains many other interesting results. For instance, evidence shows that time of day and day of week moderate the effects of temperature on assault. This is entirely consistent with any model of aggression: opportunities are needed to aggress, and opportunities vary by day of week and time of day.

One of the main conclusions of the article—that there was a significant downturn in assault as temperatures became hot—is simply not borne out by the re-

---

[3]Cohn's regression approach included linear, quadratic, and cubic terms, represented by the raw temperature (T), raw temperature squared (T^2), and raw temperature cubed (T^3). In some analyses the squared and cubed terms were kept without all of the lower order terms. This creates some difficult interpretation problems because the higher order terms are necessarily highly confounded with the lower order terms unless raw data are first converted to deviation score form. Thus, the finding that only the T^2 term yielded a significant effect in the 1985/1987 domestic violence model (Cohn's Table 7) could be misinterpreted as meaning that only a curvilinear effect occurred. However, plotting a line using the T^2 beta and T^2 scores (e.g., 40° becomes 1600, 50° becomes 2500 . . .) and then converting the x axis back to linear temperature produces the heat effect curve frequently found in this literature. At low temperatures, there were little increases in domestic violence rates with small increases in temperature, but at uncomfortably warm temperatures, further increases produced large increases in domestic violence. This is actually both a linear and a quadratic effect. Similar interpretational ambiguities exist with the 1985/1987 rape model, which included T and T^3, but not T^2.

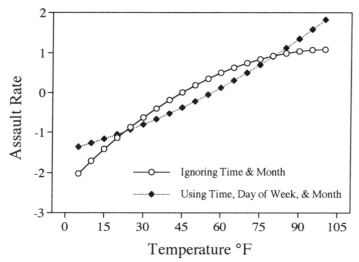

FIGURE 10.7 Relationship between temperature and standardized assault rate in Minneapolis (1987–1988). Slopes were derived from Cohn and Rotton (1997).

ported results. Conceptual, methodological, and statistical problems with this study take us well beyond this chapter (for a more thorough critique, see Bushman, Anderson, & Anderson, 1998). Two of these problems are particularly important.

The first problem concerns interpretation of the results reported in the article. Most results actually showed a clear linear relationship between temperature and assault rates, but little evidence of a downturn in assault at higher temperatures. For example, in the 56 day of week (7) × time of day (eight 3-hr blocks) analyses the linear temperature term was positively ($p < .05$) related to assault 29 times. However, the curvilinear temperature term yielded a statistically significant effect in only 10 cases, and in 7 of those the slope was positive, indicating that at hotter temperatures assault rates increased more rapidly with further temperature increases. These findings clearly contradict Cohn and Rotton's (1997) paramount conclusion that the shape of the temperature–assault relation is an inverted U; they also exemplify how overaggregation of data is problematic when analyses reveal interesting differences in effects at more microscopic levels of analysis. If the analyses that purported to show important day of week and time of day effects are accurate, then the best way to estimate the overall (or average) relationship between temperature and assault rate is to average the linear and curvilinear (quadratic) slopes across the 56 day of week (7) × time of day (eight 3-hr blocks) sets and plot the resulting equation. These averages are computed and the resulting regression line (with the diamonds) is plotted in Figure 10.7. This line shows that not only did assault rates continue to climb at the hottest of normal temperatures, but they increased at a faster rate. This is because the average curvilinear slope was positive. Even this regression line may underestimate the true heat effect because of other temperature-related "control" variables in the statistical model.

The second problem concerns the use of temperature-related "control" variables. Statistically controlling for the month of the year may have artificially reduced the effect of the linear temperature term on assault. Because month is highly correlated with temperature, removing the variance (in the assault rate) that is associated with month effects may remove much of the variance that is truly part of the temperature effect. Although Cohn and Rotton (1997) claim that removing month from the statistical model produced little change, it did in fact significantly change the shape of the temperature–assault curve. A model with month statistically controlled yielded linear and curvilinear slopes (+.0337 and –.0006, respectively) that produce a major decline in assault rates beginning at about 77°F. However, a model that differed only in the removal of month as a control variable yielded slopes that produce continued increases in assault rates through 100°F. The line with the circles in Figure 10.7 displays this latter temperature effect on assault. Other "control" variables in various models (including both models in Figure 10.7) may also have artificially deflated the statistical estimate of the linear temperature term as well. Furthermore, these two models (with and without month as a control variable) further suffer from the over-aggregation problem outlined in the preceding paragraph.

In sum, although both of the lines in Figure 10.7 already contradict the main conclusions of Cohn and Rotton (1997), there is reason to believe that statistical models that produced these lines inappropriately reduce the estimated increases in assault rates at high temperatures. The "diamond" line in Figure 10.7 is based on a statistical model that uses inappropriate temperature-related control variables. The "circle" line is based on a model that overaggregates across time and day of the week.

Other problems also warrant attention. Minneapolis is an inappropriate city to sample when testing linear and curvilinear temperature effects because the NAE downturn is posited to begin in the mid-eighties. Minneapolis reaches truly hot temperatures far less often than do southern cities, and there may well have been too few time periods with truly hot temperatures to accurately test for a hot downturn in assault. Furthermore, use of assault reporting rates is problematic when studying time of day effects because assault reports may frequently occur well after the crime has been committed. Also, heat stress may have a cumulative effect over time that is expressed later, sometimes during somewhat cooler periods of time. The point is that although the Cohn and Rotton data are useful for some purposes (e.g., testing whether there are general day of week or time of day effects, or testing the general heat hypothesis that hotter temperatures are generally related to violence), such field data are not very useful for testing specific hypotheses involving the exact shape of the temperature–aggression relationship. Thus, they cannot precisely test the NAE predicted downturn in aggression at about 85° versus a simple negative affect model predicting continued increases in violence through the normal temperature range (i.e., about 98°F).

In sum, the Cohn and Rotton (1997) results appear largely inconsistent with the NAE model and consistent with a model in which aggressive tendencies continue to increase throughout the normal temperature range. However, as noted earlier, studies of reported crime rates do not appropriately test the exact shape of the temperature–aggression relationship. More accurate tests of shape may be conducted in laboratory settings where the time and temperature of the instigation to aggress are known or in field studies that similarly assess instigation, temperature, and aggression concomitantly (e.g., Kenrick & MacFarlane, 1984; Reifman et al., 1991). As noted in other works and later in this chapter, we believe that under certain conditions a downturn at moderately uncomfortable temperatures may well occur.

HOT MONTHS

Murder

Anderson (1989) combined monthly murder rate percentages in the United States across studies by Brearley (1932), Cohen (1941), Iskrant and Joliet (1968), Lester (1979), and Michael and Zumpe (1983). An analysis of variance on these monthly percentages yielded a significant month effect ($p < .001$). The peak murder months were July and August, followed closely by December. The high December rate appears to be due to routine activities involved with Christmas, which often involve excessive alcohol consumption.

Assault

A combined analysis of monthly assault rate patterns in the United States was presented in Anderson (1989). The seven data sets came from Aschaffenburg (1903/1913), Cohen (1941), Dexter (1899), Dodge and Lentzner (1980), Michael and Zumpe (1983), and Perry and Simpson (1987). The result, displayed in Figure 10.8, was a significant month effect ($p < .001$) with a peak in the hot summer months.

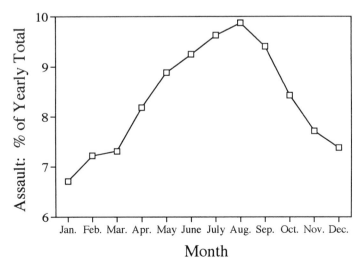

FIGURE 10.8   Monthly distribution of assaults. Adapted from Anderson (1989).

Rape

Monthly rape patterns were also examined in detail by Anderson (1989). The data sets were taken from Amir (1971), Aschaffenburg (1903/1913), Hayman, Lanza, Fuentes, and Algor (1972), Lombroso (1899/1911), Michael and Zumpe (1983), and Perry and Simpson (1987). There were eight data sets from four countries (England, France, Germany, and the United States) in these sources. An ANOVA yielded a significant month effect that paralleled the assault results, with the most rapes occurring in the hot summer months ($p < .001$).

Spouse Abuse

Several other monthly studies are reviewed in Anderson (1989), with the same general finding that aggression peaks in summer months. One of these studies deserves special mention because its findings relate to several alternative hypotheses. Some critics have suggested that assaults and rapes occur more frequently in the warmer months because of more frequent contact among potential victims and perpetrators (i.e., people get out more in the summer) and because of "women's scantier clothing" being provocative. Michael and Zumpe (1986) reasoned that if these alternative explanations were true, then wife battering should not show the typical summer increase. One could even argue that wife battering should go down, as the increase in "getting out" should decrease the time and opportunity for wife battering. If aggression is directly temperature related, though, the same summer increase observed for other violent crimes should be obtained with spouse abuse.

Michael and Zumpe (1986) examined crisis calls to 23 different women's shelter organizations in five locations during 1981–1984 (at least 2 consecutive years of data from each location). In each location the annual rhythm maximum occurred in either July or August ($p < .025$). In each case the pattern of monthly abuse means corresponded very closely to monthly temperature means. Michael and Zumpe (1986) further noted that ". . . the maxima for wife abuse in Atlanta and Texas occurred about 40 days earlier in the year than those in Oregon and California; this difference in timing corresponded (within a few days) to the differences in the rape maxima in these states, which correlated with the times of the local temperature maxima" (p. 640). Finally, they noted that the photoperiod maxima (the maximum amount of daylight, another alternative to the temperature interpretation) in these locations did not show this 40-day difference.

These data do not rule out the possibility that some type of routine activity effect also occurs independently of temperature, but they do show that the routine activity theory (or women's scantier clothing, or photoperiod shifts) cannot account for the summer increase in wife battering. Michael and Zumpe imply that it is more parsimonious to ascribe monthly effects on a variety of aggressive behaviors to the same causal factor, i.e., the direct heat effect, than to adopt different (and largely untested) explanations for different forms of affective aggression. We agree.

New Monthly Studies

A number of studies using month as the target time period have provided additional support. This section begins, however, with a study that at first appears to support the temperature–aggression hypothesis, but is actually irrelevant to it. Field (1992) reported a sophisticated time series analysis of 40 years of crime data in England and Wales, primarily as a test of routine activity theory. Field reasoned that many types of crime, including nonviolent property crimes, should be more prevalent when people are out of their homes. He further proposed that people should be out of their homes more often when the weather is nice, *relative to normal weather patterns*. He thus adjusted all the raw data for seasonal effects, i.e., monthly crime data as well as weather data were seasonally adjusted prior to the main regression analyses. The main finding was that *seasonally adjusted temperature* was a significant predictor of *seasonally adjusted crime* rates for violent crimes, sexual offenses, burglary, theft, and criminal damage, but not for robbery. On the whole, these data support routine activity theory, although the lack of an effect on robbery is problematic, as is the failure of rainfall to predict crime rates. However, these analyses are irrelevant to the temperature–aggression hypothesis, as noted by Field. The seasonal adjustment procedure essentially "adjusts out" most (or all) of the direct heat effects. Monthly crime patterns may well be influenced by both routine activities and more direct heat effects. "It is entirely possible that temperature affects the level of crime both through a direct [effect] on aggression and through the mediation of social behaviour" (Field, 1992, p. 348). Field (1992) also noted that many temperature findings, such as the Michael and Zumpe (1986) wife-battering study, ". . . (are) obviously not easily explicable in terms of routine activities" (p. 349).

A similar study, which involved time series analysis (Landau & Fridman, 1993), tested seasonal fluctuations in monthly robbery and homicide rates in Israel between January 1977 and February 1985. Landau and Fridman found an increase in robbery rates during winter months (November–February) that they explained with the routine activity explanation that cost of living increases in the winter months, which leads to stealing. A seasonal effect was not found for homicide, however. Homicides were highest in August, with March, May, and December following in frequency. Landau and Fridman state that the lack of a seasonality effect on the homicide findings contradicts the temperature–aggression hypothesis and that the strong August homicide effect is due to an increase in social interaction in that month. As Landau and Fridman note, the lack of an effect of the other summer months (June and July) on homicide does not support this routine activity theory. One additional problem with this study is that the total number of homicides in such a relatively small population is so small that monthly rates are likely to be quite unstable. Thus, it is probably wise to draw no conclusions from this one study.

Several studies, including one by Haertzen, Buxton, Covi, and Richards (1993), have examined monthly variations in aggressive behaviors by prison inmates. Haertzen et al. (1993) examined the frequency of "rule infractions" among prisoners in a Maryland correctional institution from July 1987 to March 1991. Seasonal as well as month-based analyses were reported. They found a weak correlation between average monthly temperature and relative frequency of rule infractions ($r = .25$, $N = 45$, $p < .10$). However, because rule infractions include many nonaggressive violations (about 50% according to the authors), these data do not provide a clean test of the temperature–aggression hypothesis. The authors correctly noted that to study more specific and purely aggressive incidents, a larger sample of prisons over more years would be needed.

Other (earlier) studies of prisoner aggression suffer similar problems of ambiguity of aggression measures, relative infrequency of the target behaviors, and short time spans. Ganjavi, Schell, and Cachon (1985) studied the effects of several weather and geomagnetic factors on monthly rates of major violence (e.g., murder, assault) and minor violence (minor assault, suicide, self-injury) in six Canadian prisons from January 1980 to December 1983. The major violence rate was too rare to be of value. One of the prisons was for psychiatric inmates; its rate of minor violence was too low to be useful. The biggest problem from the standpoint of testing the temperature–aggression hypothesis was the inclusion of suicide and self-injury. Apparently, minor assaults were also quite rare. For these reasons, this study was not included in Anderson (1989) and is uninformative for this chapter as well.

Pettigrew (1985) examined monthly rates of simple fighting, aggravated fighting (with a weapon or accomplice), and self-mutilation in five Louisiana prisons from 1972 to 1982. Aggravated fighting is too rare to provide appropriate tests of the temperature–aggression hypothesis, and self-mutilation is not an affective aggression act as we have defined it. The simple fighting rate measure did correlate significantly with monthly average temperature ($r = .214$, $N = 180$, $p < .05$). Similarly, an analysis of variance on the monthly rates of simple fighting showed a significant month effect, with the July rate being significantly higher ($p < .05$) than every other month except June and August. However, the author pointed out that many prisoners seemed to get into minor scrapes intentionally during the hot summer months in order to be "punished" in a way that gets them out of summer field labor. Self-mutilation rates were similarly affected by temperature and a desire to avoid field labor. As a result, these data cannot be seen as adequate tests of the temperature–aggression hypothesis.

Finally, Linkowski, Martin, and DeMaertelaer (1992) reported a study of monthly rates of violent and nonviolent causes of death in Belgium over a 5-year period. Although there appeared to be some support for the temperature–aggression hypothesis—accidental violent death rates correlated positively and significantly with temperature for both men and women—ambiguities in the meaning of the different death rate categories and in the reported data analyses make firm conclusions very risky.

SEASONS/QUARTERS

Anderson (1989) presented considerable evidence (via reanalyses, in many cases) that aggressive behaviors occur more frequently in the summer (or third quarter) than in other times of the year. Data include a variety of types of violence: simple and aggravated assaults, uprisings, family disturbances, rape, and murder.

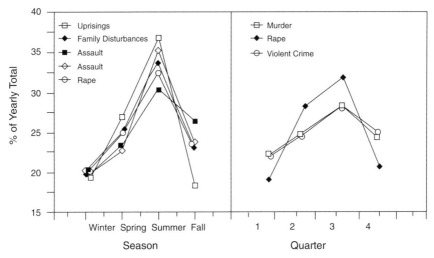

FIGURE 10.9   Quarterly and seasonal distribution of aggressive behavior. Adapted from Anderson (1989).

Data come from a variety of researchers (Anderson, 1987; Chang, 1972; Leffingwell, 1982; Lombroso, 1899/1911; Rotton & Frey, 1985), a variety of countries (e.g., England, Wales, the United States, Spain, others), and a variety of centuries (18th, 19th, and 20th). Figure 10.9 graphically summarizes these results.

Two additional studies of the temperature–aggression hypothesis with a seasonal methodology were intentionally left out of Anderson's (1989) review because of methodological problems. Both provide some support for the temperature–aggression hypothesis. Atlas (1984) studied assault rates in four Florida prisons. As noted by Anderson and DeNeve (1992), interpretational problems arise in this study because "some of the prisons had air conditioning in some places. The frequency of aggressive behaviors varied greatly from institution to institution. The number of hot, moderate, and cool days at each institution is not known" (p. 349). In addition, there did not appear to be any attempt to control for differing numbers of inmates in different months. Nonetheless, a simple reanalysis in which assaults were (a) totaled across the prisons, (b) converted to assault rates (per day), and (c) subjected to an ANOVA by quarter of the year (with three replications per quarter) produced a significant quarter effect [$F(3, 8) = 9.35$, p < .01]. The summer quarter (July, August, September) had the highest assault rate (M = 3.02, 3.20, 3.76, and 2.84 assaults per day for the first, second, third and fourth quarters, respectively). The methodological problems are severe, however, so we advise extreme caution in interpreting these particular results.

The second problematic seasonal study is the Pettigrew (1985) study of Louisiana prisons described earlier. The same interpretational problems that existed with monthly analyses also existed with seasonal ones. For the record though,

Pettigrew did find a significant increase in simple fighting among inmates in the summer ($p < .05$).[4]

YEARS

The first published study of the effect of hotter versus cooler years is a small-scale study by Anderson (1987) of violent crime rates in the United States over a 10-year period. This study found that hotter years were associated with higher violent crime rates.

More recently, Anderson, Bushman, and Groom (1997) have improved upon that earlier study in several ways in two new studies. Study 1 used time series regression procedures to test the effects of yearly average temperature and of age distribution on violent crime in the United States from 1950 to 1995. As expected, a significant ($p < .05$) positive relation between temperature and violent crime rate was observed, even after time series, age, and linear year effects were statistically controlled. On average, each 1°F increase in average temperature produced 3.68 more murders and assaults per 100,000 population. Nonviolent crimes were unaffected by average temperature.

Study 2 examined the effects of number of hot days ($\geq 90°F$) on the usual summer increase in violence. As expected, years with more hot days produced a bigger summer increase in violent crime than years with fewer hot days. Nonviolent crime was unaffected by the number of hot days.

SUMMARY OF TIME PERIOD EFFECTS

All told, time period studies produce an impressive array of support for the simple hypothesis that hot temperatures directly increase aggressive tendencies. Although routine activity theory can account for some of the results, it cannot account for all of them, as its supporters sometimes acknowledge (Field, 1992). The southern culture of violence position is totally silent on time period effects and thus cannot account for them.

CONCOMITANT STUDIES

As noted earlier, concomitant studies of the temperature–aggression hypothesis are actually a specific subcategory of time period studies. In concomitant studies, temperature and aggression are assessed at the same time. This allows stronger conclusions to be drawn in most cases because alternative explanations that rely on

---

[4]The reader should note that our criticisms of methodology should not be taken as criticisms of the researchers. We know how very difficult it is to get archival data that meet the methodological requirements of complex research questions. The first author, for instance, has tried unsuccessfully to get acceptable data on prison aggression rates. We understand, and hope that our readers will too, that researchers in this area must make do with whatever data are available.

timing differences are automatically ruled out. An additional methodological advantage is that concomitant studies can be conducted in the experimental laboratory. As noted by Anderson (1989), however, laboratory studies of the heat effect have, on the whole, produced a very mixed set of results. This section first reviews the few concomitant studies of the temperature–aggression hypothesis in naturalistic settings, then reviews the laboratory studies via meta-analytic techniques, and finally presents evidence from our laboratory that resolves many of the questions raised by prior research.

NATURALISTIC SETTINGS

Two early studies of the temperature–aggression hypothesis in naturalistic settings used horn honking as a dependent measure of aggression. Baron (1976) delayed motorists by a confederate whose car sat through a green light. Aggression was measured by latency to horn honking. The study was conducted when the temperatures were in the mid-80°F range. Subjects were classified as having air-conditioned or unair-conditioned cars. Those without air-conditioning presumably would be uncomfortably warm, and therefore should be more irritated by the confederate's blocking of the intersection and should, on average, honk sooner. Among other things, Baron (1976) found that subjects without air-conditioning honked their horns sooner than those with air-conditioning. Although this appears to support the temperature–aggression hypothesis, we advise caution in interpreting the study this way because latency to horn honking may be especially instrumental for those without air-conditioning. Thus, it is not clear that the latency measure assessed affective aggression or a more instrumental intent.

The second study of this type also investigated horn honking in response to a confederate blocking an intersection (Kenrick & MacFarlane, 1984). These researchers, though, assessed latency to honk, number of honks, and total time spent honking. The last two measures are not differentially instrumental as a function of temperature or as a function of air-conditioning and therefore may be seen as measures of affective aggression. In both cases, once one has honked the horn the instrumental role of further honking is negligible. Because all three measures were highly intercorrelated and yielded the same results, a composite of them was created and reported by Kenrick and MacFarlane (1984). This study was conducted in Phoenix with temperatures ranging from 84 to 108°F. As expected, there was a significant linear effect of temperature on horn honking ($p < .01$). Furthermore, this effect was significantly stronger for subjects without air-conditioned cars ($r = .757$) than for subjects in cars with air conditioning ($r = .12$, $Z = 2.54$, $p < .02$).

Vrij, van der Steen, and Kippellaar (1994) reported a field experiment on the heat hypothesis conducted in a police station. During a regular shooting exercise using the Fire Arms Training System, 38 Dutch police officers were randomly assigned to the hot (80°F) or comfortable (70°F) condition. The Fire Arms Training System uses video and laser discs and audio systems to provide officers with realistic scenarios to which they respond as police officers. The officers use laser "guns" in these scenarios. The scenario used in this study involved the officer responding to a burglary call at a shed and being confronted by a man holding a crowbar. The officers were videotaped during this session. After completing the scenario, each participant went to a comfortable room and completed several questionnaires measuring negative affect (annoyed and irritated), impression of the suspect (aggressive or not), impression of how threatening the suspect had been, and the officer's "tendency to shoot" the suspect. Finally, two measures of aggressive behavior were obtained based on the video tapes (percentage with firearm in hand, percentage who "shot" the suspect).

On each dependent variable, police officers in the hot condition displayed more negative responses than those in the comfortable condition. Hot participants reported more negative affect, a more aggressive impression of the suspect, a more threatening impression of the suspect, and a greater tendency to shoot the suspect; all these effects except the last one were statistically reliable. In addition, hot officers were significantly more likely to draw their weapon (41% vs 15%). Hot participants also "shot" more suspects (62%) than did cool participants (45%), but this difference was not statistically reliable.

On the whole, this work strongly supports the heat hypothesis. In all three naturalistic studies, hot participants behaved more aggressively than comfortable participants.

LABORATORY EXPERIMENTS

In many laboratory experiments, both temperature and anger have been manipulated to see if the heat effect is positive under low anger conditions and negative under high anger conditions. Anderson (1989) provides a detailed narrative review of most of the laboratory experiments on the temperature–aggression hypothesis. That article summarized the studies as follows: "On the whole, these laboratory studies . . . yield more confusion than understanding. Sometimes hotter conditions led to increases in aggression; at other times the opposite occurred. . . . The anger by temperature interaction sometimes occurred and sometimes did not. When it did occur, it usually took the form of a positive heat effect (increased heat–increased aggression) in nonangry conditions and a negative heat effect in angry conditions. In at least one instance the form was opposite" (p. 91).

Two studies were not included in that review. Baron and Lawton (1972) varied both temperature (hot versus comfortable) and whether a confederate modeled aggressive behavior. There appeared to be a weak negative heat effect in the no model conditions and a slightly positive effect in the aggressive model conditions, but neither effect approached significance. More recently, van Goozen, Frijda, Kindt, and van de Poll (1994) found no heat effect for either high dispositional anger or low dispositional anger subjects.

There has, nonetheless, been some controversy concerning whether the laboratory studies find effects consistent with the NAE model. [See Bell's (1992) comment on the Anderson (1989) review article and Anderson and DeNeve's (1992) response.] A meta-analysis was performed on the entire set of published laboratory studies in order to more objectively examine this question (Anderson & Anderson, 1996). In all, 28 comparisons of comfortable and hot conditions were found. Overall, there was no hint of consistency (d_+ = .060, 95% confidence interval = [−.114, .234]).

The NAE posits that at low levels of negative affect, further increases in negative affect will increase aggression, but at high levels of negative affect, further increases in negative affect will produce decreases in aggression because people will be focused on trying to escape rather than to aggress. Obviously, this is relevant only when escape and aggression motives lead to incompatible behaviors. The most common way of testing this interaction prediction in the temperature domain is to factorially manipulate temperature and anger. Thus, the prediction is that in high anger conditions hot temperatures should decrease aggression, whereas in low (or no) anger conditions the opposite should occur. Other context variables have also been manipulated, variables which either increase or decrease negative affect or willingness to aggress. For example, attitudinal similarity of the subject and the eventual target of aggression would decrease the negative affect whereas attitudinal dissimilarity and insult increase the negative affect. Thus, it is possible to categorize the experimental context on the basis of whether the nontemperature factors (e.g., insult, similar attitudes, cooling drink) produce a net increase in the negative affect. In the absence of hard data on the relative effectiveness of these different factors, we adopted the simple rule of assigning a +1 to positive factors (such as having similar attitudes) and −1 to negative factors (such as receiving an insult or having dissimilar attitudes). Conditions in which the net value of these nontemperature contextual factors was either positive or zero were placed in a "neutral context" category. Conditions in which the net was negative were placed in an "extra-negative context" category.

The 13 neutral context effects did yield a positive relation between temperature (hot vs comfortable), but it was just barely significantly different from zero (d_+ = .264, 95% CI = [.001, .526]). That is, hot temperatures appeared to increase aggression in these neutral context conditions, but not with great reliability. In contrast, the 15 extra-negative context effects yielded a negative heat effect, but this negative effect did not approach significance (d_+ = −.101, 95% CI = [−.333, .132]).

These results confirm Anderson's (1989) conclusions about the inconsistency of laboratory results in this domain. However, they also tend to fall in the direction predicted by NAE. Before leaving this issue, one additional caveat is needed. One of the studies that supports the NAE model at a behavioral level actually contradicts it in other ways (Palamarek & Rule, 1979). Specifically, these researchers included measures of escape motives and attributions for their affective state. Results of these measures contradict the NAE proposed mediating processes in two ways. First, the desire-to-escape measure yielded no significant effects; thus motivation to escape was not supported as a valid mediating variable. Second, subjects' ratings of the extent to which their mood was caused by the situation paralleled the aggression choices. Those in the hot angry and the cool nonangry conditions attributed their mood more to the situation than did the other subjects. Therefore, using the aggressive behavior data as supportive of the NAE model is problematic at best and misleading at worst. Furthermore, if these effects are removed from the meta-analysis, the positive heat effect in the neutral context and the negative heat effect in the extra-negative context both get even weaker (d_+ = .250, 95% CI = [−.028, .528], d_+ = −.089, 95% CI = [−.332, .154]).

Normally, we put high value on the external validity of laboratory studies (e.g., Anderson & Bushman, 1997). However, as noted in earlier works (e.g., Anderson, 1989; Rule & Nesdale, 1976) the laboratory studies of the temperature–aggression hypothesis may be especially vulnerable to artifactual processes or may not include all of the interpersonal dynamic processes that normally operate in temperature-induced aggression in naturalistic settings. In either case, the result could well be inconsistent findings. Still, we firmly believe that a better under-standing of heat effects as well as of affective aggression in general requires the precision and control available only in the laboratory. For this reason, we have (along with several others in our laboratory) been conducting laboratory research on heat and cold effects on aggressive behavior and on other aggression-related affects and cognitions. All of this work has been done in the context of a broad model of affective aggression, outlined earlier in this chapter. We turn now to a summary of what we have learned so far.

Temperature and Affect

State Hostility

In several studies we have investigated heat effects on a variety of types of af-fect. The results are quite consistent across study and paradigm. The most impor-tant affect from our perspective is what we have labeled "state hostility" (which is sometimes labeled as "anger"). The state hostility scale (Anderson et al., 1995) presents 35 statements (e.g., I feel furious) rated on five-point scales anchored at "strongly disagree" (1), "disagree" (2), "neither agree nor disagree" (3), "agree" (4), and "strongly agree" (5). Twelve items represent a lack of hostility (e.g., I feel polite); these are reverse scored. Across a number of studies we have shown that uncomfortably hot and uncomfortably cold temperatures increase state hostility (Anderson et al., 1996; Anderson et al., 1995; Anderson, Dorr, Anderson, & DeNeve, 1997). In general, participants in our studies report the least hostility at about 75–78°F. Cold temperatures in the 57–60°F range yield higher state hostil-ity ratings than comfortable temperatures, and about the same as 93–96°F.

General Negative Affect

Similar increases have been found in general negative affect in hot and cold conditions, compared to comfortable ones (Anderson et al., 1996). Specifically, self-ratings on the general descriptors "upset" and "distressed" were significantly higher in the hot and cold conditions in that study.

Hostile Attitudes

In one study (Anderson et al., 1996), participants completed the Caprara irritability scale (30 items; Caprara, Cinanni, D'Imperio, Passerini, Renzi, & Travablia, 1985) and the Velicer attitudes toward violence scale (46 items; Velicer, Huckel, & Hansen, 1989) in a comfortable (i.e., 75°F) room after doing some cognitive tasks under varying temperature conditions. All items were combined to form an overall hostile attitudes scale. The Caprara items focus on beliefs about how one has typically behaved in the past (e.g., when I am irritated, I need to vent my feelings immediately). The Velicer items focus on beliefs about various aggressive ways of behaving (e.g., university police should beat students if they are obscene). Despite the fact that all people were in a comfortable room at the time they completed these items, those who had earlier been in the uncomfortably hot or cold condition reported significantly more hostile beliefs.

Temperature and Arousal

The effects of hot and cold temperatures on physiological and subjective measures of arousal were examined (Anderson et al., 1995, 1996). It was found that hot temperatures increase heart rate but decrease perceived arousal relative to comfortable temperatures. Conversely, cold temperatures decrease heart rate but increase perceived arousal.

Temperature and Primed Cognitions

In one study, Anderson et al. (1996) used a modified Stroop procedure to investigate the possibility that uncomfortable temperatures might prime aggressive thoughts. In the modified Stroop procedure, words were flashed on a computer screen in one of five colors. On each trial the subject's task was to name the color, not the word. Some of the words were aggression related (e.g., shoot) whereas others were not (e.g., chant). If uncomfortable temperatures directly prime aggressive thoughts, then naming the color of aggressive words should be relatively harder for subjects in uncomfortable temperatures. This modified Stroop task was sensitive to a photo prime manipulation; subjects who had seen and rated gun photos took relatively longer to name the colors of aggressive words (relative to control words) than subjects who had seen and rated photos of nature scenes. However, there was no effect of temperature on the color-naming task.

Temperature and Aggressive Behavior

Two studies relating temperature to aggressive behavior in modified versions of the Taylor competitive reaction time (CRT) paradigm (Taylor, 1967) have been completed. In the standard version of this paradigm, subjects believe that they are competing with another subject on a reaction time task. On each trial the "loser" receives an electrical shock punishment. The shock intensity and duration are supposedly set by the opponent. Thus, before each trial the subject sets the intensity and duration of shock to be used against his or her opponent on that trial should the opponent lose. The actual wins and losses, as well as the trial by trial shock settings of the "opponent," are actually controlled by the experimenter. Intensity and duration as set by the subject are measures of aggression.

Experiment 1

A simple modification was made in the first study. White noise delivered through headphones was used as the punishment rather than shock. Subjects competed in 25 trials with their opponent. On each trial, participants responded to a tone by pushing a computer mouse button as soon as possible. Temperatures ranged from uncomfortably cold (56°F) to uncomfortably hot (96°F). Participants set the punishment level for their opponent prior to each trial.

In the standard paradigm as well as our first modification of it, the subject can use any of several motives in setting punishment levels. For instance, if angered the subject can set high noise levels to hurt the opponent. Because of the trial-by-trial nature of this task, the subject may refrain from setting high levels in order to prevent the opponent from responding in kind or the subject may adopt a tit-for-tat strategy in order to bring down the punishment level set by the opponent. Although the standard paradigm is well established, this ambiguity of subject motive may make it somewhat less sensitive to subtle effects, such as the heat effect, than is desired. Nonetheless, we kept this feature of the standard paradigm for our first experiment.

The pattern of punishments set by the "opponent" was also manipulated. For half of the subjects, their opponents gave consistently low punishments (selected intensities of 1–3 on the 0–10 intensity level scale). The other half of the subjects were initially given low punishment levels by their opponents, but across the 25 trials the intensity levels were increased.

As expected, subjects who received consistently low punishments by their opponent gave significantly lower punishments to their opponents than did those who received a pattern of increasing punishment. This was particularly true on the later trials, as shown by the provocation × trial block interaction $[F(2, 378) = 49.5, p < .0001]$ depicted in Figure 10.10.

As expected, provocation also increased state hostility $(Ms = 2.19 \& 1.91)$, $F(1, 212) = 15.21, p < .0001$. In addition, both hot and cold temperatures led to higher levels of state hostility than did comfortable temperatures, as shown by the significant effect of a quadratic temperature term in the model $[F(1, 184) = 7.30, p < .01]$. Similarly, escape motives, assessed via a 23 item self-report scale, were also curvilinearly related to uncomfortable temperatures, with hot and cold subjects reporting heightened motives for escape $[F(1, 181) = 5.22, p < .05]$.

However, temperature had no significant impact on noise intensity settings. This was true on the first setting, which was made prior to receiving any punishment by the opponent, as well as on each block of eight trials that followed. There are, of course, a host of reasons for an independent variable to fail to influence a dependent variable. In the present case, we believed that the standard procedure of having the subject and opponent set punishments for each other on a trial-by-trial basis instigated attempts to control the opponent. These attempts may well have overridden any increase in aggressive tendencies induced by hot or cold tempera-

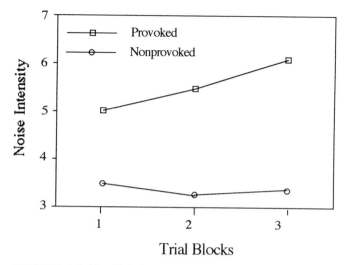

FIGURE 10.10 Noise intensity means by trial block and provocation.

tures. Alternatively, the low and high provocation manipulations themselves may have been so clear that they produced floor and ceiling effects, respectively, as soon as the subject figured out what the opponent was doing. To address these possibilities, we further modified the reaction time paradigm, and created what we call the retaliation reaction time (RRT) paradigm.

Experiment 2

In the RRT paradigm there are two sets of trials. One competitor sets punishment levels for the other on all trials in set one; the roles are reversed in set two. The real subject is always "randomly" assigned to receive punishment on the "lose" trials in set one, and therefore always sets punishment levels for the opponent in set two. This procedure allows subjects to retaliate for whatever transgressions they perceive were committed by their opponents during the set one trials, and to do so without fear of further retaliation by that opponent.

The temperature effect on aggression is likely a fairly subtle one. It may occur primarily as a brief outburst in reaction to some provocation. If this is true, then the RRT paradigm should be more sensitive to heat effects than the standard CRT, especially on the first trial in which the subject gets to set the opponent's punishment level.

This outburst by subjects in the hot and cold conditions should occur primarily when they have experienced some unwarranted aggression by the opponent, but not when the opponent's behavior during set one was either very nice (i.e., all low punishments) or very clearly not nice (i.e., systematically increasing punishment). To fully test this notion, a third pattern of opponent-set punishments was added. This set contained exactly the same frequency of each intensity setting as those in the original "high provocation" conditions, but instead of systematically increasing

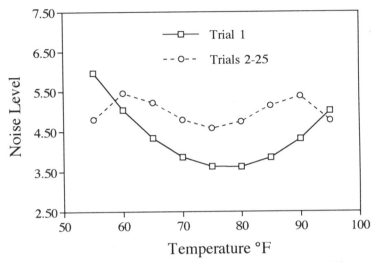

FIGURE 10.11   Noise level set by participants in ambiguous provocation conditions as a function of temperature and trial.

across trials, the various punishment settings were in a random pattern. In other words, there was no relation between trial number and intensity settings by the "opponent," thus creating ambiguity for the subject: "What is my opponent trying to do?" We expected these conditions—provocation with ambiguous intent—to be maximally sensitive to temperature effects. Here, the hostility state induced by uncomfortable temperatures can influence interpretation of the opponent's actions and of one's own state of anger. Once again, this should be especially true on the first trial for which the subject sets punishment for the opponent.

On subsequent trials the hot and cold subjects may well return to punishments that are very similar to those set by comfortable subjects. After all, the opponent has been justly punished. Indeed, for the last block of trials we expected that maximal aggression would occur by subjects in the moderately uncomfortable conditions. Hot and cold subjects may give relatively low punishments out of guilt over their earlier outburst or because that outburst fully satisfied their thirst for revenge or their desire to "set things right." Comfortable subjects may give relatively low punishments on these last trials because temperature never increased their hostility or their punishing behavior. Moderately hot and cold subjects, however, may well have increased feelings of hostility that are not expressed in an initial outburst and so they may continue to deliver moderately high punishments even in this last block.

Our results produced this very complex but meaningful pattern of aggression. On trial one punishments, there was a significant quadratic temperature × provocation interaction [$F(2, 191) = 3.74$, $p < .05$].[5] Further examination of the results

_____

[5]Temperature was converted to deviation score form prior to analysis so that quadratic and linear effects could be examined simultaneously and meaningfully.

showed that, as expected, hot and cold subjects gave the most intense punishments to their opponent, but this curvilinear effect occurred only in the ambiguous provocation condition [$F(1, 63) = 5.45, p < .05$]. Figure 10.11 displays these results.

Interestingly, this outburst in the ambiguous provocation condition ended quite rapidly; by trial two it was no longer significant. Indeed, averaging over all subsequent trials yielded a downturn in aggression at the temperature extremes, although the downturn did not quite reach the low levels of aggression displayed by the most comfortable subjects. Interestingly, people in the moderately uncomfortable conditions gave the highest punishment levels on these subsequent trials, as shown by the significant quartic temperature effect [$F(1, 61) = 3.99, p = .05$], also displayed in Figure 10.11.

SUMMARY OF CONCOMITANT FINDINGS

Although much work remains to be done to cleanly establish the causal routes through which various temperature-related effects exert their influence on aggressive behavior, we now have a good start on drawing that road map. Consider first the laboratory conditions that produced the increase in aggression at hot (and cold) temperatures. It required a paradigm that could capture an outburst (RRT) and a provocation level that was maximally ambiguous. In the real world, of course, an aggressive outburst directed at a target will typically serve as a provocation for that target. As is well known to all (e.g., Bettencourt & Miller, 1995), provocation plays a huge role in instigating further aggression. Thus, the consistent increases in aggression at hot temperatures, found in geographic region and time period studies, could well result from this outburst phenomenon.

The quartic pattern found in subsequent trials of our RRT paradigm also provides some explanatory power for the violent crime data of various types. As many people have noted, hot days also have somewhat cooler periods. The elevated aggression displayed by our subjects in moderately warm conditions could well contribute to the overall pattern of increased aggression on hot days and in hot regions.

These data do not, however, completely detail the underlying psychological processes. For instance, even though we believe that escape motives will eventually prove to play an important role, there still is little evidence that directly supports the NAE.

KEY THEORETICAL MODELS REEXAMINED

We now examine each of the main theoretical models to see how they fit with data from each triangulation perspective. We focus on southern culture of violence, routine activity theory, and our general affective aggression model.

SOUTHERN CULTURE OF VIOLENCE

Although the SCV idea is a fascinating one, temperature data provide little support at best. The strong version of SCV claims (a) that heat effects are either indirect or artifactual and (b) that regional differences in violence are due to the relative differences in endorsement of values associated with the SCV. There are several problems with this position. First, the SCV model implies that if regional differences in "southernness" are controlled in U.S. data, then heat effects must disappear. Our city violent crime data show, instead, that temperature remains a significant predictor even after controlling for southernness in various ways. Furthermore, when temperature is statistically controlled, the southernness effect disappears.

Second, the SCV model is totally silent on time period and concomitant studies of the temperature–aggression hypothesis because SCV is essentially controlled in both types of studies. The parsimonious explanation for regional differences in violent crime rates is temperature, not an additional cultural factor.

The third problem is the weak empirical base of general SCV theories as well as Nisbett's more specific culture of honor model. Note that we believe culture of honor effects exist as well as heat effects. Nisbett's studies provide hints of this (e.g., Cohen & Nisbett, 1994; Nisbett, 1993). What is needed to bolster the culture of honor model are studies showing the following: (a) Representative samples from high vs low culture of honor regions should differ in aggressive behavior, especially in public responses to public insults; (b) culture of honor scale scores should mediate the culture of honor/aggressive behavior relation in "a"; and (c) culture of honor scale scores should mediate aggressive behavior differences between "southern" and nonsouthern participants in laboratory studies. To date, none of the culture of honor laboratory studies has measured aggressive behavior. Cohen, Nisbett, Bowdle, and Schwarz (1995) measured the extent to which insulted and noninsulted southerners and northerners gave way to a large confederate in a hallway "chicken game" as well as the perceived firmness of the participants' handshakes. Insulted southerners tended to step aside later and to give firmer handshakes than northerners, but these measures relate to domineeringness. They do not meet standard definitions of aggression, and thus do not directly test the theory.

Similarly, there has not yet been a clear statement of what values and attitudes constitute the culture of honor, so there has not been an individual difference measure developed to assess culture of honor. Such a measure would be of immense value to the study of culture of honor and to violence more generally. It is hoped that future work will address these issues.

Finally, there are alternative explanations of the southern culture of violence that differ from the sociological theories and Nisbett's culture of honor model. One major historian (Wyatt-Brown, 1986) suggests that the violent aspects arose from the particular circumstances surrounding the institution of slavery and the need to maintain control. Other scholars (e.g., Pennebaker, Rimé, & Blankenship, 1996) have shown that climate plays a major role in the development of emotional expressiveness differences between cultures, a suggestion that fits well with our position that hot temperatures may contribute to the development of cultures of violence (Anderson & Anderson, 1996). In sum, although both temperature and cultural explanations are likely to play a role in the violence in modern society, the southern culture of violence notion is not a viable alternative to the temperature–aggression hypothesis. It may best be thought of as a "partner."

ROUTINE ACTIVITY THEORY

The strong version of routine activity theory also states that heat effects are either indirect, working through the kinds of activities that people normally do in various temperatures, or artifactual. If RAT is the only factor underlying observed heat effects in time period studies, then the following predictions must hold: (a) Routine activities during hotter periods of time must differ in ways that increase aggressive behavior; (b) for different types of aggressive behavior, which differ in the kinds of routines that increase or decrease them, the observed time period heat effects should differ in corresponding ways (e.g., wife battering should not increase in the summer in the same way that assault does); (c) any regional heat effects should be related to regional differences in routine activities; and (d) there should be no heat effect in laboratory experiments or in field studies where routine activities are controlled. At this point in time, there is some limited support for prediction (a). Prediction (b) is contradicted by the time period studies in that all measured violent behaviors appear to show much the same time period heat effect. To our knowledge, prediction (c) has never been examined, i.e., no studies appear to link various high violent crime routine activities to geographic regions. Indeed, one of the major shortcomings of RAT is that too little is known about what routine activities promote what kinds of aggressive behaviors, about the temporal and spatial distribution of these routine activities, and about the intra- and interpersonal dynamics that link these routine activities to aggressive behaviors. It is an area ripe for more research. Finally, concerning prediction (d), concomitant studies and even some of the day-unit time period studies cannot be handled by RAT. For instance, the Reifman et al. (1991) study of batters hit by pitched baseballs cannot be explained by RAT.

A different version of RAT, one which accepts that heat directly affects aggressive tendencies, can reasonably posit that the relationship between heat and aggression might differ as a function of routine activities. Specifically, some "routines" reduce the opportunity for aggression. In such cases we would expect the link between heat and aggression to be attenuated. The Cohn and Rotton (1997) study provides some evidence for this version of RAT.

GENERAL AFFECTIVE AGGRESSION MODEL

This theory states that heat effects are both direct and indirect. It predicts that, all else being equal, hotter regions should have higher rates of aggressive behavior for those aggressive behaviors with a large affective/impulsive component. Region studies strongly support this prediction, even when all sorts of statistical controls are imposed. The theory also predicts that hotter regions will, on average, develop more violent cultures. That is, people who grow up in hotter regions should have more positive attitudes and values toward aggressive behaviors, at least in certain kinds of circumstances. There is some support for this from the culture of honor literature (e.g., Cohen & Nisbett, 1994; Nisbett, 1993) and some from cross-cultural studies (e.g., Pennebaker et al., 1996; Robbins et al., 1972).

This theory also predicts direct heat effects in time period studies. Research consistently shows higher rates of aggression during hotter time periods in daily, monthly, quarterly, and yearly time period studies.

The general model makes a host of predictions concerning heat effects in concomitant studies, both in laboratory as well as in field settings. Research in the laboratory has resolved many of the inconsistencies found in earlier laboratory work and shows that hot temperatures do increase aggressive behavior in the laboratory. The few concomitant field studies of aggressive behavior also support the theory. In addition, the general model makes a host of predictions concerning possible routes through which hot temperatures (and cold) may influence aggressive behavior. We have shown that both affective and arousal routes may carry the heat effect from discomfort to (eventually) aggressive behavior. However, considerably more work must be done to test this model.

PROMISING DIRECTIONS

There are many promising directions for new research in this domain. We elaborate on some that are particularly exciting to us.

Development of a culture of honor scale would enable the testing of many hypotheses, both about cultures of honor as well as about individual differences in violence proneness. A culture of honor scale should be developed independently of indicators of aggressiveness so that the hypothesis that a culture of honor predicts aggressiveness can be fairly tested. Once developed, such a scale would also be useful in examining child development issues. How are these attitudes and values passed on? Are there alternative attitudes and values that could be substituted and that would be more beneficial to the individual and society?

More work is needed on the biological aspects. How can we relate biological factors (e.g., hormonal, neuronal) to heat effects on affective state, cognitions, attention, and arousal? Are some people more susceptible to such heat effects, perhaps because of their biological responsiveness to temperature?

As noted earlier, more work is needed on the specific ways that routine activities may be tied to heat effects on the one side and to violent crime on the other. Such work may be particularly important in its implications for crime control efforts.

Finally, the integrated model itself presents many research questions that, to date, do not have clear answers. Many of these questions involve temperature, of course. How does an uncomfortably hot temperature influence the interpretation of ambiguously aggressive stimuli? Does it influence attributions people make for aversive events? How do individual differences interact with temperature and other aggression-related factors such as provocation?

APPLICATIONS

Throughout this chapter we have concentrated on the more purely scientific aspects of the temperature–aggression hypothesis. What are the underlying causes? Although the potential for application may seem obvious to many readers, we feel it important to at least briefly mention a few.

The integrated model itself suggests a host of ways that society can intervene to reduce unwarranted aggression. Some of these are not new ideas arising solely from temperature research, but instead can be derived from many contemporary research programs that are congruent with our own. For instance, by reducing children's exposure to aggressive material, especially to aggression that appears to be rewarded, we might be able to produce children (and later, adults) who are less prone to making hostile attributions for observed events (e.g., Dodge & Crick, 1990; Huesmann, Eron, Lefkowitz, & Walder, 1984). The role of temperature in the broad model also has implications. Many instances of violence in society begin as small disputes that escalate. If people were more generally aware of how hot temperatures can lead to attribution and interpretation biases, perhaps they could counteract them. Public service announcements about the need to "cool" one's temper as well as one's temperature during hot periods of time might produce a reduction in heat-induced aggression.

The various field study results themselves may be useful in some settings. For instance, knowing when and where violence is likely to erupt (e.g., hot days and nights, near bars) may be used to change police presence patterns in productive ways.

Finally, most people spend much of their lives in "built" environments. By making them more comfortable, we may be able to reduce unwarranted aggression. The most obvious places (to us, at least) are schools, prisons, homes, and the workplace.

REFERENCES

Amir, M. (1971). *Patterns in forcible rape*. Chicago: University of Chicago Press.

Anderson, C. A. (1987). Temperature and aggression: Effects on quarterly, yearly, and city rates of violent and nonviolent crime. *Journal of Personality and Social Psychology, 52,* 1161–1173.

Anderson, C. A. (1989). Temperature and aggression: Ubiquitous effects of heat on occurrence of human violence. *Psychological Bulletin, 106,* 74–96.

Anderson, C. A., & Anderson, D. C. (1984). Ambient temperature and violent crime: Tests of the linear and curvilinear hypotheses. *Journal of Personality and Social Psychology, 46,* 91–97.

Anderson, C. A., Anderson, K. B., & Deuser, W. E. (1996). Examining an affective aggression frame-work: Weapon and temperature effects on aggressive thoughts, affect, and attitudes. *Personality and Social Psychology Bulletin, 22,* 366–376.

Anderson, C. A., & Bushman, B. J. (1997). External validity of "trivial" experiments: The case of lab-oratory aggression. *Review of General Psychology, 1,* 19–41.

Anderson, C. A., & DeNeve, K. M. (1992). Temperature, aggression, and the negative affect escape model. *Psychological Bulletin, 111,* 347–351.

Anderson, C. A., Bushman, B. J., & Groom, R. W. (1997). Hot years and serious and deadly assault: Em-pirical tests of the heat hypothesis. *Journal of Personality and Social Psychology, 73,* 1213–1223.

Anderson, C. A, Deuser, W. E., DeNeve, K. (1995). Hot temperatures, hostile affect, hostile cognition, and arousal: Tests of a general model of affective aggression. *Personality and Social Psychology Bulletin, 21,* 434–448.

Anderson, C. A., Dorr, N., Anderson, K. B., & DeNeve, K. M. (under review). Temperature-aggression inconsistencies resolved: Laboratory evidence of multiple functional relations between uncomfortable temperatures and aggressive behavior.

Anderson, C. A., Miller, R. S., Riger, A. L., Dill, J. C., & Sedikides, C. (1994). Behavioral and char-acterological attributional styles as predictors of depression and loneliness: Review, refinement, and test. *Journal of Personality and Social Psychology, 66,* 549–558.

Anderson, K. B., & Anderson, C. A. (1996). *Laboratory effects of hot temperatures on aggressive be-havior: A meta-analysis.* Unpublished manuscript.

Aschaffenburg, G. (1903/1913). *Crime and its repression.* Boston: Little, Brown.

Atlas, R. (1984). Violence in prison: Environmental influences. *Environment and Behavior, 16(3),* 275–306.

Bailey, W. C. (1976). Some further evidence on homicide and a regional culture of violence. *Omega, 7,* 145–170.

Bandura, A. (1973). *Aggression: A social learning theory analysis.* Englewood Cliffs, NJ: Prentice Hall.

Baron, R. A. (1972). Aggression as a function of ambient temperatures and prior anger arousal. *Jour-nal of Personality and Social Psychology, 21,* 183–189.

Baron, R. A. (1976). The reduction of human aggression: A field study of the influence of incompati-ble reactions. *Journal of Applied Social Psychology, 6,* 260–274.

Baron, R. A., & Lawton, S. F. (1972). Environmental influences on aggression: The facilitation of modeling effects by high ambient temperatures. *Psychonomic Science, 26,* 80–82.

Bazett, H. C. (1927). Physiological responses to heat. *Physiological Reviews, 7,* 531–599.

Bell, P. A. (1980). Effects of heat, noise, and provocation on retaliatory evaluative behavior. *Journal of Social Psychology, 110,* 97–100.

Bell, P. A. (1992). In defense of the negative affect escape model of heat and aggression. *Psychologi-cal Bulletin, 111,* 342–346.

Bell, P. A., & Baron, R. A. (1976). Aggression and heat: The mediating role of negative affect. *Jour-nal of Applied Social Psychology, 6,* 18–30.

Bell, P. A., & Baron, R. A. (1977). Aggression and ambient temperature: The facilitating and inhibit-ing effects of hot and cold environments. *Bulletin of the Psychonomic Society, 9,* 443–445.

Berkowitz, L. (1984). Some effects of thoughts on anti- and prosocial influences of media events: A cognitive-neoassociation analysis. *Psychological Bulletin, 95,* 410–427.

Berkowitz, L. (1993). *Aggression: Its causes, consequences, and control.* New York: McGraw Hill.

Bettencourt, B. A., & Miller, N. (1995). Sex differences in aggression as a function of provocation: A meta-analysis. Manuscript submittted for publication.

Blanchard, D. C., & Blanchard, R. J. (1984). Affect and aggression: An animal model applied to human behavior. In R. J. Blanchard & D. C. Blanchard (Eds.), *Advances in the study of aggression* (Vol. 1, pp. 1–62). Orlando, FL: Academic Press.

Brearley, H. C. (1932). *Homicide in the United States.* Montclair, NJ: Patterson-Smith.

Buchanan, C. M., Eccles, J. S., & Becker, J. B. (1992). Are adolescents the victims of raging hor-mones: Evidence for activational effects of hormones on moods and behavior at adolescence. *Psy-chological Bulletin, 111,* 62–107.

Bushman, B. J., Anderson, K. B., & Anderson, C. A. (1998). *Assaults and temperature in Minneapolis reexamined.* Manuscript in preparation.

Campbell, D. T., & Fiske, D. W. (1959). Convergent and discriminant validation by the multitrait-multimethod matrix. *Psychological Bulletin, 56,* 81–105.

Caprara, G. V., Cinanni, V., D'Imperio, G., Passerini, S., Renzi, P., & Travablia, G. (1985). Indicators of impulsive aggression: Present status of research on irritability and emotional susceptibility scales. *Personality and Individual Differences, 6,* 665–674.

Carlsmith, J. M., & Anderson, C. A. (1979). Ambient temperature and the occurrence of collective violence: A new analysis. *Journal of Personality and Social Psychology, 37,* 337–344.

Cash, W. J. (1941). *The mind of the South.* New York: Knopf.

Chang, D. H. (1972). Environmental influences on criminal activity in Korea. *Criminology, 10,* 338–352.

Church, A. T., & Burke, P. J. (1994). Exploratory and confirmatory tests of the Big Five and Tellegen's three- and four-dimensional models. *Journal of Personality and Social Psychology, 66,* 93–114.

Cohen, D., & Nisbett, R. E. (1994). Self-protection and the culture of honor: Explaining southern violence. *Personality and Social Psychology Bulletin, 20,* 551–567.

Cohen, D., Nisbett, R. E., Bowdle, B., & Schwarz, N. (1995). *Insult, aggression, and the southern culture of honor: An "experimental ethnography."* Unpublished manuscript, University of Michigan.

Cohen, J. (1941). The geography of crime. *Annals of the American Academy of Political and Social Science, 217,* 29–37.

Cohen, L. E., & Felson, M. (1979). Social change and crime rate trends: A routine activity approach. *American Sociological Review, 44,* 588–608.

Cohn, E. G. (1990). Weather and crime. *British Journal of Criminology, 30,* 51–64.

Cohn, E. G. (1993). The prediction of police calls for service: The influence of weather and temporal variables on rape and domestic violence. *Environmental Psychology, 13,* 71–83.

Cohn, E. G., & Rotton, J. (1997). Assault as a function of time and temperature: A moderator-variable time-series analysis. *Journal of Personality and Social Psychology, 72,* 1322–1334.

Cotton, J. L. (1986). Ambient temperature and violent crime. *Journal of Applied Social Psychology, 16,* 786–801.

Crano, W., & Brewer, M. (1973). *Principles of research in social psychology.* New York: McGraw-Hill.

deFronzo, J. (1984). Climate and crime. *Environment and Behavior, 16,* 185–210.

Dexter, E. G. (1899). Conduct and the weather. *Psychological Monographs, 11(10),* 1–103.

Dill, J., & Anderson, C. A. (1995). Effects of justified and unjustified frustration on aggression. *Aggressive Behavior, 21,* 359–369.

Dodge, K. A., & Crick, N. R. (1990). Social information-processing bases of aggressive behavior in children. *Personality and Social Psychology Bulletin, 16,* 8–22.

Dodge, R. W., & Lentzner, H. R. (1980). *Crime and seasonality: National crime survey report.* U.S. Department of Justice (#SD-NCS-N-15).

Erlanger, H. (1975). Is there a 'subculture of violence' in the South? *Journal of Criminal Law and Criminology, 66,* 483–490.

Feigl, H. (1958). The mental and the physical. In H. Feigl, M. Scriven, & G. Maxwell (Eds.), *Minnesota studies in the philosophy of science* (Vol. II). Minneapolis: University of Minnesota Press.

Felson, R. B. (1993). Motives for sexual coercion. In Felson & Tedeschi (Eds.), *Aggression and violence: Social interactionist perspectives* (pp. 233–253). Washington, DC: American Psychological Association.

Field, S. (1992). The effect of temperature on crime. *British Journal of Criminology, 32,* 340–351.

Ganjavi, O., Schell, B., & Cachon, J. (1985). Geophysical variables and behavior. XXIX. Impact of atmospheric conditions on occurrences of individual violence among Canadian penitentiary populations. *Perceptual and Motor Skills, 61,* 259–275.

Gastil, R. D. (1971). Homicide and regional culture of violence. *American Sociological Review, 36,* 412–427.

Geen, R. G. (1990). *Human aggression.* Pacific Grove, CA: Brooks Cole.

Greenwald, A. G., Pratkanis, A. R., Leippe, M. R., & Baumgardner, M. H. (1986). Under what conditions does theory obstruct research progress? *Psychological Review, 93,* 216–229.

Hackney, S. (1970). Southern violence. In H. Graham & T. Gurr (Eds.), *Violence in America: Historical and comparative perspectives* (pp. 505–527). New York: Bantam.

Haertzen, C., Buxton, K., Covi, L., & Richards, H. (1993). Seasonal changes in rule infractions among prisoners: A preliminary test of the temperature-aggression hypothesis. *Psychological Reports, 72,* 195–200.

Hardy, J. D. (1961). Physiology of temperature regulation. *Physiological Reviews, 41,* 521–605.

Harries, K. D., & Stadler, S. J. (1988). Heat and violence: New findings from Dallas field data, 1980–1981. *Journal of Applied Social Psychology, 18,* 129–138.

Hayman, C. R., Lanza, C., Fuentes, R., & Algor, K. (1972). Rape in the District of Columbia. *American Journal of Obstetrics and Gynecology, 113,* 91–97.

Huesmann, L. R. (1986). Psychological processes promoting the relation between exposure to media violence and aggressive behavior by the viewer. *Journal of Social Issues, 42,* 125–139.

Huesmann, L. R., Eron, L. D., Lefkowitz, M. M. & Walder, L. O. (1984). Stability of aggression over time and generations. *Developmental Psychology, 20,* 746–775.

Iampietro, P. F., Melton, C. E., Higgins, E. A., Vaughan, J. A., Hoffman, S. M., Funkhouser, G. E., & Saldivar, J. T. (1972). High temperature and performance in a flight task simulator. *Aerospace Medicine, 43,* 1215–1218.

Kenrick, D. T., & MacFarlane, S. W. (1984). Ambient temperature and horn-honking: A field study of the heat/aggression relationship. *Environment and Behavior, 18,* 179–191.

Kobrick, J. L., & Fine, B. J. (1983). Climate and human performance. In D. J. Oborne & M. M. Gruneberg (Eds.), *The physical environment at work* (pp. 69–107). Chichester, England: Wiley & Sons.

Kobrick, J. L., & Johnson, R. F. (1991). Effects of hot and cold environments on military performance. In R. Gal & A. D. Mangelsdorff (Eds.), *Handbook of military psychology* (pp. 215–232). Chichester, England: Wiley & Sons.

Landau, S. F., & Fridman, D. (1993). The seasonality of violent crime: The case of robbery and homicide in Israel. *Journal of Research in Crime and Delinquency, 30,* 163–191.

LeBeau, J. L., & Langworthy, R. H. (1986). The linkages between routine activities, weather, and calls for police services. *Journal of Police Science Administration, 14,* 137–145.

LeBlanc, J. (1975). *Man in the cold.* Springfield, IL: Charles C. Thomas.

LeDoux, J. E. (1993). Emotional networks in the brain. In M. Lewis & J. M. Haviland (Eds.), *Handbook of emotions* (pp. 109–118). New York: Guilford Press.

Leffingwell, A. (1892). *Illegitimacy and the influence of the seasons upon conduct.* New York: Scribners.

Linkowski, P,. Martin, F., & DeMaertelaer, V. (1992). Effect of some climatic factors on violent and non-violent suicides in Belgium. *Journal of Affective Disorders, 25,* 161–166.

Lombroso, C. (1899/1911). *Crime: Its causes and remedies.* Boston: Little, Brown.

Marsh, H. W., Balla, J. R., & McDonald, R. P. (1988). Goodness-of-fit indexes in confirmatory factor analysis: The effect of sample size. *Psychological Bulletin, 103,* 391–410.

Marsh, H. W., & Hocevar, D. (1985). Application of confirmatory factor analysis to the study of self-concept: First and higher order factor models and their invariance across groups. *Psychological Bulletin, 97,* 562–582.

McGrath, J. E., Martin, J., & Kukla, R. A. (1982). *Judgment calls in research.* Beverly Hills, CA: Sage.

Michael, R. P., & Zumpe, D. (1983). Annual rhythms in human violence and sexual aggression in the United States and the role of temperature. *Social Biology, 30,* 263–278.

Michael, R. P., & Zumpe, D. (1986). An annual rhythm in the battering of women. *American Journal of Psychiatry, 143,* 637–640.

Montesquieu, C. (1748/1989). *The spirit of the laws.* Translated by A. Cohler, B. Miller, & H. Stone. New York: Cambridge University Press.

Mortagy, A. K., & Ramsey, J. D. (1973). Monitoring performance as a function of work-rest schedule and thermal stress. *American Industrial Hygiene Association Journal, 34,* 474–480.

Nisbett, R. E. (1990). Evolutionary psychology, biology, and cultural evolution. *Motivation and Emotion, 14,* 255–263.

Nisbett, R. E. (1993). Violence and U.S. regional culture. *American Psychologist, 48,* 441–449.

O'Connor, J. F., & Lizotte, A. (1978). The 'southern subculture of violence' thesis and patterns of gun ownership. *Social Problems, 25,* 420–429.

Palamarek, D. L., & Rule, B. G. (1979). The effects of ambient temperature and insult on the motivation to retaliate or escape. *Motivation and Emotion, 3,* 83–92.

Pennebaker, J. W., Rimé, B., & Blankenship, G. E. (1996). Stereotypes of emotional expressiveness of Northerners and Southerners: A cross-cultural test of Montesquieu's hypothesis. *Journal of Personality and Social Psychology, 70,* 372–380.

Pepler, R. D. (1958). Warmth and performance: An investigation in the tropics. *Ergonomics, 2,* 63–88.

Perry, J. D., & Simpson, M. E. (1987). Violent crimes in a city: Environmental determinants. *Environment and Behavior, 19,* 77–90.

Pettigrew, C. G. (1985). Seasonality and lunacy of inmate behavior. *The Southern Psychologist, 2,* 41–46.

Poulton, E. C., Edwards, R. S., & Colquhoun, W. P. (1974). The interaction of the loss of a night's sleep with mild heat: Task variables. *Ergonomics, 17,* 59–73.

Ramsey, J. D., Dayal, D., & Ghahramani, B. (1975). Heat stress limits for the sedentary worker. *American Industrial Hygiene Journal, 36,* 259–265.

Reifman, A. S., Larrick, R. P., & Fein, S. (1991). Temper and temperature on the diamond: The heat-aggression relationship in major league baseball. *Personality and Social Psychology Bulletin, 17,* 580–585.

Reis, D. J. (1974). Consideration of some problems encountered in relating specific neurotransmitters to specific behaviors or disease. *Journal of Psychiatric Research, 11,* 145–148.

Robbins, M. C., DeWalt, E. R., & Pelto, P. J. (1972). Climate and behavior: A biocultural study. *Journal of Cross-Cultural Psychology, 3,* 331–344.

Rosenfeld, R. (1986). Urban crime rates: Effects of inequality, welfare, dependency, region, and race. In J. Byrne & R. Sampson (Eds.), *The social ecology of crime* (pp. 116–132). New York: Springer-Verlag.

Rotton, J. (1982). *Seasonal and atmospheric determinants of sex crimes: Time series analysis of archival data.* Paper presented at the Annual Convention of the Southeastern Psychological Association, New Orleans, March.

Rotton, J. (1986). Determinism redux: Climate and cultural correlates of violence. *Environment and Behavior, 18,* 346–368.

Rotton, J., Barry, T., & Kimble, C. E. (1985). *Climate and violent crime: Coping with multicollinearity.* Paper presented at the 95th Annual Convention of the American Psychological Association, Los Angeles, August.

Rotton, J., & Frey, J. (1985). Air pollution, weather, and violent crimes: Concomitant time-series analysis of archival data. *Journal of Personality and Social Psychology, 49,* 1207–1220.

Rule, B. G., & Nesdale, A. R. (1976). Environmental stressors, emotional arousal and aggression. In I. Sarason & C. Spielberger (Eds.), *Stress and anxiety* (Vol. 3, pp. 87–104). Washington, DC: Halsted.

Scammon, R. M. (1970). *American Votes 8: A handbook of contemporary American election statistics 1968.* Washington, DC: Government Affairs Institute, Congressional Quarterly.

Schwartz, D. C. (1968). On the ecology of political violence: "The long hot summer" as a hypothesis. *American Behavioral Scientist, July-August,* 24–28.

Taylor, S. P. (1967). Aggressive behavior and physiological arousal as a function of provocation and the tendency to inhibit aggression. *Journal of Personality, 35,* 297–310.

Timoshenko, S. P. (1953). *History and strength of materials.* New York: McGraw-Hill.

Tromp, S. W. (1980). *Biometeorology: The impact of the weather and climate on humans and their environment.* London: Heydon & Sons.

van Goozen, S. H. M., Frijda, N. H., Kindt, M., & van de poll, N. E. (1994). Anger proneness in women: Development and validation of the anger situation questionnaire. *Aggressive Behavior, 20,* 79–100.

Velicer, W. F., Huckel, L. H., & Hansen, C. E. (1989). A measurement model for measuring attitudes toward violence. *Personality and Social Psychology Bulletin, 15,* 349–364.

Vrij, A., van-der-Steen, J., & Koppelaar, L. (1994). Aggression of police officers as a function of temperature: An experiment with the Fire Arms Training System. *Journal of Community and Applied Social Psychology, 4,* 365–370.

Walters, G. D. (1991). Examining the relationship between airborne pollen levels and 911 calls for assistance. *International Journal of Offender Therapy and Comparative Criminology, 35,* 162–166.

Waynbaum, I. (1907). *La Physionomie humaine: Son mecanisme et son role social* [The human face: Its mechanism and social function]. Paris: Alcan.

Wilson, F. (1984). *Building materials evaluation handbook.* New York: Van Nostrand.

Wyatt-Brown, B. (1986). *Honor and violence in the Old South.* New York: Oxford University.

Zajonc, R. B. (1985). Emotion and Facial Efference: A theory reexamined. *Science, 228,* 15–21.

Zajonc, R. B. (1994). Emotional expression and temperature modulation. In S. H. M. van Goozen, N. E. Van de Poll, & J. A. Sergeant (Eds.), *Emotions: Essays on emotion theory* (pp. 3–27). Hillsdale, NJ: Lawrence Erlbaum Associates.

Zajonc, R. B., Murphy, S. T., & Inglhart, M. (1989). Feeling and facial efference: Implications of the vascular theory of emotion. *Psychological Review, 96,* 395–416.

INDEX